Lincoln Christian College

Studies in Church History

Subsidia

4

THE BIBLE IN THE MEDIEVAL WORLD
ESSAYS IN MEMORY OF BERYL SMALLEY

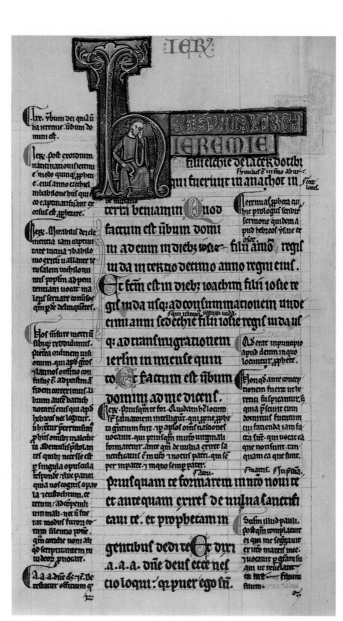

The beginning of Jeremiah, with the *Glossa Ordinaria*.
Oxford, Bodleian Library, MS Digby 226, f.96ᵛ.

THE BIBLE IN THE MEDIEVAL WORLD

ESSAYS IN MEMORY OF BERYL SMALLEY

EDITED BY

KATHERINE WALSH AND
DIANA WOOD

PUBLISHED FOR
THE ECCLESIASTICAL HISTORY SOCIETY

BY

BASIL BLACKWELL

1985

© Ecclesiastical History Society 1985

First published 1985

Basil Blackwell Publisher Ltd
108 Cowley Road, Oxford OX4 1JF, UK

Basil Blackwell Inc.
432 Park Avenue South, Suite 1505,
New York, NY 10016, USA

British Library Cataloguing in Publication Data
The bible in the medieval world: essays in memory of Beryl Smalley.—
—(Studies in Church history. Subsidia)
1. Bible——Influence——History   2. Civilization, Medieval
I. Walsh, Katherine   II. Wood, Diana
III. Smalley, Beryl   IV. Series
220   BS538.7

ISBN 0–631–14275–4

Library of Congress Cataloging in Publication Data

The Bible in the medieval world.

(Studies in church history. Subsidia ; 4)
Bibliography: p.
Includes index.
1. Bible—Criticism, interpretation, etc.—History—Middle Ages, 600–1500—Addresses, essays, lectures. 2. Europe—Church history—Middle Ages, 600–1500—Addresses, essays, lectures. 3. Smalley, Beryl—Addresses, essays, lectures. I. Smalley, Beryl. II. Walsh, Katherine. III. Wood, Diana, 1940– IV. Ecclesiastical History Society. V. Series. BS500.B545 1985   220.6   84–29033

ISBN 0–631–14275–4

Typeset by Photo·Graphics, Honiton, Devon

Printed in Great Britain by T. J. Press Ltd, Padstow

PREFACE

When we first told Beryl Smalley of our plan to produce a volume to honour her she was very reluctant to agree to it. Beryl hated flattery of any kind. Nevertheless, the genuine grief and sense of loss caused by her death, so movingly expressed to us by our contributors and others, is sufficient testimony of the great esteem and affection in which she was held throughout the learned world. Eventually she was persuaded to agree to our plan only if it would bring pleasure to those who contributed to the volume, and above all to those who edited it. Such a generous reaction was typical of her. Certainly it has brought pleasure to us, not least because of the interest she took in it, and the encouragement she gave us during the last months of her life. It was her wish that if she did not live to see its publication, it should appear as a memorial volume. She also came to agree with us that such a collection of essays would be the logical outcome of the interest she had inspired in so many scholars in the all-important subject of the Bible in the Medieval World. It is for this reason that we have had to stick so rigidly to our theme, and to exclude many distinguished medievalists who might other-wise have wished to honour her: Beryl would have hated an 'academic jumble sale', which was her description of the traditional type of *Festschrift*. She was also well aware of the danger that such a publication might become a graveyard for any piece of academic work, and she was therefore delighted to know that the volume would appear as a Subsidia to *Studies in Church History*. We are very grateful to the members of the Publications Committee of the Ecclesiastical History Society for agreeing to publish it, and in particular to Professor Michael Wilks and Dr William Sheils for much practical help and advice. Another constriction in preparing the volume has been the time limit. In the hope that it might appear before Beryl's death we had to impose almost impossible deadlines upon our contributors, which meant that several people did not feel able to contribute.

Part of the pleasure in editing the volume has lain in the knowledge that we had the support and encouragement of so many people: among these Mrs Susan Hall deserves especially warm words of thanks for compiling the indexes and for the help she has

v

given us, and Sir Richard Southern, Dr Nicholas Mann, and Mr Bruce Wilcock must also be singled out for our special thanks.

Katherine Walsh
Diana Wood

ACKNOWLEDGEMENTS

Grateful acknowledgement is made to the following: to the Bodleian Library, Oxford, for permission to reproduce MS Digby, 226, f. 96^v as the frontispiece; to the Universiteitsbibliotheek Leiden to reproduce MS Perizoniani F 17, ff. 24^v and 9^r as figs. 1 and 2 respectively, and to the Hambledon Press for permission to reproduce the Bibliography of Beryl Smalley (with additions) from *Studies in Medieval Thought and Learning from Abelard to Wyclif* (London, 1981), pp. 417–22.

CONTENTS

CONTENTS

CONTRIBUTORS

LOUIS-JACQUES BATAILLON, O.P.
Commissio Leonina, Grottaferrata, Rome

LEONARD E. BOYLE
Prefect of the Biblioteca Apostolica Vaticana

J. I. CATTO
Fellow and Tutor in Medieval History, Oriel College, Oxford

GILBERT DAHAN
Chargé de recherche au Centre national de la Recherche scientifique, Paris

DAVID d'AVRAY
Lecturer in History, University College London

ALBINIA DE LA MARE
Department of Western Manuscripts, Bodleian Library, Oxford

JEAN DUNBABIN
Fellow of St Anne's College, Oxford

GILLIAN R. EVANS
Fellow of Fitzwilliam College, Cambridge, and University Lecturer in History

ANNE HUDSON
Fellow of Lady Margaret Hall, Oxford

GORDON LEFF
Professor of History, University of York

ROBERT E. LERNER
Professor of History, Northwestern University, Evanston, Illinois

KARL LEYSER, F.B.A.
Chichele Professor of Medieval History, Oxford

DAVID LUSCOMBE
Professor of Medieval History, University of Sheffield

CONTRIBUTORS

JUDITH McCLURE
: Kingswood School, Bath

I. S. ROBINSON
: Fellow and Tutor of Trinity College, Dublin

PAUL GERHARD SCHMIDT
: Professur für Lateinische Philologie des Mittelalters und der Neuzeit, Philipps-Universität Marburg

SIR RICHARD SOUTHERN, F.B.A.
: Sometime President of St John's College, Oxford

KATHERINE WALSH
: Universitätsdozent für Geschichte des Mittelalters, Universität Salzburg

DIANA WOOD
: Lecturer in History, University of East Anglia

NOTE ON THE FRONTISPIECE

by ALBINIA DE LA MARE

The plate shows the initial for the beginning of Jeremiah in Oxford, Bodleian Library, MS Digby 226, a handsomely written and presented glossed book, with fine historiated initials, produced in England in the early thirteenth century. The manuscript contains Isaiah, Jeremiah, and Lamentations, with the *Glossa Ordinaria*, and has one particularly interesting feature. The original scribe, or a contemporary hand, gave the chapters in Jeremiah a pre-Langton numbering. In both cases he started by writing the numbers in plummet. In Isaiah he wrote roman numerals and then wrote over most of them, up to XLVI, in large red and blue numerals, and from l-cciiii in a small hand in brown ink. In Jeremiah, on the other hand, he wrote plummet numbers up to 150 in *arabic* numerals, and then broke off (at f. 177ʳ, mid 'modern' chapter 44). He then wrote over the arabic numerals in roman numerals in brown ink, but only up to lx. He wrote the arabic numerals that contained more than one digit *backwards*, so that '87' reads '78', and '150' reads '051'. This is very unusual, as indeed is the use of arabic numerals in the West for such a practical purpose at this early date. A near-contemporary hand added the 'modern' chapter numbers of Langton in the outer margins, and also added further glosses, often written in patterns, which are sometimes outlined in red and blue. This hand, or another of about the same date, copied on f.95aᵛ (a blank leaf following Isaiah) the paragraph *incipit: 'Ieremias propheta cui hic prologus ascribitur', explicit: '... insaniam provocare'*, which is part of a preface attributed to Gilbert the Universal (see Stegmüller, *Bibl.,* ii, no. 2544.1). Gilbert was the compiler of the Gloss on the books included in this manuscript, as Beryl Smalley showed, and Lamentations ends on f.234ʳ with Gilbert's subscription: '*Suffitiant hec ad expositionem lamentationum ieremie qui de patrum fontibus hausi ego Gillibertus altissiodorensis ecclesie diaconus*'.

This imposing manuscript must have been made for a client of substance, but nothing is known of its early history. It belonged in the early seventeenth century to Thomas Allen of Oxford (1540–

1632): '24', written at the top of f. 1^r, corresponds to f.24 in Allen's catalogue of 1622. Many of Allen's manuscripts had come from suppressed monasteries, and from Oxford colleges which in his time were disposing, regrettably, of unfashionable or surplus books in their collections. This manuscript was among the many that Allen bequeathed to Sir Kenelm Digby, who had it bound, like most of his other manuscripts, with his arms stamped in gilt on the cover. Then, with the rest of Digby's collection, it was given to the Bodleian in 1634.

BIBLIOGRAPHY

G. D. Macray, *Codices a viro clarissimo Kenelm Digby anno 1634 donatos = Catalogi codicum manuscriptorum Bibliothecae Bodleianae pars nona* (Oxford, 1883), col. 238; O. Pächt and J. J. G. Alexander, *Illuminated Manuscripts in the Bodleian Library*, iii (Oxford, 1973), no. 354; A. G. Watson, 'Thomas Allen of Oxford and his Manuscripts', in *Medieval Scribes, Manuscripts and Libraries. Essays presented to N. R. Ker*, ed. M. B. Parkes and A. G. Watson (London, 1978), pp. 303–4, 312; Stegmüller, *Bibl.*, ii, no. 2544.1; ix, nos. 11807–9. Gilbert's part in the Gloss is summarized by Beryl Smalley, *Bible*, pp. 60–2, with references to her earlier articles. For the introduction of arabic numerals to the West, see R. Lemay, 'The Hispanic origin of our present numeral forms', *Viator*, viii (1977), pp. 435–62, and for their use in thirteenth-century indexes, R. H. Rouse and M. A. Rouse, *Preachers, Florilegia, Sermons. Studies on the Manipulus Florum of Thomas of Ireland* (Toronto, 1979), pp. 32–3.

For those who desire it, there follows a physical description of the manuscript:

In Latin, on parchment, written in England in the early 13th cent. c.353 × 250 (213 × 132)mm.: ii + 235 + ii leaves (f.95 is double): 50 lines ruled in plummet, with text written on every second line; the Gloss written above the top line: collation, 1^8–25^8, 26^6 [?], 27^8–29^8, 30^6 [? 6 canc.?] (the binding is too tight to check the collation); original quires numbering at the end of quires in roman numerals, with a separate sequence for each work; there is also a later quire numbering (perhaps by a binder?) in a combination of dots and arabic numerals, at the beginnings of the quires; illuminated initials, some historiated, for the beginning of glosses and books, and for 'modern' chapters 2 and 4 of Lamentations (ff. 1^r, 1^v, 96^r, 96^v, 198^r, 199^r, 207^r, 224^v). Initials to verses alternately red flourished with blue and blue with red; paragraph marks in gloss and some original chapter numbering in Isaiah in red and blue. There are some running headings written by the original scribe, but no rubrics. 17th cent. calf binding with arms of Sir Kenelm Digby stamped in gilt and two clasps.

2⁰ f.–*nia que in sillaba*

For the textual contents see the account above. Isaiah *beg.* f.1ᵛ (gloss *beg.* f. 1ʳ) *ends* f.95ᵛ. F.95a was originally blank. Jeremiah *beg.* f.96ᵛ (gloss f.96ʳ) *ends* f.197ʳ. F.197ᵛ is blank. Lamentations *beg.* f.199ʳ (gloss f. 198ʳ) *ends* f.234ʳ. F.234ᵛ is blank. Ff. i–ii, 235–6, are later parchment flyleaves.

Bodleian Library, Oxford

BERYL SMALLEY AND THE PLACE
OF THE BIBLE IN MEDIEVAL
STUDIES, 1927–84

by R.W. SOUTHERN

I

IN 1927, when Beryl Smalley began to study the Bible in the Middle Ages, I think it would be true to say that the Bible had almost no place in the minds of medieval historians. The strongly constitutional emphasis of the Oxford historical school of Stubbs and the tutors in Oxford, and the elaboration of this tradition by his pupils Tout and Tait in Manchester, was distinctly hostile to the intrusion of unsubstantial intellectual distractions into the business of the historian. It was generally understood of course that the Bible became important as a moving force in politics in the sixteenth and seventeenth centuries; but it could be left out of account, so it seemed, during the preceding thousand years. And this was not just an English phenomenon. French medievalists, though they approached their historical task with rather different presuppositions, were equally dismissive. I can recall spending a whole year in 1933–4 studying the reign of the Emperor Charles the Bald with the great Ferdinand Lot. We studied every aspect of the reign—the Viking attacks, the translation of relics, the Capitulary of Quiercy, the revolt of Boso, the first cracks in the Carolingian Empire, and the early symptoms of feudalism. What was never mentioned was the image of Charles clothed in all the sanctity and power of an Old Testament ruler, which is now seen as a clue of the first importance for his habits of thought and springs of action. One has only to read the recent study of the reign by Wallace-Hadrill to realize the great change that has come over the historical scene as a result of the new appreciation of the role of the Bible.

Beryl Smalley did more than anyone to bring about this change by making all medievalists aware of the presence of the Bible in their midst. This task lay at the centre of all her scholarly activity from the time when she began to research under F.M. Powicke in 1927 till her death on 6 April 1984. She died knowing that she had completed what she set out to do and she wrote to me with the brisk clarity that is characteristic of her work, giving me some details of papers in the press, and concluding with the words 'Thanks to my surgeon's honesty, it's been possible to tailor my work to the time left to me. So no *Nachlaβ*'.

In what follows, I shall attempt to trace the progress of her work on the Bible. In her later years she branched out into several other areas in medieval history—to the scholastic background of Archbishop Becket and his helpers, to the study of Antiquity among English friars of the early fourteenth century, to the writings of medieval chroniclers and historians, and to medieval politics and political thought. But even in these works, her studies on the Bible were the foundation of what she wrote.

Let me preface my account of these years with two general observations. The first is that during the years of her early development between 1927 and 1941, when the first edition of *The Study of the Bible in the Middle Ages* appeared, those who were young in Oxford were torn apart by two rival claims on their allegiance, which may briefly be described as the claims of Rome and Moscow: a very simplistic view, it may now be thought, of all the possible choices open to mankind. Yet there were few (and Beryl was not one of them) who accounted themselves serious in their intellectual aims who did not at one time or another stand on the brink or cross the brink of one or other, or sometimes both. The choices themselves do not concern the account that I have to give of these years; but the sense of internal crisis added a poignant dimension to the successive external crisis which seemed to be moving to a long-foreseen conclusion. To continue to work on the Bible in the Middle Ages seemed at the time a gesture of defiance or despair—it was hard to know which. Even if this background of crisis is scarcely visible in the printed pages, it should be borne in mind in judging how much or how little was finally achieved.

The other observation is this. The 1930s were not a good time for getting university jobs in medieval history, more particularly for a woman, and most of all for one who was determined to follow a historical thread that seemed to have only the remotest connection with anything that could be looked on as history. All Beryl's older advisers without exception (as she finally told me) tried to dissuade her from persisting in her biblical studies. Faced with such a unanimous body of advice, what could she do? Naturally, persist despite everything. The result was that she did not have a permanent job until 1943, when she became a tutor at St Hilda's. In the previous thirteen years, she did temporary teaching at St Hilda's, in Exeter, at Royal Holloway College, London; then, by the withdrawal of the candidate of first choice, she became a research fellow at Girton, Cambridge, in 1935 until 1940, when she became a temporary war-time assistant in the Department of MSS in the Bodleian. All these moves and uncertainties, accompanied by ever recurring ill health, disturbed her work. But they gave her great freedom of movement. She moved freely between Oxford and Cambridge, spent much time in Paris, and some in Rome. She got to know the whole international community of scholars engaged in studying medieval manuscripts. So among and partly because of the troubles and worries of the time, there was the constant stimulus of new discoveries and new acquaintances, all highly congenial to a temperament which was at once fragile, tough, and determined.

II

It is time to go back to the beginning. In 1927 Beryl was in her last year as an undergraduate in the School of Modern History. I have no way of knowing how industrious she was, but I suspect she was fairly selective in choosing the parts of the history syllabus to which she gave her attention. Then, in Hilary Term, she had one of those unexpected experiences which changed the whole course of her life. Professor Powicke came from Manchester to give the Ford lectures on Stephen Langton. In those days, lecturers were not expected to need much time to prepare what they had to say. I think it was only at the beginning of 1926 that he received his invitation to lecture a year later, so he chose a subject about which he thought he could say something useful, without being epoch-making. The way in which the subject developed may be told in his own words:

> When I chose Stephen Langton as the subject of the Ford Lectures some of my friends doubted whether I could find anything new to say about him. My first intention, indeed, was to concentrate upon his share in the fight for the Great Charter and upon his later activities, but when I came to examine his

3

unpublished Lectures, I found that the subject began to have a different and greater significance in my mind. What I had thought of as a restatement, containing a few new suggestions, was changed into a tentative introduction to a fresh, almost unworked, field of study. A happy result of the change has been that I have been able to gather together a little group of students who will be able, I hope, to carry the discussion further. One of these is at work upon Langton's *quaestiones*, another on his commentaries, a third on his contemporary at Paris, Robert Curzon.

These sentences mark a new beginning not only in Beryl's career, but also in medieval history in Oxford. They contain the first suggestion by one who was soon to become Regius Professor that social, political, and constitutional history might benefit by understanding the scholastic thought of the Middle Ages. I do not think that anyone before Powicke had thought it necessary to inquire whether the theology of the schools had an influence on events outside the schools. As we have seen, the thought had come to him almost by accident; and it must be confessed that, even in his lectures, the connection between Langton's theology and his practical statesmanship was confined to a few anecdotes and generalizations from the schools. Nevertheless, the spark had been struck; and Beryl Smalley was the first—and perhaps the only one in the audience—to take fire.

As a result, she enrolled herself as a research student at Manchester for the following academic year (1927–8). In the share-out of the work referred to in the Preface which I have just quoted, she was the one to whom the biblical commentaries were allotted. This was her introduction to the subject that was to occupy her for the rest of her life.

For the next three years she worked on the confused manuscript tradition of the commentaries, chiefly in Paris and Cambridge, under the general direction of Powicke, and under the immediate friendly supervision of Mgr. Georges Lacombe, whom Powicke had discovered to be working in Paris on the related commentaries of Langton's contemporary, Prepositinus. Powicke provided the inspiration, and Lacombe the familiarity with, and enthusiasm for, unravelling the ghastly tangle of manuscripts in which the whole subject was buried. The experience was profoundly valuable for the future. But in the present it must have taken an iron resolution to keep a grip on the subject. The result was less than electrifying. It would be doing Langton no great injustice to say that he was one of the most careful, conscientious, influential, and prolific teachers of theology and Holy Scripture in his generation, but (like Lacombe himself) distinctly short on sparkle. On this subject I shall quote only Beryl's concluding remarks in her contribution to the work, which she produced jointly with Lacombe in 1931:

> A very large proportion of Langton's work is composed of extracts from the gloss, Biblical quotations, allegorical and moral excursions which recall the worst type of twelfth century sermon. It is often necessary to read through many folios of such material before arriving at an interesting 'questio' or one of Langton's incomparably pithy 'dicta'. The student of Langton's commentaries on the Historical Books (of the Bible) quickly falls into the medieval practice of collecting excerpts. As contemporaries discovered, Langton reads well that way. It may prove to be our best method of dealing with the overwhelming material he has left us.

So far no one has yet been found to carry out the programme suggested in the last sentence, and Langton did not occupy a large place in Beryl's later work. Nevertheless, her experience during the years spent on him was of fundamental importance to all that came later. To be exposed from the beginning to the intricacies of scholastic manuscripts at the central moment in scholastic development in the Middle Ages was a unique experience, which no English beginner had ever had before this time, and few have had since. The work on Langton opened up the whole field of biblical study throughout the twelfth and thirteenth centuries.

One of the first things that Dr Smalley (as she had now become) had discovered was that Langton did not start from scratch. As she mentioned in the passage I have just quoted, the first ingredient in his commentaries consisted of 'extracts from the gloss'. What was this 'gloss', which he so often referred to as G or *Glosa* or *glosa marginalis*, or *interlinearis*, or (once) *interlinearis sumpta de marginali*, or (more bewildering still) *Glosa:... sed non est glosa Ieronimi glosa ista*, or *Cantor dicit in sua glosatura quod Augustinus dixit quod numquam continetur in hac glosa?* What could all this reiteration in so many varied forms mean? One thing that it certainly meant was that Langton stood at the end of a long process of scholastic development which had produced (as schools inevitably do) a jargon of its own, presumably immediately intelligible to insiders and infinitely mysterious to outsiders—especially to outsiders more than seven hundred years later. It soon became clear that the secret of the much quoted, and so ambiguously described, Gloss would be found somewhere near the centre of the scholastic development of the twelfth century, and the greater part of Beryl's work during the years 1931 to 1935 was devoted to these central problems: where did the Gloss come from? Who had made it? What did it contain? When was it adopted as a central textbook of the schools?

The traditional answer to these questions, so far as they had ever been clearly formulated, was that the Gloss had been put together in the ninth century by a German monk Walafrid Strabo, who had assembled a large body of patristic texts and attached them to appropriate passages in the Bible. Much later in her career, Beryl was to take the trouble to track down the origin of this legend—for legend it was. But in the early 1930s there was no really reliable evidence; it was still one of the possible theories which floated around, confusing the issue. There were already other scholars who were beginning to work on the problem. In particular H.H. Glunz, in the course of his study of the text of the Vulgate, had put out some suggestions, which had the merit of pointing in the right direction—to the schools of the early twelfth century. But his suggestions were marred by errors and over-hasty conclusions, and did not help, except as an irritant, towards finding a solution of the problem. It was Beryl Smalley's work, based on her wide knowledge of the Parisian schools and their masters, gained in her study of Langton, which finally put scholars on the right track.

In reading the commentaries of Langton and his contemporaries, she had been struck by the number of times the name of Master Anselm of Laon was mentioned in connection with the Gloss. There was one particularly emphatic statement which she found in Peter the Chanter:

> It is regrettable [he wrote] that Master Anselm was prevented from glossing the whole Bible by the many demands made upon him by the canons whose dean he was.

This and several other remarks by scholars of the last years of the twelfth century pointed to Anselm, the greater teacher at Laon from about 1080 to 1120, as the originator of the work, and perhaps as the visionary scholar who had foreseen the final result.

Beryl followed this clue with immense labour and pertinacity from 1931 to 1935 and intermittently thereafter. In the course of these years she was able to define the parts of the work which could be firmly attributed to Anselm of Laon, and to distinguish the contributions of Anselm's brother Ralph, and of his pupils, Gilbert 'the Universal' and Gilbert Porreta, and finally Peter Lombard. In addition, she detected and described the work of several contributory, but independent, commentators. In these studies, she turned what had been a rag-bag of hints and allusions into a well-documented and intelligible process.

She began by accepting perhaps too literally Peter the Chanter's assertion that Anselm of Laon had intended to gloss the whole Bible. This led her to oversimplify the process whereby those parts of the Bible which Anselm had been unable to gloss had been glossed by Ralph and Gilbert 'the Universal', bringing the whole work to substantial completion by about 1130. The process turned out to have been more complicated and protracted than this, and there are still many problems to be solved about the coalescence of the various tributary streams to form the work which only in the early thirteenth century was beginning to be known as the *Glossa Ordinaria*. But it was Beryl who laid the foundations and indicated the lines of inquiry for the future. More than any other great scholastic enterprise of the twelfth century, the glossing of the Bible was the work of many hands, and it took longest to complete; but she made the origins and a large part of the process clear for the first time.

Necessarily, these arduous researches carried her further away than she had perhaps initially intended from the amalgamation of scholastic studies and historical events to which Powicke's lectures had drawn her attention. The interactions between scholastic thought and practical affairs were to be taken much further in her Ford Lectures, *The Becket Conflict and the Schools*, published in 1973. But biblical commentaries played rather little part in these lectures, and the immediate course of her work after 1935, when she had substantially completed her main work on the *Glossa Ordinaria*, did not lie in this direction, but in increasingly detailed and authoritative studies of biblical commentators, at first in the late twelfth century, and then in the schools of the thirteenth and fourteenth centuries.

In 1935, she became a research fellow of Girton College, and it became an important matter for her to write a book, both to satisfy the expectations of her College, and to help towards getting permanent employment. The origin of the Gloss had come so much to dominate her work by this time that her first idea was a volume on Anselm of Laon and the Bible. There were two considerations which turned her away from this idea. The first was that it would provide only a meagre contribution to her claim for employment to have written a book on an outlandish subject attached to the name of someone of whom no one had ever heard. The second was that she had just discovered another character, perhaps even less known than the master of Laon, but much more congenial to her. This character was Andrew of St Victor, a man whose career, when she came to piece it together, threw new light on the relations between England and the schools of Paris. Besides, she felt a warm sympathy for his character and interests. Andrew was an Englishman who became a canon of St Victor in Paris around 1125. Then, in about 1145, he returned to England as prior of the newly founded Victorine community at Shobdon, later removed to Wigmore, in Herefordshire. With one long absence, due to some obscure dispute, he remained at Wigmore till his death in 1175. He was a man with whom Beryl found many points in common. At St Victor he had been the pupil of Hugh of St Victor, the most capacious thinker of the first half of the century, who stimulated two wholly distinct types of biblical study: on the one hand, an enlargement of its symbolic interpretation; on the other, the beginning of serious study of its literal meaning. Richard of St Victor undertook the first; Andrew the second. Richard's work made him one of the great names of the Middle Ages; Andrew's consigned him to almost total oblivion till he was rescued by Beryl.

She was later able to show that his work had a considerable influence on later commentators; but, to begin with, she was attracted by his stubborn, morose independence, and his choice of obscurity: 'far be it from me to extend myself beyond the limits of my powers; much better to rest solidly on my own foundations than to be carried away into a void above myself'. And elsewhere, he wrote: *mihi ipsi vigilo; mihi ipsi laboro.* He professed to confine himself to the literal meaning of the text, because he could not afford all the commentaries necessary for the spiritual meaning: *mee paupertati, que non potest semper ⟨habere⟩ pre manibus vel commentarios vel libros glosatos, consulo.* He doubted whether what he was doing would be worth much; but there was always a little more to be found out, even when Jerome had been there before him. Even Beryl found it difficult to make his work seem interesting: he had no interest in natural science; none in doctrinal theology; he had nothing to say about the fashionable subjects of his day. 'He is distinctly prosaic', she wrote, 'This is his virtue'. She liked this independence, and saw in it perhaps a portrait of herself: 'Being merely a scholar, he is unknown to text-books, and almost unknown to modern works of reference'. She liked to think of herself in similar terms. But she also saw behind the modesty a grandeur of conception: the detailed and assiduous pursuit of the literal meaning of the Bible marked an important break with tradition: 'No Western commentator before him had set out to give a purely literal interpretation of the Old Testament, though many had attempted a purely spiritual one'. It was a break, moreover, from symbolism to 'the event that actually occurred', which could be paralleled in several other innovations of the twelfth century—in the physical sciences, in government, and in historical writing: a new respect for the physical fact. Andrew was certainly not a man of superior genius; he lacked many of the historical and linguistic skills necessary for making much progress in uncovering the literal and historical sense of Scripture. But his efforts were part of a bigger enterprise than he realized, and they had a greater future than he could have foreseen. And, at worst, his sturdy persistence in work without renown deserved all the acclaim she gave him: 'After all, the first person in Western Europe who wanted to know what the authors of the Old Testament were trying to say to the Jews has a certain value'. This was a deliberate understatement: to understand what the Old Testament meant to the Jews was an aim which appealed to all her generous instincts. At a time when anti-Jewish pogroms were among the more disgusting symptoms of the crisis of the thirties, she found relief—as Andrew had done seven hundred years earlier—in seeking the help of Jewish scholars. Such collaboration, which played an important part in her later work, dates from this time. And Andrew had been the first western scholar to make systematic and constructive use of similar collaboration.

It is not surprising, therefore, that Andrew of St Victor replaced Anselm of Laon as the central and most substantial single figure in the book which began to take shape in the Autumn of 1937, grew to its full dimensions in the course of 1938, and finally appeared in 1941.

It was Andrew, moreover, who led her to the discovery of another character, who later developed into one of her best and most sympathetic portraits. This was Herbert of Bosham. Bosham had long been known as one of the companions of Thomas Becket and as the author of an extremely verbose and undervalued biography of the martyr. But of his scholastic side little was known. Glunz had written about his edition of Peter Lombard's glosses on the Psalms and Epistles. But it was left to Beryl Smalley to give substance and shape to Bosham's mind and aims. In doing this, the essential clue was a unique manuscript of his commentary on the Psalms in the version of St Jerome, *iuxta Hebraicam veritatem*, which N.R. Ker brought to light in the Library of St Paul's Cathedral in London. In Bosham, as in Andrew, Beryl found a lonely, disconsolate, English scholar, unemployed after a career spent at the centre of great affairs, scratching beneath the surface of the biblical text and its familiar interpretations to reach the bedrock meanings which the original writer had intended to convey. Even more than Andrew of St Victor, Bosham had the independence of one who had seen greatness, who had even himself made a considerable figure in the world. Yet, having been on the winning side, he was now irretrievably excluded from office, because of the cause he had supported. He had always allowed himself considerable liberty in thinking and expressing dangerous thoughts, and this had earned him praise from his arch-enemy, Henry II. This boldness also penetrated to his inner attitudes and scholarly observations. For instance, he noted that in quoting *Psalm* lxvii.19, St Paul altered the text to fit the point he was making. The Psalmist wrote, *Ascendisti in excelsum, accepisti dona in hominibus*, and the Jewish commentators interpreted this as a reference to Moses going up Mount Sinai to receive the Law as a gift from God for men. Paul made the passage refer to the ascended Christ giving gifts to men, and to do this he changed the final words to read *dedit dona hominibus*. Bosham commented that Paul did this *auctoritate apostolica*; but he recognized that the *Hebraica veritas* meant something quite different. Like Andrew of St Victor before him, he went to the Jews for help on the literal meaning of the Old Testament, and he accepted what they told him; but he went further than Andrew in studying Hebrew for himself. One of the thoughts which troubled him was, 'Suppose the Jews turn out to be right after all: would the Christian faith still retain a value?' No other twelfth-century writer is known to have expressed this doubt or discussed this question, and it gives Bosham a place in the history of medieval doubt as well as biblical scholarship.

Of all the characters whom Beryl discovered, Bosham was the one who perhaps pleased her most: bold in action, restless in enquiry, modest in aim, solitary in the end; and, in the words of R. Loewe, 'the most competent Hebraist between Jerome and Pico della Mirandola'.

III

In speaking of the 'discovery' of Herbert of Bosham, I have already gone beyond the first phase in Beryl's biblical work, which ended with the publication of her *Study of the Bible in the Middle Ages* in 1941, for he first appears in the second edition in 1952. The other substantial addition which she made in this edition was a considerable extension in her account of the friars. Most of her later biblical work was concerned with the friars—inevitably, since it was increasingly to them that the task of biblical exegesis in the later Middle Ages fell. But, despite this limitation, the subject after 1200 became vast, unmanageable, unexplored. She was the first to recognize the change:

> This part of my book consists of travellers' tales (brought back from journeys in unknown territory). They will give my own impressions of what the thirteenth century was like: a traveller tends to find what he is looking for.

What Beryl was looking for in the first instance was a continuation of the tradition of literal exegesis initiated by Andrew of St Victor and Herbert of Bosham. And this she abundantly found: almost everywhere from Hugh of St Cher (*c.* 1230–5) through

Guerric of St Quentin (*c.* 1233–42), Bonaventura (*c.* 1253–7), Thomas Docking (*c.* 1260–5), Albert the Great (1270–80), to Aquinas (logically if not chronologically last), she found a new respect for the literal meaning of the text. And, in finding the fact, she suggested the explanation: the metaphysical and scientific works of Aristotle, with their doctrine that the hidden substance of things could be known only from their manifestation to the senses, drove out the more exaggerated forms of allegorical interpretation and directed attention to the letter, to the matters of fact in the Bible. Thus, a way of looking on the text to which Andrew of St Victor and Herbert of Bosham had been driven partly by their personal peculiarities, and partly by their loneliness, poverty, and natural stubbornness, was now supported by the greatest weight of philosophical opinion that has ever been concentrated in the European schools. The various historical, linguistic, antiquarian studies, in which this new hard-headedness manifested itself, became the main substance of the enlarged final section of Beryl's book in its second edition. I think it must be said, and I am sure she would have agreed, that, compared with the earlier part, the additions of the next decade were rather a guide to future research than a definitive history. The subject had become too vast to compress within a single volume, and it was still too unknown for a volume to be written that would embrace all its diversity.

Beryl laid the foundations for a future volume by some other hand in the papers which she wrote after 1952 (many of which are reprinted in her collected papers). They were examples of the kind of research which will be necessary before a new book can be written. Three of these may especially be mentioned, two of them for the characters which they portrayed, and the third for its importance in opening up a new field of study for the future. Taken together, they form Beryl's most important contribution to biblical exegesis in the fourteenth century.

The two studies of individual scholars are on Thomas Waleys and Robert Holcot, both Oxford Dominicans who died in or about 1349. The former had a career of remarkable diversity and hardship, in the course of which he wrote *Moralitates* on a large part of the Old Testament. The main contribution to scholarship which he made in these writings was to pursue the literal meaning of the text into the areas of ancient history and classical mythology. This extension became the subject of much of Beryl's later work, and she went on to expand the subject in her book on *English Friars and Antiquity in the Early Fourteenth Century* (1960), in which Waleys and Holcot have a prominent place.

As always, though both men formed part of the same movement, she took great pleasure in the diversity of their characters. Waleys spent much of his life abroad, involved in high-level controversies, which earned him a long period of fairly honourable confinement in papal prisons. Holcot, who had the sharper wit of the two, is not known ever to have travelled more than a hundred miles from Oxford. But, stationary though he was, he was something of a gadfly intellectually, gathering picturesque material from every kind of classical and medieval source. Beryl described him as preferring 'decoration to decorum': 'no medieval moralist (she added) ever had a stronger sense of humour'. He was evidently something of a cynic.

It will be seen that none of her favourite characters fits easily into any preconceived pattern of medieval thought or piety. They all have strongly marked idiosyncrasies, which might have made them more at home in an Oxford Common Room than a medieval lecture-room or cloister. This remark may equally apply to my last example of her later work, and the one which may be expected to have the greatest future. This was her discovery of the lost biblical lectures of Wyclif. It had long been known that Wyclif had lectured on the Bible. Indeed, as a Bachelor and then Doctor in Theology working in Oxford, with only one period of absence between 1370 and 1382, he could scarcely have failed to give *some* biblical lectures. But that he should have lectured during these years on the *whole* Bible, and that a record of these lectures should have survived, chiefly in Oxford manuscripts, was certainly not to be expected. Yet this is precisely what he did, what they did, and what Beryl discovered. The range of the lectures was itself a surprise, because, as she pointed out, Nicholas of Lyre, who finished his lectures nearly fifty years earlier, was the last lecturer to have commented on the whole Bible, so far as we know. And, as she went on to say, the last secular doctor before Wyclif with a comparable range of lectures to his credit had been Stephen Langton in Paris between 1180 and 1206. So the wheel of history, like that of her own studies, had come full circle. It was an astonishing discovery. And what is so fascinating is that it shows us the most controversial figure of his time going about his daily task of explaining the Scriptures, steadily, patiently, voluminously, year after year. The lectures allow us to see the academic face of a public figure, as we have so often seen contemporaries who were passionately involved in great causes outside the University, carrying on their daily stint of tutorials or lectures, with nothing except the occasional barbed remark, or passing reference, or recommendation for further reading, to tell the *cognoscenti* that the lecturer would be equally at home in Hyde Park—or, more likely, the *New Statesman*. Almost everything still needs to be done to bring these lectures into focus, but anyone who opens them at random will be unlucky not to find remarks which would alert a knowledgeable listener to the fact that the lecturer might say more if he would. As a university lecturer covering an important part of the curriculum, Wyclif kept to the rules, and gave the students what they needed, perhaps not without smiles from those who knew his fuller mind.

This brings me to the end of my survey of Beryl's work on the Bible. Necessarily, there is much that I have omitted. But there is one subject to which I promised to return: the question of the influence of the Bible on medieval thought and action. I started with an example of the remarkable change in historians' attitudes to the importance of the Bible in interpreting the reign of Charles the Bald. I chose that example because he lived before the main period of exegesis which Beryl Smalley has so brilliantly illuminated. We must now ask whether any similar change can be observed in the recognition of the importance of the Bible by historians of the period within which most of her biblical work has lain. I think the answer to this question is 'no', or at least 'not yet'. And it is right that I should try to explain why this should be so.

There seem to be two reasons. The first is that in order to achieve anything of substantial solidity, it was necessary for her to confine her attention to biblical study in the schools and universities of Europe. I have described the circumstances which led her to start her work with Stephen Langton. This starting-point naturally led to more studies of the academic tradition of biblical exegesis. Nearly everything that she wrote on the Bible thereafter kept within the orbit of the schools. Certainly they provided enough, and more than enough, work for one lifetime, and the work needed to be done before any full account of the Bible in the Middle Ages could be given. And yet it was not through biblical exegesis that the schools most effectively influenced the world. No doubt many sermons came directly from the *Glossa Ordinaria* and from the lectures in which the friars supplemented the Gloss in the fourteenth century. But until sermons become too dangerous to be tolerated, they will seldom do more than reinforce influences that are already being more effectively exercised through other channels. It cannot be said that there was anything very inflammatory in the exegesis of any of the authors I have mentioned in these pages—until Wyclif. And that is why I have expressed the view that Beryl's discovery of his university lectures will prove to be her most important contribution to the study of the Bible in the later Middle Ages: they bridge the gap between the Bible in the schools and the Bible in the world.

The universities certainly influenced the world more powerfully in the Middle Ages than at any time before the nineteenth century. But this influence was exerted not by biblical exegesis, but by scholastic theology and canon law. Indeed, this was the main lesson of Beryl's book on *The Becket Conflict and the Schools*: the exegetical influence was almost entirely absent, except in that one shady corner in which an odd translation of *Nahum*, i.9, produced the formula *non iudicat Deus bis in idipsum*. The association of this text with courts of law did not come from biblical commentators, but from the lawyers who dominated the whole dispute. It is significant that Herbert of Bosham took to exegetical work only in his retirement: when he had ceased to have any practical influence. Like his predecessor in literal exegesis, Andrew of St Victor, he might have said *Mihi ipsi vigilo; mihi ipsi laboro*.

The exegesis of the schools was not, I think, an important force in bringing the Bible into medieval life. Indeed, the increasing concentration on the literal sense, however pleasing in some of its manifestations, was itself a debilitating force when it came to the application of the Bible to political or corporate life: take away the symbolism, and the result was apt to be antiquarianism. There were many reasons why the Old Testament type of kingship should have withered away in the twelfth century; but the decline of biblical symbolism was certainly a symptom, perhaps a cause, of its decline. It is of course possible to find many examples of the influence of the Bible outside the schools in the later Middle Ages; but for these examples we must look to the followers of Abbot

Joachim of Fiore, whose method of biblical exegesis had been quietly and firmly stripped of all scholastic credibility by Thomas Aquinas; and next we must look to the mystics, and poets, and the rebels. In the ninth, and even in the eleventh, century biblical imagery had been a central influence in the conduct of business and in the concept of established government. That is something we shall not find in the centuries with which these pages have been concerned, and we shall not find it again in comparable strength until the seventeenth century.

It may seem ironical that the final result of Beryl's biblical studies should have been to refine rather than disprove, to display rather than destroy, the foundations of the old generalization that the Bible ceased to influence society and government in the period from the twelfth to the fourteenth centuries. Her work had begun, partly at least, as a reaction against the crude version of this generalization which was then current. Clearly, in one sense, that old generalization was absurd, and needed to be upset. The Bible was the primary source of scholastic theology and canon law, which were the dominating influences in the practical life of the later Middle Ages. Nevertheless, though the Bible was the foundation of these disciplines, it was philosophy and doctrine which were the moving forces in later medieval practice. Was the success of the Gloss one of the agents in diminishing the influence of the Bible by smothering it in interpretations? And did the Bible recover its importance only when these wrappings were removed? These are questions which must be left for later studies.

If there is any irony here, Beryl would have welcomed it. The ironies of life gave her great pleasure, and her work gave her many opportunities for appreciating them. They did not disturb her. She knew that she had transformed the whole shape of the subject which she had undertaken to study, and which she had carried forward against every kind of discouragement and difficulty. She left it rejuvenated and ready for the next step, which will bring the Bible out of the schools into the world again, immensely enriched by her work. From this point of view her firm 'No Nachlaß!' was certainly wide of the mark. No one has left more unfinished work for others to complete.

Oxford

BEDE'S *NOTES ON GENESIS* AND THE TRAINING OF THE ANGLO-SAXON CLERGY

by JUDITH McCLURE

IT has long been recognized that the mainspring of Bede's intellectual work throughout his life was pastoral. Recently it has become increasingly apparent that his dedication to the continuing demands of the conversion of the Anglo-Saxons was stimulated and informed by the ideas of Gregory the Great.[1] What is less clear is the relationship between the great bulk of Bede's exegetical writings and his conception of the precise needs of those priests and monks whom he was seeking to prepare for pastoral responsibility. He had a certain amount of immediate personal experience of the range of technical problems involved in communicating the essentials of Christian doctrine and liturgy to an illiterate people who were ignorant of Latin. It seems that frequently he had advised monoglot Anglo-Saxon priests, *idiotae* in his terms, and equipped them with the bare essentials of conversion: the Creed and the Lord's Prayer in their own tongue.[2] Such personal contacts must have been considerably reinforced in conversation with experienced missionaries like Acca, who had accompanied Wilfrid on preaching missions and had visited Willibrord, and obviously by his accumulation of material for the *Historia Ecclesiastica*.[3] But, inspired by the writings of Gregory, and with the whole-hearted support of Acca, Bede chose to focus his activities not on the provision of vernacular material, but on the creation of an Anglo-Saxon clergy educated to at least some degree in the Latin exegetical tradition.[4]

[1] Most recently, A. Thacker, 'Bede's Ideal of Reform' in *Ideal and Reality in Frankish and Anglo-Saxon Society: Studies presented to J.M. Wallace-Hadrill*, ed. P. Wormald with D. Bullough and R. Collins (Oxford, 1983), pp. 130–53.
[2] *Letter to Egbert*, 5: Plummer, *Bede*, i, pp. 408–9.
[3] D. Whitelock, 'Bede and his Teachers and Friends' in G. Bonner, ed., *Famulus Christi* (London, 1976), pp. 26–7.
[4] H. Mayr-Harting, *The Coming of Christianity to Anglo-Saxon England* (London, 1972), pp. 191–219, especially pp. 216–19, 240–8.

One result of this commitment was that the backbone of Bede's literary work, regularly supplemented over thirty years or so, was a long series of notes on various scriptural books.[5] Research has begun to demonstrate that these items, given pride of place in Bede's own bibliography of his writings, are not merely extracts from the Fathers, but are worthy in themselves of sophisticated analysis to uncover Bede's principles of choice and personal contribution; nonetheless, notes they essentially remain.[6] This should not be seen in any sense as a denigration of Bede's intellect or as a condemnation of his assessment of the needs of missionaries; on the contrary, his working methods reveal him as the natural heir of the Late Antique exegetical tradition, making excerpts from those of the established authorities available to him on each scriptural book, and adding clarifications of meaning and interpretation of his own where he judged it necessary.[7]

The resulting compilations were clearly entirely satisfactory to Bede's principal recipient, Acca, who had all the qualifications to judge their immediate utility. Acca's heavy demands for additional material often cut across the rhythm of work which Bede had established for himself, and led him, in the case of his comments on the Book of Genesis, to put together sections of notes that had been separately conceived in order to fulfil them.[8] But fundamentally Bede followed, albeit on a reduced scale more appropriate to the intellectual limitations of his readers, methods of commenting on the text which would have been familiar to Jerome.[9] It is worth remarking that his compilations were not the written product of a series of exegetical homilies orally delivered, as was the case with

5 *HE*,v, 24: Plummer, *Bede*, i, p. 357.
6 C. Jenkins, 'Bede as Exegete and Theologian' in A. Hamilton Thompson, ed., *Bede: His Life, Times and Writings* (Oxford, 1935), pp. 170–3; C.W. Jones, 'Some Introductory Remarks on Bede's Commentary on Genesis', *Sacris Erudiri*, xix (1969–70), pp. 115–98; P. Meyvaert, 'Bede the Scholar', *Famulus Christi*, pp. 52–3.
7 Smalley, *Bible*, p. 36; H.F. Sparks, 'Jerome as Biblical Scholar', *CHB*, i, pp. 510–41; J.N.D. Kelly, *St Jerome. His Life, Writings and Controversies* (London, 1975), pp. 144–52, 220–5, 290–5; J. McClure, 'Gregory the Great: Exegesis and Audience' (unpublished D. Phil., Oxford, 1978), pp. xix–xx.
8 Bede, *In Genesim*, *CC*, cxviiiA, ed. C.W. Jones, Introduction, pp. vii–viii, *Praefatio*, pp. 1–2; *In Lucae Evangelium Expositio*, *CC*, cxx, ed. D. Hurst, *Prologus*, p. 5; *Expositio Actuum Apostolorum et Retractatio*, ed. M.L.W. Laistner (Cambridge, Massachusetts, 1939), p. 3.
9 Kelly, *Jerome*, pp. 144–52.

so much Late Antique exegesis.[10] Bede's habit of preparing his comments alone with his books may be the result of the fact that he did not hold a central position of spiritual authority at Wearmouth-Jarrow, and was thus not expected to preach frequently to the monks; or quite simply it could be because he did not have the advantage of scribes who could take down material for him.[11] However, given the predominantly derivative nature of his notes, what is particularly instructive about their form and content is the amount they reveal of what Bede and his contemporaries believed necessary for the training of an educated Anglo-Saxon clergy.

The *Notes on Genesis* are especially useful in this respect, as they are now available in an excellent edition, which greatly facilitates source identification, and their editor, C. W. Jones, has uncovered the several layers of work represented in the final compilation.[12] Their purpose and content make them especially appropriate for analysis. In the dedicatory letter Bede elaborated on Acca's request for a collection of excerpts from the many profound patristic writings on the beginning of Genesis for the benefit of weaker readers. He described the aim of his notes as the provision of a basic beginner's guide for the *rudis lector*, which would also be a starting-point for the more erudite.[13] In this work, or at least in the first section of it, we have the kind of material desired by a bishop with experience of missionary activity, written with the express purpose of informing Anglo-Saxon priests and monks, who had learned Latin but not very much more, on a scriptural text fundamental to any teaching they would be called upon to give about the creation, the fall, and the promise of salvation. It is therefore a very suitable work on which to base any argument about Bede's conception of the training of the Anglo-Saxon clergy.

The fragility of the evidence makes the precise dating of the different layers of the *Notes on Genesis* impossible, but the sequen-

---

[10] Despite Jones's unwillingness to distinguish between Bede's conception of homily and that of exegesis, Gatch is surely right to stress the need for a detailed consideration of the different categories of preaching: *In Genesim*, Introduction, p. viii; M. McC. Gatch, *Preaching and Theology in Anglo-Saxon England: Aelfric and Wulfstan* (Toronto and Buffalo, 1977), p. 31.

[11] *In Lucae Evangelium*, p. 6, '*Ipse mihi dictator simul notarius et librarius existerem*'.

[12] *In Genesim*, Introduction, pp. iii–ix.

[13] *Ibid.*, Praefatio, p. 1, '*...quae rudem adhuc possent instituere lectorem, quibus eruditus ad altiorem disceret fortioremque maiorum ascendere lectionem*'.

tial pattern of Bede's concentration on the text seems clear. Although it is possible to question Jones on various characterizations or on points of detail, his full examination of the structure of Bede's work, in which he develops the brief observations of Martène and Laistner, is most illuminating.[14] He has established that the present Book I of Bede's *Notes* represents the first recension in two books sent to Acca. He suggests that the first part of this recension was already long composed when Acca sent his request, and that it was a sustained and careful selection of a wide range of patristic comment on the Hexameron, or six days of creation in Genesis. The second part would then have been added on receipt of Acca's letter, possibly in some haste and from a much smaller selection of sources, to take the notes as far as the expulsion of Adam from paradise.[15] This would certainly have formed a short but useful guide to a number of primary themes, and as such it enjoyed a limited circulation, as the three surviving manuscripts of this recension attest.[16] Even at this stage Bede intended to return to Genesis, but he wanted first to work on Ezra and Nehemiah, a previous commitment or at least intention interrupted by Acca's request.[17] Subsequently he did so, adding to the first recension three further books to continue his commentary on the text as far as Abraham and the birth of Isaac.[18] The four books, which were the product of this third and final stage of Bede's work on Genesis, thus had a unity of their own, and dealt with some of the earliest and most crucial episodes in the presentation of Christian teaching. The surviving accounts of the most primitive form of missionary preaching, whether in Anglo-Saxon England or on the Continent, though they provide an unsatisfactory basis on which to build a complete picture of its likely content, nevertheless inevitably contain references to these themes.[19] Bede must have been aware of the practical relevance of his undertaking.

The *Notes on Genesis* reveal that Bede expected future preachers to have seen something of the fundamental problems of Latin

[14] M.L.W. Laistner, *A Hand-list of Bede Manuscripts* (Ithaca, New York, 1943), p. 41.
[15] *In Genesim*, Introduction, pp. vii–ix; Jones, 'Bede's Commentary', p. 115.
[16] Laistner, *Hand-list*, p. 41; *In Genesim*, Introduction, p. vi.
[17] *In Genesim*, *Praefatio*, p. 2.
[18] *Ibid.*, Introduction, pp. ix–x.
[19] R.E. Sullivan, 'The Carolingian Missionary and the Pagan', *Speculum*, xxviii (1953), pp. 705–40, especially pp. 715–16.

exegesis, despite their doubtless hardly acquired knowledge of that language, obtained through his own grammatical textbooks.[20] The development of scriptural understanding in the patristic period had inevitably been determined by men educated in schools of grammar and rhetoric, and Origen's concept of a divine language with its own complex rules underlay their interpretations. It was regarded as axiomatic that every word in the Scriptures was of profound significance and potentially capable of multiple levels of interpretation.[21] So even the most simplified approach, one capable of being understood by men of much inferior education in textual analysis, had to include some training in sensitivity to the complexity of the language used by God. Bede's use of Augustine's comments on the creation of light and darkness is instructive here.[22] In the context of a polemical commentary against the Manichees, the text was of crucial importance for Augustine in that it could be used to justify the Manichaean doctrine of two separate principles of light and dark: *Et divisit Deus inter lucem et tenebras, et vocavit Deus diem lucem, et tenebras vocavit noctem.*[23] Augustine explained the function of the verb *divisit*, instead of *fecit*, to reinforce his assertion that darkness was simply the absence of light, as silence was the cessation of sound. For Bede, the significance of this passage, and no doubt the reason why he noted it down at length, was not its controversial application, but its insight into the care to be taken in examining the precise usage of words in the Scriptures, a point to which he often returned. This analytical method could also serve to avoid an anthropomorphic conception of God, one of its earliest uses: thus Bede continued Augustine's comment to explain that *vocavit*, with God as subject, meant *vocari fecit*, as he was pure intellect, beyond the confines of human languages.[24] Bede's inclusion of this passage reveals that patristic

[20] R.B. Palmer, 'Bede as Textbook Writer: A Study of his *De Arte Metrica*', *Speculum*, xxxiv (1959), pp. 573–84; on Bede's didactic writings and his educational influence, C.W. Jones, Preface to *Opera Didascalica*, CC, cxxiiiA, pp. v–xvi; C.B. Kendall, Introduction to *De Arte Metrica et De Schematibus et Tropis*, p. 74.

[21] M.F. Wiles, 'Origen as Biblical Scholar,' *CHB*, i, pp. 454–89.

[22] *In Genesim*, I, i, 5, p. 9; Augustine, *De Genesi Contra Manichaeos*, I, ix, 15, *PL* xxxiv, 180.

[23] *Genesis*, i. 4–5.

[24] *In Genesim*, p. 9, '*Sed apud Deum purus intellectus est sine strepitu et diversitate linguarum*'. Bede seems to have changed Augustine's *vocavit* to *appellavit*, no doubt to match his text: otherwise he abridged Augustine accurately, even adding from further on another example to explain the passive usage.

excerpts, despite being isolated from their original context and often reduced thereby in significance, could provide a basic initiation into exegetical techniques, and the starting-point for topics of theological inquiry raised by such an interpretation of the scriptural text.

An understanding of the concept of a divine language, infinitely more sophisticated than human language but susceptible to similar methods of analysis, was the first stage in Latin exegesis of the process of gradually uncovering the different levels of meaning in every scriptural word and phrase. The theoretical basis of this approach had been explained by Augustine in the *De Doctrina Christiana*, which included Tyconius' useful short list of rules of interpretation; subsequently additional handbooks had provided collections of common scriptural expressions and their allegorical equivalents, and references to patristic bibliography on individual books.[25] Many exegetes took the provision of several levels of interpretation very seriously, including Bede's mentor Gregory the Great, who had actually intended to give three layers of meaning, literal, allegorical, and moral, for every phrase in his homilies on Job, and probably in all his lost homilies too.[26] Bede was facing a very different audience. Gregory had been surrounded by a group of earnest, highly educated Roman monks, who were searching for the most subtle points of spiritual guidance in the Scriptures, who delighted in lengthy and illuminating digressions, and who included among their number skilled *notarii* well able to take down every word from the lips of their spiritual father.[27] Bede worked alone with his superb patristic library for readers and listeners who had to be led very gently to recognize any subtlety in the text. He did include spiritual interpretations of some passages, making explicit the change from a literal explanation.[28] He pointed out apparent oddities in typology, such as the use of evil characters to represent good,[29] and obviously dealt at length with subjects where the literal interpretation alone would cause difficulty, as with the

---

[25] McClure, 'Gregory the Great', pp. xii-xvii, xxii, xxiv–xxvii.
[26] *Moralia in Iob*, Letter of Dedication, III, *PL* lxxv, 513.
[27] McClure, 'Gregory the Great', pp. 2–4, 7–9, 20–1.
[28] *In Genesim*, II, iv, 3–4, p. 81; II, vi, 16, p. 108; II, viii, 15–18, p. 126; III, xi, 8–9, p. 157; IV, xxi, 9–10, p. 240.
[29] *Ibid.*, IV, xx, 16, p. 236.

description of the daughters of Lot sleeping with their drunken father in order to repopulate the earth.[30] The account of the flood was a useful point at which to include extended sections of allegorical analysis, and Bede noted the traditional interpretations of the ark of Noah as the Church, its door as the unity of faith, and the rainbow as the sign of the divine covenant.[31] These precise textual comments were coupled with general explanations of the need for such a spiritual understanding of the Scriptures, especially the Old Testament.[32] This section of the *Notes on Genesis*, produced in the third stage of Bede's work, ended with a summary of the significance of Noah, and illustrates clearly the way in which a suitable topic could be used by a skilled teacher to draw out many fundamental lessons of theology and scriptural interpretation.[33] Though Bede produced his initial compilation alone, there can be little doubt that he had in mind, as he selected his excerpts, areas capable of being amplified in this way, which would then become the basis of sessions of oral instruction. It could well be that his *Notes* should be viewed as much in this light, as a collection of opinions and ideas upon which a teacher would expand, as a handbook for an individual's private study.

Nonetheless, Bede did intend his *Notes* to be coherent and informative enough for private use. He was generally concerned to refer to other books of Scripture and to indicate their relevance to Genesis, which encapsulated the history of salvation.[34] He frequently referred to his sources, and expected his audience to have some perception of the great wealth of the patristic tradition: his dedicatory letter to Acca, which naturally circulated with both the first and final recensions, is a masterly summary of the available Latin writings on Genesis, and gives in itself a striking insight into the range and depth of the library at Wearmouth-Jarrow.[35] Like previous exegetes he was not concerned to remark on the original purpose of a particular commentary, even if it were polemical, but he did expect his audience to be aware of the existence of heretical

---

[30] *Ibid.*, IV, xix, 31–2, pp. 229–31.
[31] *Ibid.*, II, vi, 16; ix, 13–15, pp. 108, 135.
[32] *Ibid.*, II, vii, 16–17, p. 117.
[33] *Ibid.*, II, ix, 27–9, pp. 140–1.
[34] *Ibid.*, I, i, 2, p. 4; I, i, 24, p. 23.
[35] *Ibid.*, *Praefatio*, p. 1.

opinions. Some of these, for instance on the legality of marriage, would be relevant; others, relating to long-dead heresies, seem to have been included simply to draw attention to the possibilities of error.[36] Bede may well have been particularly sensitive on this score as a result of his own experience; despite the range of material available to him on Genesis, he also consulted the two volumes of Augustine and Filastrius on heresies.[37] More broadly, he included any precise pieces of erudition that would help illuminate the text, or generally inform and interest his readers. As Jones points out, the Hexameron had traditionally provided the opportunity for including instruction on diverse items of natural history, chronology, and scriptural geography.[38] Bede's readers might well have found his *Notes on Genesis* quite rich and various in content, as they encountered information on bitumen, about the Hebrew months, and on the reason for the name of the Dead Sea.[39]

A more surprising element in the *Notes on Genesis*, which it might be thought at first sight inappropriate for an audience with only a rudimentary knowledge of exegesis, is Bede's inclusion of discussion of textual criticism and scriptural translation. He was prepared to note down fairly complex accounts of variant readings and their significance, to the extent of considering in some detail uses of a word in both Latin and Greek.[40] It might seem reasonable to alert his readers to the existence of discrepancies in the text, which they could conceivably encounter were they to travel and thereby to use codices in other libraries. However, Bede went further than this: he even pointed to the possibility of detailed scholarly work on the Scriptures to isolate additions made by Ezra during the reconstitution of the text after the exile.[41] Moreover, he frequently drew attention to the original scriptural languages, sometimes examining Hebrew grammatical usages and the relationship between the original language and the Septuagint and

---

[36] *Ibid.*, I, i, 25, p. 24; III, xi, 8–9, p. 161; IV, xxi, 9–10, p. 239.

[37] *Ibid.*, I, i, 25, p. 24.

[38] Jones, 'Bede's Commentary', pp. 118–21; Mayr-Harting, *The Coming of Christianity*, pp. 211–14.

[39] *In Genesim*, II, vi, 14–15, pp. 105–6; II, vii, 11–12, pp. 115–16; III, xiv, 3, p. 183.

[40] *Ibid.*, II, vi, 1–2, pp. 99–100; III, xiii, 14–15, p. 180; II, vi, 16, p. 110.

[41] *Ibid.*, III, xiii, 18, p. 181, '*Qualia multa in scripturis ab eo addita periti litterarum sanctarum reperiunt*'.

Vetus Latina translations.[42] His references to the *Hebrew truth* show what he had drawn from the work of Jerome, to one of whose letters on consulting contemporary Jews Bede actually refers.[43] Inevitably such notes on the text and on translations reflect Bede's own intellectual interests. They may also suggest that at least some of his immediate pupils at Wearmouth-Jarrow were capable of appreciating this level of comment, despite the fact that none of them was drawn to continue their master's work. They must represent the readers for whom the *Notes on Genesis* were merely a starting-point, the *diligentes lectores*, who were sometimes shown what further attention they could devote to the text, and what reading would be relevant.[44]

For the weaker students, the content of Bede's *Notes* would provide a basic commentary on each phrase in the text of Genesis covered, with a certain degree of coherence and logical development provided by transitional sentences, references forward and back, and rhetorical questions.[45] The care with which the individual excerpts were linked, together with the explicit introduction of the occasional theological excursus and the emphasis and sometimes repetition of significant points of doctrine, suggest that Bede envisaged that his *Notes* might well be studied by individual readers working alone.[46] It is hard to imagine, however, that they could have been of use to what must have been the majority of Anglo-Saxon priests and monks, who would have known little or nothing of Latin, except as mediated through a monastic teacher or educated bishop. This, presumably, is what Acca had in mind in his constant pressure on Bede to produce compilations. A learned man in his own right, he would have had no difficulty in teaching his

---

[42] *Ibid.*, II, iv, 7, p. 75; II, v, 5, p. 94; III, xi, 12, pp. 163–4.

[43] *Ibid.*, I, ii, 2, p. 32; I, ii, 8–9, p. 46; II, iv, 24, p. 90 (quoting Jerome, *Ep.* xxxvi).

[44] *Ibid.*, III, x, 32, pp. 151–2; III, xiv, 20, p. 192, '*Haec de Melchisedech paucis sint dicta prout nostro operi sufficere videbantur. Ceterum qui plene de illo deque eis quae figuravit ille sacramentis scire desiderat, totam ad Hebreos epistolam sedulus legat*'; IV, xviii, 1, p. 210, '*Si quis vero hanc lectionem altius discutere querit, totam spiritales redolere sensus inveniet*'.

[45] *Ibid.*, I, i, 1–2, p. 4; I, i, 20, p. 22, '*...ut supra docuimus*'; I, i, 26, p. 24, '*Nunc apparet evidentius*'; p. 25, '*...nunc autem manifestius*'; III, xii, 1–2, p. 168, *et passim*.

[46] *Ibid.*, III, xiv, 18–20, p. 189, '*De cuius expositione versus et sacerdotio ac regno Domini Iesu Christi, quod in Melchisedech figuratam est, ideo nostram parvitatem hoc in loco brevissime loqui ac tractare opportet*'; IV, xviii, 1–3, pp. 211–12, on the Trinity.

own clergy with the aid of Bede's *Notes*, in which the groundwork of assembling the patristic material had already been accomplished. It would be interesting to know if the *Notes on Genesis* formed the basis of the vernacular instruction of monks and priests. It is possible to see, from what has already been said, how this would have been done. There are also indications that Bede included material which would have been extremely pertinent for those whose future concern would be preaching to the laity. For instance, he used a long excerpt from the *Contra Faustum*, in which Augustine was responding to Faustus' denial that the Old Testament predicted Christ. In reply, Augustine had enumerated passages which, by allegory, verbal allusion, or in historical narrative referred to Christ, and the material drawn from *Genesis* was noted by Bede.[47] Early missionary teaching does seem to have been constructed almost as a chronological account of the creation of the world, man's sinfulness, and the promise of redemption through Christ, so this section would have an obvious relevance for the preacher.[48]

Such passages notwithstanding, there are manifest weaknesses in the form and content of the *Notes on Genesis* seen as an aid to the training of the Anglo-Saxon clergy. The sophistication of much of the language, especially in the excerpts from Augustine, the scholarly nature of a proportion of the subject matter, and the lack of an orderly division of content, an inevitable result of the commentary form, meant that the *Notes* would have been of real value only in the hands of an experienced teacher or of a relatively advanced student. It is not surprising that the Lorsch codex of the first recension should also include a more digestible list of questions and answers on Genesis, taken not only from the major Fathers but also from the handbooks of Isidore, Eucherius, and Junilius.[49] Bede did not see the need to produce any kind of scriptural handbook

---

[47] *Ibid.*, II, vi, 13–14, pp. 102–5.

[48] R.E. Sullivan, 'The Carolingian Missionary', pp. 715–16; see Eddius' account of the preaching of Wilfrid 'on the wondrous doings of the Lord in the face of idolatry from the beginning of the world', to the pagans of Selsey: B. Colgrave (ed.), *The Life of Bishop Wilfrid by Eddius Stephanus* (Cambridge, 1927), ch. 41, p. 82.

[49] Oxford, Bodleian Library, MS Laud Misc. 159, f. 16v. A recension of the *Exameron Bedae* is followed, at f. 29r, by a *Liber Questionum*.

himself, presumably because his own programme of instruction at Wearmouth-Jarrow rendered it unnecessary. For the student with a grounding in the Latin language and in basic exegetical theory and techniques, the *Notes* would indeed provide a most useful start to the understanding of the essentials of patristic comment on the Book of Genesis and a stepping-stone to advanced works. Indeed, the existence of so much other material probably meant that Bede's *Notes* did not enjoy the popularity of his other scriptural introductions, to judge by the number and provenance of the surviving manuscripts.[50] But this should not be pressed too far, as the circulation of Bede's works in general and their subsequent use does suggest that they really did fulfil their author's intention and played an important role in exegetical education.

The priests and monks who benefited from the *Notes on Genesis* and its companion works were the subjects of what might be called the Gregorian model of clerical training. They would have spent many hours of their lives in listening to and reading the Scriptures; they would have been able to perceive some of the problems of the text and its translation, and, with a basic appreciation of patristic techniques of analysis, they would have been able to explore the different levels of meaning in each word and phrase of the books they had studied. Above all, they would have been trained to find the essential teachings of Christian theology and the main guide to their spiritual lives hidden in the words and phrases of the Scriptures. To the undoubted strengths of this model must be added its weaknesses. In late sixth-century Rome, Gregory had been able to rely on the survival of the late Roman schools, with their extensive training in rhetoric as well as grammar; he saw no need to offer technical advice on the presentation of Christian teaching to uneducated congregations.[51] Even in his own city this had meant a lack of emphasis on preaching liturgically.[52] His advice to bishops in the *Pastoral Rule* was concerned with their personal spirituality and with the subtle guidance of their immediate

---

[50] Laistner, *Hand-list*, p. 41; Jones, *In Genesim*, Introduction, pp. i–iii. To the eleven manuscripts listed by Jones, two more should now be added: M.M. Gorman, 'The Encyclopedic Commentary on Genesis prepared for Charlemagne by Wigbod', *Recherches Augustiniennes*, xvii (1982), p. 195 n. 87; pp. 197, 199.
[51] McClure, 'Gregory the Great', pp. 46–51.
[52] *Ibid.*, pp. 162–74; Gatch, *Preaching and Theology*, pp. 27–32.

brethren, not with the adaptation of sophisticated teaching to the simpler or at least less-educated minds of the Christian laity.[53] Not surprisingly, Augustine and his followers were in many ways ill prepared for the nature of their missionary task in Kent, not least for the problem of communicating the essentials of the Faith to a completely alien audience.

Bede naturally accepted the Gregorian model, though not without modification. His own *Notes* were put together in an entirely different context from that of Gregory's monastic homilies, and he eschewed their long digressions and frequent concentration on the moral level of interpretation as a means of giving advice to a spiritual élite. Thus, as has been seen, Bede owed more to Jerome than to Gregory for the form of his *Notes*. Unlike Gregory, Bede had personal experience of some of the more fundamental demands of missionary teaching. While Gregory searched deep in the Scriptures for the justification of his ultimately sensible advice to Augustine on precise problems raised by the Anglo-Saxon mission, Bede simply urged the sending out of priests, with the barest grasp of the Christian message, to remote hamlets.[54] But Bede wanted something much more: a clergy trained by Gregory's methods. In the end he found no effective means to bridge the gap, for nothing he had learned from Gregory showed him how he could equip priests and monks to preach to the Anglo-Saxons. On the one hand, he translated the Creed, the Lord's Prayer, and the Gospel of John; on the other, he prepared Latin exegetical notes.[55] But he did not put together a typical sermon suitable for an uneducated audience, as Augustine had tried to do in the *De Catechizandis Rudibus*; nor did he compose a rhetorical handbook.[56] For Bede, those popular homilies he had read, far from exemplifying the informal discourse known to Late Antique rhetoric, and encouraging him to attempt something on the same lines to aid Anglo-Saxon preachers, must have seemed as subtle and complex in their

[53] McClure, 'Gregory the Great', pp. 104–30.
[54] *Libellus Responsionum*: *HE*, i, 27: Plummer, *Bede*, i, pp. 48–62; *Letter to Egbert*, 5: ibid., p. 409.
[55] For Bede's translations, see Cuthbert's Letter to Cuthwine on the death of Bede, Plummer, *Bede*, i, p. lxxv; *Letter to Egbert*, 5, ibid., p. 409.
[56] J.J. Murphy, *Rhetoric in the Middle Ages: A History of Rhetorical Theory from Saint Augustine to the Renaissance* (Berkeley, California, 1974), pp. 76–80.

composition as anything in patristic Latin. He does not seem to have preached to a lay congregation himself, and certainly not in the vernacular: the notion of circulating popular homilies, as the more enterprising of the sixth-century Gallic episcopate had done, does not seem to have occurred to him. Despite his emphasis, and that of the Council of Clofesho, on preaching, its form, content, and context remain even now elusive.[57] Like Gregory, Bede interpreted the person and role of the preacher in the broadest sense; even though, unlike Gregory, he did think very seriously about the basic problem of communicating the Christian message, some potential solutions escaped him.

Such an interpretation of Bede's view of the conversion of the Anglo-Saxons is confirmed by the accounts in his reworking of the *Life of Cuthbert* and in the *Historia Ecclesiastica* of those outstanding saints who travelled widely spreading the Christian faith: Bede made much of their aims and achievement without anywhere examining the content of their message.[58] Another aspect of the conversion period, however, did receive full attention in his treatment of the Church of his day: the significance of kings in furthering and consolidating the process of evangelization.[59] This perception was not simply a product of Bede's old age, for it appeared much earlier, in his exegetical writings. It was certainly in his mind during the composition of the *Notes on Genesis*, especially after the completion of the first recension sent to Acca. He turned his attention at this point to the Books of Ezra and Nehemiah, in which he discovered a unity of theme missing in many of his other exegetical compilations: that of the building of the visible Church.[60] It may well be that Bede was drawn to this work not only by a request of Acca, but by the similarity of its content, the rebuilding of the Temple after the exile, to that of the fortieth book of Ezechiel on the first Temple, which had been the subject of a

---

[57] Gatch, *Preaching and Theology*, pp. 32–3; Thacker, 'Bede's Ideal of Reform', pp. 150–1; *Councils and Ecclesiastical Documents*, ed. A.W. Haddan and W. Stubbs, 3 vols (Oxford, 1869–78), iii, pp. 360–76, for the Council of Clofesho on preaching.

[58] Bede, *Life of Cuthbert*, chs. 3, 8, 9: ed. B. Colgrave, *Two Lives of St. Cuthbert* (Cambridge, 1940), iii, pp. 160–4; viii, pp. 180–4; ix, pp. 184–6; Thacker, 'Bede's Ideal of Reform', pp. 138–42, 144.

[59] J. Campbell, 'Observations on the Conversion of England', *Ampleforth Journal*, lxxviii (1973), pp. 12–26.

[60] *In Ezram et Neemiam, Prologus*, ed. D. Hurst, *CC*, cxixA, p. 237.

series of monastic homilies given by Gregory the Great.[61] He took the opportunity, as Gregory had done, to enlarge on the position of preachers in the Church.[62] He was free to comment more personally on books not already overlaid with many layers of patristic exegesis, and his references to the Church of his own day reveal that his subject matter was close to his heart, and certainly more congenial than his labours on Genesis.[63] His reflections on the needs of the contemporary Church provoked by the text of Ezra and Nehemiah reveal that he was preoccupied even then by the failures of bishops and priests in his day, and, moreover, convinced of the importance of the role of Christian kings in spreading the faith.[64] But Bede had no personal contact with the Northumbrian kings of his day. Future programmes for the training of the clergy and the evangelization of the people were to require not only a more radical break with the Gregorian model than Bede had been able to accomplish, but also the positive collaboration of powerful kings.

Kingswood School, Bath

[61] McClure, 'Gregory the Great', pp. 217–249.
[62] *In Ezram*, I, 359–64, p. 250.
[63] *Ibid.*, I, 1446–52, p. 277; I, 1463–71, pp. 277–8; I, 1488–1502, p. 278.
[64] *Ibid.*, II, 993–5, p. 312, '*Obsecro autem ne sit grave lectori breviter textum huius epistolae percurrere et quantum personae christianorum regum conveniat videre*'.

THE MACCABEES AS EXEMPLARS IN THE TENTH AND ELEVENTH CENTURIES[*]

by JEAN DUNBABIN

WHEN the court chaplain Wipo produced his *Gesta Chuonradi* in 1046 as an instruction in kingship for the young Henry III, he prefaced it with an indictment of contemporary writers' laziness in failing to chronicle the deeds of their great men, although convenient models had been provided by pagan authors and Old Testament historians. The latter, in describing David's single combats, Solomon's counsel, Gideon's magnanimity, and the battles of the Maccabees, had created a remarkable series of biographies illustrative of the different ways in which a man could serve the common weal.[1] Their achievement deserved imitation. The main drift of Wipo's argument is unfortunately too broad a theme for discussion here. What concerns us is simply that for him the Maccabees were the archetypes of heroic warriors, and that he expected his audience to be as familiar with their exploits as he was himself.

Here it is unlikely that he was disappointed. For despite the opinion—challenged by Augustine—that they were uncanonical, Jerome had included Maccabees books I and II in his translation of the Bible. Although apparently little read in the patristic age, in the first half of the ninth century these books were the subject of an extensive and influential commentary by the Carolingian scholar Rabanus Maurus,[2] which was later copied and included among his own writings by Rabanus' pupil Walafrid Strabo.[3] Rabanus ex-

---

[*] I would like to thank Dr Henry Mayr-Harting and Dr Paul Binski for helpful suggestions.

[1] *Die Werke Wipos, MGH SRG*, p. 5. On Wipo see Smalley, *Historians*, pp. 72–3. Wipo was clearly concerned with Matthias and his sons, not with the Maccabean martyrs, whose fate was described in II *Maccabees*, vii, and whose feast was kept on 1 August. This paper shares the same concern.

[2] *PL*, cix, 1125–1256.

[3] *Ibid.*, cxiv, 63.

plained the text on three levels: firstly he clarified its literal meaning by exploiting Josephus and other sources to recreate the historical background; then he showed how the story prefigured events in the New Testament; and lastly he elaborated its allegorical meaning, as a parable of the Christian Church's struggles against its enemies. He was apparently unconscious of any irony in paralleling the Maccabees' wars on behalf of the integrity of Judaism with those of the Church against, among others, the Jews.

By his contemporaries, Rabanus' commentary was perhaps more admired than understood. But it certainly popularized a story which had, for readers of the later ninth and tenth centuries, all the elements of a topical best-seller. How Matthias and his five sons faced oppression, led Israel through massacres, sieges, and battles, and finally triumphed, the very stuff of high adventure, was easily transposed into the world they knew. So, when Rabanus had endorsed it as morally improving, its currency in the more educated circles of later Carolingian society was assured.

In the Old Testament, comparatively little attention is devoted to the individual characters or achievements of Matthias, Judas, Jonathan, or Simon; they are presented rather as a family group, ably backed by the whole corps of uncorrupted Jews. It is almost the nation-in-arms that is the hero. This aspect impressed the artists who produced the illuminations of MS Leyden University, cod. Perizoniani F 17, a work reminiscent of, though more crudely executed than, the famous Utrecht Psalter.[4] Among the thirty illustrations that accompany the text of I Maccabees in this manuscript, the many battle scenes strike the eye with compelling vividness (see figs. 1 and 2). Drawn in pen, with some colour tint, these are full of movement and tension; and they focus on the army as a whole, rather than on its leaders. The models for these scenes are probably antique;[5] they may perhaps also be affected by traditional illustrations of Vegetius' *De Re Militari*, which follows I

---

[4] On this see A. Merton, *Die Buchmalerei in St. Gallen* (Leipzig, 1912), pp. 64–6; A. Goldschmitt, *German Illumination*, 2 vols. (Florence, 1929), i, p. 22, and plates 72 and 73; J. Hubert, J. Porcher, and W.F. Volbach, *Carolingian Art* (London, 1970), p. 174, and plates 163 and 164.

[5] R.L. McGrath, 'The Romance of the Maccabees in Medieval Art and Literature' (Ph. D. thesis, Princeton, 1963), Fine Arts, University Microfilms inc., Ann Arbor (Michigan), p. 127 takes it for granted that they are, quoting 'the venerable adage that the medieval artist never invents unless he is obliged to do so'. Goldschmitt, i, p. 22, seems less sure.

Figure 1   The Leyden Maccabees
MS Leyden University, cod. Perizoniani F 17, f. 24ᵛ

Figure 2   The Leyden Maccabees
MS Leyden University, cod. Perizoniani F 17, f. 9ʳ

Maccabees in the manuscript. Yet some updating has taken place: some warriors sport stirrups;[6] and the very simple and crude fortifications seem like reflections of tenth-century building.

It is generally agreed among art historians that the bulk of the Leyden Maccabees was produced at St Gall in the early tenth century, probably before 925 when the St Gall library was moved to Reichenau.[7] Conceptually it has much in common with the rather earlier Golden Psalter, also a product of the St Gall *atelier*, which is similarly preoccupied with warfare; and it is also reminiscent of Notker of St Gall's famous verbal picture of Charlemagne and his army at the siege of Pavia.[8] Clearly the monks of that ancient and famous house on Lake Constance were far from pacific by temperament. Nevertheless, it is worth wondering why they should devote so much time to I Maccabees—the only book in the Vulgate which does not so much as mention the name of God—and pair it with the entirely secular Vegetius text; and then why they should illustrate their production so lavishly. The answer may lie in the Hungarian raids southern Germany was suffering at the time. The *Annales Alamannici* and the *Annales Sangallenses maiores* record incursions in 900, 902, 908, 909, and 913, while in 926 St Gall itself was sacked.[9] Interestingly enough, the chroniclers describe the Hungarians as *Agareni* — a good Old Testament name. Therefore it may not be too fanciful to believe that, in illuminating their text, the monks were calling on God for a replay of the miraculous Maccabean triumph. It would take less stretching of the imagination to think that they had their eye on the noble youths being educated in their own outer school.[10] In driving home vividly the lesson that God protects those who fight in his name, the monk-artists were also offering a few practical hints as to how warriors might do it.

If the Leyden Maccabees was intended to provide inspiration in a time of crisis, its creators were in tune with the Carolingian

---

6 See fig. 1.

7 Merton, pp. 65–6.

8 *Einhard and Notker the Stammerer. Two Lives of Charlemagne*, trans. L. Thorpe (London, 1969), pp. 162–4.

9 J. Duft, *Die Ungaren in Sankt Gallen. Mittelalterliche Quellen zur Geschichte des ungarischen Volkes in der Sanktgaller Stiftsbibliothek = Bibliotheca Sangallensis*, i (Zurich—Constance/Lindau, 1959), pp. 9–13.

10 W. Horn and E. Born, *The Plan of St. Gall*, 3 vols. (Berkeley and Los Angeles, 1979), ii, pp. 168–75.

tradition that prized the Bible as a 'guidebook for good living'.[11] Old Testament history was conventionally viewed from the didactic angle, felicitously expressed by Bede: 'Should history tell of good men and their good estate, the thoughtful listener is spurred on to imitate the good'.[12] In this conviction, clerics ransacked Holy Writ for compelling models to press on their lay lords. When John Scotus Eriugena hailed Charles the Bald as the heir of David, he aimed not simply to flatter, but to set standards for Charles's conduct.[13] When the author of Otto the Great's epitaph compared the Emperor with David, Solomon, Hezekiah, and Josiah,[14] he was less concerned with honest obituary writing than with impressing on Otto's heir the multifarious demands of good kingship. So Old Testament history became a chronicle of the great and good to which Jesus' words, 'Go, and do thou likewise', (*Luke*, x. 37) were automatically attached.

In 930 the violent, self-seeking Arnoul, Count of Flanders, fell ill. Fearing approaching death, he called to his bedside the monastic reformer Gerard of Brogne, under whose tutelage he prepared to face the Almighty. But miraculously Arnoul recovered and lived for thirty-five years more, during which time he displayed all the fervour of a recent convert in forwarding Gerard's religious aims. The Damascus-road episode achieved its earliest outward expression in the restoration of St Peter's, Ghent, an abbey harmed by Viking raids and in the reformers' eyes at least, morally decadent. By 941 the building had been restored; then those inmates who refused to accept the Benedictine rule were forced to flee, and the church was rededicated with great solemnity. To mark the occasion, Arnoul issued a charter which began thus:

> It is read in the book of the Maccabees, long ago committed to writing, that the temple of God at Jerusalem was destroyed by Antiochus, the most wicked of kings; after many great triumphs in battle, Judas Maccabaeus rebuilt it, decorating it with gold and silver acquired from the spoils of his enemies. By this deed he believed that the assistance of the King of Heaven would be with him. Moved by eager longing to follow

[11] J.M. Wallace-Hadrill, *The Frankish Church* (Oxford, 1983), p. 241.
[12] Colgrave and Mynors, *Bede, EH*, p. 3.
[13] Wallace-Hadrill, p. 246.
[14] *MGH SS*, IV, p. 636.

this example, I, most humble Arnoul, aspired to be a participant in the great mental struggle of those who keep the Lord's
precepts and transform their earthly patrimony into treasures
in heaven.[15]

The charter then goes on to specify those lands, once the property
of St Peter's, later annexed either by Arnoul or by his father,
Baldwin II, which were now being returned in perpetuity to the
abbey; it lays down that the Benedictine rule is to be observed
within the monastery walls, and that the monks are to elect their
abbot, though the Count is to validate the election.[16]

To read this charter is to admire Gerard of Brogne's ingenuity in
teaching Arnoul to identify with Judas Maccabaeus. The comparison was flattering, in that the endowment of St Peter's, Ghent,
hardly involved heroic self-sacrifice on a Maccabean scale. Nevertheless, it was apt, in that Judas's opponents were not only Greeks
in the pay of the Seleucid dynasty, but also those among the Jews
who favoured Greek religious influences: when the temple fabric
had been restored, Judas chose 'priests without blemish' (I *Macc.*,
xiv. 42) to purify it from past corruption. So Arnoul, having made
good Viking depredations, washed away the defilement of less-
than-perfect monasticism by appointing Gerard abbot over a truly
Benedictine community.

From Arnoul's point of view, the adoption of Judas Maccabaeus
as his examplar was just as happy. As his great-grandfather,
Charles the Bald, had grown in stature when equated with David,
so now Arnoul was magnified in finding his own niche within
biblical tradition. It was an appropriate one in that Judas remained
to the end of his life a warrior; so there was no need for Arnoul to
change his nature. Besides, just as Judas's initiative lay behind the
cleansing of the temple, and the 'priests without blemish' were
consulted on his authority, so Arnoul remained firmly in charge of
the reform movement in Flanders; Gerard was his counsellor, not
his master.[17] Then again, Judas had become prince in Israel, in

---

[15] *Diplomata belgica ante annum millesimum centesimum scripta*, ed. M. Gysseling and
A.C.F. Koch (Brussels, 1950), p. 144.
[16] On this see E. Sabbe, 'Deux points concernant l'histoire de l'abbaye de St. Pierre
du Mont Blandin (x—xi siècles)', *RB*, xlvii (1935), pp. 52–71.
[17] H. Platelle, 'L'oeuvre de Saint Gerard de Brogne à Saint-Amand', *RB*, lxx (1960),
pp. 127–41.

virtue neither of inherited right nor of constitutional position, but because he and his brothers were the only Jews both sufficiently warlike and sufficiently confident in their faith to do so. While Arnoul prided himself on his royal blood, derived from his grandmother, Judith, he and his successors were every bit as proud of the fact that, through the male line, their family's reputation rested more on heroic deeds than on noble blood.[18] Had Arnoul claimed identity with one of the kings of Israel, he would have infringed on a specifically royal image. As it was, Judas's cloak rested lightly on his shoulders; it provided emotional security, it permitted self-dramatization, it attracted popular approbation, and—he hoped—even divine approval.

Times changed. External raids slowly disappeared; ecclesiastical confidence in strong princely defenders was shaken. The monastic reformers of the later tenth and the early eleventh centuries no longer cared to expatiate to lay lords on the virtues of one so masterful as Judas Maccabaeus. On the other hand, he became relevant to a new class of militantly acquisitive abbot: André of Fleury in his life of Gauzlin, the aristocratic monk who later became Archbishop of Bourges, compared Gauzlin's reclamation of Fleury's lands with Judas's extension of Israel's territory.[19] But for some reformers this crudely materialistic use of the text repelled. William of Poitiers in his *Gesta Guillelmi Ducis* came close to Rabanus Maurus' allegorical interpretation when he described the holy men Maurille and Gerbert as Maccabean in their striving after spiritual perfection.[20] Yet this kind of metaphor never really caught on, perhaps because it involved too gross a contortion of the literal meaning of the story. It began to look, by the later eleventh century, as though the Maccabees were now out-of-date models, both for the laity and for the clergy.

However, the polemic of the Investiture Contest gave them another airing. This time, though, it was not the warrior Judas who was the focus of attention, but his brothers Jonathan and Simon, each of whom had been high priest in Israel. Their blend of political

[18] J. Dunbabin, *France in the Making \843–1180* (Oxford, 1985), pp. 127, 248.
[19] *Vie de Gauzlin, abbé de Fleury*, ed. R.H. Bautier and G. Labory (Paris, 1969), p. 38.
[20] *Guillaume de Poitiers: Histoire de Guillaume le Conquérant*, ed. R. Foreville (Paris, 1952), pp. 134–5.

and religious authority appeared to Wenrich of Trier, one of the more thoughtful pamphleteers, as the counterpart of that of late eleventh-century German bishops. In his letter written to justify Bishop Theoderic of Verdun's conduct in 1080–1.[21] Wenrich put before Pope Gregory VII a moderate but wide-ranging statement of the imperial position. On the royal right of investiture, he admitted that there could be a case in principle against it. Nevertheless, it was well-established in custom, and benefited from the endorsement both of Gregory the Great and of Isidore. Besides, there were precedents in Scripture: 'If those glorious men through whom Israel was saved, the Maccabees, had believed that for honours to be distributed according to the wish of royal dignity was a stain on their religion, they would never have acquiesced in receiving their priesthood from alien kings, impious men who were contemptuous of the divine law'.[22] So Wenrich posed a question: because Jonathan and Simon were good men, was it not legitimate to imitate them, especially since the German emperor who would bestow the staff and ring was a far nobler figure than a Seleucid king?

At once the gulf between Wenrich and Arnoul is obvious. Arnoul's approach to his model was imaginative; he identified with Judas at the dramatic climax of his career and drew inspiration from the act. Wenrich, the product of a more intellectual age, distanced himself from Jonathan and Simon. In calling to mind their conduct, his real concern was not with whether they ought to be imitated, but whether his opponents in debate would be embarrassed by the argument. In this hope he was rapidly disillusioned. Manegold of Lautenbach's counterblast, while furious in intellectual passion, was remote from religious feeling. He began by dissecting in scholarly fashion the circumstances in which Jonathan had accepted the high priest's robes; he concluded that Jonathan had already been elected to office by the people of Israel. He then twisted I *Maccabees*, x. 17–20, on which Wenrich had relied, to argue that Alexander merely expressed his acceptance of the people's decision; therefore, in despatching the high priest's robes to Jonathan his action was not

---

[21] I.S. Robinson, *Authority and Resistance in the Investiture Contest. The Polemical Literature of the Late Eleventh Century* (Manchester, 1978), pp. 153–6.
[22] *MGH Lib.*, I, p. 298.

constitutive. But, either because Manegold realized his interpretation was open to question, or because he saw that there might still be a case for royal investiture as a symbol of acquiescence, he went further. In a characteristically blunt punch-line, he pointed out that the matter was irrelevant, since the books of Maccabees were not part of the canon of Scripture, and therefore had no authority.[23] In committing himself to what was ultimately to be orthodoxy among the Protestant churches of Europe, Manegold was taking a more dogmatic line than most of his contemporaries were prepared to accept.

Manegold's careful examination of the text, his distinctions, and his concern with precise authority, were somewhat ahead of his time—he would have found it easy to hold his own among the philosophers and theologians of Paris more than a century after his death. His approach to Scripture opened exciting challenges to subsequent generations of scholars, and facilitated the development of true exegetical studies. In following where he led, twelfth-century clerks tacitly accepted that the old exemplarism was naïve; though they might on occasion employ a Maccabean simile for rhetorical effect, they no longer thought of it as prescriptive. Israel's past had lost its unique meaning.

But for the laity, the clergy's preoccupation with scholasticism was emotionally impoverishing. So in compensation they began to develop through the medium of epic and romance their own form of exemplarism: Charlemagne or King Arthur took the place of David or Solomon in the new portrait gallery of models, Christian chivalry replaced Old Testament blood-and-thunder. But there was one notable throw-back: within the panoply of the new secular heroes, Judas Maccabaeus took his place, as a 'verray, parfit, gentil knyght', the defender of Jerusalem against the Saracen foe. The transformation admittedly owed something to Latin literature, to the concluding lines of Hildebert of Lavardin's *Carmen de Machebeis*,[24] and to pseudo-Turpin, who had pictured Charlemagne communing with Judas.[25] But it was in vernacular poetry, above all

[23] *Ibid.*, p. 406.
[24] *PL* clxxi, 1301–2.
[25] *Liber sancti Jacobi: Codex Calixtinus*, ed. W.M. Whitehill (Santiago de Compostela, 1944), p. 337.

that of thirteenth-century Picardy, that Judas Maccabaeus re-emerged as a 'mirror of princes' in a guise very different from, but as compelling as, that which Gerard of Brogne had set before Arnoul the Great. Gauthier de Belleperche's *Roman de Judas Machabée* and Pierre du Riés' *Chevalerie de Judas Macabé*, along with the pictures that accompanied these poems in the manuscripts, were central in Judas's transformation into a feudal lord and a crusader.[26] And for these authors, as for Gerard de Brogne, Judas remained above all a model for imitation:

> Prions Deu qu'il nos doinst ausi
> Signor, par tout, qui auteus soit
> Comme li Macabés estoit.
> A lui doivent li roi entendre,
> Li duc, li conte, pour aprendre
> Comment il doivent justicier
> Les anemis Deu, et jugier
> Caus ki ne font bien ne droiture
> Et u il n'a foi ne mesure.[27]

St Anne's College, Oxford

---

[26] McGrath, pp. 19–32, 179–238.
[27] J.R. Smeets, *La chevalerie de Judas Macabé* (Assen, 1955), Vv. 7918–26.

LIUDPRAND OF CREMONA, PREACHER AND HOMILIST*

by KARL LEYSER

I N THE history of medieval Bible studies the tenth century in
Beryl Smalley's own words brought a sudden interruption, a
dramatic pause, and any reader of her *magnum opus* must come
away with the strong impression of a hiatus between the Carolingian commentators and the great teachers of the eleventh century,
Fulbert of Chartres, Berengar of Tours, Drogo of Paris, and
Lanfranc.[1] Strangely enough she did not mention Atto of Vercelli's
elaborate and weighty *Expositio in Epistolas S. Pauli*, written not
long after 940, which at least continued and used the massive
labours of the ninth-century scholars. As Beryl saw this interlude,
its foremost spirits turned away from literary studies towards
liturgy, and the great abbots of Cluny in their sermons and
meditations concentrated on the dramatic and emotional aspects of
Scripture. Their method, as she put it, might be called exclamatory. The sermons of Abbot Odo of Cluny, of Atto of Vercelli and
Rather of Verona which we possess seem to bear out these
characteristics. They were addressed to clerical and monastic
communities in a tone of forthright instruction. Sometimes they
expounded their texts directly, more often they employed them to
drive home a lesson or a moral. For instance, as death came about
through the fault of a woman, the joy of the Resurrection was
conveyed to the disciples through a woman, St Mary Magdalen, so
that the original opprobrium was forever removed from the sex

---

* In presenting this study in memory of Beryl Smalley I have ventured on what was
in part new ground for me. I am very grateful to Professor Bernhard Bischoff for
letting me have an advance copy of his edition of Liudprand's sermon. My
indebtedness to his *apparatus criticus* will be obvious and is gladly acknowledged. I
should like to thank no less Sir Richard Southern, Alexander Murray, and
Henrietta and Conrad Leyser for their suggestions, advice, and encouragement.
[1] Smalley, *Bible*, pp. 44–5.

(Odo).[2] The pre-pascal diet of *lactuca agrestis*, bitter herbs (*Numbers*, ix. 11), must change ill will in the heart and turn it to sighs, laments, and true peace before the worshipper can partake of Easter fare (Rather).[3] A Whitsun sermon of Atto's is propounded in a shortened version lest the vulgar are bored, suggesting that it might have been addressed or translated to a lay crowd. Here the more merciful dispensations of Christ's laws are contrasted with the sternness of Mosaic dicta. For this very reason it became imperative not to lose time for penitence.[4]

Some of the foremost Ottonian bishops were renowned as preachers, and praised by the historians and biographers of the tenth and early eleventh centuries for their power of the word. Of Archbishop Frederick of Mainz (937–54), Widukind wrote that he was great in prayer and in the largesse of his alms but outstanding in his preaching, albeit a consistent enemy of Otto I.[5] Gerhard, St Udalrich of Augsburg's biographer, dwelt long and lovingly on the Saint-bishop's *ammonitio* of clergy and people and on his regular visitations, *causa regendi, praedicandi et confirmandi*.[6] Ruotger did not omit to extol Archbishop Brun of Cologne (953–65) for his preaching of the word of God, and Thietmar of Merseburg praised Archbishop Willigis of Mainz (975–1011) above all for his *praedicatio*.[7] He was like a sun illuminating the hearts of laggards. On another occasion he mentioned that Archbishop Adalbert of Magdeburg (968–81) delivered an excellent sermon. Of his own, Thietmar spoke modestly only in passing.[8] Otloh, the biographer of St Wolfgang, especially noted that his hero avoided intricate and sophistic expositions. By his simple, austere, and admirable mode

---

[2] *Sancti Odonis Abbatis Cluniacensis secundi Opera Omnia, Sermo* ii, PL cxxxiii, 721. On Carolingian sermons and homilies see R. McKitterick, *The Frankish Church and Carolingian Reforms, 789–895*, RHS (London, 1977).

[3] *Ratherii Veronensis Episcopi Opera Omnia, Sermo* iv, PL cxxxvi, 721–2.

[4] *Attonis Vercellensis Episcopi Opera Omnia, Sermo* xii, PL cxxxiv, 849–50.

[5] *Widukindi Monachi Corbeiensis Rerum Gestarum Saxonicarum Libri Tres*, III, 15, ed. P. Hirsch and J.E. Lohmann, MGH SRG, (Hanover, 1935), p. 112.

[6] *Gerhardi Vita S. Ouldalrici Episcopi*, chs. 4, 6, MGH SS, IV, pp. 391, 394.

[7] *Ruotgeri Vita Brunonis Archiepiscopi Coloniensis*, c.33, ed. I. Ott, MGH SRG, ns, X (Weimar, 1951), pp. 33–4. For Willigis see *Thietmari Merseburgensis Episcopi Chronicon*, III, 5, ed. R. Holtzmann, MGH SRG, ns, IX (Berlin, 1955), p. 102.

[8] Thietmar, *Chronicon*, III, 1, pp. 96–8. For Thietmar's own preaching see *ibid.*, VI, 70, p. 360.

of address he drew enormous crowds of both sexes, and many of his hearers went away moved to tears.[9] The mid-eleventh-century *Vita* of Archbishop Heribert of Cologne (999–1021) described a Palm Sunday sermon of his when he harangued—the word often used is *disputare*—clergy and people on the ruinous disobedience of the first man and the hope of resurrection and glory.[10]

Of these eight bishops three came to be venerated as saints, and a fourth, Willigis, had an office composed in his honour in the twelfth century.[11] That they and others should have fulfilled their duty of preaching is not unexpected. Bishops were meant to preach, and it was felt to be desirable that priests should too. All the same, it may come as a surprise that Liudprand of Cremona's name must be added to this list of eminent and appealing tenth- and early eleventh-century homilists. Hitherto he has been known to us for two of the most vivid, not to say lurid, historical works of the Ottonian age, and a third, a justification of Otto I's doings at Rome—the *Antapodosis* begun in 958 and not yet finished in 962—the *Legatio*, his polemic about his embassy to Constantinople, written in 969, and the *Historia Ottonis* of 964–5. To these must now be added an Easter sermon composed sometime between 958 and 961. We owe its discovery to Bernhard Bischoff, who has edited the text from a renowned Freising manuscript which had once belonged to Bishop Abraham of Freising (957–94) and is now Clm 6426 of the State Library in Munich.[12]

Bishop Abraham was a great patron, who during his long but troubled pontificate commissioned and acquired an impressive number of *codices* for his cathedral. Clm 6426, however, with the Liudprand homily, occupied a very special place among them and was more intimately linked with its owner than all the others. It is a handbook, an episcopal *vade-mecum* with blessings, essential and

---

[9] *Othloni Vita Sancti Wolfgangi Episcopi*, c.19, MGH SS, IV, p. 535.

[10] *Lantberti Vita Sancti Heriberti Archiepiscopi*, c.9, MGH SS, IV, p. 747.

[11] See *MGH SS*, XV, 2, pp. 742–3, 746–8.

[12] B. Bischoff, 'Eine Osterpredigt Liudprands von Cremona (um 960)', in his *Anecdota Novissima Texte des vierten bis sechzehnten Jahrhunderts, Quellen und Untersuchungen zur Lateinischen Philologie des Mittelalters*, vii (Stuttgart, 1984), pp. 20–34. On the manuscript see also Bischoff, 'Über gefaltete Handschriften vornehmlich hagiographischen Inhalts', in his *Mittelalterliche Studien*, i (Stuttgart, 1966), pp. 93–100.

befitting *formulae*, but above all missionary aids in Slavonic, which Bishop Abraham needed for the arduous and urgent tasks that confronted him in the vast Carinthian temporalities of his see. In this remote Alpine bastion a large Slav population still awaited conversion. The gathering with Liudprand's text was joined to these important and unusual helps for the bishop's day-to-day use. That Liudprand's sermon should have found a place just here reveals how much Abraham must have valued it. There is, moreover, clear evidence that the Bishop of Freising cared also for Liudprand's historical writings, the *Antapodosis* and the *Historia Ottonis*, for he possessed both in another of his manuscripts, now Clm 6388, where his own hand has been detected.[13]

The sermon in Bishop Abraham's handbook is headed: ΟΜΙΛΕΙΑ ΤΟΥ ΛΙΟΥΤΖΙΟΥ ΤΟΥ ΙΤΑΛΙΚΟΥ δίακόνου, thus unmistakably revealing its authorship, and Liudprand himself may have penned the Greek letters of the title. Bernhard Bischoff, moreover, has identified the Fulda-North-German hand of this, at one time folded, fascicule in the codex.[14] It has been suggested that Abraham acquired it perhaps at Corvey, where he was exiled after taking a prominent part in Henry the Wrangler's and his mother's, the duchess Judith's, conspiracy against Otto II in 974.[15] We cannot be at all sure about this. Most likely Abraham knew Liudprand personally at the Ottonian court, both before and after his promotion to the see of Freising in 957. That Liudprand, after difficult beginnings, was able to join the clerical *familia* of Otto I, and serve him in his chapel as a refugee from Italy, is known.[16] Whether Abraham too was one of Otto I's *capellani* has been much debated and remains uncertain, but it cannot by any means be ruled out.[17] As a bishop he attended Otto's *curia* at Regensburg in February 961, and he may even have heard Liudprand deliver his homily in some

---

[13] N. Daniel, *Handschriften des zehnten Jahrhunderts aus der Freisinger Dombibliothek* = *Münchener Beiträge zur Mediävistik und Renaissance-Forschung*, xi, Arbeo-Gesellschaft (Munich, 1973), pp. 105–6.

[14] Bischoff, *Mittelalterliche Studien*, i, p. 93, and Daniel, *Handschriften*, p. 106.

[15] Daniel, *Handschriften*, pp. 79–87, and esp. p. 83.

[16] J. Fleckenstein, *Die Hofkapelle der deutschen Könige*, ii: *Die Hofkapelle im Rahmen der Ottonisch-Salischen Reichskirche*, MGH Schriften, XVI/ii (Stuttgart, 1966), pp. 46, 50.

[17] Fleckenstein, *Hofkapelle*, ii, pp. 45–6, but see also p. 216, n. 403, where he thought it very doubtful.

form, which according to Bischoff should be dated between 958 and 961.[18] During these years Liudprand, as we know, was working on the *Antapodosis*, which of all his writings thus stands nearest to the homily. It is here that we must look for affinities between Liudprand the preacher and Liudprand the historian. Let us listen to what the future Bishop of Cremona had to say to his audience and readers.

His themes were, as befitted the occasion, the central tenets of Christian belief, the Incarnation, the Redemption, and the Trinity. Liudprand however chose to cast his *exposé* of the articles of faith in the form of a vigorous dialectic. They were to be vindicated against the doubts and objections of a Hebrew. Liudprand in his homily thus reveals himself not only as a well-schooled theologian, but his sermon must also be seen as a forceful contribution to the continuous and troubled debate between the Church and Judaism at a time when that debate was as yet unaccompanied by wholesale massacres and plunder.[19]

Throughout, the Jew is called *infelix*, and once he is addressed in Greek as ὦ ἄπιστε, but Liudprand never becomes vehemently abusive. The Jew feared and refused to hear the Christian message. In the words of the Apostle James's letter (i. 23) he listened to the message, but did not act upon it. Liudprand opens his sermon magnificently, not only with a ringing statement of the Creed, but also its dogmatic exposition. The Hebrew then enters the argument: If God is omnipotent, to which I agree, what need had he, the Uncreated, to become *creatura* to set free his creation?[20] By his might alone he could liberate man from the power of the apostate angel whom he had cast down. To this the preacher replies: 'You sin, for by proclaiming only God's power you deny his true justice.

---

[18] Bishop Abraham's presence appears from Otto I's diploma for a clerk, Diotpert, dated Regensburg, 961 February 13. See *MGH Dip Otto I*, no. 221.

[19] On Christian-Jewish relations and exchanges in the tenth century see B. Blumenkranz, *Juifs et chrétiens dans le monde occidental 430–1096 = Etudes juives*, ii, Ecole Pratique des Hautes Etudes (Paris and The Hague, 1960). For a debate between Church and Synagogue, which the author dates in the middle of the tenth century, see his *Les auteurs chrétiens latins du moyen âge sur les juifs et le judaisme = Etudes juives*, iv (Paris and The Hague, 1963), no. 188. See also F. Lotter, 'Zu den Anfängen deutsch-jüdischer Symbiose in frühottonischer Zeit', *Archiv für Kulturgeschichte*, lv (1973), pp. 1–34, and esp. now J.M. Wallace-Hadrill, *The Frankish Church* (Oxford, 1983), pp. 390–403.

[20] Bischoff, 'Osterpredigt', p. 24, lines 12–14.

If God had freed fallen man by his power alone and not also by reason where would his justice be by which the prophet had affirmed him to be the just judge?' Liudprand here followed Augustine, *De Trinitate*, xiii, 13, but he did so with a vivacity all his own. By power, he averred, God could have coerced the proud angel to forego his pride, but the angel had wanted to make himself the equal of his creator by his own volition. Where there was a will to sin there must also be an ability to do so. God created the angels so that they should either of their own will enjoy eternal bliss or be punished by perpetual damnation. Wishing to refurbish the *ordo* which had been diminished by the lapse of the unclean spirits—and here Liudprand again followed Augustine—the Lord therefore created man *ex limo terrae* to punish the devil all the more by man's possible transition to his, the devil's, former glory. The devil, touched by envy and in his hatred of the Creator, now sought to bring it about that man through an act of disobedience should not be able to reach the beatitude from which he, the fiend, had lapsed.[21]

The preacher then described Eve's temptation, the Fall, and its consequence, death.[22] 'And, O Hebrew, so that I anticipate your silent question', Liudprand continues, 'well did God allow man to be tempted when he foreknew that he would yield to temptation'.[23] Throughout, the idea of justice is profoundly linked with the ability to choose, to decide for better or for worse. Temptation and the chance to resist it was the permanent condition of mankind. Liudprand continues: God, grieving that man whom he had created, had been deceived by the devil's fraud wanted to free him from the jaws of due death not by power alone but by power joined to holy reason. If the opponent said, 'Why did God wish to liberate only man and not the fallen angel?' it was because the latter had sinned of his own malice, whereas man burdened by the weight of his flesh was incited by the serpent's insinuation, and so man alone was to be liberated by divine grace. And since the merit of no angel could suffice for the redemption of the whole world, God wanted to free man *per principium hoc est creatorem increatum*. That, Liudprand explained, was God's son.[24]

---

[21] *Ibid*, pp. 24–5 and notes 5 and 7 for Augustine's exposition.
[22] *Ibid*., pp. 25–6.
[23] *Ibid*., p. 26, lines 67–9.
[24] *Ibid*., p. 26, lines 85–90.

This brings the preacher to the Trinity and the opponent's question, an often-voiced one in the Christian-Jewish debate: How can divinity without contagion and corruption adhere to the flesh? Good question, Liudprand replies, 'and unknown to yourself, O Hebrew, you have sent missiles by which you yourself will be injured'. He added that he was really forbidden to unfold the mysteries of the Lord to one who did not and would not believe: 'yet shall I try as best as I can, to explain for the sake of the simplicity of certain believers'.[25] Human frailty cannot speak worthily about God. Our language cannot really describe him or compare him with anything, but—and here Liudprand continues to address the simple—only by comparison with visible things can we arrive at an understanding of invisible ones. Yet his discussion and analysis of the concepts of 'word' and 'substance' here is far from simple and unfolds, as Bischoff noted, Liudprand's schooling in the *artes*.[26] He then turns to the familiar simile of the sun, its fire, splendour, and heat. If there were three words, *sol*, *splendor*, and *calor*, theirs was not a diverse, but one and the same, substance, and since their nature, substance, and functioning were the same, we don't speak of three suns, three lights, and three heats, but one sun; yet so that when you name it you have not named the words heat or splendour but have understood the substance of the words to be one. The analogy with the Trinity is then drawn: Why should the Hebrew believe that God the Father, God the Son, and God the Holy Spirit were three gods and not one? When Abraham greeted the three angels he called upon one God. Again and again Liudprand appeals to the Old Testament as irrefragable evidence for the New. 'Hence Abraham, when he saw the angels, in three persons understood deity's one essence'.[27]

From this confident demonstration of the Trinity Liudprand comes to speak of the Incarnation. Only the Son was incarnated so that by this mystery he could free us from the devil's grip, not by power alone, but by just and true reason. Liudprand here approached the central drama of Easter. The devil did not believe that Christ was at once God and man, but trusting in his victory over the first man he sought to ensnare him by temptation.

[25] *Ibid.*, pp. 26–7, lines 95–106.
[26] *Ibid.*, p. 22.
[27] *Ibid.*, p. 28, lines 161–3.

Vanquished by our redeemer he thought that if he could encompass the death of him who was without sin, the whole world would be subject to him, since there is no one else without sin. In causing Christ to be crucified by the Jews, the devil sought to snatch what was forbidden, and so lost justly what he held and had acquired. Liudprand here returns to his earlier theme. 'Consider God's power joined to just, holy, and true reason'.[28] It was just that the devil by this act, his attempt to extinguish the man without sin and God on the cross and to drag him to the shadows of death, where he boasted he held the whole human race justly, should by the power of the immortal and just God rightly lose what he trusted he rightly possessed. Nor must it be believed, Liudprand continued, that Christ did an injury to the devil. Death fled when he saw life approach, whose onset he could not bear. 'This, O Hebrew, is why I exalt and wish to put forward a philosophical dilemma'. Dialecticians say that two opposites cannot be together *in eodem*. When one is there, the other must be absent. You cannot deny that God is life and the devil death. Since it is so, nay, because it is so, death prejudiced himself in having life come to him when he could not bear its presence. For this we Christians celebrate Easter.[29]

Liudprand here is heir to a long tradition, well affirmed in Carolingian writings, a tradition, moreover, which outlived him for more than a century: the idea that the devil by the first man's sin and lapse had acquired just rights over all mankind, which he forfeited only by his transgression against Christ.[30] Gilbert Crispin was to argue still in this vein, although the prologue of his *Dialogue* with the Jew from Mainz was addressed to St Anselm, who decisively broke with this haunting view.[31] It is noteworthy in Liudprand's sermon that he treated the devil's rights with studied ambiguity and reserve. In the critical passage, *que tenebat, iuste perdidit adquisita* could mean that it was just that he lost what he had

[28] *Ibid.*, p. 30, lines 204–6.

[29] *Ibid.*, p. 30, lines 215–23.

[30] On this see J. Rivière, *Le dogme de la rédemption au début du moyen âge, Bibliothèque Thomiste*, xix (Paris, 1934), pp. 7–61, and above all R.W. Southern, *Saint Anselm and his Biographer A Study of Monastic Life and Thought 1059–c.1130* (Cambridge, 1963), pp. 85–7, 93–7.

[31] *Gisleberti Crispini Disputatio Iudei et Christiani et Anonymi Auctoris Disputationis Iudei et Christiani Continuatio*, ed. B. Blumenkranz, *Stromata Patristica et Mediaevalia*, iii (Utrecht and Antwerp, 1956), p. 50 and Southern, *Saint Anselm*, pp. 90–1.

held, but it might also describe the devil's title, the same *iuste* covering both—the past and the state of mankind after Christ's sacrifice.[32] In what follows Liudprand spoke of rights which the devil boasted he had, and rights that he confidently thought he possessed, rather than rights which he did lawfully possess.[33] He wanted to show that divine power and divine justice had triumphed together through Christ's voluntary act followed by the harrowing of hell and the Resurrection.

Liudprand then turned to the yet unanswered question: How could immortal God adhere to corruptible and mortal man without compromising his nature? He answered it again with spiritual interpretations of Old Testament texts, *Prov.*, ix. 1 and *Psalms*, viii. 5–8, as well as another appeal to the likeness of the sun. If the sun was not soiled by the filth its rays traversed, or divided by the tree it saw cut down, so let the Jews not wonder that the immortal God could without detriment to himself take on the humanity he had come to liberate. Here Liudprand washes his hands of the Hebrew and does not want to 'litigate' with him any longer. He now comes to the most urgent part of his homily.[34]

In the last part of his sermon the preacher turns from soteriological teaching to pàstoral practice. Having demonstrated how man had gained the chance of his own salvation, Liudprand now wishes to show how he might attain it and how he must strive for it. He strikes a new note of entreaty, and the homiletic here really begins. 'Therefore, dearest brethren'—and this is the first time he refers to his audience again after his opening words—'because we celebrate Holy Easter, let us inwardly imitate what we are outwardly seen to have solemnized'.[35] Deeds must follow words. Easter is called a *transitus*. We keep it reverently if we leave behind vices and go over to virtues. The whole of this section is dominated by a telling reminder of divine judgement to come. The wicked sometimes forsook their misdeeds because they feared earthly rulers and the death-penalty of the body, but for the sake of immortal God, the king of kings who can punish body and soul eternally, they gave up

---

[32] 'Osterpredigt', p. 30, lines 204–5.
[33] *Ibid.*, '...ad mortis tenebras in quibus se iuste humanum genus gloriabatur habere ... ab immortalis et iusti Dei potentia iuste perderet, quod se iuste possedisse confideret'.
[34] *Ibid.*, pp. 30–1, line 233: ὦ ἄπιστε'.
[35] *Ibid.*, p. 32, lines 270–1. ·

nothing. Earthly execution can often be avoided by bribes, influence, or the expectation of making amends, but eternal torments can be averted only by one's own good works in this life. He who has no oil for his lamp at the end, that is, good works in his conscience, will not be able to borrow it. Liudprand is here the brilliant stylist both his admirers and his critics have acknowledged. His image, from *Matthew*, xxv, then leads him to quote St Paul, II *Cor.*, vi. 2: *Ecce nunc tempus acceptabile, ecce nunc dies salutis.*[36] Now is the time, let us now prove ourselves as God's ministers. Liudprand is here clearly haranguing his own *ordo*, his fellow clerks, whose task it is to preach God's mercy, but who must also avow that he is a just judge. Through us, his unworthy servants, Christ continues to act and to declare how eternal reward might be gained and eternal condemnation escaped. He knew also that we could not ascend to heaven by our own goodness, and therefore he sought to prepare a ladder for us by which if we wish it we can fly there.

We are not left long in suspense about what constituted this ladder. God did not wish some to be poor and others to be rich from any want of power. He mercifully wanted there to be poor in this life for the salvation of the rich, so that the rich could by the love of charity make them partners of their wealth, and so themselves partake with them in eternal bliss.[37] Liudprand seems to think that the poor had a much better chance of salvation. Every one of us must consider the plight of the wretched and the disabled and set it against his own relative good health and prosperity. It might all have been the other way about. Charity was therefore the greatest and most acceptable sacrifice we can offer to God. Liudprand here vastly enhances the urgency and effect of his discourse by breaking into dialogue, between himself and his audience, between them and God. 'What are we doing for God by which we might earn these things, namely wealth and good health? Nothing, I say. What could we do? Nothing better than what we have learned by his grace: love God and love your neighbour. But you say, "I do love my neighbour". "How", speaks God, "do you love your neighbour whom you don't visit when he is ill and don't

---

[36] *Ibid.*, p. 32, lines 293–5.
[37] *Ibid.*, p. 33, lines 307–10.

hear when he cries to you for help". Our behaviour, my brethren, is detestable'.[38] At this point Liudprand appealed pungently to one of the strongest and most important social bonds his world knew: *familiaritas*. When we see the *familiares* of the kings and princes of this life, we receive them with great honour and beg them to accept the gifts we press upon them again and again, even if they don't want them. We offer them not trash, but things we ourselves value. Now the poor were the *familiares* of Our Lord Jesus Christ, but not only do we not give them presents, but we don't deign to look at them, and if we respond to their cries and afflictions, we don't do it in person; and the paltry things we offer them we send not by an honoured but by some low servant.[39] Liudprand then grimly depicts the retribution that awaited those who behaved like this. Here he recited Abraham's words to the rich man in the torments of hell.[40] The homily ends with a dialogue between a bishop, whose locked barns are full of freshly harvested grain, and one of the *clerici* of the audience. Some bishops preferred to throw away old and rotting grain which might yet help to relieve distress rather than distribute it. 'If it is like this, my brethren, I don't defend myself nor anyone else who does such things, but denounce him vehemently and deem him, though alive, to be already dead'. The exhortation rises once more to a shrill climax: It won't help you to share the torments of false bishops. Their 'woe, woe' is of no use to your 'woe', and companionship in suffering does not relieve the pain of burning.[41] May he who was made man for our sake avert it from us. Liudprand then concludes by returning to the theme of Easter.

There is no doubt that his sermon was addressed to relatively well-to-do and privileged clerks such as he was himself. Judging by the final, imaginary dialogue between one such member of his audience and a bishop, it is at least possible that he, Liudprand, was already marked out for promotion to an Italian see, a bishop-designate as it were, when he wrote and perhaps delivered his sermon. Otto I's expedition to Italy, where Liudprand of course

---

[38] *Ibid.*, p. 33, lines 318–27.
[39] *Ibid.*, p. 33, lines 327–35. On *familiaritas* see K.J. Leyser, *Medieval Germany and its Neighbours* (London, 1982), pp. 75, 94 and esp. 99–100.
[40] *Luke*, xvi. 25.
[41] 'Osterpredigt', p. 34, lines 345–6, 354–6.

accompanied and served him, assembled in August 961, but had been planned at least since Christmas 960. Easter in 961 fell on 7 April, but we do not know where the King kept it. He was on his way to Saxony. In the last sentences of his homily Liudprand appears to identify himself with the erring prelate who preferred to throw away spoiling victuals rather than distribute them. He himself is one of the scribes to whom he alluded through *Matthew*, xxiii. 3, where it is enjoined that one should do what they say but not follow their deeds. The humility- and modesty-*topos* would fit in all the better if Liudprand was about to rise above the ranks of his fellow clerks. Whether the future bishop of Cremona referred to an actual famine, specific events or persons in his homily must remain uncertain. The St Gallen Annals reported a hard year, widespread dearth, and many deaths through shortages under the date 959–60.[42]

As an exponent of dogma Liudprand can bear comparison with his foremost Italian colleagues of whom we possess Easter sermons, Atto of Vercelli and Rather of Verona. His vividness and dialogue are distinctive and all his own. They may have come across better than Rather's more profound but morose spirits. Atto too could be vivid and to the point as well as brief, and his vision of contemporary Italian society was acute, but Liudprand in his homily harnessed his insights more forcefully to his immediate purpose. As for so many of his clerical contemporaries, charity was above all a means of salvation.[43] He was nothing if not self centred: the poor were there to enable the rich to earn their way to heaven. The deep division between the well-off, privileged, and relatively secure higher clergy and the *vulgus* is evident in what he wrote about the *familiares* of the great, and in his effort to present the poor as the *familiares* of Christ who might possess influence in the highest court and tribunal of them all. It was an effective image to drive home and so temper the rigours of the social cleavage.

The question must now be asked where Liudprand's homily stands in relation to his historical works, above all whether his personality as a writer, already complex enough, has become even

---

[42] *Annales Sangallenses Maiores*, 959 (960), *MGH SS*, I, p. 79.
[43] On tenth-century almsgiving see Leyser, 'The German Aristocracy from the Ninth to the Early Twelfth Century', *PP*, xli (1968), p. 26 and *Medieval Germany*, p. 162.

more bewildering and full of contradictions now. Here we shall look solely at the *Antapodosis* and not at the *Historia Ottonis* and the *Legatio*. Both these were *livres d'occasion*, while in conception and in composition the *Antapodosis* overlapped the date of the sermon, as has already been noted. For the question here raised it is for many reasons the most relevant text. Now with very few exceptions, modern scholars have portrayed Liudprand as a brilliant, albeit vain, subjective, entertaining, not to say scabrous and risqué, writer. Robert Holtzmann commented many years ago that his theological schooling stood far below that of Atto of Vercelli, and he also remarked on his vanity and conceit towards Byzantium's ruling circles. In the *Antapodosis*, he thought, the polemic pushed aside the initially didactic and edifying purposes.[44] Helmut Beumann reflected on Liudprand's subtlety and ambivalence. He was too clever by far.[45] Auerbach, who examined Liudprand's style, slated him more severely: courtier and diplomat, he was an ecclesiastic only in name. His literary talent was considerable but superficial, journalistic and anecdotic. As a man he thought him vain, vengeful, and indiscreet.[46]

Liudprand's editor for the *Scriptores Rerum Germanicarum* in the *Monumenta*, Joseph Becker, laid the foundations for all this censure. He too felt that Liudprand belonged only outwardly to the clerical *ordo*, and while he did not wish away the many theological utterances in his historical works, he thought that they were a mere varnish rather than signs of inner piety. Liudprand was vain, self-pleasing, and fond of lascivious and piquant tales. He wanted to entertain and, it is true, to edify. Becker thus saw that Liudprand in his histories wished to show the hand of God at work rewarding good and punishing evil, yet at the same time he remarked on his passionate and temperamental make-up. He was the most personal of early-medieval writers.[47] Only Karl Hauck guarded himself, and

[44] W. Wattenbach, R. Holtzmann, *Deutschlands Geschichtsquellen im Mittelalter Deutsche Kaiserzeit*, i, 2, 2nd ed. (Tübingen, 1948), p. 320.
[45] H. Beumann, 'Der Schriftsteller und seine Kritiker im frühen Mittelalter', *Studium Generale*, xii, (Berlin, Heidelberg, and New York, 1959), pp. 502–4 and his *Wissenschaft vom Mittelalter* (Cologne and Vienna, 1972), pp. 21–4.
[46] E. Auerbach, *Literary Language and its Public in Late Latin Antiquity and in the Middle Ages*, translated from the German by R. Manheim (London, 1965), p. 153.
[47] *Die Werke Liudprands von Cremona*, 3rd ed. J. Becker, *MGH SRG* (Hanover and Leipzig, 1915), pp. xiii–xiv, xvii, xx.

warned his readers against these judgements, and saw in Liudprand one of the earliest propagators of a divinely willed and legitimated royal and imperial rule for Otto I.[48] It is possible to go further still and to insist on Liudprand's urgent and unremitting homiletic purposes throughout the *Antapodosis*. Here too he at times preached, and interpreted critical moments and events in Otto I's struggles for his kingship with the help of biblical example and precept. Only through the sacred texts could Otto's survival and victories in these critical years, especially 939, be explained. There was no other way. Let us follow him.

The *Antapodosis* is a parallel history of kings and princes 'of part of Europe' from the late ninth to the mid-tenth century. It had at one moment wanted to be more ambitious, a history of the whole of Europe, but even so Liudprand's design was formidable, and has no match in the historical writings of the tenth century.[49] It was addressed to and professedly written at the request of Bishop Recemund of Elvira, a servant of the Umyad Khalif of Cordoba. Liudprand had met him as Abd ar-Rahman III's envoy at Frankfurt in 956. The proem of the book not only describes its purposes, but also its method. Liudprand's *neniae* must be regarded as the modest self-depreciation required of an author in Carolingian and post-Carolingian convention, and if he wished to divert, it was a *utilis comediarum risus* that justified his stories.[50] The stressmark lies on *utilis*. He would speak of the deeds of enervate kings and effeminate rulers only to unfold their just divine repression. Above all, Liudprand throughout the *Antapodosis* is the sworn enemy of all wheeling and dealing between Christian rulers and the attackers and invaders of contemporary Christendom, Saracens and Magyars.

Bernhard Bischoff has pointed out certain linguistic affinities between the sermon and the *Book of Revenge*. Liudprand was fond

---

[48] K. Hauck, 'Erzbischof Adalbert von Magdeburg als Geschichtsschreiber', *Festschrift für Walter Schlesinger*, ii, ed. H. Beumann, *Mitteldeutsche Forschungen*, 74/II (Cologne and Vienna, 1974), pp. 298–305.

[49] See *Antapodosis*, p. 1 and I, 1, p. 4 in *Die Werke*, as n. 47, above.

[50] On Liudprand's encounter with Recemund see Becker's Introduction, *Werke*, pp. viii-ix. For 'utilis comoediarum risus' see *Antapodosis*, I, 1, p. 4, and see Beumann, *Wissenschaft*, p. 24.

of graecisms, and one at least is used conspicuously in both works, *amphibologia*, meaning *ambiguity*.[51] He has also drawn attention to the use of dialogue in the *Antapodosis* no less than in the homily to enliven the narrative. Moreover, Liudprand, in the midst of relating calamities like the Saracen onslaught on Southern Italy, pauses in his story to insert a whole chapter, very like his sermon, rehearsing for his readers the Saviour's beneficence, his providence, his sacrifice, and his constant wish for man's good. If, for the time being, he castigates us because we do not respond to his blessings, he then again re-animates the Christian spirit of resistance, so that the Saracens should not mock and say, 'Where is their God?'[52] Despite all the embroilments, the interplay of war, intrigue, ambition, and license, which he describes without embellishment in the *Antapodosis*, Liudprand wanted to make it quite clear that divine guidance and not chance governed human affairs.

Nowhere did he demonstrate this so effectively as when he dwelt on Otto I's, to him, miraculous victory over his enemies in the war waged against his disaffected brother, Henry, and Duke Giselbert of Lotharingia in 939. Otto had marched to the Lower Rhine from Saxony, and some of his mounted men had already crossed it near Xanten when Henry and Giselbert, with superior forces, advanced upon the detachment now stationed on the left bank by Birten. There was no time nor shipping to come to their aid, and Otto met the crisis by praying in front of the Holy Lance with the nails of the Cross, which accompanied him on his journeys. There was nothing else he could do. His men on the far side, however, were victorious against the odds, and according to Liudprand suffered no casualties. Widukind, who also gave a good account of the battle, made it clear that Otto lost men and there were many wounded. In his narrative too the King prayed, but it was a *ruse de guerre* which won the encounter.[53]

In the *Antapodosis* Liudprand not only narrated at length how Otto's father, Henry I, had acquired the Holy Lance, but he also

---

[51] 'Osterpredigt', pp. 22, 28, line 162; *Antapodosis*, III, 47, p. 99, further IV, 12, p. 111 and also IV, p. 120, an important example, not indexed.

[52] *Antapodosis*, II, 46, p. 58.

[53] *Anapodosis*, IV, 24, pp. 117–18, Widukind, *Res Gestae Saxonicae*, II, 17, pp. 82–3, and see R. Köpke and E. Dümmler, *Kaiser Otto der Große, Jahrbücher der Deutschen Geschichte* (Leipzig, 1876), pp. 82–4 and Hauck, 'Erzbischof Adalbert', p. 304.

wrote what can only be described as a sermon, a homily, to explain and magnify Otto's unexpected success. Purposefully he digressed to present the victory of the few over the many as the work of divine providence, whereby God wished to make known to wavering men, and indeed to Otto himself, how dear he was to him. At first sight it may seem strange that in order to do so Liudprand resorted to *John*, xx. 25–8, the story of doubting Thomas. He himself in his pulsing prose entered into a dialogue with the Apostle. It is also evident that Liudprand mastered the interpretation of the text resting on St Augustine and Gregory the Great. Heretics, Manicheans, who did not believe Christ to have risen in the body, were refuted by it, and above all Thomas's doubts were not accidental, but part of the economy of divine providence. By them the faith of the many was confirmed and strengthened. It was just this idea Liudprand applied to Otto I's victory at Birten. Not Otto's faith, but that of the weaker brethren, those who believed only in superior numbers, human prowess, or chance, was enhanced by the victory through prayer. Men must be roused by it to place their hopes in God, and also learn that Otto, their king, belonged to the elect.[54] Loyalty as a religious duty could hardly have been propagated more forcefully.

Liudprand continued in this vein, and the next events in Otto's struggle against his formidable rivals, Henry, the Frankish Duke Eberhard, and Giselbert, are transposed into a further homily. Otto here overcame not only his visible but also invisible enemies, his own passions and temptation. God sometimes allowed sinners to worst their adversaries, but it was given only to a few to uphold unshakeable strength of spirit, not to be elated by success or broken by adversity. This stoic equanimity, which Einhard had set forth as one of Charlemagne's qualities, is here Christianized and becomes a form of piety.[55] The fight at Birten had settled nothing, and when,

---

[54] *Antapodosis*, IV, 26, pp. 120–2. On the medieval interpretation of *John*, xx. 24–9 and its history see U. Pflugk, 'Die Geschichte vom ungläubigen Thomas (Johannes 20, 24–29) in der Auslegung der Kirche von den Anfängen bis zur Mitte des sechzehnten Jahrhunderts' (unpub. dissertation, Hamburg, 1965), esp. pp. 116, 126, 141. He does not comment on Liudprand's use of the story, though, and leaves a notable gap between the ninth and the twelfth century in his survey. I am greatly indebted to Alexander Murray for enabling me to read this work.

[55] *Antapodosis*, IV, 28, p. 123 and cf. *Einhardi Vita Karoli Magni*, chs. 7, 8, 6th ed. O. Holder-Egger, *MGH SRG* (Hanover and Leipzig, 1911), pp. 10–11.

later in the year, Otto with a Saxon host surrounded the fortress of Breisach his situation changed for the worse. His camp began to empty through desertions, and he was short of warriors. When a count with a sizeable following sought to exploit his situation and press for the grant of the abbey of Lorsch as the price for continued service, Liudprand had the King reply: *Nolite sanctum dare canibus* (*Matthew*, vii. 6), and not only this, but even expound the passage thus: Although the learned teach that it must be understood spiritually, I reckon that I am giving the holy to the dogs if I grant the lands of monasteries, which pious men gave to those warring for God, i.e., monks, to those fighting in the *saeculum*.[56] The count collapsed. Liudprand crowns his homily with the observation that the devil, having seen that he could not harm Otto by mobilizing so many enemies against him, prompted the count to ask for the saints' patrimony so that the King might incur God's wrath. 'But because he could not do this we shall now set forth how the pious prince grew in stature because of his constancy in this temptation, God fighting for him'. Liudprand finally interpreted the decisive battle at Andernach, in which Eberhard and Giselbert lost their lives, by *Psalm* lxxx. 15. Because he, Otto, walked in the Lord's ways, the Lord laid his hands upon his persecutors.[57]

Here, then, Otto's survival and eventual victory was the outcome of biblical precept observed, temptation resisted. Liudprand wanted to show not only why rebellion against such a ruler was in itself sinful, but also that resistance to temptation worked and could be seen to lead to triumph. The preacher in him was no stranger to the historian. This does not mean that we have explained him in full. His macabre tales and obsessions still pose serious problems. Once we find him use in a very light-hearted, not to say shameless, way a biblical image which his sermon had employed as a solemn appeal, the story of Lazarus blessed and *dives* in torment. In the sermon this had served as a dire warning. In *Antapodosis* it became the witty plea by which Liudprand elicited a further gift from the Emperor Constantine Porphyrogenitus in the course of his first embassy to the Byzantine court (949–50). He had already been given one, as was customary, when the Emperor made him attend

---

[56] *Antapodosis*, IV, 27, 28, pp. 122–4.
[57] *Ibid.*, IV, 29, pp. 124–5.

the annual pay parade of the higher dignitaries. Liudprand saw the spectacle, the display of enormous wealth and, at the same time, ceremonial orderliness, but when Constantine had him asked through the logothete how he liked it, he replied that it would please him very much if it was of any use to him, just as Lazarus' blessed ease in heaven would have pleased the parching rich man in hell if it had profited him in any way. Because this could not happen, how, I pray, could it please?[58] Here, then, Liudprand turned the parable on its head, nor could he forbear telling the story. Yet for all his cheek, underlying his writings is a passionate concern to tell his readers and listeners that it was not chance, but divine direction, *ratio*, justice, and judgement that governed their lives and awaited them often enough here, and certainly in the next world.

Liudprand's arguments have been surveyed but shortened here. In his sermon he often liked to pause, to draw out, enlarge, and glitter with rhetorical flourishes like beats on a tympanum. Where, then, finally, does he stand as an expositor of scriptures? His method too might be called 'exclamatory', and he certainly had a strong sense for the dramatic and emotional features of his texts, to return to Beryl Smalley's characterization of the tenth century. It would, however, be mistaken to regard this period altogether as one of stagnation in the history of medieval Bible studies. The Carolingian legacy here as elsewhere was huge and very much alive, calling for great effort and cultivation. With preachers like Atto, Rather, Odo of Cluny, Aelfric, and now Liudprand, it would seem that that effort was made, and it must not be thought that the eleventh-century scholars started with *tabula rasa*.

All Souls College, Oxford

---

[58] *Ibid.*, VI, 10, p. 158.

THE BIBLE IN THE INVESTITURE CONTEST: THE SOUTH GERMAN GREGORIAN CIRCLE

by I.S. ROBINSON

BERYL Smalley has often pointed to the importance of the eleventh-century cathedral schools in the history of biblical studies, but she has also emphasized the difficulties of investigating the study of the sacred page in this century. 'We have to eke out our knowledge by guesswork .... We are beginning to see a great movement. Though we cannot yet discern the detail, we can trace its outline, at least provisionally'.[1] At first the outlook appears bleak. Abbot Williram of Ebersberg is found complaining *c*.1060 that scholars concentrate on grammar and dialectic and neglect the Scriptures: a charge echoed a few years later by Otloh of St. Emmeram in Regensburg.[2] However, the complaints of these monastic polemicists run directly contrary to the information coming out of the cathedral schools. Here the news is of masters abandoning profane learning in favour of sacred studies. A letter of Gozechin, *scholasticus* of Mainz, to his former pupil, Walcher, written *c*.1065, lists a number of eminent scholars who have rejected *sophistica disputatio* and *necessaria argumentatio* 'and, making use of wise counsel, have withdrawn into *theologiae otium*'. These masters were Herman of Rheims, Drogo of Paris, Huzman of Speyer, Meinhard of Bamberg, 'and many other outstanding men of special authority'.[3] Their withdrawal into *theologiae otium* does

---

[1] Smalley, *Bible*, pp. 46–9, 66–77; 'La *Glossa Ordinaria*: quelques prédécesseurs d'Anselme de Laon', *RTAM*, ix (1937), pp. 365–400; 'Les commentaires bibliques de l'époque romane: glose ordinaire et gloses périmées', *Cahiers de civilisation médiévale*, iv (1961), pp. 15–22, reprinted in: *Studies*, pp. 17–25.

[2] Williram, *Prologus in Cantica*, ed. J. Seemüller, *Quellen und Forschungen zur Sprach- und Kulturgeschichte*, xxviii (1878), pp. 1–2; Otloh, *Dialogus de tribus quaestionibus: praefatio*, PL cxlvi, 60. See Smalley, *Bible*, pp. 45–6.

[3] *Gozechini scholastici epistola ad Valcherum*, ch. 33, PL cxliii, 902: '*Haec omnia sapienter despexit Herimannus Remensis, Drogo Parisiensis, Spirensis Huoremannus, Bavenbergensis Meinbardus et praeterea multi et praestantes et praecipuae auctoritatis viri, qui praecisis speciebus et abdicatis laboribus studiis valefecerunt et sapienti consilio usi in theologiae otium concesserunt*'.

not mean that these masters had ceased to teach: at least ten years after Gozechin wrote his letter, Herman was still teaching in Rheims, and Meinhard was still *scholasticus* in Bamberg.[4] Gozechin was perhaps thinking of Augustine's definition of *otium* in his comment on *Psalm* xlv. 11: '*Agite otium et agnoscetis quia ego sum Dominus*: not the leisure of idleness but the leisure of meditation'.[5] The four distinguished masters, like many of their colleagues, had renounced grammatical and dialectical *studia* in favour of meditation on the Scriptures; and some of the fruits of this *theologiae otium* have survived. Glosses on the Pauline Epistles labelled 'Drogo' are extant, which may be the work of Drogo of Paris, the friend of Berengar of Tours.[6] Meinhard of Bamberg composed a treatise *De fide*[7] and (according to the twelfth-century bibliographer Wolfger of Prüfening) a commentary on the Song of Solomon.[8]

Meinhard's *De fide* marks that conversion from profane to sacred studies for which Gozechin applauded him. The author had been the pupil of Herman of Rheims;[9] and it was presumably from him that Meinhard had received his thorough grounding in the Latin culture of antiquity. The sixty-six letters which Meinhard composed while teaching in the school of Bamberg demonstrate the conscious classicism of his style and above all his devotion to Cicero. He writes of the difficulty of transcribing a manuscript of the Verrine orations; he recommends the reading of Cicero as a preparation for Augustine.[10] His training in the arts qualified him

---

[4] J.R. Williams, 'The cathedral school of Rheims in the eleventh century', *Speculum*, xxix (1954), p. 663; C. Erdmann, *Studien zur Briefliteratur Deutschlands im elften Jahrhundert*, MGH *Schriften*, I (1938), pp. 19–20.

[5] Augustine, *De vera religione*, XXXV, 65, PL xxxiv, 151: '*non otium desidiae, sed otium cogitationis, ut a locis et temporibus vacet*'.

[6] Smalley, 'La *Glossa Ordinaria*', pp. 372–99; *Bible*, pp. 47, 63–5, 70–2.

[7] C.P. Caspari, *Kirchenhistorische Anecdota*, i (Christiana, 1883), pp. 251–74, edited *De fide* as the work of Meginhard, monk of Fulda (†888). See N. Fickermann, 'Eine bisher verkannte Schrift Meinhards von Bamberg', *Neues Archiv*, xlix (1931–2), pp. 452–5.

[8] Wolfger, *De scriptoribus ecclesiasticis*, ch. 111, ed. E. Ettlinger, *Der sog. Anonymus Mellicensis de scriptoribus ecclesiasticis* (Karlsruhe, 1896), p. 95: '... *in canticum canticorum explanationum opus eximium*.'

[9] *Weitere Briefe Meinhards von Bamberg*, 4, *Briefsammlungen der Zeit Heinrichs IV.*, MGH *Briefe*, V, p. 196.

[10] *Die Hannoversche Briefsammlung*, 65, MGH *Briefe*, V, p. 113; *Weitere Briefe Meinhards von Bamberg*, 1, p. 193. See Erdmann, *Studien zur Briefliteratur*, pp. 16–24.

to compose a treatise on dialectic (not extant), *libellus de maxima propositione*.[11] However, in the treatise *De fide* (dedicated to Bishop Gunther of Bamberg, and therefore completed by 1064, the year of his death) Meinhard sets the *artes* aside. The author reproves those scholars who, *perditi magis quam periti*, presume to extend the authority of *ratio* to sacred things: 'in studying the divine Scriptures you must obtain faith, which leads the way to understanding'.[12] The ensuing treatise is largely a collection of Augustinian *sententiae*, culminating in a list of heresies which most offended against the Nicene Creed, compiled from Augustine's *Liber de haeresibus* and Gennadius's *De ecclesiasticis dogmatibus*. *De fide* confirms the approving judgement of Gozechin, that Meinhard of Bamberg rejected the *sophistica disputatio* of Berengar of Tours. It was because he was 'second to none in learning, genius, and eloquence'[13] that Meinhard was invested in 1085 with the bishopric of Würzburg. His promotion bears witness to Emperor Henry IV's concern, during his conflict with the reform papacy, to appease German reforming opinion by the respectability of his episcopal appointments: the Gregorians must not appear to have a monopoly of learned bishops.[14]

Meinhard of Bamberg ended his career as the principal ornament of the Henrician ecclesiastical settlement in Germany. His most famous pupil ended his career in a Saxon monastery, the author of a polemic 'in bitter language' against Henry IV demonstrating 'how noxious and hateful was the emperor to the Saxons'.[15] This was Bernhard, master of the cathedral school of Constance in the pontificate of Bishop Rumold (1051–69) and subsequently *scholasticus* of the cathedral of Hildesheim from *c.*1072 to *c.*1085.[16] Bern-

---

[11] *Die Hannoversche Briefsammlung*, 80, p. 130.
[12] Meinhard, *De fide*, ed. Caspari, pp. 255–6: '... in divinis vero scripturis, ut intelligas, oportet te fide, quae praecessit, promereri'.
[13] Frutolf of Michelsberg, *Chronica* 1085, *Ausgewählte Quellen zur deutschen Geschichte des Mittelalters*, xv (Darmstadt, 1972), p. 98.
[14] J. Fleckenstein, 'Heinrich IV. und der deutsche Episkopat in den Anfängen des Investiturstreites', *Adel und Kirche. Festschrift für Gerd Tellenbach*, ed. J. Fleckenstein and K. Schmid (Freiburg im Breisgau, 1968), p. 235; 'Hofkapelle und Reichsepiskopat unter Heinrich IV.', *Investiturstreit und Reichsverfassung*, ed. J. Fleckenstein, *Vorträge und Forschungen* xvii (Sigmaringen, 1973), pp. 135–6.
[15] Sigebert of Gembloux, *Liber de scriptoribus ecclesiasticis*, 165, PL clx, 585.
[16] The fact that Bernhard was Meinhard's pupil was established by Erdmann, *Studien zur Briefliteratur*, pp. 218–21, 308–11, who also worked out the chronology of his career.

hard was composing his learned *Liber canonum contra Heinricum IV* at precisely the time that his former master was being installed as imperial anti-bishop of Würzburg.[17] However, while pupil and master ended their lives in hostile camps, their intellectual development had been remarkably similar. Bernhard, like Meinhard, had abandoned profane *studia* for *theologiae otium*. The letters which Bernhard wrote as part of his duties as *scholasticus*, in the name of the Bishop of Hildesheim, quote Virgil, Terence, Ovid, Persius, Juvenal, Cicero, Sallust, and in particular Horace—fragments of Meinhard's teaching of the *artes*.[18] In the letter which Bernhard addressed on his Bishop's behalf to the cathedral chapter of Bamberg—and which would reach the eye of the *scholasticus* Meinhard—the pupil strove to imitate the style of the master.[19] These, however, were the outward flourishes, not the true scholarly personality. For Bernhard of Hildesheim had forsaken 'the frivolous lyre of Horace' in favour of 'the mystical lute of David, more profitable both to himself and to his hearers (*auditores*)'.[20] If the term *auditores* has here the meaning usual in the cathedral schools, of 'pupils attending a lecture', we can conclude that Bernhard lectured on the sacred page in Hildesheim.

We owe our knowledge of Bernhard's 'conversion' to two correspondents from the cathedral school of Constance in the year 1076, who valued the former master of their school as 'more diligent and more discreet than other men in sacred literature'.[21] These correspondents were a senior member of the cathedral clergy of Constance, Adalbert, and a young clerk, Bernhard's former pupil, Bernold, the future chronicler, canonist, liturgist, and defender of the Gregorian reforms in his numerous polemical writings. Their letter sought Bernhard's advice concerning the

---

[17] Bernhard's *Liber canonum* (*MGH Lib*, I, pp. 472–516) was composed in response to the synod of Mainz of May 1085 which witnessed Henry IV's reorganization of the German church: see G. Meyer von Knonau, *Jahrbücher des Deutschen Reiches unter Heinrich IV. und Heinrich V.*, iv (Leipzig, 1903), pp. 22–3, 25–6, 43, 547–50..

[18] Erdmann, *Studien zur Briefliteratur*, pp. 206–11, 304–8.

[19] *Hildesheimer Briefe*, 24, *Briefsammlungen der Zeit Heinrichs IV.*, pp. 56–9. See Erdmann, *Studien zur Briefliteratur*, p. 220.

[20] Adalbert and Bernold of Constance, *De damnatione scismaticorum, epistola*, 3, *MGH Lib*, II, p. 47: '... sacerdoti Bernardo, non iam nugacem liram Horatii, sed misticam cytharam David fructuosius sibi et suis auditoribus amplexanti'.

[21] *Ibid.*, *epistola*, 1, p. 28.

legality of the sentence passed by the Pope on the bishops who had participated in King Henry IV's synod of Worms, in January 1076, and concerning the validity of the sacraments administered by excommunicate and simoniac clergy. Bernhard sent to his 'venerable father' Adalbert and 'the spring blossom' Bernold a reply on uncompromisingly Gregorian lines.[22] Adalbert and Bernold were seeking the advice of their former colleague in their quarrel with Bishop Otto of Constance (1071–86), who opposed recent papal reforms; and they could be confident of Bernhard's sympathy, knowing the important role which he had played in the struggle against Bishop Otto's predecessor, the simoniac Bishop Charles (or Carloman). The latter had been deposed by the synod of Mainz in August 1071 after the cathedral clergy of Constance had proved that he had bought the bishopric from King Henry IV and recovered his expenses by robbing the cathedral treasury. In order to obtain publicity for their accusations, the cathedral clergy had written to Pope Alexander II; and it seems likely that Bernhard, at this time still *magister scholarum* in Constance, composed this letter, as well as the letter of accusation which the canons of Constance presented to the synod of Mainz.[23]

It was undoubtedly the crisis in Constance provoked by Charles's simony which destroyed Bernhard's confidence in the 'imperial Church system' ordered by the Salian King. The events of 1071 inspired the ecclesiastical-political opinions which caused Bernhard to diverge so sharply from the attitudes of his master, Meinhard of Bamberg. The scandal of the Bishop's simony and the resolution of the clergy to withdraw from communion with him stimulated the research of Bernhard and other clerks into the *disciplina aecclesiasticae regulae*.[24] This research in the cathedral library of Constance seems to have turned up a codex of the *Opusculum LV capitulorum* of Hincmar of Rheims.[25] In this treatise Bernhard found a theme

---

[22] This reply, the original inquiry, and a subsequent letter by Adalbert and Bernold, were edited by Bernold as a single treatise, of which the only complete extant manuscript exemplar is Stuttgart, Württembergische Landesbibliothek, MS HB.VI.107. See J. Autenrieth, *Die Domschule von Konstanz zur Zeit des Investiturstreits* (Stuttgart, 1956), pp. 135–42.

[23] This is argued by I.S. Robinson, 'Zur Arbeitsweise Bernolds von Konstanz und seines Kreises', *DA*, xxxiv (1978), pp. 99–101.

[24] Berthold of Reichenau, *Annales* 1071, *MGH SS*, V, p. 275.

[25] Robinson, 'Arbeitsweise Bernolds', pp. 95–7, 100.

relevant to the situation of 1071—the deposition of a delinquent bishop—and in particular a discussion, with biblical and canonical authorities, of the *ordo iudiciarius* appropriate in a case of notorious ill-fame.[26] In 1071 Bernhard set aside 'the frivolous lyre of Horace' and applied himself to *sacrae literae*, seeking in the Bible, the Fathers, and canon law the norms by which Christian society should be ordered. After Bernhard's departure for Hildesheim, these researches were continued in the cathedral library of Constance by his pupil Bernold and other clerks, who sought *auctoritates* in support of their opposition to Bishop Otto.

No learned centre of the late eleventh century has been studied—perhaps can be studied—in the same detail as the cathedral library of Constance. Although most of the Constance collection was sold to the abbey of Weingarten in 1629–30, and the whole collection was dispersed throughout Germany in the subsequent secularization, it has proved possible to trace many of the original Constance codices in the current holdings of the libraries of Stuttgart, Fulda, Karlsruhe, St. Gallen, Freiburg, and Darmstadt. Johanne Autenrieth has published important studies of fifty codices which belonged to the cathedral library of Constance in the late eleventh century.[27] She has shown that these biblical, patristic, and canon-law manuscripts were being studied intensively in the late eleventh century. They bear numerous glosses written in at least three different hands: marginal notes summarizing passages of text which seemed significant to students working in the cathedral library at this period. Autenrieth identified these glossators as three clerks of Constance: Wolferad, 'Anonymous A', and Bernhard's pupil, Bernold.[28] Bernold's methods of study can be examined in far greater detail than is possible for any other eleventh-century scholar; since so many codices survive which contain his handwriting, or which were written under his supervision and bear his

---

[26] Hincmar, *Opusculum LV capitulorum*, 28, PL cxxvi, 400–1. Cf. Bernhard, *De damnatione scismaticorum, epistola*, 2, pp. 31, 32–3.

[27] Autenrieth, *Domschule*; 'Bernold von Konstanz und der Codex Sangallensis 676', *Friedrich Baethgen zu seinem 65. Geburtstag* (typescript in the Library of MGH, Munich, 1955), pp. 1–17; *Die Handschriften der Württembergischen Landesbibliothek*, ii, 3: *Die Handschriften der ehemaligen Hofbibliothek Stuttgart*, beschrieben von J. Autenrieth (Wiesbaden, 1963).

[28] Autenrieth, *Domschule*, pp. 22–6, 121–34, 143–68.

corrections. Using the glossed passages in the Constance codices, Bernold compiled manuals of canonical and patristic *sententiae*, of which three survive: Stuttgart, Württembergische Landesbibliothek, MS HB.VI.107, St. Gallen, Stiftsbibliothek, MS 676, and Sélestat, Bibliothèque municipale, MS 13.[29] These compilations served Bernold as the basis of his treatises; and they were directly used also by other polemicists who defended the cause of Gregory VII in South Germany. *Auctoritates* from Bernold's sentence collections are found in the writings of his master, Bernhard of Hildesheim, of Archbishop Gebhard of Salzburg, and of an anonymous polemicist of the monastery of Hirsau. The distinguished reformer and polemicist Manegold of Lautenbach—a significant but mysterious figure in the history of biblical studies in the eleventh century—used both the sentence collections and the completed treatises of Bernold as the *fontes formales* of his *Liber ad Gebehardum*.[30] These writers form a 'South German Gregorian circle', their polemics showing a common dependence on the scholarly research in the cathedral library of Constance in the 1070s.

The main emphasis in Autenrieth's research has been on canon-law studies in the cathedral library of Constance, and their role in the intellectual formation of Bernold of Constance, a crucial figure in the history of Gregorian ecclesiology and legal thought.[31] However, more numerous than the canon-law holdings of the eleventh-century library were the patristic codices, and in particular patristic commentaries on the Bible. The library possessed an exemplar of Ambrose's *Hexaemeron*, copied *c.*800 in the abbey of

[29] Autenrieth, *Domschule*, pp. 106–15; *Handschriften der Hofbibliothek Stuttgart*, pp. 100–5; 'Codex Sangallensis 676', pp. 1–17; Robinson, 'Arbeitsweise Bernolds', pp. 55–61.

[30] Robinson, 'Arbeitsweise Bernolds', pp. 89–122. On Manegold and the study of the Bible see most recently W. Hartmann, 'Psalmenkommentare aus der Zeit der Reform und der Frühscholastik', *SGre*, ix (1972), pp. 319–26.

[31] Autenrieth, *Domschule*, pp. 121–42; 'Bernold von Konstanz und die erweiterte 74-Titelsammlung', *DA*, xiv (1958), pp. 375–94; 'The Canon Law Books of the *Curia episcopalis Constantiensis* from the ninth to the fifteenth century', *Proceedings of the Second International Congress of Medieval Canon Law 1963, Monumenta Iuris Canonici, series C: Subsidia* i (Vatican City, 1965), pp. 3–15. See also O. Greulich, 'Die kirchenpolitische Stellung Bernolds von Konstanz', *HJb*, lv (1935), pp. 1–54; H. Weisweiler, 'Die päpstliche Gewalt in den Schriften Bernolds von St. Blasien aus dem Investiturstreit', *SGre*, iv (1952), pp. 129–47.

Reichenau, and Carolingian copies from Tours and from South Germany of the Pseudo-Ambrosian commentary on the Pauline Epistles.[32] Jerome's biblical commentaries were represented by a mid-ninth-century Reichenau exemplar of the *Liber hebraicarum quaestionum in Genesim*, an early ninth-century Reichenau exemplar of the commentary on Ecclesiastes, an early eleventh-century exemplar of that on Isaiah copied in Constance for Bishop Eberhard I (1034–46), and a copy of the commentary on Matthew made c. 800 in the abbey of St. Gallen, which also contains Pseudo-Jerome on Mark and on the Pauline Epistles.[33] Of the scriptural commentaries of Augustine the library possessed the *Enarrationes in Psalmos* and the *Tractatus in Iohannis evangelium* in five Carolingian codices from South Germany.[34] The library held also the greater part of Gregory I's *Moralia in Iob* in five South German codices, ranging from the late eighth to the early eleventh century, Bede's *Expositio in Proverbia Salomonis et in librum Tobiae* in a late ninth-century South German codex and an early ninth-century Tours codex of Pseudo-Chrysostom on the Gospels.[35] The numerous glosses and *nota-sigla* in these manuscripts are clear evidence of interest in biblical studies among the scholars of the cathedral of Constance in the later eleventh century. It is noteworthy that of the surviving Constance codices which contain eleventh-century glosses, only one is a work of profane literature: the exemplar of Juvenal's *Satyrae* copied in the time of Bishop Eberhard of Constance, with many marginal and interlinear glosses (BL, Add. MS 30861).[36] This solitary exception certainly suggests a neglect of the *artes* in favour of *theologiae otium*; and this is made explicit in a gloss by Wolferad in the Constance codex of Jerome's commentary on

---

[32] Autenrieth, *Domschule*, pp. 37, 51; A. Holder, *Die Reichenauer Handschriften*, i = *Die Handschriften der Badischen Landesbibliothek in Karlsruhe*, v (Leipzig, 1906,) pp. 492–3; K. Löffler, *Die Handschriften des Klosters Weingarten* (Leipzig, 1912), pp. 59, 65.

[33] Autenrieth, *Domschule*, pp. 38–40, 52–4, 92–4; Löffler, *Weingarten*, pp. 60, 65; Holder, *Reichenauer Handschriften* i, pp. 498–500.

[34] Autenrieth, *Domschule*, pp. 30–2, 54–5, 59–63; Löffler, *Weingarten*, pp. 59, 61, 63, 66.

[35] Autenrieth, *Domschule*, pp. 32–7, 51–2, 79–80, 91–2; Löffler, *Weingarten*, pp. 60, 63, 65–7.

[36] *The New Palaeographical Society*, series I, ii (London, 1903–12), plate 211: facsimiles of ff. 31ʳ, 52ᵛ.

Isaiah, xiii. 8 (Stuttgart, MS HB.VII.7, f. 3ʳ): 'The shrewd arguments of Aristotle are of no use to you, when you are accused by your own conscience'.[37]

The glosses in the patristic commentaries on the Bible were the work of Wolferad and Anonymous A, while their colleague Bernold concentrated almost exclusively on the canon-law codices of the cathedral library of Constance. The passages glossed or marked with a *nota-siglum* in these canonical manuscripts consistently correspond with *auctoritates* cited in Bernold's treatises;[38] and likewise the glosses and signs of *lectio continua* in the biblical commentaries have correspondences in the writings of two other 'South German Gregorians', Bernhard of Hildesheim and Manegold of Lautenbach. The *auctoritates* in their polemics corresponding to marked passages in the Constance codices are noticeable for their unusually precise attributions: *Ieronimus in primo libro super Matheum, Augustinus in psalmo XXXIIII*[39]— immediately suggesting that the polemicists had direct access to their patristic sources and did not use *florilegia*. The *Liber canonum contra Heinricum IV* of Bernhard of Hildesheim contains such passages from Jerome's *Liber hebraicarum quaestionum in Genesim* and commentary on Matthew and from Augustine's *Enarrationes in Psalmos* and *Tractatus in Iohannis evangelium*.[40] The *Liber ad Gebehardum* of Manegold of Lautenbach draws more frequently on these same works and also on passages from Gregory I's *Moralia in Iob* which are marked in the Constance codices.

A comparison of the glossed codices of Jerome *In Matthaeum* and Gregory's *Moralia* with Manegold's quotations from these works reveals a striking correspondence between the scholarly interests of Anonymous A and the polemical interests of Manegold. On f. 33ʳ of the Constance codex (Stuttgart, MS HB.VII.9) Anonymous A glossed Jerome, *In Matthaeum* I.10.34: 'Note that the whole world was divided against itself and each household had unbelievers and

---

[37] Autenrieth, *Domschule*, pp. 93, 149: '*Nil tibi prosunt acuta argumenta Aristotelis ubi propria conscientia accusaris*'; a comment on Jerome, *In Isaiam*, VI, *PL* xxiv, 217.

[38] Autenrieth, *Domschule*, pp. 122–32; Robinson, 'Arbeitsweise Bernolds', pp. 59–61, 91–2.

[39] Manegold, *Ad Gebehardum*, 20, 40, *MGH Lib*, I, pp. 345, 381.

[40] Bernhard, *Liber canonum*, 10, 14, 21, 45, *MGH Lib*, I, pp. 483, 484, 487, 491–2, 514–15.

believers; and so a good war was sent so that an evil peace might be broken up'.[41] This gloss contains the main argument of chapter 48 of Manegold's polemic, defending the papal absolution of the vassals of Henry IV from their oaths of fealty and concluding with the same *auctoritas* of Jerome.[42] Likewise Anonymous A's gloss on Jerome, *In Matthaeum* III.21.12–13 (f. 85ʳ), pointing out the applicability of Christ's cleansing of the Temple to the modern condition of the Church—'Note that the Lord casts out of his Temple bishops, priests, deacons, and laymen selling and buying spiritual things'—relates directly to Manegold's chapter 20, *de dampnatione symoniacorum*, where the same point is made by means of the same passage of Jerome.[43] Gregory I's *Moralia in Iob* particularly attracted the attention of Anonymous A because of its numerous references to the heresies of the early Church; and the Constance codices of this work are full of the glossator's summaries and definitions on this subject. His comment on *Moralia* III, xiv, 56.74 (Stuttgart, MS HB.VII.25, f. 167ʳ), describing how Emperor Tiberius Constantine caused the heretical writings of Eutychius to be burned, corresponds with a similar explanation in Manegold's polemic.[44] Anonymous A's gloss on *Moralia* IV, xxxiii, 26, taking up Gregory I's definition, 'Zion means "looking out"', corresponds with the salutation at the beginning of Manegold's *Liber ad Gebehardum*, where Archbishop Gebhard of Salzburg is addressed as 'Gebhard, most vigilant look-out of the citadel of Zion'.[45] In his use of all these patristic commentaries available in the cathedral library of Constance, Manegold was evidently guided to the *auctoritates* which he used in his polemic by the glosses of Anonymous A.

---

[41] Autenrieth, *Domschule*, p. 39: '*Nota quod totus orbis contra se divisus sit et unaquęque domus habuit infideles et credentes et ideo bonum bellum missum esse ut mala pax rumperetur*'.

[42] Manegold, *Ad Gebhardum*, 48, pp. 392–5.

[43] Autenrieth, *Domschule*, p. 40: '*Nota quod dominus eiciat de templo suo episcopos, presbiteros, diaconos et laicos pendentes [? vendentes] et ementes spiritalia*'. Cf. Manegold, *Ad Gebhardum*, 20, p. 345.

[44] Autenrieth, *Domschule*, p. 35. Cf. Manegold, *Ad Gebhardum*, 10, p. 331.

[45] Stuttgart, MS HB.VII.26, f. 95ᵛ: '... *sion speculatio dicitur*' (Gregory I, *Moralia in Iob* IV. xxxiii. 26, *PL* lxxvi, 702). Cf. Manegold, *Ad Gebhardum*, preface, p. 310: '*Gebehardo arcis Syon speculatori vigilantissimo*'. On the identity of this Gebhard see P. de Leo, 'Ricerche sul *Liber ad Gebehardum* di Manegoldo di Lautenbach', *Rivista di Storia e Letteratura religiosa*, x (1974), pp. 112–53; and the contrary arguments of W. Hartmann, *DA*, xxxii (1976), pp. 260–1.

Manegold must either have copied his quotations directly from these Constance manuscripts or have used a collection of *sententiae* compiled on the basis of the research of Anonymous A.

An examination of other Constance codices reveals further parallels between the scholarly interests of Anonymous A and those of Manegold. For example, Sélestat, Bibliothèque municipale, MS 13, copied in Constance under the supervision of Bernold, contains a small number of glosses in the hand of Anonymous A which are clearly related to the text of the *Liber ad Gebehardum*. Such a gloss appears on f. 136^v: a sentence attributed to *Isodorus* (Anonymous A's usual spelling) concerning law and custom, a paraphrase of Isidore of Seville, *Synonyma*, I. 45–6. This sentence appears verbatim in Manegold's polemic.[46] On f. 2^v Anonymous A's gloss *david* marks a passage in the text of the treatise of Bernold of Constance, *De prohibenda sacerdotum incontinentia* I (composed in 1075), referring to David's receiving the shewbread from Ahimelech (I *Samuel*, xxi. 5). An extended version of the same passage appears in the *Liber ad Gebehardum*.[47] The single word *david* appears as a frequent gloss in the hand of Anonymous A: for example, glossing the words *propheta* and *psalmista* in the text of Gregory I's *Moralia* (Stuttgart, MS HB.VII.26, ff. 95^v, 145^r). The same preoccupation occurs in the Constance codex of the *Decretum* of Burchard of Worms (Freiburg, Universitätsbibliothek, MS 7) where, on f. 215^v, Anonymous A glossed *Decretum* XV.39, a sentence of Isidore concerning the qualities necessary in a king, with the words *de humilitate david exemplum*. This *exemplum* is developed in chapter 11 of the *Liber ad Gebehardum*.[48] Further investigation is needed of the glosses of Johanne Autenrieth's 'Anonymous A'. If that investigation does not demonstrate that Anonymous A and Manegold of

---

[46] Robinson, 'Arbeitsweise Bernolds', p. 62: '*Isodorus. Adime consuetudinem serva legem. Usus auctoritati cedat. Pravum usum lex et ratio vincat*'. Cf. Manegold, *Ad Gebehardum*, 66, p. 418.

[47] Bernold, *De prohibenda sacerdotum incontinentia* I, MGH Lib, ii, p. 9: '*...cum et ipse David, quem Dominus secundum cor suum elegit, panes propositionis non accepisset, priusquam a sacerdote percunctatus se triduo continuisse respondisset*'. Cf. Manegold, *Ad Gebehardum*, 22, p. 350: '*nec David ille, quem Dominus secundum cor suum elegerat, ... proposicionis panes ... edere cum suis presumeret, nisi triduanam per continenciam vasa puerorum sancta, Abimelech sacerdote percontante, promisisset*'.

[48] Burchard, *Decretum*, XV, 38, PL cxl, 905 (Isidore, *Sententiae* III, 49, PL lxxxiii, 720–1). Cf. Manegold, *Ad Gebehardum*, 11, p. 333.

Lautenbach are one and the same, it will at least show that they were remarkably unanimous about what was most relevant in the codices of the cathedral library of Constance.

The activities of Anonymous A and Wolferad as biblical scholars can most easily be studied in the two Constance Bible codices, now Fulda, Hessische Landesbibliothek, MSS Aa 10, 11.[49] The two codices were copied in the early ninth century in South Germany. Fulda, MS Aa 10, ff. 1ᵛ – 15ʳ contains the text of Genesis, together with glosses by Wolferad. On f. 21ᵛ Wolferad began to gloss Exodus, but abandoned the task after a single comment on *Exodus*, iv. 25. Wolferad's glosses on Genesis are drawn from two commentaries, Jerome's *Liber hebraicarum quaestionum in Genesim* and the *Commentarius in Genesim* of Remigius of Auxerre, equal use being made of the two works. Occasionally Wolferad combined his two authors together in a single gloss, as in his comment on *Genesis*, vi. 3, 'His days shall be a hundred and twenty years' (f. 2ᵛ):

> *Non igitur humana vita, ut multi errant, in centum viginti annos contracta est, sed generacioni illi a die qua Deus loquebatur Noe centum viginti anni ad penitenciam dati sunt. Multos enim legimus post diluvium pluribus vixisse annis.*

Here the first sentence is from Jerome, the second from Remigius.[50] A similar case is the gloss on *Genesis*, xxiii. 16, 'Abraham agreed with Ephron' (f. 8ʳ):

> *Efron primum dictum est perfectus sed postquam precium ex sepultura accepit, licet cogente Abraham immutatum est nomen eius et dictum est Efran, id est inperfectus vel infirmus. Audiant hoc qui sepulchra venditant et non coguntur ut accipiant precium sed a nolentibus quoque extorquent, immutari nomen suum et perire quid de merito eorum, cum etiam ille reprehendatur, qui invitus acceperit.*

The first thirty words of this gloss come from Remigius' commentary, then from the words *sepulchra venditant* Jerome is quoted verbatim.[51] Elsewhere glosses drawn mainly from one author are

---

[49] Autenrieth, *Domschule*, pp. 57–9.

[50] Jerome, *Liber hebraicarum quaestionum in Genesim*, PL xxiii, 948; Remigius, *Commentarius in Genesim*, 6, PL cxxxi, 73.

[51] Remigius, *Commentarius*, 23, col. 97; Jerome, *Liber*, col. 973.

found to contain words or phrases from the other; as in the gloss on
Genesis, x. 11, 'From that land he went into Assyria, and built
Nineveh' (f. 4^r): *Ninus beli filius ninum condidit, quam hebrei appellant
niniven.* This sentence is from Remigius, except for the word
condidit, which was inspired by Jerome.[52] The gloss on *Genesis*,
xxiv. 63, 'Isaac went out to meditate in the field in the evening',
blends together phrases from the two commentators (f. 9^r):

> *Alii codices habent 'ad exercitandum in agro', alia translacio 'ut
> loqueretur in agro'. Vir sanctus post solis occasum ut spiritales Deo
> oracionis victimas immolaret, id est per oraciones, Deo loqueretur in
> agrum egressus.*[53]

The passages which Wolferad quoted from Jerome's *Liber hebraicarum quaestionum* are found also in the *Commentariorum in Genesim* of
Rabanus Maurus; but it can be demonstrated that Wolferad used
Jerome rather than Rabanus, since the Constance codex of Jerome's
commentary (Karlsruhe, Badische Landesbibliothek, Augiensis
perg. CCXVIII) shows Wolferad at work, collecting material for
his glosses on Genesis. The occasional passages in the *Liber
hebraicarum quaestionum* marked by Wolferad are used in his glosses
in Fulda, MS Aa 10.[54] Some of Wolferad's glosses occur also in the
Glossa Ordinaria;[55] but this is presumably coincidental: there is no
reason to suppose that Wolferad influenced the compiling of the
Gloss on Genesis.

Anonymous A is found at work in Fulda, MS Aa 11, f. 200vb. In
the right-hand column of f. 200^v, left blank by the early ninth-
century scribe responsible for the preceding text of the Old

---

[52] Remigius, *Commentarius*, 10, col. 80; Jerome, *Liber*, col. 953.

[53] Remigius, *Commentarius*, 24, col. 99: '*Quidam codices habent "ad exercitandum in
agro". Alia quoque translatio dicit "ut loqueretur in agro". Inclinata iam die. Quia vir
sanctus iam post nonam horam diei ad vesperam inclinatam egressus fuerat solus ut Deo
spiritales victimas immolaret, hoc est, ut orationes et hymnos persolveret'*. Jerome, *Liber*,
col. 975: '... *vel nona hora, vel ante solis occasum, spirituales Deo victimas obtulisse'*.

[54] Autenrieth, *Domschule*, p. 52.

[55] E.g. *Genesis*, iii. 17, *maledicta terra*: '*Opera hic non ruris colendi, ut plerique estimant,
sed peccata significant*' (Jerome, *Liber hebraicarum quaestionum*, col. 943). Cf. *Glossa
Ordinaria*, marginal gloss on *Genesis*, iii. 17, 'Hieron.' *Genesis*, x. 5, *unusquisque
secundum linguam suam*: '*Hoc per prolepsin, id est per preoccupacionem accipiendum est.
Necdum enim divisio linguarum facta est*' (Remigius, *Commentarius*, 10, col. 79–80).
Cf. *Glossa Ordinaria*, interlinear gloss on *Genesis*, x. 5.

Testament, Anonymous A inserted, in a small, cramped hand, a series of *sententiae* on the Gospels. The *sententiae* begin with brief surveys of the lives of the evangelists, in which Luke mysteriously appears as the second evangelist and Mark as the third.[56] These are followed by definitions of the terms *breviarium, capitulum, canon*. Anonymous A's principal source was perhaps the work of Sedulius Scotus, *Explanationes in praefationes sancti Hieronymi ad Evangelia*;[57] but Anonymous A added further details and developed Sedulius' definitions in his own words. Anonymous A's study of the Gospels can also be investigated in the Constance codex of Jerome's commentary on Matthew and of Pseudo-Jerome on Mark (Stuttgart, MS HB.VII.9). Glosses on Jerome's prologue to his *Commentarius in Matthaeum* and on Pseudo-Jerome's prologue to the *Expositio in Marcum evangelistam* illustrate Anonymous A's interest in the careers of the evangelists.[58] His gloss on the *Passio sancti Marci* in the mid-eleventh-century Constance passional (Stuttgart, MS HB.XIV.16, f. 71ᵛ) summarizes the Evangelist's life in a manner similar to that of the biography in Fulda, MS Aa 11.[59] Once more a parallel can be drawn with the scriptural material in the work of Manegold of Lautenbach. In the *Liber ad Gebehardum* the career of St Mark is cited as an *exemplum* in defence of the legatine journeys of Hildebrand, who, like the Evangelist, was an *interpres Petri apostoli*.[60]

---

[56] Inc.: *Matheus primus in ordine evangelistare ponitur quia ipse primum ante alios in Iudea evangelium hebreo sermone scripsit.* Expl.: *matrem suam iens ad crucem commendavit, ut virginem virgo servaret.*

[57] Sedulius, *Explanationes in praefationes sancti Hieronymi ad Evangelia*, PL ciii, 331–52.

[58] Autenrieth, *Domschule*, pp. 39–40.

[59] Fulda, Hessische Landesbibliothek, MS Aa 11, f. 200ᵛᵇ: '*Petri apostoli in baptismate filius et in divino sermone discipulus et interpres Petri apostoli ... Qui ex tribu Levi ortus, ante fidem in Iudea sacerdos fuit, sed conversus ad fidem Christi evangelium suum in Italia scripsit. Hic etiam post conversionem suam sibi pollicem amputavit, ut indignus sacerdocio haberetur, sed predestinatio Dei ob hoc in eo non mirius implebatur. Fuit enim et evangelista et episcopus Alexandrie*'. Cf. Stuttgart, MS HB.XIV.3, f. 71ᵛ (Autenrieth, *Domschule*, pp. 102–3): '*Hic igitur Marcus, qui ut Iohannes matrem Mariam levitici generis habuit et ante conversionem sacerdotium in Israel gessit, deinde predicatione beati Petri conversus eius in baptismo factus est filius et postmodum interpres. In tantum autem humilis extitit, ut pollicem sibi amputaret, quatinus sacerdocio temporali reprobus haberetur. Sed divina in eo gratia in tantum prevaluit, ut non solum secundum evangelium digito scriberet sed etiam Alexandrie episcopus fieret*'.

[60] Manegold, *Ad Gebehardum*, 10, p. 331: the polemicist is defending Hildebrand against the charge of being a *gyrovagus*, or unstable monk.

It is instructive to compare the scholarly activity visible in Fulda, MSS Aa 10, 11 with polemics from the 'South German Gregorian circle' making use of similar research. For example, the use of the Bible in the *Liber canonum* of Bernhard of Hildesheim suggests a close dependence on research like that of Wolferad and Anonymous A. In chapter 36 the polemicist likens the participants in Henry IV's council of Mainz in 1085 to the magi of Pharoah in *Exodus*, vii–viii, who used their secret arts to conjure up plagues in competition with Moses and Aaron.

> Like Moses in the first plague they turned the waters into blood, in the second they produced croaking frogs; but when it came to the gnats, seeing that they were resisted by the Holy Spirit which was in Moses, they said: 'This is the finger of God.' Gnats, by means of which third plague the pride of the Egyptians was reduced to submission, are flies born of the slime, so tiny that they are hardly to be seen, so restless that they attack when driven away, settling on the body and boring into it with their sharp stings. They signify the heretics, savouring of the slime, restless, tormenting with the subtle sting of cunning.[61]

This is a very learned insult. The main point, that the gnats (*scinifes*) of *Exodus*, viii. 16–18 are to be interpreted allegorically as the heretics, derives from the *Quaestiones in Exodum* of Isidore of Seville.[62] The magi's recognition that they were being resisted by the Holy Spirit comes from Augustine's *Quaestiones in Heptateuchum*.[63] The description of the habits of the *scinifes* is a patchwork of details from Origen, *Homilia IV in Exodum*, extracted by Rabanus Maurus in his *Commentaria in Exodum*.[64] It is worth

---

[61] Bernhard, *Liber canonum*, 36, p. 506: 'Hi enim, cum item ut Moyses ... in prima dehinc plaga aquas in sanguinem verterent, in secunda loquaces ranas producerent, in tercia, cum iam ventum esset ad scynifes, sibi videntes resisti a sancto, qui in Moyse erat, Spiritu, dixerunt: "Digitus Dei est iste". Scinifes, qua tercia plaga Aegyptiorum cedebatur superbia, sunt muscae de limo ortae minutae, ut vix videantur, inquietae, ut irruant, cum abiguntur, qua corpus tetigerint acerbo terebrantes stimulo. Significant autem hereticos limosa sapientes, inquietos, subtili stimulantes calliditatis aculeo'.

[62] Isidore, *Quaestiones in Exodum*, 14, *PL* lxxxiii, 293: 'Hoc ergo animalis genus subtilitati haereticae comparatur'. Isidore quotes as part of his exposition II *Timothy*, iii. 8–9, which is also cited by Bernhard after his description of the *scinifes*.

[63] Augustine, *Quaestiones in Heptateuchum*, II. 25, *CC* xxxiii, 79–80.

[64] Origen, *In Exodum homilia*, IV. 6, *PG* xii, 322; Rabanus, *Commentaria in Exodum*, I. 15, *PL* cviii, 36.

noting that in this passage Bernhard refers to every patristic comment on *Exodus*, viii. 18–19 found in the *Glossa Ordinaria*.[65] As in the case of Wolferad's glosses on Genesis, this is presumably coincidental: it is unlikely that Bernhard had access to the ancestor of the Gloss on Exodus. However, the resemblance must prompt the suggestion that Bernhard's account of the third plague of Egypt, with its unusual range of patristic comments, was based on a set of glosses on Exodus.

The biblical studies in the cathedral library of Constance, undertaken in an atmosphere of growing conflict between the supporters and the opponents of Gregorian reform, came to furnish Gregorian intellectuals with arguments and *exempla* for their polemical writings. The dependence of Manegold of Lautenbach on these biblical studies has already been mentioned. The sacred page is exploited for polemical purposes in his two controversial writings, *Liber contra Wolfelmum* and *Liber ad Gebehardum*, on a scale unusual even in late eleventh-century polemical literature. The *Liber contra Wolfelmum*, attacking the teaching of 'Wolfhelm of Cologne'— evidently abbot Wolfhelm of Brauweiler (1065–91) is meant[66]— takes as its targets six doctrines of the pagan *philosophi* which endanger Christian belief: Pythagoras' theory of the transmigration of souls (ch. 1), Macrobius' and Chalcidius' theory of the world soul (ch. 2), the theory that the soul is blood (ch. 3), Macrobius' theory of the antipodes (ch. 4), Plato's theory of the creation of the world (ch. 8), and Macrobius' theory of the nature of bodies (ch. 22). Each of these false doctrines is refuted by the authority of the Bible.[67] In the *Liber contra Wolfelmum*, therefore, profane learning is directly confronted by *sacrae literae*: the treatise amounts to a South German Gregorian manifesto in defence of *theologiae otium*. In his final chapters Manegold links together two totally different groups of opponents, intending that the reader should regard them as

---

[65] See in particular the Gloss on *Exodus*, viii. 19, labelled 'Rabbanus': '... *ciniphes nati sunt in terra Aegypti de limo, muscae scilicet minutissimae, inquietissimae ... in oculos ruentes ... dum abiguntur redeunt*'.

[66] Manegold, *Liber contra Wolfelmum*, preface, *MGH Quellen*, VIII, 39. On the identity of Wolfhelm see W. Hartmann, 'Manegold von Lautenbach und die Anfänge der Frühscholastik', *DA*, xxvi (1970), pp. 60–4.

[67] Manegold, *Contra Wolfelmum*, pp. 45–6, 49, 51, 52, 58–60, 94–8. Cf. Hartmann, 'Manegold von Lautenbach', pp. 64–71.

identical: both those who hold the doctrines of the *philosophi* and those who oppose Pope Gregory VII belong to the body of Satan.[68] In the same way that he makes 'Wolfhelm of Cologne' the representative of the adherents of pagan philosophy, Manegold makes the polemicist Wenrich, *scholasticus* of Trier, stand for all anti-Gregorian intellectuals. Wenrich writes 'in the manner of the rhetoricians of the schools who, when they have taken up a theme, pay no attention to what actually happened, but sharpen up their tongues on fictitious cases'.[69] Just as Wolfhelm and the adherents of the pagan *philosophi* prefer the *dogmata prophana Grecorum* to the teachings of Christ,[70] so Wenrich and the anti-Gregorians prize the *artes* more than *sacrae literae*, and devote themselves to the techniques of the *grammatici* and *rethori* rather than to *theologiae otium*. Both the adherents of the *philosophi* and the supporters of King Henry IV distort the truth of the sacred page.

Manegold developed this complaint in the *Liber ad Gebehardum*, composed at approximately the same period as the *Liber contra Wolfelmum*.[71] Here the attack on Wenrich of Trier, begun in the final chapter of the polemic against Wolfhelm, becomes the central theme. Wenrich had composed a polemic against Gregory VII, which was the more effective because the polemicist claimed to be a well-wisher, embarrassed because he could find no answers to the accusations of Gregory's opponents: 'he pretends to be a friend so that, in the guise of an inquirer, he may pour forth all the venom of [the pope's] enemies'.[72] Manegold proposed to refute in detail the arguments and *exempla* from the Bible and from Church history which Wenrich had cited in order to impugn Gregory's actions. The resultant *Liber ad Gebehardum* is a disorganized compilation of scriptural and patristic *auctoritates* and quotations from eleventh-century works, strung together often without editorial comment.

---

[68] Manegold, *Contra Wolfelmum*, 23–4, pp. 98–108.

[69] *Ibid.*, 24, p. 107.

[70] *Ibid.*, 6, p. 56.

[71] P. Ewald, 'Chronologie der Schriften Manegolds von Lautenbach', *Forschungen zur deutschen Geschichte*, xvi (1876), p. 385 argues that Manegold began work first on the *Liber ad Gebehardum*, then temporarily set it aside to write the *Liber contra Wolfelmum*. See also W. Hartmann, introduction to Manegold, *Liber contra Wolfelmum*, MGH Quellen, VIII, pp. 12–13.

[72] Manegold, *Contra Wolfelmum*, 24, p. 107. Cf. Wenrich, *Epistola*, 3, MGH Lib, I, p. 288.

Despite its formlessness, however, the polemic has a unifying theme in Manegold's preoccupation with the correct interpretation of *auctoritates*, especially the authority of the sacred page. Wilfried Hartmann has investigated Manegold's treatment of Scripture in the *Liber ad Gebehardum*, looking for evidence of scholastic method. He concludes that Manegold was not content, like many pre-scholastic theologians, to overwhelm opponents by the sheer weight of *auctoritates* which he had accumulated: he wished also to seize upon his opponents' *auctoritates* and by means of skilful interpretation to harness them to his own arguments.[73] The emphasis in the *Liber ad Gebehardum*, therefore, is on the status of the biblical *auctoritates* used by the opponent and on the varieties of biblical language.

Manegold derived at least some of the inspiration for his biblical arguments from the school of Constance: to be more precise, from the early treatises of Bernold of Constance. The exemplar of Bernold's *De prohibenda sacerdotum incontinentia* which Manegold actually used survives as Sélestat MS 13, ff.1ʳ–17ᵛ, with traces of *lectio continua*, probably in Manegold's own hand.[74] *De prohibenda* was particularly relevant to the preoccupations of the *Liber ad Gebehardum*; for Bernold was concerned to prove the inauthenticity of his opponent's *auctoritas*, 'a certain chapter in the history which is called *Tripartita*' describing how Paphnutius exhorted the council of Nicea to permit priests to keep their wives.[75] Bernold's opponent, Alboin, had cited in defence of his recommendation of clerical marriage the *exemplum* of Lot and his daughters in Sodom (*Genesis*, xix. 8).[76] Bernold's treatment of this *exemplum* attracts signs of *lectio continua* in Sélestat, MS 13, f. 14ᵛ, and reappears in chapter 56 of the *Liber ad Gebehardum*. Bernold applied the opinion of Augustine, *Contra mendacium*, XV.32, that certain biblical *exempla* have a negative function, to be a warning to the faithful rather than a model of right conduct: *vitanda potius quam imitanda sacrae scripturae exempla.*[77]

[73] Hartmann, 'Manegold von Lautenbach', pp. 129–140.

[74] Robinson, 'Arbeitsweise Bernolds', pp. 69–74, 119–21.

[75] Bernold, *De prohibenda sacerdotum incontinentia*, I, p. 7. Cf. Cassiodorus, *Historia Tripartita*, II, 14, *CSEL*, lxxi, pp. 107–8. See I.S. Robinson, *Authority and Resistance in the Investiture Contest* (Manchester, 1978) pp. 166–7.

[76] *De prohibenda sacerdotum incontinentia*, IV, p. 17.

[77] *Ibid.*, V, p. 22; Manegold, *Ad Gebehardum*, 56, p. 409. Cf. Augustine, *Contra mendacium*, XV, 32, *CSEL*, xli, pp. 512–3.

Sélestat, MS 13, ff. 17ᵛ–41ʳ contains a second treatise by Bernold, his *Apologeticus* of 1075, which is the principal *fons formalis* of the *Liber ad Gebehardum* (chapters 16–22 are paraphrases of Bernold's work; chapters 71–3 transcribe *Apologeticus*, chapters 17–19). Once again the *lectio continua* in the Sélestat codex identifies the passages used by Manegold. Here he came upon Bernold's denunciation of the *perversa interpretatio* of Scripture: as, for example, when the advocates of clerical marriage claim that the saying of the Apostle, 'Each man should have his own wife' (I *Corinthians*, vii. 2), applies equally to clergy and laity.[78] More important, Manegold found in *Apologeticus* a discussion of the status of *auctoritates* from the Old Testament which determined his response to the Old Testament *exempla* cited by Wenrich of Trier. Bernold's concern in the *Apologeticus* was with the use made by the opponents of Gregorian decrees against clerical marriage of Old Testament *auctoritates* in favour of the marriage of priests. He concluded that such *auctoritates* were invalid as a guide to conduct in Christian society:

> The Old Testament is composed partly of mysteries and partly of moral precepts; with the coming of Christ, however, its mysteries and carnal observances ceased, because he is the end and fulfilment of the Law, but its moral precepts still remain, because it is necessary always to observe 'you shall love your neighbour as yourself' (*Leviticus*, xix. 19, *Matthew*, xix. 19, xxii. 39, *Galatians*, v. 14, *James*, ii. 8) and so forth. Therefore, if any man teaches that any carnal observance from the Law must be observed in opposition to the New Testament, without doubt he is judaizing like the Galatians, or rather, like the Ebionites.[79]

The marriage of priests was a *carnalis observantia*: it was necessary in Old Testament times because admission to the sacerdotal office was restricted to members of one priestly tribe. 'In our own time priests

---

[78] Bernold, *Apologeticus*, 13, *MGH Lib*, II, p. 74. Cf. Manegold, *Ad Gebehardum*, 42, p. 384.

[79] Bernold, *Apologeticus*, 12, p. 72: '*Vetus testamentum partim in misteriis partim in moralibus preceptis continetur, sed adveniente Christo cessavit in mysteriis et carnalibus observantiis, quia ipse est finis sive completio legis, in moralibus autem preceptis adhuc manet, quia semper est observandum:* Diligas proximum tuum sicut te ipsum *et reliqua. Quicumque igitur ex lege aliquam carnalem observantiam novo quidem testamento adversam adhuc observandam esse dogmatizat, procul dubio cum Galathis immo cum Hebionitis iudaizat*'.

can be chosen from every class (*genus*) and marriage is rightly forbidden to them, since nowadays they do not need to have heirs'. This argument offered Manegold a means of coping with Wenrich's demonstration that the practice of Old Testament times was directly contrary to Gregorian views of the relations of *regnum* and *sacerdotium*.[80]

Manegold's principal criticism of Wenrich's use of the Bible was that he paid no attention to the *circumstantiae*, the context, of the passages which he extracted. 'Many proofs from the Scriptures are introduced there, all of which, if understood soberly and considered piously, are found to be unfavourable to [our opponents] and advantageous to us, as we learn from the context of the places from which they have been pilfered'.[81] Wenrich's practice was to tear a quotation from its *circumstantiae* and to 'bend it to [his] own point of view by a violent interpretation'.[82] The importance of *circumstantia* in deciding the meaning of a text is a frequent theme in the writings of Augustine, notably in *De doctrina christiana*, III, 4, 8: *circumstantia ipsius sermonis, qua cognoscitur scriptorum intentio*.[83] Manegold may have learned to emphasize the *circumstantiae* of a biblical *auctoritas* from Augustine, or once again he may have learned from the school of Constance. For Bernold of Constance also stressed the necessity of examining the *circumstantia* of a text in his treatise on the interpretation of canon law, *De fontibus iuris ecclesiastici*. 'The context of a passage provides us with much that the single chapter does not contain, and without which it cannot be fully understood; but the collation of different laws with each other helps us greatly, because one often throws light on another'.[84]

---

[80] Manegold, *Ad Gebehardum*, 42, pp. 383–4.

[81] *Ibid.*, 42, p. 383: '*Inducuntur enim ibi multa scripturarum testimonia, que videlicet omnia sobriȩ intellecta, pie considerata, illis inveniuntur contraria, nobis proficua, sicut in omnibus unde furata sunt loȩorum docet circumstantia*'. Cf. *ibid.*, 43, p. 385. See Hartmann, 'Manegold von Lautenbach', pp. 130–2.

[82] Manegold, *Ad Gebehaṛdum*, 6, p. 321.

[83] Augustine, *De doctrina christiana*, III, 4, 8. Cf. *De mendacio.*, XVI, 31; *De Genesi ad litteram*, X, 18; *De civitate Dei*, XXII, 18; *Epistolae*, CXL, 23; CXLIX, 24; *Sermo* L, 9.

[84] Bernold, *De excommunicatis vitandis, de reconciliatione lapsorum et de fontibus iuris ecclesiastici*, *MGH Lib*, ii, p. 139: '*Ipsa enim circumstantia lectionis multa nobis prescribere solet, quae unum singulare capitulum non habet, sine quibus tamen pleniter intelligi non valet, sed diversorum statutorum adinvicem collatio multum nos adiuvat, quia unum sepe aliud elucidat*'.

Manegold urgently needed these aids to interpretation, faced as he was with the claim of Wenrich of Trier that the actions of Gregory VII contravened 'very many passages of holy Scripture, instructions of the Law and the Gospels'.[85] Wenrich's most damaging contention was that biblical authority favoured Salian control of the imperial Church and the papacy against Gregorian demands for the freedom of the Church. The Old Testament depicted a society—that of God's chosen people—in which the secular ruler deposed and replaced the high priest. King Solomon deposed Abiathar, even though he had been a loyal servant of King David, and put Zadok the priest in his place (I *Kings*, ii. 26–7, 35).[86] Those glorious men the Maccabees felt it no stain on their religion to receive the high priesthood from impious foreign kings (I *Maccabees*, x. 20; xiv. 38).[87] How can the Gregorians argue, therefore, that the royal power should not dispose of the priesthood and the papacy?

Manegold's reply is spread over three chapters of the *Liber ad Gebehardum*, and is as incoherent as every other argument in the work.[88] In the case of the *exemplum* of the Maccabees he accuses Wenrich of falsely interpreting the text. The passages which Wenrich cited, purporting to demonstrate that Jonathan received the high priesthood from King Alexander, and Simon from King Demetrius, must be compared with I *Maccabees*, ix. 29–31, which states that Jonathan was chosen by the people. The explanation of this contradiction is that the high priests in reality owed their position to the Jewish people, while the foreign kings' claim to appoint them was an empty boast. If the author of Maccabees recorded their claim, this does not mean that he accepted its validity, any more than the evangelists approved of the mockery of Jesus which they recorded. However, even if Wenrich's interpretation of I *Maccabees*, x. 20 and xiv. 38 had been accurate, it would have availed him nothing; 'for proofs from doubtful sources should not be put forward in support of doubtful and controversial arguments. Although the Books of the Maccabees have been

---

[85] Wenrich, *Epistola*, 3, p. 288.
[86] *Ibid.*, 4, pp. 288–9.
[87] *Ibid.*, 8, p. 298.
[88] Manegold, *Ad Gebehardum*, 42, 55–6, pp. 383–4, 406–9.

published for the edification of the Church, they were nevertheless not received into the canon by the Hebrew church'.[89] Jerome, Origen, and Gregory I confirm that they are not canonical.

The *exemplum* of Solomon is disposed of by a similar combination of arguments. Firstly, Solomon's deposition of Abiathar is interpreted in the light of I *Samuel*, ii. 27–36: the King was not acting on his own behalf, but rather fulfilling God's curse on the house of Eli.[90] In addition, the account in I *Kings*, ii. 26–7, 35 must be read in conjunction with that in I *Chronicles*, xxix. 22, which makes it clear that it was the Jewish people, and not Solomon, who appointed Zadok as high priest.[91] If the author of the account in Kings says that Solomon substituted Zadok for Abiathar, this is simply the *mos scripturarum*, a manner of speaking. It is this author's custom to say that an action was performed by a king, when he means simply that the action occurred in that king's reign.[92] Having argued thus far from the *circumstantiae* and from the *collatio* of different accounts of the same events, Manegold changed his approach and introduced Bernold's argument concerning the *carnalis observantia* of the Old Testament. Wenrich's citing the conduct of Solomon towards Abiathar as an *auctoritas* is tantamount to recommending the Jewish *lex talionis*, the practice of taking revenge for personal injuries, as acceptable conduct for Christians: 'when he preaches retaliation, he incites Christianity to accept the vicious doctrine of the heresiarch Ebion and commends Jewish superstition so as to tread the Gospel underfoot'.[93] Even conceding Wenrich's account of events to be accurate, it is obvious that many practices were permitted in Old Testament times which are forbidden under 'the better covenant' (*Hebrews*, vii. 22).[94] For good measure Manegold throws in Bernold's argument about the biblical *exempla* which are to be avoided rather than imitated by the faithful, notably the *exemplum* of Lot and his daughters.[95]

[89] Ibid., 55, p. 408: '*Ad confirmandas enim dubias et que in contentionem venerint res de dubiis testimonia non sunt proferenda. Machabeorum autem libri, quamquam ad edificationem ecclesie prolati, in canone ab Hebrea ecclesia tamen non sunt recepti*'.

[90] Ibid., 42, p. 384.

[91] Ibid., 56, p. 409.

[92] Ibid.

[93] Ibid., 42, p. 384: '*... dum talionem predicat, ad pravum dogma Hebionis heresiarchae tempora christiana provocat et Iudaicam superstitionem ad evangelii conculcationem commendat*'.

[94] Ibid., 56, p. 409.

[95] Ibid.

These three chapters of the *Liber ad Gebehardum* contain an impressive range of exegetical techniques; but the overall impression which they convey is one of uncertainty about their application. In tackling Wenrich's *exempla* from Maccabees and Kings, Manegold first produced a plausible refutation according to the literal sense, and demonstrated that Wenrich was guilty of *perversa interpretatio*. However, Manegold could not rest content with these arguments according to *hystoria*.[96] He must reach for a bludgeon which would obliterate Maccabees, Kings, the whole of the Old Testament, as a source of *auctoritates* for anti-Gregorian polemicists: the Books of Maccabees are not canonical; the *carnalis observantia* cannot be regarded as a guide to Christian conduct. He ends by rejecting the literal sense, 'the letter that kills', [97] as a valid subject for investigation. The effect, of course, is to invalidate his own arguments according to the literal sense—the elaborate examination of the *circumstantiae* and the *mos scripturarum* with which he first attempted to refute Wenrich's interpretation.

Manegold of Lautenbach remains a figure of mystery. The twelfth-century bibliographer Wolfger of Prüfening—normally very reliable on the subject of 'the South German Gregorian circle'[98]—identified the polemicist Manegold as the author of glosses on Isaiah and Matthew and of a commentary on the Psalter.[99] The search for the Psalm commentary in particular has preoccupied scholars in recent years, without, however, reaching a generally agreed identification.[100] Wolfger's remark about Manegold's work on Matthew—*super Matthaeum vero glosas continuas scribit*—ought to make us pay particular attention to the extensive use of Jerome, *In Matthaeum*, in the *Liber ad Gebehardum*, to the glosses by Anonymous A in the Constance codex of Jerome's *In Matthaeum*, and to Anonymous A's *sententiae* on the evangelists in Fulda, MS Aa 11. However, even if no further biblical commentary or glosses by Manegold of Lautenbach chance to turn up, there is

---

[96] *Ibid.*, 55, p. 407.
[97] *Ibid.*, 42, p. 384.
[98] Robinson, 'Arbeitsweise Bernolds', p. 75 n. 85; and also my introduction to the forthcoming *MGH* edition of the chronicles of Berthold and Bernold.
[99] Wolfger, *De scriptoribus ecclesiasticis*, ch. 105, ed. Ettlinger, p. 91. But see F. Chatillon, 'Recherches critiques sur les différents personnages nommés Manegold', *Revue du moyen âge latin*, ix (1953), pp. 153–70.
[100] See the summary of research by Hartmann, 'Psalmenkommentare', pp. 319–24, 356–66.

enough material in the *Liber ad Gebehardum* to enable us to form a judgement on Manegold as a biblical scholar. Here he appears unsure where his methods are leading him, compelled to take up adventurous arguments by the polemical needs of the moment. It was the topical debates of the Investiture Contest which caused him first to experiment with, then to discard, the literal sense of the Old Testament. There survives a response to Manegold's polemic composed by an anti-Gregorian calling himself 'Hugo orthodoxus'. He denounces Manegold's doctrine with the words: *O nova lex! o dogma novum, noviter fabricatum!*[101] In fact, however, Manegold was no innovator. The *auctoritates* and the methods of argument in the *Liber ad Gebehardum* are both rooted in the solid learning of the cathedral school of Constance.

Trinity College, Dublin

---

[101] *Versus Hugonis contra Manegoldum, MGH Lib*, I, 431. See B. Smalley, 'Ecclesiastical attitudes to novelty *c.*1100–*c.*1250', *SCH*, xii (1975), p. 113, reprinted in *Studies*, p. 97.

BIBLISCHES UND HAGIOGRAPHISCHES KOLORIT IN DEN *GESTA HERWARDI*

von PAUL GERHARD SCHMIDT

HEREWARDS Kämpfe gegen Wilhelm den Eroberer haben ihn zu einem der 'Folk Heroes of Britain'[1] gemacht. Zu seinen historisch gut bezeugten Taten, der Plünderung von Peterborough im Juni 1070 und dem bis 1071 von Ely aus gegen die Normannen geführten Partisanenkrieg, treten farbige Erzählungen über seine Jugend, die er als Verbannter in der Fremde verbracht haben soll, über seine Kämpfe gegen Untiere und Berserker, seine Werbung um die schöne Turfrida und seine Kundschaftergänge und Handstreiche, zu denen er sich bald als Töpfer, bald als Fischer verkleidete. Als edler Outlaw und Vorbild einer der über Robin Hood erzählten Episoden ist er kürzlich von M. Keen[2] und J.C. Holt[3] gewürdigt worden. Ähnlich wie Robin Hood eignet sich auch Hereward zum Helden der Unterhaltungsliteratur; im 19. und 20. Jahrhundert entstanden mehrere Kinderbücher, zwei vermutlich nie aufgeführte Dramen und drei historische Romane über den 'letzten Engländer'.[4]

Am bedeutendsten und bekanntesten ist der Roman 'Hereward the Wake', den Charles Kingsley 1866 verfaßte, als er eine Geschichtsprofessur in Cambridge innehatte.

Kingsley folgte hauptsächlich dem Bericht der *Gesta Herwardi*, die er als zuverlässige Quelle ansah. Sein positives Urteil über diesen Text wurde bereits wenig später von Freeman revidiert und eingeschränkt.[5] Noch ungünstiger urteilte eine Studie aus dem Jahr

---

[1] Ch. Kightly, *Folk Heroes of Britain* (London, 1982), pp. 119–47 (Ch. 5: 'The English Resistance. Hereward and the Fenland Revolt against William the Conqueror').

[2] M. Keen, *The Outlaws of Medieval Legend*, 2nd ed. (London, 1977), pp. 23–38.

[3] J.C. Holt, *Robin Hood* (London, 1982), pp. 62–5.

[4] W.E. Dring, *Hereward's Isle. Books on the Fenland* (Ely, 1962), pp. 14ff. [List of Ely County Library holdings].

[5] E.A. Freeman, *The History of the Norman Conquest of England* (Oxford, 1871) iv, pp. 454–81 und pp. 804–13; 2nd ed. (1876), pp. 450–485 und pp. 826–33.

1906 über Kingsleys wichtigste Quelle. Sie wird mit folgenden Worten charakterisiert: Die *Gesta Herwardi* sind eine in schlechtem und dunklem Latein geschriebene Chronik, die nach Liebermann um 1150 von dem Mönch Richard von Ely verfaßt worden ist.[6]

Meine Absicht ist es, das hier zitierte Urteil über die literarische Gattung, die Latinität und den stilistischen Rang der *Gesta* zu überdenken, die Notwendigkeit einer Neuedition zu begründen und auf einige in der Diskussion bisher übersehene Aspekte des Werks aufmerksam zu machen. Auf das noch offene Problem der Datierung und Verfasserschaft der *Gesta* möchte ich dagegen nur kurz eingehen. Seit Liebermann[7] gilt der Mönch Richard von Ely als Verfasser der *Gesta Herwardi*. Seine Vermutung stützt sich auf eine Notiz im *Liber Eliensis*. Diese vor 1174 verfaßte Kompilation enthält längere Passagen, die der Sache und vielfach auch der Formulierung nach mit entsprechenden Abschnitten der *Gesta Herwardi* übereinstimmen. Der *Liber Eliensis* nennt nun als seine Quelle: *In libro autem de ipsius gestis Herewardi, dudum a venerabili viro ac doctissimo fratre nostro beate memorie Ricardo edito, plenius descripta inveniuntur.*[8] Der Mönch Richard von Ely, der 1174 als verstorben bezeichnet wird, kann nicht mit dem Prior Richard von Ely identisch sein, der noch gegen 1195 nachweisbar ist.[9] Wann der Mönch Richard lebte und seine *Gesta* abfaßte, läßt sich nicht exakt bestimmen. Aus ihrem Prolog geht hervor, daß Verfasser und Empfänger der Schrift selbst noch Kampfgefährten Herewards gesehen haben, was eine Abfassungszeit vor der Mitte des 12. Jahrhunderts nahelegt. Ein Umstand deutet auf das erste Viertel des 12. Jahrhunderts. Da die *Gesta Herwardi* sich zumindest für ihren ersten Teil als Übersetzung aus einem altenglischen Werk des Diakons Leofric ausgeben, und da für den Episkopat Bischofs Hervey von Ely (1109–1130) eine Übersetzung altenglischer Texte in Ely bezeugt ist, wäre eine Entstehung der *Gesta* unter diesem Bischof nicht unwahrscheinlich.[10] Bestreitet man aber die Identität

---

[6] L. Dicke, 'Charles Kingsleys "Hereward the Wake". Eine Quellenuntersuchung'. (Diss. phil., Münster, 1906), p. 6.

[7] F. Liebermann, 'Über ostenglische Geschichtsquellen des 12., 13., 14. Jahrhunderts, besonders den falschen Ingulf', *Neues Archiv*, xviii (1893), pp. 225–67, bes. pp. 238–43.

[8] *Liber Eliensis*, ed. E.O. Blake, CSer, 3, xcii, (London, 1962), p. 188.

[9] Liebermann, 'Ostenglische Geschichtsquellen', p. 243.

[10] R.M. Wilson, *The Lost Literature of Medieval England*, 2nd ed. (London, 1970), p. 72 und pp. 113–15.

der im *Liber Eliensis* genannten *Gesta Herewardi* Richards mit den
uns vorliegenden, anonym überlieferten *Gesta Herwardi* oder geht
man von der Annahme tiefgreifender Bearbeitungen der *Gesta
Herewardi* Richards aus, so gelangt man zu anderen Datierungs-
vorschlägen. Eine Tübinger Dissertation, die diesen Standpunkt
vertritt, kommt zu dem Ergebnis, daß die *Gesta* erst nach dem Jahr
1224 verfaßt seien.[11] Der *terminus ante quem* ist dagegen nicht
umstritten. Er wird durch die Handschrift der *Gesta* ·(Peterborough, Chapter Library MS 1) gegeben, eine gegen 1250 von Robert
von Swaffham angelegte Sammlung auf Peterborough bezüglicher
Urkunden und Chroniken.[12] Der Codex Swaffhams diente leider
nicht als Basis für die *editio princeps* der *Gesta*; Thomas Wright
benutzte für die 1839 veröffentlichte Erstedition eine neuzeitliche,
sehr fehlerhafte Abschrift des Swaffhamcodex in Cambridge, Trinity College.[13] Wrights zweite Ausgabe, 1850 im Anhang zu
Gaimars *Estoire des Engles* publiziert,[14] brachte zwar Änderungen,
aber keine Verbesserungen der Textgestalt. Damit war die Spur für
die weitere Entwicklung gelegt. Eine von zwei Lokalhistorikern
1895 besorgte zweisprachige Ausgabe folgte trotz der Benutzung
von Swaffhams Handschrift weitgehend Wrights fehlerhaftem und
mitunter unverständlichem Text.[15] Auch C.T. Martin, der für
seine 1888 in der *Rolls Series* gedruckte Edition statt der Cambrid-
ger Abschrift den Swaffhamcodex selbst benutzte, konnte sich dem
Einfluß seines Vorgängers Wright nicht entziehen. Über den
Schreiber der Handschrift und über den Autor der *Gesta* fällte er

---

[11] J. Benecke, *Der gute Outlaw*. Studien zu einem literarischen Typ im 13. und 14.
Jahrhundert=Studien zur englischen Philologie, N.F., xvii (Tübingen, 1973), p.
21.
[12] J.D. Martin, *The Cartularies and Registers of Peterborough Abbey*=
Northamptonshire Record Society, xxviii (1978), pp. 7–12. Der Codex wird
derzeit in der University Library Cambridge aufbewahrt.
[13] Wrights 1839 erschienene Ausgabe ist enthalten in F. Michel, *Chroniques Anglo-
Normandes* (Rouen, 1836 [!]), ii, pp. 1–98. In seinem auf den 20. Juni 1838 datierten
Vorwort urteilt Wright über die von ihm benutzte Abschrift des Antiquars Gale in
Trinity College Cambridge: 'Cette transcription est excessivement incorrecte, et
dans de certains passages il est impossible d'y retrouver le sens'.
[14] *The Anglo-Norman Metrical Chronicle of Geoffrey Gaimar*, ed. by Th.
Wright=*Caxton Society's Publications*, ii, (London, 1850), App. 46–108.
[15] *De Gestis Herwardi Saxonis*, transcribed by S.H. Miller and translated by W.D.
Sweeting=*Fenland Notes and Queries*, iii, (Peterborough, 1895). Eine Bearbeitung
dieser englischen Übersetzung veröffentlichte Trevor Bevis [*Hereward. The Siege
of the Isle of Ely ... together with De Gestis Herwardi Saxonis*, 2nd ed. (Peterborough,
1982)].

folgendes Urteil: 'The scribe was comparatively ignorant of Latin, and the author was probably not much his superior in that respect'.[16]

Aus den Vorarbeiten zu der von mir geplanten Neuedition der *Gesta Herwardi* ergibt sich, daß dieses Urteil einer kritischen Überprüfung nicht stand hält. Stellvertretend für zahlreiche andere Fälle sollen hier drei Beispiele erörtert werden, die Schreiber und Autor in einem günstigeren Licht erscheinen lassen.

In dem Bericht über Herewards Heimkehr in das von den Normannen eroberte England heißt es in Wrights erster Ausgabe: *At quodam vespertino tempore tum ad sui patris mansionem quandam quae vocatur Brunne recessit, et apiro cujusdam sui patris, militem Aseredum nomine, in extremis ejusdem villae hospitatus est.*[17] Das unverständliche *apiro* änderte Wright in seiner zweiten Ausgabe zu einem Eigennamen, außerdem wandelte er den Akkusativ *militem* in einen Ablativ um. In dieser Form, *et a Piro cuiusdam sui patris milite, Aseredum nomine*, diente der Passus auch Sweeting für seine englische Übersetzung als Vorlage: 'And then one evening he arrived at his father's mansion, called Bourne, and was hospitably entertained by a certain Pirus, a soldier of his father's, Asered by name'.[18] Ungewöhnlich an dem lateinischen Text ist u. a. der passivische Gebrauch des Deponens *hospitari*, das in der Regel mit *apud* verbunden wird, und die Tatsache, daß zwei Namen eine Person zu bezeichnen scheinen. Heißt Herewards Gastgeber Pirus und Asered zugleich? Die schöne Literatur gebraucht nur einen Namen für diese Nebenperson, die übrigens nur an dieser Stelle der *Gesta* begegnet. In Kingsleys Roman und in Stedmans Drama erscheint Pirus als Pery, der in seiner Hütte die Heimkehr Herewards ersehnt.[19] Der von Martin in der *Rolls Series* gebotene Text hebt die Doppelnamigkeit des Pirus Aseredus wieder auf. Er folgt der vom Swaffhamcodex überlieferten Namensform und nennt den Ritter Oseredus. Anstelle des seiner Meinung nach verderbten *apiro cujusdam sui patris militem* schlägt Martin die Emendation *a servo*

---

[16] Th. D. Hardy, u. C.T. Martin, *Geffrey Gaimar, Lestoire des Engles, RS* 91 (London, 1888), i p. lii. Martins Edition der *Gesta* findet sich auf pp. 339–404.

[17] Wright, *Chroniques* (1836 bzw. 1839), p. 39.

[18] Miller/Sweeting, *De Gestis* (1895), p. 32; ähnlich Bevis, *Hereward* (1982) p. 21.

[19] D.C. Stedman, *Hereward. A Romance* (Dublin, 1908), (2. Akt, 1. Szene: The Hut of Pery, Bourne).

cujusdam sui patris militis vor, womit jedoch die Apposition *Oseredum nomine* schlecht vereinbar scheint. Auch der ungewöhnliche Sprachgebrauch *hospitatus a quodam* ist durch Martins Konjektur nicht beseitigt. Anstelle des von Wright suggerierten rätselhaften *apiro* bietet der Swaffhamcodex ein wesentlich bekannteres, an dieser Stelle auch notwendiges und passendes Wort: *apud*. Da der Schreiber gelegentlich ein *d* schreibt, dessen Oberlänge nicht senkrecht nach oben, sondern fast waagerecht nach links zeigt, kann ein eindeutig von ihm als *apud* geschriebenes Wort vom Betrachter als *apiro* gelesen werden. Der Passus lautet nunmehr: *ad sui patris quandam mansionem secessit et apud quendam sui patris militem, Oseredum nomine, ... hospitatus est.* 'Old Pery' in seiner Hütte ist damit eliminiert. Dieses erste Beispiel gestattet es, dem Autor an dieser Stelle einen korrekten lateinischen Satzbau zu attestieren; einzig der Abschreiber muß sich einen geringfügigen Fehler—*cuiusdam* schrieb er anstelle von *quendam*—vorhalten lassen.

Bei Osered rüstet sich Hereward zu einem nächtlichen Überfall auf die im Haus seines erschlagenen Bruders lärmend feiernden Normannen. In drei der vorliegenden Editionen lautet der Text übereinstimmend so: *induit se scilicet tunica, loricam et galeam nigro panno detectam sub pallio quidem ancillae cum gladio accepit.* Wenn auch wenig ansprechend formuliert, scheint die Aussage selbst klar verständlich. In sagengeschichtlichen Studien wird denn auch wiederholt auf die Verkleidung Herewards als Frau verwiesen.[20] Aber die angeführten Parallelen zeigen, daß in anderen Texten die Verkleidung von Männern für die Handlung von konstituierender Bedeutung ist; in den *Gesta Herwardi* dagegen kommt es nicht zur Demaskierung einer angeblichen Magd. Die Verkleidung *sub pallio ancillae* ist funktionslos und überflüssig. Hat der Autor nur eine Vorsichtsmaßnahme Herewards, nur eine seiner vielen Verkleidungen nennen wollen? Der Swaffhamcodex erlaubt es, Wrights Text in zwei Punkten zu korrigieren. Er bietet *sub* statt *scilicet*, was Martin in seine Edition aufnahm. Nicht von Martin wurde die Interpunktion und Satzgliederung des Codex übernommen. Nach

---

[20] F. Panzer, 'Erzbischof Albero von Trier und die deutschen Spielmannsepen', *Germanistische Abhandlungen. Festschrift für Hermann Paul* (Straßburg, 1902), pp. 303–32, bes. p. 324. Außerdem G. Noack, 'Sagenhistorische Untersuchungen zu den Gesta Herwardi' (Diss. phil., Halle-Wittenberg, Halle, 1914), pp. 19–23.

detectam hat der Abschreiber einen Punkt gesetzt. Den Beginn des folgenden Satzes hob er außerdem mit einer roten Majuskelinitiale hervor: *Sub pallio ancille cum gladio accepit.* Dieser objektlose und damit scheinbar mißglückte Satz mag zu den Urteilen über die Ignoranz des Abschreibers beigetragen haben. Das von der Handschrift gebotene *ancille* ist jedoch nicht, wie Wright durch seine Schreibung *ancillae* es suggerierte und Martin es wiederholte, ein Genitiv; vielmehr handelt es sich um das an dieser Stelle erforderliche Akkusativobjekt. Das der gehobenen Literatursprache angehörende Wort *ancille* bzw. *ancile* begegnet übrigens in ähnlicher Verbindung noch einmal in den *Gesta Herwardi*.[21] Der fragliche Abschnitt lautet also in der vom Verfasser intendierten Form: *induit se sub tunica loricam et galeam, nigro panno detectam.*[22] *Sub pallio quidem ancile cum gladio accepit.* Der Abschreiber hat demnach hier den Text in einer bis in die Interpunktion hinein korrekten Form wiedergegeben; der Autor verfügt, wie das *ancile* des zweiten Beispiels lehrt, über einen anspruchsvollen Wortschatz und er weiß die Stilhöhe zu wahren. Eine burleske oder schwankhafte Verkleidung wäre mit der in dieser Situation erforderlichen Würde des Rächers Hereward nicht vereinbar gewesen.

Mit Panzer, Helm, Schild und Schwert bewaffnet zieht Hereward—so lautet die dritte Stelle—gegen die weinseligen Okkupanten des väterlichen Hauses aus. Seine Absicht ist es, *superpropinare eis, pro fratris morte, potum arundinis et vina doloris.*[23] Ein Ausdruck in dieser drohenden Ankündigung, nämlich *potus arundinis*, bietet Verständnisprobleme. Die englische Übersetzung begegnet ihnen folgendermaßen: 'designing to pledge them, for his brother's death, in a draught of a spear-shaft, and in wine of sorrow',[24] versteht also den Ausdruck als Kenning für Blut. Gegen diese Übersetzung ist einzuwenden, daß *arundo* in der Regel das als Waffe ungeeignete schwache Rohr meint; es kann zwar auch den Pfeil oder Pfeilschaft, nie aber den Speerschaft bezeichnen. Der Editor der *Rolls Series* löste das Problem auf andere Weise. Er sah in *arundinis* eine Korruptel, die er durch die Konjektur *amaritudinis*

---

[21] Martin, *Geffrey Gaimar*, p. 397: '... *cum nudo ense et ancile*'.
[22] Eine Auslassung an dieser Stelle ist möglich; vielleicht ist *capiti imposuit* nach *detectam* zu ergänzen.
[23] Martin, *Geffrey Gaimar*, p. 366.
[24] Miller/Sweeting, *De Gestis* (1895), p. 34.

heilen wollte. Eine Korrektur des überlieferten Textes ist jedoch
nicht erforderlich. So wie *propinare vinum* eine Formulierung der
Bibel (*Amos*, ii. 12) ist, läßt sich auch *potus arundinis* auf einen Passus
der Bibel zurückführen. Bei der Beschreibung von Christi Tod
heißt es (*Matt.*, xxvii. 48): *unus spongiam implevit aceto et imposuit
arundini, et dabat ei bibere.* Der *potus arundinis* ist der am Rohr
gereichte Essigtrank, der letzte bittere Trank in der Todesstunde.

Diese offene Anspielung auf den Passionsbericht, die wiederum
die Zuverlässigkeit der Handschrift bestätigt, läßt zugleich einen
Mangel der bisherigen Editionen empfinden, die die biblischen
Zitate und Wendungen nicht kenntlich gemacht haben. Für ein
zutreffendes Textverständnis sind aber diese Nachweise mitunter
unentbehrlich. Daß ein lateinschreibender Kleriker des Mittelalters
vorgeformte Wendungen aus Liturgie und Bibel gebraucht, ist
nicht anders zu erwarten; Umfang und Art der Verwendung
biblischer *termini* sind jedoch im Einzelfall zu überprüfen und auf
mögliche Intentionen des Autors zu befragen. Die in den *Gesta*
gebrauchte Formulierung *rogabant ea, quae pacis sunt*[25] z. B. über-
nimmt eine Wendung des Lukasevangeliums (xiv. 32), ohne daß
damit weitere Implikationen verbunden wären. Auch wenn das
Zitat nicht erkannt ist, gelangt der Leser der *Gesta* zum richtigen
Verständnis der Stelle. In anderen Fällen dagegen muß er von der
biblischen Herkunft einer Formulierung wissen, wenn er nicht
Gefahr laufen will, den Text gründlich mißzuverstehen. Als Bei-
spiel mag ein Passus der *Gesta* dienen, der von Herewards erster
Heldentat, der Bezwingung eines gefährlichen Bären, handelt. Der
Sieg trägt Hereward Ruhm, Bewunderung, aber auch Neid ein.
Die *Gesta* beschreiben die Reaktion seiner Umgebung u. a. mit den
Worten: *provinciales eum in laudibus praeferebant, et mulieres ac puellae
de eo in choris canebant, quod gravius inimicis erat.*[26] Wer nun den
biblischen Bericht über Davids erste Heldentat, den Sieg über
Goliath, nachliest, findet dort (I *Reg.*, xviii. 6) eine ähnliche
Beschreibung: *egressae sunt mulieres de universis urbibus Israel, can-
tantes, chorosque ducentes ... atque dicentes: Percussit Saul mille, et David
decem millia.* Wie man weiß, war Saul über das David so reichlich
gespendete Lob so erzürnt, daß er bald danach den nichtsahnenden

---

[25] Martin, *Geffrey Gaimar*, p. 388.
[26] Martin, *Geffrey Gaimar*, p. 344.

David mit einem Speerwurf zu töten suchte. Der Autor der *Gesta* hat sich ganz sicher den biblischen Bericht zum Vorbild genommen; ihm entnahm er das ausschmückende Detail, daß die erste Tat des jungen Helden David von Frauen besungen wurde, und übertrug es auf die erste Tat seines Helden Hereward. Wer diese Anspielung auf die biblische Vorlage nicht erkennt und den Bericht der *Gesta* als Aussagen ihres Autors über ein tatsächliches Geschehen versteht, zieht daraus u. U. zu weitgehende Schlüsse. R. M. Wilson etwa gelangt zu folgendem Ergebnis: 'Although the written English version of the Hereward story appears to have been lost at a comparatively early date, there is evidence to show that he long continued popular. According to the Gesta, his deeds were celebrated by the country people, and women and girls sang of them in their dances'.[27] Meines Erachtens kann die Existenz altenglischer Tanzlieder auf Hereward aus dem Text der *Gesta* nicht erschlossen werden. Denn ihre Darstellung ist von der Davidszene abhängig. Diese Abhängigkeit läßt sich an einem weiteren Detail zeigen. Unmittelbar im Anschluß an die Tanzlieder folgt in beiden Texten der Lanzenwurf eines Neiders gegen den nichtsahnenden Helden. Wie David entgeht Hereward im letzten Augenblick dem heimtückischen Wurf eines Mannes, den er für seinen Freund halten mußte.

Der Nachweis der in den *Gesta Herwardi* begegnenden Anklänge an biblische Themen, Szenen und Formulierungen soll der Edition vorbehalten bleiben. Auf einige auffällige Entlehnungen aus dem Neuen Testament möchte ich abschließend noch aufmerksam machen. Der Autor der *Gesta* hat, als wollte er seinen reichen Wortschatz demonstrieren, die Verkleidungen Herewards in variierenden Formulierungen beschrieben. Neben *seipso transfigurato, mutato habitu* und *varia usus specie* gebrauchte er auch die Wendung *aspectu exinanire se*.[28] Dieser Ausdruck nimmt *Phil.*, ii. 7 *semetipsum exinanivit formam servi accipiens* wieder auf. Herewards Verkleidungen erscheinen damit als freiwilliges Opfer eines Höherstehenden, der sich wie Christus seiner Gestalt entäußert und Knechtsgestalt annimmt. Wie Christus vom Gefolge des Pilatus so

[27] Wilson, *The Lost Literature*, p. 114.
[28] Martin, *Geffrey Gaimar*, p. 388.

wird Hereward von der Dienerschaft König Wilhelms verspottet.[29] Obwohl Pilatus Christus freilassen will, gibt er dem Volk nach, das Christi Tod verlangt; ganz ähnlich verhält sich König Wilhelm, der dem Wunsch der Neider nachgibt und Hereward ins Gefängnis werfen läßt.[30]

Auch hagiographische Texte sind vom Autor der *Gesta* als Vorbilder benutzt worden. Zwar ist Hereward keineswegs ein Heiliger—er bezeichnet ihn sogar ausdrücklich in biblischer Wendung als *vir sanguinum*[31]—dennoch ist ein in Heiligenviten häufiges Motiv auf ihn übertragen worden. Aufgrund einer Vision, so berichtet der Autor, habe Hereward die in Peterborough geraubten Schätze zurückgegeben. Als er sich danach mit seiner Schar auf der Flucht vor den Feinden im nächtlichen Wald verirrte, habe ihm Gott einen weißen Wolf gesandt, der sie sicher an ihren Bestimmungsort führte. Göttliche Hilfe durch geleitende Tiere ist festes Stereotyp der Heiligenlegende.[32]

Die *Gesta Herwardi* weisen zwar biblisches und hagiographisches Kolorit auf, Hauptziel ihres Verfassers ist es aber, Hereward als vorbildlichen Ritter zu zeigen. Im Prolog und an anderen Stellen seines Werks gibt der Verfasser zu erkennen, daß er das Leben eines großmütigen, hervorragenden Ritters darstellen wollte. Er wendet sich an ein Publikum, das an wahrer Ritterschaft interessiert ist. Die *Gesta* lehren, wie ein *miles* kämpft, daß er einen überwundenen Gegner schont, die Regeln des Zweikampfs streng einhält und trotz drohender Niederlage die Hilfe seiner Gefährten zurückweist. Sie zeigen ihn schlagfertig bei höfischer Unterhaltung, vertraut mit Musikinstrumenten, als erfolgreichen Friedenstifter und als jemanden, der situationsgerecht sich bald bescheiden im Hintergrund hält, bald durch ein stattliches Gefolge seinen Rang betont. Durch seine Beachtung höfischer Normen und eines ritterlichen Verhaltenskodex erscheint Hereward als Vorbild echten Rittertums. Die *Gesta* berichten denn auch, daß selbst während seiner Kämpfe

---

[29] Martin, *Geffrey Gaimar*, p. 386: *illudentes eum—Matt.*, xxvii. 29: *illudentes ei.*

[30] Martin, *Geffrey Gaimar*, p. 401: *rex ... ut eis [sc. invidentibus] tamen satisfaceret—Matt.*, xxvii. 18: *per invidiam; Marc*, xv. 15: *Pilatus volens ... satisfacere.*

[31] Martin, *Geffrey Gaimar*, p. 396—*Ps.* v. 7, u. ö.

[32] Belege bei H. Günter, *Psychologie der Legende* (Freiburg im Breisgau, 1949), pp. 180ff. und C.G. Loomis, *White Magic. An Introduction to the Folklore of Christian Legend* (Cambridge, Mass., 1948), pp. 6off.

gegen König Wilhelm sich Höflinge des Eroberers im gegnerischen Lager aufgehalten haben sollen, um sich von Hereward in der *milicia* unterweisen zu lassen.[33]

Ein Werk solchen Inhalts und Zuschnitts läßt sich nicht einer einzigen literarischen Gattung zuordnen. Es ist sicher falsch, die *Gesta Herwardi* als Chronik zu bezeichnen. Das Werk nennt keine einzige Jahreszahl; es informiert nur über seinen Helden, nicht über die Ereignisse der Zeit. Die *Gesta* dienen erkennbar nicht dynastischen oder genealogischen Interessen und sie sind auch nicht als didaktisches Lehrbuch oder als Ritterspiegel angelegt. Dem äußeren Schema nach handelt es sich um eine *Vita*, die von der Kindheit zum friedlichen Tod des Helden führt. Das Explicit des Swaffhamcodex hebt das Besondere dieser *Vita* hervor, die nicht eine Heiligen- oder Fürstenbiographie, sondern die *Vita Herwardi incliti militis*, eine Rittervita, ist. Zugleich trifft auch die im *Incipit* der Handschrift verwendete Bezeichnung *Gesta* zu. Dieser vielseitige und dehnbare Begriff umschließt auch die vielen Einschübe in das Werk, die Nebenerzählungen, z. B. über die gegen Hereward wirkende Hexe oder über den anderweitig nicht bekannten Brumannus, der normannische Prälaten auf ihrem Weg zu englischen Klöstern abfing und in einen großen Sack steckte.[34]

Die Mischung von Realem und Wunderbarem, von Erbauung und Unterhaltung, von Fakten und Fiktion kennen wir aus anderen Werken des 11. und 12. Jahrhunderts. Im vierten Jahrzehnt des 12. Jahrhunderts entstanden zwei Werke dieser Art: Die *Gesta Regum Britanniae* Geoffreys von Monmouth, die sich wie die *Gesta Herwardi* als Übersetzung aus dem Altenglischen geben, und die fast gleichzeitige *Historia Karoli Magni* des Pseudo-Turpin, die in wirkungsvoller Weise hagiographische Elemente in eine Geschichtsschreibung romanhaften Charakters einfügte; die *Historia* scheint außerdem einen Roman über Karls Jugend zu kennen, die er im spanischen Exil verbrachte. In die gleiche Kategorie gehört auch der lateinische Konstantinroman, der seinen weltlichen Inhalt in biblischen Formulierungen und nach biblischen Erzählmustern vorträgt.[35] Liebermann hat für die *Gesta Herwardi* die Bezeichnung

---

[33] Martin, *Geffrey Gaimar*, p. 393.

[34] Martin, *Geffrey Gaimar*, p. 374.

[35] *Incerti auctoris de Constantino Magno eiusque matre Helena libellus*, ed. E. Heydenreich (Leipzig, 1879). G. Landgraf, *Die Vulgata als sprachliches Vorbild des Konstantinromans= Jahresberichte der Kgl. Studienanstalt Speier* (1881), pp. 68–74.

historischer Abenteuerroman vorgeschlagen.[36] Ich möchte diesen
Ausdruck aufgreifen. Dem schillernden Charakter des Werkes, das
als Roman unter dem Einfluß verschiedener Gattungen steht, wird
diese Bezeichnung am ehesten gerecht. Die *Gesta Herwardi* sind
zudem keine Einzelerscheinung. Es gibt mehrere solcher historischer Abenteuerromane, deren Held ein unfreiwillig in die Fremde
ziehender Ritter ist, der den Namen einer historisch bezeugten
Gestalt trägt und mit deren Schicksal zumindest in einem Punkt
eine gewisse Übereinstimmung aufweist. Die Haupt- und Titelper-
son solcher *Gesta* wird auf ihrer Reise in romanhafte Abenteuer
verwickelt, die von Treulosigkeit, Kämpfen und Friedensschluß,
dem Aufenthalt an einem fremden Hof, einer erfolgreichen Braut-
werbung, dem Gewinn eines hervorragenden Tieres, einer wun-
derbaren Waffe, eines Kleinods oder einer Reliquie handeln und
zum Schluß den Helden in seinen alten Besitz zurückkehren oder
ihn ein eigenes Reich gewinnen lassen. Lebensumstände einer oder
mehrerer Nebenpersonen werden im Lauf der Erzählung epi-
sodenartig vor dem Leser ausgebreitet. Eine innere Wandlung und
Entwicklung des Helden ist nicht gattungsimmanent; die belehren-
den und moralischen Partien solcher *Gesta* erfüllen in erster Linie
eine Alibifunktion.

Dank dieser Mischung von Historie, Belehrung und Unterhaltung wurden die *Gesta Herwardi* nicht zufällig zur Blütezeit des
historischen Romans im 19. Jahrhundert als Stoff aufgegriffen;
Kingsley und andere fanden im historischen Abenteuerroman des
Mittelalters eine ihren Intentionen gemäße Gattung.

Philipps-Universität Marburg

---

[36] Liebermann, 'Ostenglische Geschichtsquellen', p. 238.

INNOCENT III AND VERNACULAR
VERSIONS OF SCRIPTURE

by LEONARD E. BOYLE

LOTHARIO dei Conti di Segni became pope as Innocent III in 1198, at the age of thirty-seven, and for the eighteen years of his pontificate he had two chief preoccupations: to regain the Holy Land for the Church and to restore the true Faith in Europe. It is with the latter that I am concerned here, and with just one moment in his endeavour to counter the heretical tendencies and movements which had been threatening the stability of the Church for a century or more by 1198. This is the problem of vernacular versions of the Scriptures, a problem which arose, seemingly for the first time ever at this level, at the very beginning of Innocent's pontificate. It is a well-known if not celebrated moment, and has had a place in every modern discussion of the question of vernacular versions of the Bible in the Middle Ages, since the days when S. Berger first gave it prominence in his *La Bible française au moyen âge* (Paris, 1884).[1]

In English-speaking scholarship the best-known treatment of Innocent's position is that of the late Margaret Deanesly in *The Lollard Bible and Other Medieval Biblical Versions* (Cambridge, 1920). This brilliant book, written when she was a very young scholar indeed, has had an extraordinary impact over the years, and probably accounts as much as any other for certain views of Innocent III and his attitude towards vernacular versions which still prevail today. These views so associate Innocent with suppression of vernacular versions that a recent historian, getting things a little muddled, states baldly that the Fourth Lateran Council, under Innocent, 'set limits to the translation of the Bible into the

---

[1] Notably, H. Rost, *Die Bibel im Mittelalter* (Augsburg, 1939), pp. 73–9, G. De Poerck and R. Van Deyck, 'La Bible et l'activité traductrice dans les pays romans avant 1300', in *Grundriß der romanischen Literaturen des Mittelalters*, VI. 1: *La littérature didactique, allégorique et satirique* (Heidelberg, 1968), pp. 21–48, especially pp. 31–7, C.A. Robson, 'Vernacular Scriptures in France,' *CHB*, ii, pp. 436–52.

vernacular', where in fact the Council has nothing whatever on the matter.[2]

What Margaret Deanesly, as a prologue to her discussion of the Wycliffite Bible, drew to the attention of English-speaking and other scholars, was a small batch of letters, three in all, from the second year of Innocent's pontificate—letters which had already been the object of study by Berger and others. These letters were and are readily to hand in the last volumes of Migne's *Patrologia latina*, and recently have had a critical edition, in the edition of the registers by the Austrian School in Rome, now in progress.[3] They concern a situation which had arisen in the diocese of Metz, and about which the Bishop of Metz had written in, perhaps, June 1199. In Metz, according to the Bishop, a 'multitude' of laymen and women was gathering in secret and devoting itself to studying and preaching to each other versions in French of the Gospels, Epïstles of Paul, the Psalms, the *Moralia* of Gregory the Great, and many other such books. By way of placating the Bishop, who clearly wanted a confirmation of some repressive measures he had taken or wished to take, Innocent answered him with two letters, one to the 'dissidents' in question and the clergy and people of Metz, in, probably, mid-July 1199, the other to the Bishop himself, at the same time or a day or two afterwards; then he followed these up after about five months with a third on 9 December, in which he commissioned three local or near-local Cistercian abbots to conduct an inquiry and report back to him.

I do not wish to engage in this paper in a point-by-point discussion of Deanesly's presentation of these three letters of Innocent. In general, and at the risk of appearing ungenerous to someone who was kindness itself to me as a young student, I may say that her translation and summary of the first letter is misleading, her version of the second is somewhat at sea, and that her treatment of the third verges on the tendentious. For all that Deanesly allows that Innocent displayed much reluctance to condemn the versions out of hand in the first two letters, she states of the third, that to the three abbots, that Innocent 'spoke as if he had

[2] H.E. Mayer, *The Crusades*, trans. J. Gillingham (Oxford, 1972), p. 207.
[3] *Die Register Innocenz' III 2: Pontifikatsjahr, 1199/1200*, ed. O. Hageneder, W. Maleczek and A.A. Strnad (Rome, 1979), pp. 271–6, 432–4.

already condemned the translation'. And again, for all that she goes on at once to qualify this remark (incorrectly, as it happens) with 'though he had actually only condemned its users', she scraps this qualification a few paragraphs later when she states that Innocent 'displayed a broader mindedness than the local archbishop, but ended [in the third letter] by confirming what the latter desired: the suppression of the translation'.[4]

This is Margaret Deanesly's conclusion, and a conclusion which has had a wide following over the past sixty years. It surely is at the back of the mind of a commentator in the second volume of the *Cambridge History of the Bible* (1969) when he asserts that Innocent 'speaks as if he had condemned these particular translations'.[5]

Should this conclusion be taken for granted? I suppose the only way to find out is to take each letter in turn, a process I shall now engage in at the risk of over-simplification.

The first letter of Innocent III is to the people and clergy of Metz, the 'dissidents' included, in July 1199. This is the fullest of the three letters and is the only one of the three to be included in the Decretals of Gregory IX, the first official collection of canon law, in 1234. Like any letter of yours or mine, this has a beginning, a middle, and an end; but unlike our letters, no papal letter may be taken *tout court* in its entirety as expressing the mind of the writer. The beginning normally consists of the addressee of the letter, a greeting, and an arenga or rhetorical flourish stating in general, lofty terms the pope's competence in the matter in hand. The second part of the letter is the *corpus*, where the pope gets down to business, and this in itself falls into three parts:

— a *narratio* of whatever the problem is that has come to the pope's attention
— a speculative or legal reflection on the problem leading to the all-important point
— the *dispositio* or papal judgement on the case.

The third part rounds off the letter, with threats of excommunication etc. and the date. In the present case the *narratio* in the *corpus* is entirely taken up with what the Bishop of Metz had written to

---

[4] *The Lollard Bible*, pp. 32–3.
[5] H. Hargreaves, 'The Wycliffite Versions,' *CHB*, ii, pp. 387–415, at p. 391.

Innocent sometime before July 1199. Although Deanesly rightly translates the beginning of the *narratio* as 'The bishop of Metz has signified to us that ...', she in fact seems to take what follows in the *narratio* as the opinion of Innocent III himself. What is more, she gives a translation of the *narratio* which is not at all accurate.[6]

The Bishop, Innocent says, had informed him that a multitude of laymen and women, 'not a little swayed by a certain desire for the scriptures' (Deanesly: 'led to a large extent by a desire of understanding the scriptures'):

(1) had had translations into French made of the Gospels, the letters of Paul, the Psalter, the Moralia [in] Job, and many other books;

(2) were so taken up with *relying* on this translation ('would that it were prudently as well') that they presume to debate these matters of the Scriptures in secret gatherings and to preach one to the other (Deanesly wholly misrepresents this phrase, *translationi huiusmodi adeo libenter ... intendens, ut,*[7] when she translates, 'They *intend* that with this translation, made thus at their own discretion (would that it had been made with prudence as well), laymen and women shall presume to hold forth on such matters, and to preach to each other ...');

(3) repudiate those who spurn these gatherings, who do not bother themselves with like matters, who do not give their ears and minds to such things (Deanesly has nothing on this point or the next);

(4) laugh at the simplicity of their priests, and when the word of salvation is proposed to them by these priests, murmur behind their backs, asserting that they themselves have better things in their own books and are in a better position to speak prudently.

Up to this, Innocent has simply been rehearsing or narrating (with just one personal comment: 'would that it were prudently as well') what the Bishop of Metz had told him. Now he begins in the second part of the *corpus* or body of the letter to reflect and

---

[6] *The Lollard Bible*, p. 31.
[7] *Register Innocenz' III*, p. 271.

comment on the situation. Margaret Deanesly has given snippets from this part of the *corpus* in her translation, but without any hint of the change-over in the letter from narration to Innocent's personal reflection on the problem as narrated by the Bishop of Metz. What is interesting about this long and closely-argued passage of personal reflection on Innocent's part is that Innocent never once mentions the translations. What he is really concerned about is what he sees as the usurpation by these people at Metz of the office of preaching, an office which does not belong to anyone and everyone in the Church.

Although, Innocent says, the 'desire of understanding the Holy Scriptures and a zeal for preaching what is in the Scriptures is something not to be reprimanded but rather to be encouraged', there is good reason in the present case why the laity in question should be taken to task (*merito arguendi*—perhaps 'rightly to be argued with'), because

(*a*) they hold gatherings in secret,
(*b*) they usurp the office of preaching,
(*c*) they deride the simplicity of priests,
(*d*) they spurn the company of those who do not join them.[8]

Now Margaret Deanesly, while rendering these four points faithfully, has the Pope saying that these laypeople of Metz 'appear to be justly accused' under these four heads in their zeal for the Scriptures and preaching. In fact, he says no such thing. What he says is *in eo tamen apparent merito arguendi*, meaning not 'appear to be justly accused', as though Innocent were condoning any action already taken by the Bishop of Metz, but rather 'they appear indeed worthy of being taken to task—argued with—on this account'. And after listing the four heads above with which they should be confronted, Innocent goes on at much length to take each of the four points in turn, noting in particular with respect to the apparent usurpation of the office of preaching at Metz, that preaching is to be engaged in only by those who are sent. And, he goes on, 'If anyone should reply by way of arguing the point, that the sending [in the present case] is an invisible one and from God ... then one may reasonably reply that because that mission is an interior one and

[8] *Ibid.*, p. 272.

hidden, it is not at all sufficient simply to claim to have been sent by God (any heretic can do this)—there should also be some confirmation of that invisible mission by a miracle or by a special witness of Scripture itself', as there was in the case of Moses and John the Baptist.[9]

In other words, in this long second part of the *corpus* of Innocent's first letter, all that the Pope does is propose guidelines for the people and clergy of Metz on how to confront these lay preachers with rational and scriptural arguments against their apparent usurpation of the office of preaching. As Innocent put it to the Bishop of Metz in his second letter, 'In the letter which we have sent to the generality of the people [of your city and diocese], we have shown you a way of recalling them and convincing them out of the Scriptures with respect to those things which we have noted to be reprehensible'.[10]

Much of the *corpus* of the first letter was included in this second, that to the Bishop of Metz, which, presumably, was sent out on the same day and by the same messenger as the first. Again there is the repetition of what the Bishop had told the Pope in his original letter, and again there is the point about *merito arguendi videantur*, but the exemplary caution of the letter is manifest from the outset. There is no doubt, Innocent says, that prelates have a duty 'of catching the little wolves who are trying to ruin the vineyard of the Lord'. All the same, this should be done prudently as well as diligently. Above all else, prelates should take care not to try to root out the cockle before the harvest time, lest they should destroy the grain in the process. Of course, the Pope says, one should not tolerate heresy, but on the other hand one should be careful not to turn simple people into heretics by impatient action. Because, he goes on, the Bishop has not really shown in his letter just how these laypeople in Metz are at variance with the Faith of the Church, and because the Pope has no idea of what the way of life is of those 'who have translated the sacred Scriptures in this fashion', or of the way of life of those 'who teach the Scriptures as they have been translated'—neither of which is possible *sine scientia litterarum*—Innocent felt he was in no position to proffer any sort of prudent

[9] *Ibid.*, p. 273.
[10] *Ibid.*, p. 276.

judgement. Hence, the better to inform himself, Innocent ordered the Bishop to do certain things (and this is the third and really important part of any papal letter: the *dispositio* or personal decision of the pope). First of all:

(*a*) Convince the people in question by means of rational and scriptural argument to give up whatever appears to be at variance with faith; then:

(*b*) Find out the truth about the following points:
    (1) who is the author of the translation?
    (2) what was his intention as translator?
    (3) what is the quality of faith of those who use the translation?
    (4) why do they persist in teaching?
    (5) are they reverent towards the apostolic see and the Catholic Church?

Six months later, Innocent's third and last letter on the problem at Metz was issued. By then he had had a reply from the Bishop to his queries, and obviously was not at all satisfied with what the Bishop had to report. In order to inform himself further, Innocent therefore appointed a commission of three Cistercian abbots to conduct an inquiry at Metz. In his letter to these of 9 December 1199, Innocent states in his *narratio* that from the reply of the Bishop of Metz to his queries, he had learned that some of the suspect laity at Metz had refused to pay any attention to his letter of July, and that some publicly, some in private, had said that their only obedience was to God. As for the translation of the Scriptures of which they were so fond, some of them, according to the Bishop, had asserted that they would not cease to stick to it even if the Pope himself were to decree to have it abolished. This was all a bit provocative, Innocent admitted, but all the same (and here we reach the *dispositio*), lest he should seem to be acting too hastily, he ordered the abbots to go to Metz, get together with the Bishop and 'those who adhere to the said translation', and if they found anything worthy of correction in these laypeople, take steps to correct it. And if these laypeople refused to mend their ways, then the abbots were to question them on the points specified in Innocent's letter to the Bishop in July, and then send a messenger with the replies to the Pope, so that he might work out what was to be done. But he urged the abbots to proceed with the utmost care and caution. This was not simply a local matter. It touched the whole Church and the whole Christian Faith.

In Margaret Deanesly's rendition of this letter we get a rather different picture, and one which leads to the widespread conclusion with which I am at variance here. According to Deanesly, Innocent 'told the abbots that at Metz: "No small multitude of laymen and women presume to hold forth among themselves at secret conventicles, in order to learn a certain translation of holy scripture, ... even when prohibited'.[11] Actually, and at the risk of being pedantic, I may say that Innocent 'told them' nothing of the sort. What he 'told' them was simply what the Bishop of Metz had said. Nothing more. And he did not tell the abbots that these laypeople of Metz were gathering together secretly 'in order to learn a certain translation of holy scripture, ... even when prohibited'. What he stated on the authority of the Bishop of Metz was that these people were still usurping the office of preaching, and were so devoted to the translation that they used in their preaching that they would not drop it 'even if we [the Pope himself] were to order it to be abolished'.[12]

The crucial question, of course, is whether or not Innocent eventually abolished the translation in the light of what the abbots reported. We do not know. All that we know about Innocent's part in this Metz affair is what we have in these three letters, and the only time that an 'abolition' of the translation occurs in these letters is in the report of the Bishop of Metz, as rehearsed by Innocent to the abbots, that the people in question would not drop the translation 'even if we were to order it to be abolished'. Nor do we have any account or even inkling of what the three Cistercian abbots reported back to Innocent on the completion of their inquiry. The matter never comes up again in the remaining seventeen years of Innocent's pontificate.

There is, however, an account in a chronicle of the Cistercian Alberic of Trois Fontaines (c. 1250) which states under the year 1200 that 'when a sect called Vaudois was prospering in the city of Metz certain abbots were sent to preach. These abbots burned certain

[11] The Lollard Bible, p. 32.
[12] Register Innocenz' III, p. 433.

books which had been translated from Latin into Romance and extirpated the said sect'.[13] Deanesly has taken these 'certain abbots' to be Innocent's three Cistercian commissioners, and switching rather neatly from Innocent's letter to the abbots to Alberic's chronicle, says:

> These [commissioners] had been told [by Innocent] to summon before them ... 'those who favour these things and adhere to the aforesaid translation'; as the Metz chronicler says, 'they burnt certain books translated from Latin into Romance, and extirpated the aforesaid sect'.[14]

Perhaps the Cistercian abbots did burn the translations, but I feel that Deanesly is not playing fair with the facts here, no more than she is when she states a little earlier that Innocent told the abbots they were to go to Metz, 'and, with the archbishop, summon before them "those who favour these things and adhere to the aforesaid translation"—with the result that they burnt all that they could find of such books'.[15]

If the abbots did burn any books, then it was not, as Margaret Deanesly implies, on the strength of Innocent's letter—unless, of course, the abbots misunderstood the phrase, 'even if we were to order it [the translation] to be abolished', as Deanesly and others in her wake have interpreted it. There is not in fact the slightest hint that Innocent ever spoke in any way, hypothetically or not, of suppressing the translations. The passage in which the hypothetical statement occurs, and which Deanesly has taken as a fact, is indeed not at all Innocent's, but his report to the abbots of what the Bishop of Metz had said that the dissidents at Metz had stated when the Bishop asked them to stop preaching and expounding their translations. Again, as in the interpretation by Deanesly and others of the first letter, there is a fatal methodological flaw: *narratio* is taken for *dispositio*.

For my part, I am convinced that Innocent's only interest in the Metz translations was that they provided a spur for preaching by people who by definition were not qualified for the office of

---

[13] *Chronica Albrici monachi Trium Fontium*, ed. P. Scheffer-Boichorst *MGH Scriptorum*, XXIII (Hanover, 1874), pp. 631–950, at p. 878.
[14] *The Lollard Bible*, p. 34.
[15] *Ibid.*, p. 33.

preaching, or could not show that they had a divine mission to this effect.[16] He never, for example, asks if the translations are accurate, though he does express a curiosity about the learning of the translator. More importantly, if Innocent really were concerned with the translations as such and with the whole phenomenon of vernacular translations, then he would surely have included a prohibition of translations in the constitutions he drew up fourteen or fifteen years later for the Fourth Lateran Council of late 1215, and which sum up so many of his preoccupations since the beginning of his pontificate in 1198. It is at least remarkable, though I have not found anyone to remark on it, that when, in his long constitution on heretics, Innocent speaks of those who 'appropriate to themselves the authority to preach', and repeats his point in the first Metz letter about the importance of a 'mission' to preach, there is not even a whiff of a reference to vernacular versions of Scripture.[17]

I am of the opinion, further, that Innocent has been much maligned by historians who see a denunciation of translations, or of the reading or study of the Scriptures by the laity, in his citation in that first letter to Metz of *Matthew*, vii. 6: 'Do not give to dogs what is holy and do not cast your pearls before swine'. To Margaret Deanesly, this quotation 'had been taken [by the three abbots] as discountenancing the use of the Waldensian translations, as they were probably intended to do. This was', she continues, 'in accordance with the whole tenor of the letter ...'.[18]

In fact, as I have noted before, Innocent never comments on the translations as such in that first letter. And when he quotes *Matthew*, vii. 6, what he is arguing against is not translations of Scripture or even preaching and reading the Scriptures, but, oddly as it may seem in the light of what Deanesly and others say, against those who maintain (as some bishops and preachers did) that the 'holy things' of Scripture and the 'pearls' were only for the elect. To Innocent, on the contrary, the 'holy things' and the 'pearls' are for all without exception who willingly and gratefully accept them,

---

[16] See also C.R. Sneddon, 'The "Bible du XIIIe siècle": Its Medieval Public in the Light of its Manuscript Tradition', in *The Bible and Medieval Culture*, ed. W. Lourdaux and D. Verhelst (Louvain, 1979), pp. 127–40.

[17] *Conciliorum Oecumenicorum Decreta*, ed. Centro di Documentazione, Istituto per le Scienze Religiose, Bologna (Freiburg, 1962), pp. 209–11.

[18] *The Lollard Bible*, p. 32.

but they are not to be given to those who do not revere the Scriptures and the sacraments of the Church—who are heretics.[19]

Perhaps, in conclusion, one is making too much of all this. I do not think so. The plain fact is that while everyone admits, as the *Cambridge History of the Bible* does, that 'no universal and absolute prohibition of the translation of the Scriptures into the vernacular nor of the use of such translations by clergy or laity was ever issued by any council of the Church or any pope', these three letters of Innocent III are repeatedly adduced, as they are by this same *Cambridge History*, as letters 'which could reasonably be taken to represent condemnation of translations'.[20]

Biblioteca Apostolica Vaticana

[19] *Register Innocenz' III*, p. 272.
[20] Hargreaves, 'The Wycliffite Versions', p. 391.

PETER COMESTOR

by DAVID LUSCOMBE

D URING her own career Beryl Smalley greatly expanded our knowledge of Peter Comestor. When she first discussed his works, Peter's links with Peter Lombard and his activity as a commentator upon the Gospels had only recently been established. She went on to show Peter's connections with the school of St Victor and, before she died, she explored some aspects of Peter's glosses on the Gospels. It may therefore be appropriate to try to fit together some of the pieces of the jigsaw that we now have, and to follow the lines along which, as we can now see, Peter's career evolved.[1]

Peter Comestor was a close follower of Peter Lombard. This was firmly established by R. Martin and A. Landgraf in 1931.[2] In more recent years Fr. Brady has shown that Peter Comestor, Dean of Troyes since 1147, came to Paris before 1158–9, when Peter Lombard stopped teaching, and that he reported Peter Lombard's oral teaching in the course of writing a series of theological questions. He knew the Lombard's Four Books of Sentences, and, in addition, enjoyed a personal acquaintanceship that amounted to discipleship, for he often preferred to follow Peter Lombard's teaching, as his questions show: *inquit, dicit Magister, dubitat Magister, Magister noster, determinat Magister, Magister solvebat, concedebat, explicabat*, etc. After Peter Lombard's election to the bishopric of Paris, and after his death in 1160, Peter Comestor taught in the

---

[1] The last short appraisal of Peter Comestor's achievement in the light of available evidence was published by S.R. Daly, 'Peter Comestor, Master of Histories', *Speculum*, xxxii (1957), pp. 62–73.

[2] R. Martin, 'Notes sur l'oeuvre littéraire de Pierre le Mangeur', *RTAM*, iii (1931), pp. 54–66. A.M. Landgraf, 'Recherches sur les écrits de Pierre le Mangeur', *RTAM*, iii (1931), pp. 292–306, 341–72. See also H. Weisweiler, 'Eine neue frühe Glosse zum vierten Buch der Sentenzen des Petrus Lombardus', *Aus der Geisteswelt des Mittelalters=Beiträge zur Geschichte der Philosophie und der Theologie des Mittelalters*, Supplementband iii, 1 (Münster in Westfalen, 1935), pp. 360–400, and R.M. Martin (ed.), *Pierre le Mangeur, De sacramentis=Spicilegium sacrum Lovaniense*, xvii, Appendix (Louvain, 1937).

DAVID LUSCOMBE

Paris schools.[3] Walter of St Victor, writing *c*.1177, mentions him anonymously as a disciple of Peter Lombard, and, more striking, Peter Comestor glossed Peter Lombard's Books of Sentences, and introduced them thereby into the schools as a textbook and as the basis of regular teaching and study in theology.[4] However, it is less clear who were Peter Comestor's earliest masters. He must have been a mature associate of Peter Lombard in the latter's last years in the schools, not a young beginner. In his Questions Peter Comestor mentions two of his teachers. One of these is the obscure John of Tours, whom Peter may have heard in Tours; at least an anonymous glossator of the Lombard's Sentences tells us that Peter Comestor was himself once in Tours.[5] The other is Peter Abelard, whom Peter Comestor once heard teaching, and who had stopped teaching by 1140.[6] The indications are therefore that Peter Comestor began his studies in the schools of Paris and Tours before 1140 and before he became Dean of Troyes in 1147.

Wherever Peter Comestor went and worked in the 1140s and 1150s, he was sufficiently well known in Paris in 1168 to have been appointed Chancellor by that year, and he held this office until his death in 1178 or 9. In his last years he retired to the abbey of St Victor in Paris, where he died and was buried, as we learn from the

[3] I. Brady, 'Peter Manducator and the Oral Teachings of Peter Lombard', *Antonianum*, xli (1966), pp. 454–90; I. Brady (ed.), *Magistri Petri Lombardi ... Sententiae in IV Libris Distinctae. Editio tertia ... tomus II. Liber III et IV=Spicilegium Bonaventurianum*, v (Grottaferrata, 1981), p. 39*. The Questions of Peter Comestor are questions 288–334 in J.P. Pitra's edition of the *Questiones Magistri Odonis Suessionis=Analecta novissima Spicilegii Solesmensis. Continuatio altera*, ii (Paris and Frascati, 1888), pp. 98–197.

[4] Walter of St Victor, *Contra IV Labyrinthos Franciae*, ed. P. Glorieux, 'Le Contra Quatuor Labyrinthos Franciae de Gauthier de Saint Victor', *AHDLMA*, xix (1952), pp. 187–335, at p. 320, lines 12–35. See on this Brady, *Petri Lombardi ... Sententiae, ... tomus II. Liber III et IV, Prolegomena*, pp. 40*–42*.

[5] The evidence is set forth by Brady, 'Peter Manducator and the Oral Teachings of Peter Lombard', pp. 484–5 and 465. The anonymous writer of a gloss on the fourth book of the Sentences mentions the case of a Breton who became a monk and priest at St Martin of Tours, and who died while still unbaptized: '*Quesitum est a magistro Johanne, quid faciendum de illo, vel utrum salvus esset. [Sed se dixit] omnino ignorare. Hoc idem dicit M[agister] P[etrus] Man[ducator], qui ibidem erat quando hoc contigit*'. Furthermore, in question 326 (ed. Pitra, p. 167) Peter Manducator indicates that John of Tours had taught him.

[6] See again Brady, 'Peter Manducator and the Oral Teachings of Peter Lombard', p. 465 '*M[agister] P[etrus] A[baelardus] dicebat ... sic audivi illum docentem*' (Question 298, ed. Pitra, p. 113).

necrology of St Loup in Troyes, which informs us also that Peter had become a canon of St Loup as well as Dean of the cathedral there.[7] He appears to have remained both Dean of Troyes and Chancellor of Paris to the end.

Peter Comestor's attachment to St Victor, like that of Peter Lombard before him, involved more than residence in the abbey. Like the Lombard he was deeply influenced by Victorine theological teaching, and in ways that only Beryl Smalley has revealed.[8] The biblical Glosses that were produced at Auxerre by Gilbert the Universal and in the school of Laon under the brothers Anselm and Ralph opened the way to teaching more parts of the Bible than the Psalter and the Letters of St Paul. The continuous *Glossa Ordinaria* on the whole of Scripture came into being in the schools of Laon and of Paris during Peter Comestor's lifetime. Peter Comestor's compendium of all biblical history, known as the *Historia scholastica*, owes much to it, not least in its attempt to come to terms with the whole of Scripture. But Peter also owed much to the Victorine emphasis, itself a renewal of Jerome's emphasis, on the literal study of the Bible, which largely approximated to the study of *Hebraica veritas*.[9] As well as seeing allegories in the Old and the New Testament, the Victorines appreciated the historical value of Scripture, and read it not only in terms of typology, of prefiguration, and of spiritual meaning, but also and initially as history. Hence their interest in the Old Testament as the historical account of what happened before the coming of Christ. Hence also the approaches they made to Jewish interpreters of the Old Testament, for Jewish

---

[7] '*XII Kal. Nov. [21 October]: Obiit magister Petrus Manducator, Sancti Petri decanus et canonicus Sancti Lupi, qui sepultus est apud Sanctum Victorem Parisiensem*', ed. A. Longnon, *Obituaires de la Province de Sens* (Paris, 1923), IV (*Diocèses de Meaux et de Troyes*), p. 297C. The day of his death is said to be *XI Kal. Nov.* [22 October] in the necrology of Notre Dame, Paris, which describes Peter as *Petrus Manducator, cancellarius*, ed. B. Guérard, *Collection des Cartulaires de France, VII. Cartulaire de l'Eglise Notre Dame de Paris* (Paris, 1850), IV, 172. See too Brady, 'Peter Manducator and the Oral Teachings of Peter Lombard', pp. 483–4. Peter is described as *noster canonicus* in the obituary of St Victor. See A. Molinier, *Obituaires de la Province de Sens, I. Diocèses de Sens et de Paris = Recueil des historiens de la France, publiés par l'Académie des inscriptions et belles-lettres. Obituaires*, 1 (Paris, 1902), p. 593 and it is possible that he was counted as one of the community in his last years.

[8] See especially Smalley, *Bible*, chapter 5. See further Smalley, 'The Bible in the Medieval Schools', *CHB*, ii, pp. 197–220, at p. 206.

[9] See especially Smalley, *Bible*, chapters 3 and 4.

scholars did not read the Old Testament in terms of prefigurations of the life of Christ, and Jewish exegesis was always associated with the literal sense. Peter Comestor benefited from these changes of attitude among biblical scholars not only in general ways and through use of the *Glossa Ordinaria*, but also by direct influence from particular Victorine masters. Beryl Smalley found that he produced comments made on Genesis by Hugh of St Victor that are not to be traced in Hugh's *Notulae super Genesim*.[10] She showed also that in his *Historia* Peter borrowed extensively, although without acknowledgement, from the commentaries of Andrew of St Victor, especially from his Commentary on the Octoteuch.[11] Peter Comestor often appeals in his writings to the *Hebraeus sermo* and the *Hebraei*, to what the *Hebraei tradunt* or *exponunt*, and when he does so he not infrequently draws material from the writings of Andrew of St Victor in particular. He showed himself more conscious than the Victorines of the desire of students to have convenient aids to study. Hence the single-volume *Historia scholastica*.[12] But he was far from alone in the second half of the twelfth century in Paris in teaching students according to the example set by the Victorines. His successors, particularly Stephen Langton, were in many ways of a similar outlook, and it is perhaps surprising that Beryl Smalley gave more attention in her *Study of the Bible in the Middle Ages* to Stephen Langton than to Peter Comestor in her discussion of the Victorine achievement, because in fact Peter Comestor's influence was to prove more potent and enduring than that of Stephen Langton in the history of medieval biblical scholarship.

It is then as a supporter of the traditions established by both Peter Lombard in the school of Notre Dame and by the Victorines that Peter Comestor is to be seen. It would be difficult to trace the development of his teaching and writing in terms of a progression from one set of influences to another. Hugh of St Victor, whom

---

[10] *Ibid.*, pp. 98–9.
[11] *Ibid.*, pp. 178–80; Smalley, 'The School of Andrew of St. Victor', *RTAM*, xi (1939), pp. 145–67. Also (briefly) Smalley, 'L'exégèse biblique du xii⁰ siècle', *Entretiens sur la renaissance du xii⁰ siècle sous la direction de M. de Gandillac et E. Jeauneau=Décades du Centre culturel international de Cerisy-la-Salle*, ns, ix (1968), pp. 273–93, at p. 279.
[12] Smalley, *Bible*, p. 200.

Peter Comestor may well have heard teaching, died in 1141, by which time Peter Lombard was already settled in Paris and living at St Victor. Andrew of St Victor produced his Commentary on the Octoteuch by about 1147, and shortly afterwards Peter Lombard produced the first draft of his Glosses on the Epistles of St Paul. The double set of influences developed simultaneously rather than successively. But they were also somewhat exclusive of other influences. Peter Comestor, unlike other Parisian theologians such as Robert of Melun, gives no indication of having taught the arts, still less of being interested in applying dialectic to the teaching of theology, and in this respect he considerably narrowed the programme of study outlined by Hugh of St Victor in his *Didascalicon*. Moreover, Peter Comestor shows no personal interest in following the debates occasioned by the lectures of Gilbert of Poitiers, even though Gilbert's teachings in and after 1148 were keenly contested by Peter Lombard.

It would be difficult to arrange Peter Comestor's writings in a strict chronological sequence, but it is reasonable to turn first to his professional activities as a teacher of theology in the school of Notre Dame, and to those writings that may not have been intended for a wider readership than that of familiar students and masters. It seems best to begin with Peter Comestor's glosses on the four Gospels. They are unprinted and have been very little studied, except by Beryl Smalley.[13] They survive only in the form of reports by hearers or students. They reflect the intra-mural and repetitive activity of a lecturer within his classroom. But the glosses were securely identified by Landgraf,[14] and the known manuscripts have been listed by Fr. Stegmüller.[15] Beryl Smalley has shown us their historical significance. Behind the polished and carefully edited work for which Peter is best known, his *Historia scholastica*, lies the patient and unglamorous activity of reading through Scripture in front of students within the period between 1159 and 1178. Peter Comestor, like Peter Lombard, used the glosses that were becoming standard as the *Glossa Ordinaria*; he tried to arrange these glosses and to handle them critically. He also used the earlier

---

[13] B. Smalley, 'The Gospels in the Paris Schools in the late Twelfth and early Thirteenth Centuries, I', *Franc Stud*, xxxix (1979), pp. 230–54, at p. 231.
[14] Landgraf, 'Recherches' pp. 366–72.
[15] Stegmüller, *Bibl.*, iv, nos 6575–8.

expositio of Rabanus. In addition, he used recent commentaries, including that on the Gospels by Zachary of Besançon (1140–5), as well as a commentary on St Matthew written by an unknown religious in the 1140s.[16]

The question of how original Peter Comestor was in choosing to gloss the Gospels is difficult to settle definitively at present, but he was clearly in an *avant garde*. Traditionally the Psalter and the Letters of St Paul were the biblical books that were singled out for teaching and glossing. Commenting the Gospels was only beginning to cease to be rare, one reason for this being that the literal Gospel narratives required less exposition; the traditional challenge facing a teacher was to explore the allegories detected in the books of the Old Testament and the interpretation of the New Testament advanced by St Paul. But the rapid development of the schools in the twelfth century provided encouragement to masters to lecture on more books of the Bible. Anselm of Laon glossed the Gospel of St John. He died in 1117, and it is doubtful that Peter Comestor ever encountered him, but for a while Peter Comestor was taught by Master John of Tours, who had studied under Anselm. Moreover, Peter Comestor correctly mentions Anselm's brother Ralph as the writer of the gloss on St Matthew, and he gives us reason for thinking that the masters of Laon read their glosses in the course of lecturing on the Gospels in the schoolroom. This tradition was introduced to Paris by Peter Lombard, and also a little earlier by *L*, whose lectures on St Luke were discovered by Beryl Smalley[17] and were cited by Peter Comestor. *L* himself alluded to

---

[16] Smalley, 'Gospels in the Paris Schools', p. 231; Smalley, 'Peter Comestor on the Gospels and his Sources', *RTAM*, xlvi (1979), pp. 84–129, at p. 95. The *Enarrationes in S. Matthaeum* are attributed to Anselm of Laon in the incomplete edition of *PL* clxii, 1227–1500. On Peter Comestor's sources see especially Smalley, 'Some Gospel Commentaries of the Early Twelfth Century', *RTAM*, xlv (1978), pp. 147–80, at pp. 150–7 and 166–80.

[17] B. Smalley, 'An Early Paris Lecture Course on St Luke', '*Sapientiae Doctrina*': *Mélanges de théologie et de littérature médiévales offerts à Dom Hildebrand Bascour O.S.B.=RTAM*, numéro spécial, i (1980), pp. 299–311. In this paper Beryl Smalley brought to light an anonymous secular clerk or priest who gave the first-known Paris lecture course on a Gospel. He prepared his Commentary before Peter Comestor gave his own lectures on the Gospels and perhaps after *c*.1156; his Commentary survives in the notes made by the Master himself, who used a glossed text of St Luke, as did Peter Lombard and Peter Comestor. The importance of her discovery is that Peter Comestor now appears less original on account of his lectures on the Gospels, but he also appears more competent and

others who had glossed the Gospels before him. *L*, Peter Lombard, and Peter Comestor all constructed their expositions with the aid of the glosses being read in front of students and to be found mostly in the *Glossa Ordinaria*. We would not know so much about Peter Lombard's glosses were it not for Peter Comestor's references to them,[18] and it would seem that Peter Comestor adapted himself to a scheme of teaching that was sufficiently new for a participant to feel himself to be an innovator also, but sufficiently indebted to Peter Lombard for Peter Comestor to feel that he was his direct successor, and for us to be indebted to Peter Comestor for knowledge of Peter Lombard's own unpublished and unprinted glosses. As regards his opinions, by examining what Peter Comestor said about poverty and other issues Beryl Smalley was able to show how middle of the road he was: 'he upheld uses and denounced only abuses', and he did not think that churchmen were obliged to be poor.[19] A time for disputes over the obligation upon clerics to practise poverty was coming, but had not yet arrived. And yet, if Peter Comestor avoided controversy and provocation, he altered the character of Bible studies, as Beryl Smalley showed particularly well, by widening the range of materials for study so as to include the evidence of the liturgy, of pictures, and of relics. He

---

able than his unknown predecessor, who belongs to the 'lesser fry of the schools'. On p. 303 she mentions that the author cites two opinions on the priest's part in the remission of sin: '*Solvite hac pena, secundum magistrum Hugonem, vel solvite, id est ostendere solutum in culpa, secundum magistrum Petrum, quia quecumque solveritis hac pena, secundum magistrum Hugonem, vel solveritis, id est ostendens, secundum magistrum Petrum, erunt soluta et in celo*'. Hugh is clearly Hugh of St Victor, but Beryl Smalley may be too confident in identifying Peter with Peter Lombard. Peter Lombard held the view here attributed to him, but so did Peter Abelard, and in general writers in the twelfth century who contrasted the teachings of Hugh and of Peter were writing in the course of the disputes between the adherents of the 'schools' of St Victor and of Abelard. See for detail D.E. Luscombe, *The School of Peter Abelard* (Cambridge, 1969), pp. 195–6, 278–9. None of the evidence cited by Beryl Smalley certainly proves that the writer was teaching after Peter Lombard composed his Sentences (1155–8). An earlier date for these lectures, perhaps as early as the late 1130s, is not out of the question, and might explain better why their author shows no knowledge of Peter Comestor's own lectures.

[18] Brady (ed.) *Magistri Petri Lombardi ... Sententiae, ... tomus II. Liber III et IV, Prolegomena*, pp.42*–44*. Brady believes that Peter Comestor provides sure evidence that Peter Lombard glossed, besides the Psalter and St Paul, Luke, Matthew, and Mark, as well as the Twelve Minor Prophets.

[19] Smalley, 'Gospels in the Paris Schools', pp. 231–2; Smalley, 'Peter Comestor on the Gospels', pp. 124–8.

made a special use of the history, topography, and antiquities of Palestine, and these obvious characteristics of the *Historia scholastica* were already well developed in Peter's lectures.[20]

Peter Comestor's lectures on the Sentences of Peter Lombard were also innovatory. That he glossed the Sentences has been well established. The Prologue to his gloss survives; the gloss itself has not been securely identified, apart from fragments, but the gloss was cited by Peter of Poitiers, and the Prologue was a prologue to a gloss on all the Lombard's Four Books, not just on parts of the whole work.[21] Peter Comestor probably wrote his Prologue between 1165 and 1170, when the Lombard's Sentences were about ten years old. We may assume that the Lombard had sufficiently well established a tradition of teaching through sentences that a later Parisian master such as Peter Comestor found in his published Books of Sentences an unavoidable and serviceable textbook. Peter Comestor's Prologue was probably the first of its kind, as it clearly influenced a whole series of subsequent Prologues by other students or masters, who themselves provided glosses on the Lombard's Sentences.[22] Peter Comestor's glosses, like theirs, were probably originally entered into the margins of a copy of the Sentences, and therefore came to be overlaid by additional glosses added by later copyists or adapted by later glossators. They are found in this way, along with those of other masters, in the copy of the Lombard's Sentences found in the Naples MS VII.C.14. Peter Comestor's glosses, like a stream into which flow other waters, quickly lost much of their identity, and cannot always be isolated and authenticated, but they were a considerable influence upon Peter of Poitiers. Stegmüller has also found evidence that Peter Comestor may have glossed another work by Peter Lombard, his Commentary on the Psalter, for there are glossed copies of this work in two manuscripts of the thirteenth century, from Clairvaux and from Valasse, both

---

[20] Smalley, 'Peter Comestor on the Gospels', pp. 115–23.

[21] The Prologue was published by Martin, 'Notes sur l'oeuvre littéraire de Pierre le Mangeur', pp. 60–4. He had discovered it in Madrid, Real Academia de la Historia, MS 24 (F.208). See too Weisweiler, 'Eine neue frühe Glosse'.

[22] See Landgraf, 'Recherches' pp. 350–7; also O. Lottin, 'Le Prologue des Gloses sur les Sentences attribuées à Pierre de Poitiers', *RTAM*, vii (1935), pp. 70–3. The same may be true of Peter Comestor's Prologue to the Gospel glosses; BN, MS lat., 16794, a twelfth-century MS from St Martin des Champs, has a commentary on St Matthew which begins with an abbreviation of Peter Comestor's Prologue.

bearing an attribution to Peter Comestor, and extracts from glosses on the Psalter attributed to Peter Comestor are also found in a Berlin manuscript.[23]

More clear-cut evidence of Peter Comestor's debt to Peter Lombard's Sentences is his own *De sacramentis*, which was successfully identified by Martin and by Landgraf, and which was edited by Martin.[24] In three manuscripts it is attributed to Peter Comestor, and it is similarly attributed to Peter Comestor in quotations made from the work by other masters such as Guy of Orchelles. In addition, there are parallel passages in other works by Peter Comestor. However, the *De sacramentis* does not appear in the manuscripts in a fixed form.[25] In its longest form it provides a reasonably full guide to teaching on the sacraments in general, and it is clearly meant to be a summary of Peter Lombard's Sentences, for it is shaped by this work, while improving upon it by the coherent arrangement of material, and by the addition of more documentation from the Bible and the Fathers and from Gratian. But in the main it is an abridgement, and it preluded a series of other abbreviations of the Lombard's text, such as those by Master Bandinus, by the author of the *Filia magistri*, and by Gundulph of Bologna, whose own work may have soon followed that of Peter Comestor. The purpose for which Peter Comestor sought to revise and condense the Lombard's Sentences was probably to provide a convenient manual for priests, for a priest who consulted this work would find, for example, advice not to say Mass more than once a day, how to distribute the Eucharist, and how to administer the sacrament of penance. He would also learn what the word 'Mass' means and what the fire of purgatory consists of. In other words, the *De sacramentis* is written in a practical, pedagogic way to meet the needs of men in training for or already charged with pastoral responsibilities. It was written perhaps between 1165 and 1170, and together with his glosses on the Sentences confirms the impression of a master who was perhaps the first, and certainly the most

---

[23] Stegmüller, *Bibl.*, 6574, 1, 3 and 4. The MSS are Troyes 770 and Rouen 129 (A 518); also Berlin (GDR), Deutsche Staatsbibliothek, MS Lat.Fol.848.
[24] See above, n. 2.
[25] For example, the BL, MS Add. 34807 lacks the section on penance, and in the Trinity College, Dublin, MS C.2.14 the extracts on the Eucharist and on penance are arranged in a different order.

vigorous among the earliest, to promote Peter Lombard's work as a basis of teaching in the schools and also of reading when away from them. His ambition and his example were quickly shared by a small host of like-minded Parisian masters.

Mention has already been made of Peter Comestor's written questions, which no doubt arose from his question sessions in the schoolroom of Notre Dame. In addition to the activities of glossing and of discussing questions, a theology master had to preach. Recently Peter Comestor's career as a teacher of clerics has been set in a fresh light through the growing realization of the importance of his sermons. He was expected to preach to clerics as well as being called upon to preach to synods. Numerous manuscripts of sermons bearing his name survive, and they have now been listed. The total number of sermons composed by Peter Comestor is smaller than some have believed. But Peter Tibber has recently revealed how very popular and influential these sermons nonetheless were, for they circulated widely, and Peter Comestor had a distinctive and influential preaching style. The obligation to preach was clearly a principal feature of the duties of a theology master.[26]

Peter Comestor's *Historia scholastica* should be set against the background of years of repeated lecturing on the Bible and on the Lombard's Books of Sentences. It is, of course, the work for which he has always been best known, and he dedicated it to William aux Blanches Mains, who was elected Archbishop of Sens in 1168.[27] But why did he write the *Historia scholastica* in addition to glossing the Gospels? In what ways did his purposes in preparing it differ

[26] About 150 sermons are attributed to Peter Comestor with varying degrees of reliability in MSS of the late twelfth and early thirteenth century. Fifty sermons by Peter are printed in Migne; some of these are under the name of Hildebert in *PL* clxxi, 339–964, others in *PL* cxcviii, 1721–1844. Landgraf, 'Recherches' p. 292, n. 3, indicated the existence of unprinted collections of sermons attributed to Peter Comestor. In two important articles M.M. Lebreton, 'Recherches sur les manuscrits contenant des sermons de Pierre le Mangeur', *Bulletin d'information de l'Institut de Recherche et d'Histoire des Textes*, ii (1953), pp. 25–44; iv (1955), pp. 35–6 (Additions et corrections), compiled a list of sermons which could be claimed for Peter Comestor on grounds of style and of other characteristic features of expression such as the use of distinctions. She listed 155 sermons collected from 36 MSS. More recently Peter Tibber has revised Lebreton's conclusions, and has established the contents of what he calls the 'standard collection' of Peter's sermons in 'The Origins of the Scholastic Sermon, 1130–1210' (unpub. D. Phil., Oxford, 1983). This consistently presents 40 sermons and is found in at least 30 MSS of the late twelfth and early thirteenth centuries. Tibber has therefore

from those that guided him when lecturing to students? How do the contents of the *Historia* compare with those in the glosses? To answer some of these questions we have to look again at Peter Comestor's links with the school of St Victor. He wrote his *School History* at the end of his life, and finished it between 1169 and 1173, after he had retired from teaching in Notre Dame and had gone to live in the abbey of St Victor.[28] Many years earlier Hugh of St Victor had urged the study of the whole Bible in its literal and historical sense before attempting an allegorical interpretation. Peter Comestor was in effect fulfilling Hugh's wish for a continuous and comprehensive commentary which took the form of an *historia*. All readers of the work quickly become aware of the wide range of Jewish, pagan, and Christian writers cited by Peter Comestor. He used his sources to explain the structure of the different biblical books, and to elucidate scriptural persons and events. For the Old Testament, Josephus is the most frequently consulted writer, and he is followed, but from a wide distance, by Jerome. From Daniel onwards Peter weaves into his survey of Jewish history an account of ancient history generally; he no longer reports *incidentia* or isolated events in pagan history, but synchronizes the history of Greece and Rome with that of the Jews before and after the coming of Christ. One surprise is that Peter Comestor does not treat each Gospel individually, but takes all together as Zachary had done, but as Peter had not done in the schools. But he is clearly not wholly satisfied with this, and after describing the calling of the disciples and explaining the meanings of their names, he compares the merits of an *unum ex quattuor* presentation of the Gospels with the better way.[29] Henceforth, he notes, the order of

---

reduced the number of sermons claimed for Peter by Lebreton, but has increased their importance by showing how widely and rapidly they were disseminated. Tibber's admirable work is shortly to be published. What Peter Comestor said in his Sermons about Christ, the Church, Virtues, and Vices has been carefully examined by J. Longère, *Oeuvres oratoires de maîtres parisiens au XII⁰ siècle. Etude historique et doctrinale*=*Etudes augustiniennes* (Paris, 1975), i, pp. 20–1, 96–114, 302–10; ii, pp. 19–20, 85–93, 233–7.

[27] *PL* cxcviii, 1053–1644. A critical edition is much needed and would help many kinds of student since Peter Comestor's work was so very widely read during the Middle Ages.

[28] Smalley, 'Some Gospel Commentaries of the Early Twelfth century', p. 150.

[29] *PL* cxcviii, 1558. He associates the former approach with Ammonius of Alexandria, Eusebius of Caesarea, and Theophilus of Antioch.

the events narrated begins to vary for a while in the different Gospels.

There are occasional references to differences of opinion found in his secondary sources, but in the main Peter is concerned to collect the fruits of his reading and to present them succinctly in order to provide a constructive historical, geographical, and chronological basis for reading Scripture, as well as to alert the reader to textual problems and to difficult words that have arisen in the process of translation and of copying. He does not seek to raise theological questions, but he is far from being uncritical and uninquiring, and his method is not mere compilation. There is as much criticism, both implicit and explicit, as there is exposition. He very readily accepts that the authorities disagree, and does not hesitate in the interests of compression or of clarity to record the differences he finds among orthodox Christian expositors of the Bible. He is, in addition, always willing to add his own criticism or disagreement. Unlike the previous generation of masters, he did not defensively suggest that disagreements between Catholic authors were more apparent than real. He read his authorities, as he read the Bible, in a literal way, and did not seek to dispel apparent inconsistencies or contradictions by the application of hermeneutical principles. Still less did he seek to bridge the differences between pagan philosophy and scriptural truth by applying the principles of allegorical inter-pretation to pagan writings as well as to the Scriptures themselves. While Peter often found confirmation or amplification of the historical events of the Old Testament in the works of pagan historians, he had no interest in trying to reconcile Plato's teaching on the formation of the universe with the account found in Genesis. Peter Comestor repeatedly attacks Plato, and clearly thereby implies his opposition to the earlier ambitions of the 'Chartrains' such as Thierry of Chartres and William of Conches. Plato, he writes, wrongly regarded the ideas and *ile* as well as God as eternal.[30] He wrongly depicted the Holy Ghost as the *anima mundi* or soul of the world.[31] He wrongly thought that both good and bad demons inhabited the empyrean.[32] Plato wrongly said that God

---

[30] *Ibid.*, 1055 C.
[31] *Ibid.*, 1057 A.
[32] *Ibid.*, 1061 D.

created souls and angels created bodies.[33] He wrongly believed that
a tree could not be a tree of life and a tree of good and evil.[34]
Throughout, Peter shows a relaxed confidence in his own judgements and an ease in handling and in abstracting his materials. And
Fr. Stegmüller has shown how very selective Peter was.[35] For
example, for Ruth he considers only chapter xxiii, for Tobias only
chapter i, for Jeremiah only chapters xl–xlii, for Ezechiel only
chapters i–iv, for Judith only chapters viii–x. As is well known,
Peter intended to go no further than the ascension of Christ, so that
the section on the Acts of the Apostles was not provided by him,
but added by Peter of Poitiers.[36]

   The *corpus* of writings by Peter Comestor is flanked by a series of
spurious and dubious works associated with his name. Martin's
acceptance in 1931 of Peter Comestor's authorship of the *Allegoriae
in epistolas Pauli* was rejected by Landgraf.[37] If Landgraf is right,
Peter Comestor is bereft of any claim to have written a surviving
commentary on St Paul, whether in the form of *Allegoriae*[38] or of
Quaestiones.[39] This would be surprising, since Peter Comestor had
a long career as a teacher, and is hardly likely to have lectured only
on the Gospels. His own master, Peter Lombard, published his
Gloss on Paul, and we might expect Peter Comestor to have
wanted to follow his master in glossing both Paul and the Gospels.
Martin's argument concerning the *Allegoriae* was simple: in several
manuscripts the *Allegoriae* are attributed to Peter Comestor, and the
writer of the *Allegoriae* refers to the *Quaestiones super epistolas Pauli*
for a better presentation of one of his opinions. But the *Quaestiones*
contain teaching which conforms with Peter Comestor's known
teaching. Therefore both works are by Peter Comestor. This

---

[33] *Ibid.*, 1066 C.

[34] *Ibid.*, 1067 D.

[35] Stegmüller, *Bibl.*, iv, 6543–65.

[36] *PL* cxcviii, 1645–1722. See P.S. Moore, *The Works of Peter of Poitiers, Master in
   Theology and Chancellor of Paris (1193–1205)* (Notre Dame, Indiana, 1936), pp.
   118–22.

[37] Martin, 'Notes', pp. 56–7. Landgraf, 'Recherches', pp. 357–66. See also P.S.
   Moore, 'The Authorship of the *Allegoriae super vetus et novum testamentum*', *New
   Scholasticism*, ix (1935), pp. 208–25.

[38] The *Allegoriae* are printed in *PL* clxxv and the section on Paul is found at columns
   879–924.

[39] *PL* clxxv, 431–634.

argument rests chiefly on the shaky premiss that manuscript attributions may be trusted, and Landgraf was right to examine the problem from other points of view. But neither singly nor cumulatively are Landgraf's objections convincing. He noted that the *Allegoriae* are part of a larger work, the *Liber exceptionum* or *Excerptiones allegoricae;*[40] but it is possible that work by one author could subsequently have been incorporated into the larger *Excerptiones* by another. He noted too that no allegorical exposition of Scripture is mentioned by Peter Comestor in his Prologue to the *Historia scholastica*; but neither does he mention there any other work by him, such as his glosses on the Gospels. Landgraf drew attention to the fact that Stephen Langton stated in his Gloss on the *Historia scholastica* (written in 1193) that Peter Comestor had intended to write a work of allegory after writing a work of history, but that he had not found it.[41] But here Landgraf's argument can be stood on its head, for Langton's remark increases the possibility that Peter Comestor may have written a work of allegory, albeit one that Langton could not find fifteen years after his death. Landgraf mentions manuscripts which attribute the *Allegoriae* to the writer of the *School History*, and which do so in a way that suggests that Peter Comestor, having explained Scripture according to the historical sense, now provides further allegorical interpretations: *Allegorie Hystoriarum magistri Petri dicti Comestoris.* But Landgraf believed that these *Allegoriae* need not be by the same author, for Hugh of St Cher expressly says that Peter Comestor dealt only with the historical sense. But Hugh of St Cher may well have meant that Peter Comestor only dealt with the historical sense of Scripture in the *Historia*. Landgraf also noted that the *Allegoriae in epistolas Pauli* were not always included in manuscript copies of the longer *Allegoriae* on the New Testament, nor were they announced by the Prologue to the *Allegories* on the New Testament in which *Allegories on the Gospels* alone were mentioned. The *Allegories* on Paul's Epistles are sometimes found separately in the

---

[40] The first part of the *Excerptiones allegoricae* is printed in *PL* clxxvii, 191–284; the *Allegoriae* are the second part.

[41] Landgraf, 'Recherches', p. 361: '*Proposuerat enim forsitan componere allegorias, quod tamen non invenimus fecisse Magistrum*', ed. G. Lacombe, 'Studies on the Commentaries of Cardinal Stephen Langton (Part I)', *AHDLMA*, v (1930), pp. 5–151, at p. 44.

manuscripts. As for the *Quaestiones in epistolas Pauli*, they contain teachings from Peter Comestor, but may not be by him since the writer departs, without being explicit in his dissent, from Peter Comestor's known views. One may question, therefore, whether Peter Comestor's part in the writing of a work or works of interpretation was satisfactorily explained in the 1930s.

In the following decades discussion of the authorship of the *Allegoriae* was reopened, and it was not satisfactorily concluded until F. Châtillon produced his fine edition of the whole *Liber exceptionum* of Richard of St Victor.[42] The *Allegoriae* on the Old and New Testaments constitute books i–ix and xi–xiv of the second part of this *Liber exceptionum*. The first part offers a summary of knowledge concerning the arts, geography, and history; the second part provides allegories arranged according to the plan of the first. But the *Allegoriae* also circulated separately from the *Liber exceptionum*, having abandoned the first part and book x of the second. On their own the *Allegoriae* offer a continuous exposition of the Old Testament (books i–ix) and then comments on the New Testament (books xi–xiv). In some manuscripts containing the *Allegoriae* without the rest of the *Liber exceptionum*, the *Allegoriae* follow Peter Comestor's *Historia scholastica*, and in some of these manuscripts the *Allegoriae* on the Old and New Testaments are attributed to Peter with a title such as *Allegoriae magistri Petri Comestoris*. Robson explains the association of the work with both Peter Comestor and Richard by positing Richard's collaboration with Peter in drafting an allegorical interpretation of Scripture which follows step by step the literal interpretation of the *Historia scholastica*.[43] But the *Allegoriae* were never finished, owing to Richard's death in 1173, and their inclusion in the *Liber exceptionum* was made posthumously. Robson's conjecture was based on the argument that the twenty-two books of the *Historia scholastica* were written on twenty-two quires, and that Richard used the same method to edit books v–ix of the *Allegoriae* on the Old Testament,

---

[42] J. Châtillon (ed.), *Richard de Saint-Victor, Liber exceptionum. Texte critique avec introduction, notes et tables = Textes philosophiques du moyen âge*, v (Paris, 1958), pp. 75–7, 78–81.

[43] C. A. Robson, 'The *Pecia* of the Twelfth-Century Paris School', *Dominican Studies*, ii (1944), pp. 262–79, and *Maurice of Sully and the Medieval Vernacular Homily* (Oxford, 1952).

though he did not live to complete his revision of the remaining books. When revised, the *Allegoriae*, Robson suggested, correspond closely to the order and contents of the *Historia scholastica*, and each chapter was meant to fill exactly one column of the side of a parchment leaf. Of this ingenious hypothesis Châtillon provided conclusive disproof. Not only was the *pecia* system of copying books unknown before the thirteenth century,[44] but the chapters of the *Allegoriae* are not equal in their length, and the parallelism between the *Allegoriae* and the *Historia* is not a strict one. Moreover, the *Allegoriae* is not as unfinished a work as Robson maintained. The *Liber exceptionum*, which Châtillon believes was written between 1153 and 1162, is a single work, the unity of which is evinced by its prologues, by its tables of contents, and by internal cross-references. This unity was provided by the author, Richard, and there is no reason to suppose his collaboration with Peter or a posthumous compiler. Châtillon's argument is firmly based on an exhaustive study of 124 manuscripts containing the *Liber exceptionum* or the *Allegoriae*. The manuscripts enable an evaluation to be made of the attribution of the latter work to Peter. In most manuscripts (seventy-four) the *Liber exceptionum* and the *Allegoriae* are anonymous, and in a further twenty manuscripts the name of an author—such as Richard or Hugh or Peter—was provided only by later hands. It is reasonable to suppose that the thirteen books of the *Allegoriae*, since on their own they provide a reasonably self-contained work of allegory, became separated from an anonymous copy of the complete *Liber exceptionum*, and therefore themselves circulated without title and anonymously. In time the *Allegoriae* came to be seen as a suitable sequel to Peter Comestor's *Historia*, and in twenty manuscripts a copy was attached to the *Historia*. In this way the attribution of the *Allegoriae* to the author of the *Historia* which preceded it in the manuscripts became a likely possibility. But all but eight of the manuscripts bearing Peter's name are English, and in these the name is usually an addition by a later hand. The supposed authorship of Peter therefore arose during the copying tradition and has no real basis of truth.

---

[44] Graham Pollard has recently traced its beginnings to the University of Bologna about the year 1200, 'The *Pecia* System in the Medieval Universities', *Medieval Scribes, Manuscripts and Libraries. Essays presented to N.R. Ker*, ed. M.B. Parkes and A.G. Watson (London, 1978), pp. 145–61.

More recently G. Raciti has sought to claim for Peter Comestor the authorship of *De spiritu et anima*, as well as of a group of related treatises: the *Meditations* of St Bernard, *De conscientia*, *Manuale*, and *De diligendo deo*.[45] In addition, Raciti claimed for Peter the *Libellus in laude beate virginis totus ex dictis auctenticis contextus*.[46] The *De spiritu et anima* is a compilation of extracts, chiefly from Augustine, and is printed in the appendix to Augustine's works. It was much studied in the thirteenth century, when Vincent of Beauvais claimed that Hugh of St Victor had put it together. Raciti explored the Victorine features of the work, the traces of Hugh's writings that are found in it as well as the traces of the *De anima* of Isaac of Stella (*c*.1167) and of the *De discretione animae, spiritus et mentis* by Richard of St Victor (†1171). A date of composition during the career of Peter Comestor is clearly possible, but Raciti suggests as well that Peter Comestor is the author. The reasons he offers include the fact that the writer must have been used to compiling manuals and must have had a vast knowledge of patristic literature as well as being alive and active *c*.1167. But since the work is a compilation of little value, and merely a disorganized and banal ragbag of teachings from various authors, Peter Comestor (Raciti argues) may well be its author since he was a second-rate figure[47] and an uncritical writer, as his *Historia* shows, but one who also breathed the Victorine atmosphere in which biblical, patristic, and didactic-ascetic compilations were made and encouraged. The author, in the other related treatises, also describes himself as a wise, capable, and intelligent man, endowed with a good memory.[48]

Against Raciti's attribution of *De spiritu et anima* to Peter Comestor four objections may be made. First, Raciti puts aside the warning given by Dom Wilmart that it is always more tempting to deal with a known author than with an anonymous one.[49] Secondly,

---

[45] G. Raciti, 'L'autore del *De spiritu et anima*', *Rivista di filosofia neoscolastica*, liii (1961), pp. 385–401. *De spiritu et anima* is printed in *PL* xl, 779–832, the *Meditations* in *PL* clxxxiv, 485–507, *De conscientia* in *PL* clxxxiv, 507–552, the *Manuale* in *PL* xl, 949–68, and *De diligendo Deo* in *PL* xl, 847–64.

[46] Raciti, 'L'autore', p. 398 and note.

[47] *Ibid.*, p. 397.

[48] *Ibid.*, p. 399.

[49] A. Wilmart, *Auteurs spirituels et textes dévots du moyen âge latin* (Paris, 1932; reprinted 1971), p. 175, n.3, hesitated over ascribing the work to Alcher of Clairvaux simply because 'il est toujours plus commode d'avoir affaire à une personne qu'à un traité anonyme': cited by Raciti, 'L'autore', p. 386.

there is no attribution in the manuscripts of the work to Peter Comestor. Thirdly, to fasten a Victorine-type work upon Peter Comestor merely on grounds of a general suspicion that it is characteristic of his methods of work is insufficiently persuasive. Fourthly, to regard Peter Comestor as a likely author of a badly organized, banal compilation is to adopt a low view of the qualities shown by the author of the *Historia scholastica*.

As regards the group of four related writings (*De diligendo deo*, *Meditations* of St Bernard, *De conscientia*, and *Manuale*), these are found together with the *De spiritu et anima* in one of the earliest manuscripts which was written *c.*1200: MS CCXXXVI of the Archivio della abbazia di S. Scolastica (Subiaco). Internal features, both of style and of content, common to all these treatises, including *De spiritu et anima*, tell strongly in favour of a single compiler using the writings of Bernard and of Augustine. Finally, the *Libellus in laude beate virginis totus ex dictis auctenticis contextus* contains at its end ten verses normally attributed to Peter Comestor.[50] As Raciti explains, the *Libellus*, itself a compilation somewhat like the *De spiritu et anima*, is normally attributed to Vincent of Beauvais, who himself, however, attributed to Peter Comestor, besides the *Historia scholastica, alia opuscula*, and, following these, *versus in laudem B. Virginis*. But in the Milan manuscript the *Libellus* is attributed to Peter Comestor, the ten verses follow at the end and are themselves followed by the epitaph of Peter Comestor. The *Libellus* is also attributed to Peter, and found in the fifteenth-century Brussels, Bibliothèque royale, MS 542–7 (1556). On these grounds Raciti attributes the *Libellus* to Peter Comestor, and he adds that it was under the name of Peter Comestor that it was printed at Antwerp in 1536 and again at Paris in 1540, on the latter occasion by a Victorine canon, Nicholas Grenier. It would appear then that to accept for Peter Comestor any of these treatises would entail the attribution to him of all of them, but the case for doing so is doubtful, as it depends rather heavily on the evidence of manuscript attributions and on a somewhat unfavourable assessment of Peter Comestor's skill in compilation.

---

[50] The *Libellus* is found in Milan, Biblioteca Ambrosiana, MS E.69 sup., s.XV, perhaps from Chiaravalle in Milan.

The extent to which Peter Comestor's school teaching was reported and discussed is astonishingly great, as Landgraf first revealed in 1931, when he published references made to him in fourteen works.[51] The authors of these, when they can be named, include Prepositinus, Peter the Chanter, Peter of Capua, Stephen Langton, Geoffrey of Poitiers, Gerald of Wales, and Guy of Orchelles. None of their references consists of a quotation from or allusion to the contents of the *Historia scholastica* or Peter's Sermons. All reflect Peter's teaching in the schools; there are references to his glosses on the Lombard's Sentences, and there are reports of Peter's teaching in theological question collections that probably reflect Peter's known participation in the activity of teaching by means of question sessions. The topics are varied, and range from the fate of the unbaptized to the need to wear vestments when saying Mass. There is much emphasis on points of morality and penance. Landgraf strangely observed that mention of Peter Comestor's opinions—and such mentions are always sparse or brief—usually amount to a disagreement, but in fact very many are sympathetic and supportive of Peter. Yet there was opposition to him, or at least to what Peter Comestor's work might lead to, from Peter the Chanter. Peter the Chanter was probably already a master in Paris in 1173, and he became a great inspirer of students for more than two decades. He certainly knew Peter Comestor's *Historia scholastica* and his Gospel commentaries. But without naming his colleagues he was, we suspect, very critical of him and of Peter of Poitiers, or at least of their more naïve and uncritical followers, on account of what he held to be futile ways of glossing Scripture. The matters on which such men concentrated—'places, dates, genealogies and descriptions of buildings such as the tabernacle and the temple image'—are unimportant. 'Scripture was given to us not so that we should seek out what is vain and superfluous but faith and moral doctrine and counsels and answers to the countless matters arising in church affairs'.[52] In his own work *De sacramentis*, which

---

[51] Landgraf, 'Recherches', pp. 293–306. Also Martin, 'Notes', pp. 64–6.
[52] Smalley, 'The Gospels in the Paris Schools', pp. 233–4, citing Peter the Chanter, *Verbum abbreviatum*, *PL* ccv, 27–8. This was written in 1191/2.

was finished after 1191–2, Peter the Chanter put his precept into practice: the Bible should be explained; the quest for literal understanding should be abandoned. Biblical history should not be studied for its own sake; the Bible should be read for the lessons it offers to solve questions of faith and morals.[53] Peter the Chanter turned his teaching towards the practical side of the religious life, to moral issues, and to questions of reform.

The strictures of Peter the Chanter, which may have been aimed more at Peter Comestor's readers and followers than at Peter himself, did nothing to prevent Peter Comestor's *Historia* from rising to lasting fame. It was copied extraordinarily widely and frequently during the Middle Ages.[54] Abbreviations were made; excerpts were taken from it; it was given a new Prologue;[55] it was translated into French, German, Dutch, Portuguese, and Czech; it was rendered into verse and adapted by popular dramatists. Peter of Poitiers wrote a *Genealogy of Christ* which was sometimes placed at the head of the *Historia* to serve as an introductory table or genealogical tree.[56] The *Historia* attracted glosses and comments, and Stephen Langton apparently glossed the *Historia* in a manner akin to his gloss on Peter Lombard's *Sentences*.[57] However, the *Historia* did not become as regularly glossed in the schools as Peter Lombard's *Sentences* were. It was a reference work from which all might learn and acquire knowledge; it was not, unlike the *Four Books of Sentences* and unlike Gratian's *Decretum*, a collection of questions on which continuous debate and speculation might be founded. But Peter Comestor's reputation was not less enduring than theirs, and Dante placed him in heaven in the Circle of the Sun alongside Peter Lombard and Hugh of St Victor.[58] Peter Comestor's Sermons also enjoyed a burst of considerable fame, but after the early thirteenth century this was mostly exhausted. His glosses

---

[53] *Summa de Sacramentis et Animae Consiliis*, ed. J.A. Dugauquier, *Analecta Mediaevalia Namurcensia*, 4, 7, 11, 16, 21 (1954–67), 16, p. 163.

[54] Stegmüller, *Bibl.*, iv, pp. 288–90 lists the MSS. See further *CHB*, ii, pp. 320, 382–3, 430, 448, 471.

[55] Stegmüller, *Bibl.*, iv, 6566.

[56] Smalley, *Bible.*, pp. 214–15.

[57] *Ibid.*

[58] Dante, *Divine Comedy*, III, cant. xii, 134.

and questions also received attention for a while in more restricted scholastic circles, but once the generation of his own students had passed away they ceased to matter much in the developing work of commentary and disputation within the thirteenth-century universities.

University of Sheffield

LES INTERPRÉTATIONS JUIVES DANS LES COMMENTAIRES DU PENTATEUQUE DE PIERRE LE CHANTRE

par GILBERT DAHAN

PARMI les apports majeurs de Beryl Smalley à notre connaissance des études bibliques au moyen âge ne figurent pas seulement la redécouverte d'André de Saint-Victor et la mise au jour de son influence considérable dans la seconde moitié du XIIe siècle et au début du XIIIe; c'est aussi par elle qu'a été révélée l'importance de l'oeuvre exégétique de Pierre le Chantre. Certes, avant les travaux de la savante historienne, Pierre le Chantre n'était pas un inconnu, mais l'on s'intéressait essentiellement à la partie plus spécifiquement théologique de son oeuvre: à son *Verbum abbreviatum*, qui fut longtemps son seul ouvrage imprimé, à sa grande *Summa de Sacramentis*, récemment publiée, à son recueil de *distinctiones*, la *Summa Abel*, encore en partie inédite.[1] Beryl Smalley a été la première à utiliser d'une manière conséquente les commentaires bibliques de cet auteur, particulièrement dans son étude de ce qu'à la suite de Martin Grabmann[2] elle appelait 'the biblical moral school', c'est-à-dire les trois principaux maîtres parisiens du dernier tiers du XIIe siècle: Pierre Comestor (le Mangeur), Pierre le Chantre et Etienne Langton.[3]

---

[1] *Verbum abbreviatum*, PL ccv, 21–370; *Summa de sacramentis et animae consiliis*, éd. J.-A. Dugauquier (Louvain et Lille, 1954–67); *Summa Abel*, fragments publiés par J.-B. Pitra, *Spicilegium solesmense*, ii (Paris, 1855), pp. 1–521, et iii (Paris, 1855), pp. 1–276. On observera le peu de place consacrée aux commentaires bibliques dans la notice 'Pierre le Chantre' de l'*HLF*, xv, pp. 283–303, ou dans la monographie de F.S. Gutjahr, *Petrus Cantor Parisiensis, sein Leben und seine Schriften* (Graz, 1899), pp. 52–5. De même, l'ouvrage admirable de J.W. Baldwin, *Masters, Princes and Merchants. The Social Views of Peter the Chanter and his Circle*, 2 vols. (Princeton, 1970), qui renouvelle tant nos connaissances sur le milieu dans lequel a vécu Pierre le Chantre, ne s'intéresse pas aux commentaires bibliques.

[2] M. Grabmann, *Die Geschichte der scholastischen Methode*, 2 vols. (Freiburg im Breisgau, 1909–11), ii, pp. 476–501 (sur Pierre le Chantre, pp. 478–85).

[3] Smalley, *Bible*, pp. 196–263; 'The School of Andrew of St Victor', *RTAM*, xi (1939), pp. 145–67. Bien sûr, ces trois maîtres ne sont pas seuls: on trouvera, sur les principaux contemporains de Pierre le Chantre, de substantielles notices dans l'ouvrage de Baldwin, i, pp. 17–46.

C'est très précisément située dans ce groupe d'auteurs que l'oeuvre exégétique du Chantre prend toute sa signification. Chacun de ces maîtres, en effet, se donne pour but de présenter la totalité de la Bible, et y réussit, de sorte que l'on a en un laps de temps assez bref une succession d'oeuvres qui, tout au moins à Paris, détrônent la *Glossa Ordinaria* et deviennent tour à tour les commentaires de référence, jusqu'à ce que les 'expositions' d'Etienne Langton soient elles-mêmes remplacées par la *Postille* de Hugues de Saint-Cher. Entre-temps, les commentaires de nos trois maîtres parisiens auront été assez abondamment recopiés, comme en témoignent les listes impressionnantes fournies par le *Repertorium biblicum* de Fr. Stegmüller.[4] Plus que l'*Historia scholastica* du Mangeur, qui la précède, et différemment des commentaires d'Etienne Langton, qui la suivent,[5] l'oeuvre de Pierre le Chantre se présente comme l'aboutissement (provisoire) de l'exégèse de son temps. D'abord au niveau des sources: aux auteurs traditionnellement cités—le Josèphe latin, Origène, S. Jérôme, S. Grégoire, Isidore de Séville, Raban Maur—le Chantre ajoute S. Bernard, Raoul de Flay (pour le commentaire du *Lévitique*) et, comme les autres maîtres de l'"école biblique morale', fait usage de la *Glossa Ordinaria*; mais encore, ce qui est la marque distinctive de ces trois maîtres, il utilise assez souvent André de Saint-Victor, sans le nommer; il recopie également, et toujours anonymement, son prédécesseur le plus proche, Pierre Comestor. Au carrefour des traditions exégétiques, l'oeuvre de Pierre le Chantre l'est surtout par la diversité des éléments dont sont tissés ses commentaires: exégèse spirituelle, où allégorie christique et tropologie ont une part égale; exégèse 'scientifique', attentive aux diverses implications de la lettre du texte, qu'il s'agisse de l'examen du contexte

---

[4] Stegmüller, *Bibl.*, iv, pp. 248–75 (Pierre le Chantre), pp. 280–301 (Pierre Comestor), et v, pp. 232–301 (Etienne Langton).

[5] L'*Historia scholastica* se donne pour un résumé général de la Bible: '*Causa suscepti laboris fuit instans petitio sociorum. Qui cum historiam sacrae Scripturae in serie, et glossis diffusam lectitarent, brevem nimis et inexpositam, opus aggredi me compulerunt… A cosmographia Moysi inchoans rivulum historicum deduxi, usque ad ascensionem Salvatoris, pelagus mysteriorum relinquens*' (*PL* cxcviii, 1053–4). Les commentaires d'Etienne Langton présentent assez souvent le caractère de gloses fragmentaires ou elliptiques.

historique et des traditions variées attachées à tel récit,[6] de la comparaison minutieuse des versions différentes de certains versets,[7] ou du recours à l'hébreu.[8]

Nous voudrions étudier ici l'un des éléments de son exégèse 'littérale': les interprétations attribuées aux Juifs. Elles nous semblent présenter un double intérêt: d'une part, elles nous montreront avec précision l'utilisation que fait de ses prédécesseurs Pierre le Chantre; d'autre part, surtout, il s'agit aussi d'un élément caractéristique de l'exégèse de nos maîtres parisiens, par lequel s'affirme nettement leur dette à l'égard d'André de Saint-Victor.[9] Sans doute, avant eux et avant André, les interprétations juives ne sont-elles pas totalement absentes de certains commentaires: outre les exemples anciens de Raban Maur, d'Angelome de Luxeuil ou de Rémi d'Auxerre,[10] il faut mentionner à cet égard dans la première moitié du XIIe siècle notamment la *Glossa Ordinaria* et Rupert de Deutz.[11] Mais, la plupart du temps, les mentions de la sorte

---

[6] Cf. la discussion sur la date de Pâques, à propos de *Nombres*, ix. 1 (Oxford, Balliol Coll. MS 23, f. 18ra); cette note sur *Deut.*, i. 1: '*Videtur liber iste non editus a Moyse, qui Iordanem non transiit. Videtur etiam a Iosue esse compositus, quia cum hec recapitulatio facta sit a Moyse et adhuc esset citra Iordanem, Iosue retinens eam memoriter, uerbotenus scripsit eam postquam transiit Iordanem*' (ms cité, f. 60rb); ou cette autre note sur *Deut.*, ii. 18; '*Ar metropolis est moabitarum super ripam torrentis Arnon, olim possessa a gente ueterrima Emim*' (ms cité, f. 63va).

[7] Notamment la version des Septante (c'est-à-dire la *Vetus latina*, en réalité), qu'il connaît par S. Augustin (cf. ms cité, f. 81rb: 'Hic ponit Augustinus litteram .lxx.').

[8] Cf. cette note sur *Nombres*, xxi. 13: '*Contra Arnon; nomen fluuium est, sed quia sequitur relatiuum femininum, uidetur quod hebrei non seruant regulam nostram in nominibus fluminum*' (ms cité, f. 35va). Voir également ci-après les textes 5, 10, 16, 17, 18, 34. Il n'est pas dans les intentions de ce travail d'étudier ces recours à l'hébreu; nous ne citerons les textes qui en contiennent que dans la mesure où ils se réfèrent en même temps à des interprétations juives.

[9] Voir notamment Smalley, 'The School of Andrew of St Victor'.

[10] Voir notamment Ch. Merchavia, *The Church versus Talmudic and Midrashic Literature, 500–1248* [en hébreu] (Jérusalem, 1970), pp. 42–55 (Raban Maur), et pp. 55–8 (Angelome); A. Saltman, 'Rabanus Maurus and the Pseudo-Hieronymian *Quaestiones hebraicae in libros Regum et Paralipomenon*', *HTR;* lxvi (1973), pp. 43–75, ainsi que B. Blumenkranz, *Auteurs chrétiens latins du moyen âge sur les Juifs et le judaïsme* (Paris/La Haye, 1963), *passim*. La présence de ces 'interprétations' chez Rémi d'Auxerre ne semble pas avoir encore fait l'objet de recherches.

[11] Nous signalons ci-après, à titre d'exemple, la présence d'interprétations juives communes avec Pierre le Chantre, chez Rupert de Deutz; il ne faut, bien sûr, y voir aucune filiation possible; sur l'exégèse de cet auteur, outre les nombreux travaux de H. Silvestre, voir H. de Lubac, *Exégèse médiévale*, ii. 1 (Paris, 1961), pp. 219–38.

remontent, directement ou non, à S. Jérôme. Avec les Victorins, André surtout, la situation change: les interprétations se multiplient et paraissent être de 'première main': s'il semble bien qu'André ne savait pas assez d'hébreu pour lire tout seul la littérature rabbinique, il a pu néanmoins prendre connaissance de nombre de traditions relatives aux récits bibliques par des échanges oraux avec des Juifs.[12] Ses successeurs parisiens reprennent beaucoup de ces interprétations qui, sans doute grâce à eux, se retrouveront dans plusieurs commentaires du XIIIe siècle, y compris la *Postille* de Hugues de Saint-Cher, et ce probablement jusqu'à Nicolas de Lyre, dont les mérites d'hébraïsant ont parfois été surestimés et qui a dû recourir assez souvent à des gloses remontant à André de Saint-Victor, voire directement au Victorin lui-même.[13] Chez les maîtres parisiens du dernier tiers du XIIe siècle, à côté des interprétations juives issues des commentaires d'André de Saint-Victor, en figurent également qui ne sont pas fournies par celui-ci: on peut supposer que la tradition des contacts scientifiques avec les Juifs s'est prolongée.

˙ Dans les commentaires de Pierre le Chantre sur les cinq livres de Moïse nous avons pu relever une cinquantaine de mentions explicites d'interprétations juives, plus de la moitié se trouvant dans le commentaire de la *Genèse*; nous en donnons le texte ci-après. Les observations qui suivent supposent que le lecteur a bien voulu s'y reporter préalablement (les textes sont identifiés par les références des versets qu'ils commentent). Le problème essentiel qui se pose à propos de ces interprétations est celui de leurs sources. Dans la plupart des cas, il s'agit d'emprunts de Pierre le Chantre à ses prédécesseurs. Mais, quand il est possible de reconstituer dans sa totalité la chaîne d'une tradition donnée, de qui s'inspire-t-il directement? Soit un texte de S. Jérôme: il figure dans la *Glossa Ordinaria*, elle-même mise à contribution par André de Saint-Victor; celui-ci à son tour est recopié par Pierre Comestor et ce

---

[12] Cf. A. Graboïs, 'The *Hebraica Veritas* and Jewish-Christian Relations in the Twelfth Century', *Speculum*, l (1975), pp. 613–34; B. Smalley, 'L'exégèse biblique du xiie siècle', *Entretiens sur la renaissance du xiie siècle* = Décades du Centre culturel international de Cerisy-la-Salle, ns, ix, pp. 273–93.

[13] L'étude consciencieuse de H. Hailperin, *Rashi and the Christian Scholars* (Pittsburgh, 1963), en majeure partie consacrée à Nicolas de Lyre, n'accorde pas assez d'importance à celui-ci par rapport à ses prédécesseurs chrétiens.

même texte apparaît enfin chez Pierre le Chantre. Mais il n'est pas sûr que celui-ci s'inspire de son plus proche prédécesseur, le Mangeur. Il semble bien que Pierre le Chantre ait eu à sa disposition, au moins pour certains passages, l'ensemble des commentaires qui viennent d'être cités; ce sera alors la plus grande conformité textuelle à l'un d'entre eux qui nous indiquera sa source immédiate, bien qu'il soit dans plusieurs cas difficile de trancher. Nous mènerons notre rapide examen en allant du plus proche dans le temps au plus lointain.

1 *Les sources latines*

a) *Pierre Comestor.* Pierre le Chantre ne paraît pas avoir suivi l'enseignement du Mangeur,[14] mais il utilise abondamment l'*Historia scholastica*, d'où proviennent directement la moitié environ des interprétations juives mentionnées dans ses commentaires du Pentateuque. Plusieurs des interprétations procurées par Pierre Comestor remontent à André de Saint-Victor (*Gen.*, iv. 24; iv. 26; xxii, 2; xlix. 10; *Ex.*, iv. 25–26) mais la plupart à la *Glossa ordinaria* (*Gen.*, vi. 16; xvii. 5; xvii. 15; xix. 33; xxv. 1; xxxv. 21; xxxvii. 36; *Deut.*, v. 21). Le commentaire de *Gen.*, vi. 16 fournit un exemple d'interprétation présente également chez André de Saint-Victor, mais c'est la *Glossa* qu'a dû utiliser directement Pierre Comestor:

Glossa	André	Pierre Comestor
Fenestram in hebraeo meridianum facies arcae. Symmachus: dilucidum arcae facies … Hanc tradunt Iudaei crystallum fuisse (éd. Anvers, 1634, col. 145–6).	*Fenestram. In hebreo meridianum. Fenestram hanc tradunt Iudei cristallinam fuisse, ut aquas non admitteret et lucem ministraret* (BN, ms lat. 356, f. 20rb).	*Fecit in ea Noe fenestram quam Hebraei cristallinam fuisse tradunt, quae in hebraeo vocatur meridianum, a Symmacho diluculum* (*PL* cxcviii, 1083).

Quelques interprétations proposées par Pierre Comestor et reprises par Pierre le Chantre apparaissent pour la première fois, à notre connaissance, dans des textes latins. Il en est ainsi de *Gen.*, i. 6, pour lequel la *Glossa*, recopiant S. Jérôme, propose une explication différente *secundum Hebraeos*:

---

[14] Sur la formation de Pierre le Chantre, voir Baldwin, i, pp. 3–16.

Hier. lib. I *contra Iovinianum*: Notandum etiam quod huius diei secundi opera secundum Hebraeos non dicuntur bona, cum bona sint sicut caetera; quod fit propter binarium principem alternitatis, qui primus ab unitate discedit ... (éd. Anvers, 1634, col. 13).

L'explication le plus couramment fournie par les textes juifs est celle de l'inachèvement du second jour; le *Midrash Rabba* sur la *Genèse*, qui parle également de division, est plus proche de S. Jérôme;[15] nous n'avons pas retrouvé celle que donne Pierre Comestor[16]—le Talmud babylonien, traité *Pesahim* 54a, disant: 'Pourquoi n'est-il pas affirmé "il est bon" au second jour? Parce qu'alors fut créée la lumière de la Géhenne'. Pour *Gen.*, v. 24, la source probable (utilisée par l'informateur juif de Pierre Comestor?) est un recueil d'homélies datant du VIIIe ou du IXe siècle, *Pesiqta de-Rab Kahana.*[17] Les interprétations mentionnées à propos d'*Ex.*, xxxii. 33; *Num.*, xxvii. 3; *Deut.*, xxiii. 1 et xxvi. 12, rappellent assez les gloses de Rashi sur ces versets.[18]

---

[15] Voir L. Ginzberg, *The Legends of the Jews*, 6 vols. (Philadelphia, 1910–46), i, p. 15, et v, p. 18. Le *Midrash Rabba* est un recueil de commentaires du Pentateuque et des cinq 'rouleaux' (Lam., Ruth, Eccl., Esther, Cant.) composés vraisemblablement entre le Ve et le IXe siècles, et qui reprennent nombre de traditions plus anciennes, notamment d'ordre légendaire (*agadot*); on désignera ces commentaires par la suite d'une manière abrégée et hybride, ainsi: *Gen. R.* (*Midrash Rabba* sur la *Genèse*), *Lam. R.* (*Midrash Rabba* sur les *Lamentations*), etc. Il en existe une traduction anglaise, *The Midrash Rabbah*, sous la direction de H. Freedman et M. Simon, n. éd., 5 vols. (London, 1977). Pour la littérature rabbinique ancienne, nous renvoyons, une fois pour toutes, au manuel de H.L. Strack, *Einleitung in Talmud und Midrasch*, 5. ed. (Munich, 1920), traduction anglaise, *Introduction to the Talmud and Midrash* (Philadelphia, 1931).

[16] '*Tradunt enim hebraei quia hac die angelus factus est diabolus Satanael, id est Lucifer, quibus Hebraeis consentire videntur qui in secunda feria missam de Angelis cantare consueverunt...*' (*PL* cxcviii, 1058). Les sources indiquées par Merchavia, *The Church*, p. 180, ne rendent pas exactement compte de la tradition de la chute de Satan au second jour; le chapitre consacré à Pierre Comestor dans cet ouvrage est d'une grande richesse (pp. 167–93); l'étude de E. Shereshevsky, 'Hebrew Traditions in Peter Comestor's *Historia Scholastica*', *Jewish Quarterly Review*, lix (1968–9), pp. 268–89, utile en ce qu'elle fournit des rapprochements avec les sources juives, ne tient cependant pas compte de toutes les sources latines dans lesquelles le Mangeur a trouvé la plupart des interprétations juives qu'il rapporte.

[17] Source indiquée par Merchavia, *The Church*, p. 173.

[18] Le commentaire de Rashi (Salomon ben Isaac, Troyes ou environs, *c*.1040–1105) est vite devenu le commentaire 'standard' de la Bible pour les Juifs; ses disciples ont pu avoir une influence sur les commentateurs chrétiens de la France septen-

b) *André de Saint-Victor*. Le commentaire de *Deut.*, xxxiii. 2 illustre la difficulté qu'il y a parfois à déterminer la source précise des emprunts de Pierre le Chantre: ici, la citation n'est pas littérale et l'on peut se demander si c'est du Mangeur ou d'André qu'il s'inspire:

Pierre Comestor	André de Saint-Victor
Tradunt Hebraei quod Dominus misit angelos suos ad Idumaeos et ad Ismaelitas in Pharan et obtulit eis legem suam. Quam cum recipere nollent, venit ad Iudaeos in montem Sina, cum multis millibus angelorum (*PL* cxcviii, 1260).	*Tradunt etiam hebrei dominum misisse angelos suos ad ydumeos et ad illos de monte Pharan, hysmaelitas scilicet, et legem suam illis obtulisse; quam postquam recipere noluerunt, uenit ad iudeos in monte Syna et cum eo multa milia angelorum* (BN, ms lat. 356, f. 93va).

En tous cas, il s'agit ici d'un *midrash* extrêmement répandu, présent dans la mémoire de la plupart des Juifs quelque peu frottés de culture rabbinique et pour lequel les sources hébraïques abondent.[19]

Dans une douzaine d'occurrences, l'emprunt à André n'est pas douteux, même si parfois les interprétations se retrouvent aussi chez Pierre Comestor (*Gen.*, xiv. 18; *Num.*, xxi. 14; xxi. 15; *Deut.*, xxxiv. 6). André lui-même emprunte quelquefois à la *Glossa* (*Gen.*, xlix. 27; *Ex.*, iii. 2) ou directement à S. Jérôme (*Gen.*, vi. 4; xiv. 18). Mais le plus souvent il s'agit, nous l'avons dit, d'interprétations nouvelles dans les commentaires latins. Plusieurs d'entre elles s'apparentent à l'enseignement de Rashi (*Gen.*, iv. 2; iv. 10b; *Ex.*,

---

trionale (voir Smalley, *Bible*, pp. 149–56). Il existe plusieurs traductions du commentaire du Pentateuque, notamment une traduction française, *Le Commentaire de Rachi sur le Pentateuque*, trad. par I. Salzer, J. Bloch, etc., 2 vols. (Paris, 1957). Dans aucun des cas, nous n'avons pu découvrir, dans les interprétations présentes chez Pierre le Chantre, d'adaptation littérale d'explications venant de Rashi—ce qui confirmerait encore le caractère oral des sources juives de nos maîtres parisiens; mais la substance s'y retrouve parfois. Cf., par exemple, sur *Ex.*, xxxii. 33: 'Voici mon ange et non pas Moi-même' (traduction citée, i, p. 401): sur *Num.*, xxvii. 3: 'Il était mort uniquement pour son propre péché... R. Aqiba dit que c'était le ramasseur de bois'.

[19] Notamment dans le *Midrash Rabba: Num. R.* xiv. 10; *Cant. R.* v. 9; *Lam. R.* iii. 1; voir encore *Pirqe de-R. Eliezer*, ouvrage 'midrashique' du VIIIe s., ch. xli (traduction anglaise, G. Friedlander, London, 1916, pp. 318–20); rappelé également par Rashi.

xv. 16b; *Num.*, xxi. 15);[20] dans deux cas (*Ex.*, xv. 16a; *Num.*, xxi. 14) leur source remonte à des textes midrashiques assez répandus, le *Midrash Rabba* sur les *Nombres* et la *Mekhilta de-R. Ishma'el.*[21] Cependant, pour *Gen.*, ix. 27, nous n'avons pas trouvé de texte rabbinique contenant l'explication proposée; elle figure également chez Rupert de Deutz et Pierre Comestor, qui ne l'attribuent pas aux Juifs, et sera reprise par Nicolas de Lyre.[22] De même pour *Deut.*, xxxiv. 6, également présent chez Pierre Comestor et Nicolas de Lyre; Pierre le Chantre accompagne de quelques considérations le texte bref d'André, reproduit tel quel par Pierre Comestor:

> Et non cognouit homo. *Iudei autumant hoc ideo factum ne iudei, semper ad ydolatriam proni, mortuum tamquam deum colerent* (BN ms lat. 356, f. 94vb).

On classera également ici l'explication juive du pluriel de *Gen.*, i. 26 qui apparaît pour la première fois, semble-t-il, chez Hugues de Saint-Victor[23] et qui sera constamment reprise par la suite (notamment dans les *Sentences* de Pierre Lombard);[24] elle correspond effectivement à une donnée très fréquente dans les commentaires

---

[20] Voici un exemple: 'Quem possedisti (*Ex.*, xv. 16) *in hereditatem, unde Iacob funiculus hereditatis eius. In hebreo 'comparasti' uel 'emisti', in quo notatur quod caros et preciosos eos habebat'* (BN ms lat. 356, f. 52ra); cf. Rashi: 'Tu as acquis: *tu le chéris plus que les autres peuples. Tel un objet acquis à grand prix et par conséquent très cher à un homme*' (trad. citée, i, p. 271).

[21] Traduction anglaise de J.Z. Lauterbach, *Mekilta de-Rabbi, Ishmael*, 3 vols. (Philadelphia, 1933), ii, pp. 74–6.

[22] Nicolas de Lyre: '*Aliqui descendentes de Iapheth habitent in tabernaculis Sem, id est in tabernaculo et templo, quia in festiuitatibus solemnibus aliqui gentiles qui descenderant de Iapheth, ascensuri erant causa orationis in tabernaculum et templum*' (éd. d'Anvers, 1634, *Biblia sacra cum glossis*, i, col. 175–6). Le traité *Yoma*, f. 10a, du Talmud de Babylone parle cependant du second Temple à propos du même verset, mais avec une implication différente.

[23] 'Faciamus hominem etc. *Nec propterea consilium inducit, quin aeque possit facere et magna et parva; sed ut dignitatem creati hominis ostenderet, et ut nos cautos reddat, ne dedignemur consilium accipere et ab aequalibus et a minoribus; cum ipse ad angelos ita loquatur, quorum ministerio forsitan formatum est corpus hominis. Vel, quod melius est, accipiamus consilium Trinitatis fuisse et per verbum plurale distinctionem personarum*' (*PL* clxxv, 37); on observera que la problématique chez Rashi est la même, avec cette leçon de modestie.

[24] Pierre Lombard, *Sententiae*, éd. de Quaracchi (Grottaferrata, 1971–81), i, p. 406: 'Ex persona enim Patris hoc dicitur ad Filium et Spiritum Sanctum, non, *ut quidam putant*, angelis…'.

rabbiniques,[25] dans lesquels elle prend au XIIe siècle une connotation polémique anti-chrétienne.[26]

c) *Glossa Ordinaria.* Malgré le renouvellement des méthodes, la *Glossa* continue à être un outil de travail fondamental pour les commentateurs jusqu'au XIIIe siècle. Pierre le Chantre l'utilise assez et la cite parfois nommément: *Glosa Gileberti* ou *Interlinearis*. Il lui emprunte plusieurs interprétations juives. Celles qui concernent des versets de la *Genèse* (xiv. 2; xvi. 2; xix. 30; xxiv. 2; xxii. 21) remontent aux *Hebraicae quaestiones* de S. Jérôme; celles qui concernent les *Nombres* (iii. 39), aux Homélies d'Origène sur ce livre. La tradition rapportée en *Deut.*, xxv. 17 se trouve dans les *Quaestiones hebraicae in libros Regum* du pseudo-Jérôme.[27] Nous n'avons pas trouvé de source latine pour les quelques autres interprétations. La légende mentionnée sur *Ex.*, xxxii. 20 remonte peut-être à un passage des *Pirqe R. Eliezer.*[28] Sur *Deut.*, x. 10 plusieurs commentaires juifs,[29] sans être aussi précis, présupposent le même décompte. Sur *Deut.*, xxiii. 4 nous n'avons pas non plus repéré de source hébraïque: il est possible que l'explication soit tirée du texte biblique lui-même.[30].

Dans bien des cas, les interprétations fournies par la *Glossa* figurent aussi chez d'autres commentateurs chrétiens antérieurs à Pierre le Chantre, notamment Rupert de Deutz (*Gen.*, xiv. 2; xix. 30; xxii. 21; xxiv. 2; *Ex.*, xxxii. 20; *Deut.*, xxv. 17), André de Saint-Victor (*Gen.*, xxii. 21; xxiv. 2), Pierre Comestor (*Gen.*, xix. 30; xxii, 21; xxiv. 2; xxxii. 20; *Deut.*, xxv. 17). Mais la ressemblance textuelle nous fait penser à un emprunt direct de Pierre le

---

[25] Cf. Ginzberg, *The Legends of the Jews*, i, pp. 52–5, et v, pp. 69–73.

[26] Ainsi chez Joseph Bekhor Shor, auteur français du XIIe siècle, l'un des successeurs de Rashi: 'Et si un hérétique (*min*) te dit: "C'est à cause de la Trinité que le pluriel est employé"...' (éd. Ad. Jellinek, Leipzig, 1856, p. 6). Dans les textes plus anciens, il y a également connotation polémique, mais à l'adresse des polythéistes.

[27] *PL* xxiii, 1402.

[28] *Pirqe R. Eliezer*, ch. 45: 'Every one who had kissed the calf with all his heart, his upper lip and his bones became golden and the tribe of Levi slew him' (trad. citée, p. 356).

[29] Ainsi Rashi ou Joseph Bekhor Shor (éd. A. Zweig, Breslau, 1914, p. 22).

[30] *Deut.*, xxiii. 5 parle de pain *et* d'eau.

Chantre à la *Glossa*, comme le montre l'exemple suivant (*Gen.*, xxii. 21):

Glossa	Pierre Comestor	André
Buz] a quo Buzites dicitur, quem Hebraei putant Balaam fuisse (éd. Anvers, 1634, c.271–2).	*Hus de cuius stirpe descendit Iob ... et fratrem eius ex cuius genere Balaam qui secundum Hebraeos dicitur in Iob Eliu Buzites* (*PL* cxcviii, 1105).	Buz. *Ab isto Eliu Buzites dicitur, quem hebrei Balaam putant fuisse* (BN, ms lat. 356, f. 31rb).

De même, il semble bien qu'une fois (à propos de *Gen.*, xxvii. 11), quoique l'interprétation juive mentionnée figure également dans la *Glossa* et chez le Mangeur, le Chantre ait eu directement recours à S. Jérôme.[31]

2 *Sources juives?*

Un certain nombre d'interprétations juives rapportées par Pierre le Chantre ne se trouvent dans aucune de ces sources latines. Faut-il admettre l'hypothèse selon laquelle cet auteur aurait poursuivi la tradition du recours à des Juifs connaisseurs en Ecriture Sainte? Avant de répondre définitivement à cette question, il faudrait être sûr de posséder toute la tradition exégétique latine du XIIe siècle— ce qui n'est pas encore le cas. Pourtant rien n'interdit cette supposition. Pierre le Chantre étudia dans sa jeunesse à Reims, cité qui abritait une communauté juive—sur laquelle on est cependant mal renseigné et dont les maîtres, semble-t-il, n'ont pas laissé d'oeuvres à la postérité;[32] en tous cas, les Juifs de Reims apparaissent ici ou là dans le *Verbum abbreviatum*.[33] De même, de tels contacts auraient été possibles durant la période parisienne—la communauté juive ayant cette fois une tradition savante bien établie.[34]

---

[31] *CCSL* lxxii (voir p. 34 le comment. de *Gen.*, xxvii. 11 et 15).

[32] Voir H. Gross, *Gallia Judaica. Dictionnaire géographique de la France d'après les sources rabbiniques* (Paris, 1897), pp. 633–4, et B. Bl[umenkranz], art. 'Rheims', *Encyclopaedia Judaica*, 16 vols. (Jerusalem, 1971), xiv, col. 142.

[33] Mentions soigneusement relevées par Baldwin, *Masters*, i, pp. 5, 94, 153, et 328.

[34] Voir Gross, *Gallia Judaica*, pp. 496–534. On notera aussi dans les textes que nous publions ci-après quelques indications assez concrètes sur des usages juifs: interdiction de la polygamie (texte 26), circoncision (textes 17 et 33).

Les interprétations juives mentionnées sans doute pour la première fois par Pierre le Chantre ne sont, pour la plupart, pas très courantes chez les Juifs mêmes: on ne trouve chez Rashi que la première explication donnée à *Gen.*, i. 22 et celle de *Gen.*, iii. 1. Les autres ne figurent pas dans les commentaires courants (*Gen.*, xxix. 30; *Ex.*, iv. 10—le début se retrouve chez Nicolas de Lyre; *Lev.*, xix. 18;[35] *Num.*, iii. 2; *Deut.*, x. 10[36]). Le commentaire de *Gen.*, xi. 28 présente un cas extrêmement intéressant: il s'agit d'un *midrash* sur la jeunesse d'Abraham, dont une partie seulement figure chez d'autres auteurs latins,[37] qui s'inspirent de S. Jérôme.[38] Pierre le Chantre nous en donne une version complète et détaillée: l'origine en est le *Midrash Rabba* sur la *Genèse*;[39] mais il s'agit d'une légende très répandue chez les Juifs[40] sous une forme orale et il nous semble bien voir là une preuve du caractère oral de ces échanges avec des Juifs, qui expliquerait aussi peut-être les passages pour lesquels nous n'avons pas trouvé de source écrite. Mais là aussi il ne peut s'agir que d'une conclusion provisoire, la réponse appartenant aux spécialistes de la littérature rabbinique.

On nous permettra cependant quelques observations rapides sur le caractère de ces interprétations juives—ces remarques ne s'appliquant pas seulement aux traditions nouvellement rapportées par Pierre le Chantre mais à l'ensemble des textes ici retenus. Contrairement à ce que l'on pense parfois, il ne s'agit pas simplement d'interprétations littérales proprement dites: dans la plupart des cas, nous avons affaire à des *agadot*, c'est-à-dire à des légendes formées à partir des textes bibliques et perçues comme telles par les Juifs;[41]

---

[35] Il s'agit, en fait, ici, d'une extension d'une interprétation donnée aux versets concernant le prêt à intérêt.

[36] Présent aussi chez Nicolas de Lyre (éd. d'Anvers, 1634, col. 1532).

[37] Voir ci-après. André de Saint-Victor ne fait qu'une rapide allusion à cette légende: 'Mortuus est Aran ante Thare. *Vel ante oculos eius obiit in ignem, quem adorare noluit, ut tradunt hebrei, proiectus, uel ante mortuus est quam Thare pater suus*' (BN, ms lat. 356, f. 25rb).

[38] *Hebr. quaest.*, *CCSL* lxxii, p. 15 (mais ne contient pas d'allusion à la légende de Terah marchand d'idoles).

[39] *Gen. R.* xxxviii. 13 (trad. citée, i, pp. 310–11), mais avec une variante (les idoles se sont disputées parce qu'elles voulaient le plat qu'une femme leur avait apporté).

[40] Voir Ginzberg, *The Legends of the Jews*, i, pp. 186–217, et v, pp. 208–18.

[41] Voir R. Bloch, 'Ecriture et tradition dans le judaïsme', *Cahiers sioniens*, viii (1954), pp. 9–34; E.H., art. 'Aggadah', *Encyclopaedia Judaica*, i, col. 354–64.

l'effort historique et grammatical des successeurs de Rashi[42] transparaît assez peu, c'est davantage l'aspect anecdotique ou mythique, contre l'abus· duquel s'étaient insurgés quelques maîtres juifs du XIIe siècle,[43] qui se trouve retenu. Mais on n'oubliera pas que les frontières entre histoire et légende, réalité et mythe sont imprécises chez beaucoup de commentateurs médiévaux, qu'ils soient chrétiens ou juifs.

Ces interprétations sont mentionnées sans aucun esprit polémique par Pierre le Chantre; quand elles sont contestées, elles le sont sans acrimonie et sans ironie. L'apport de l'exégèse juive est donc accueilli avec une certaine sympathie par les maîtres parisiens du XIIe siècle, qui y voient une contribution sérieuse, susceptible d'éclairer les difficultés des récits bibliques[44] et cela, quelle que soit par ailleurs leur position à l'égard des Juifs et du judaïsme. Nous avons montré ailleurs comment l'article *Iudei* de la *Summa Abel* de Pierre le Chantre traduit le durcissement de l'Eglise envers les Juifs,[45] durcissement qui devait prendre une forme officielle un peu plus tard lors du IVe Concile du Latran (1215).[46] Il semble y avoir en fait une sorte de dichotomie entre l'attitude *théorique*, telle qu'elle se manifeste dans les oeuvres spécifiquement théologiques,[47] et cette ouverture qui autorise dialogue et discussion et dont la présence des interprétations juives dans les oeuvres exégétiques nous permet de croire qu'elle orienta l'attitude concrète et réelle, du moins dans une partie de l'élite cultivée. Le dernier maître de l'école biblique morale', Etienne Langton, recopiant Pierre le

---

[42] Voir notamment B.J. Gelles, *Peshat and Derash in the Exegesis of Rashi* (Leyde, 1981).

[43] Cf. M. Signer, 'Exégèse et enseignement: les commentaires de Joseph ben Simeon Kara', *Archives juives*, xviii (1982), pp. 60–3; E. Touitou, 'Concerning the Methodology of R. Samuel b. Meir in his Commentary to the Pentateuch' [en hébreu], *Tarbiz*, xlviii (1979), pp. 248–73; le même, 'La méthode exégétique de R. Samuel b. Meir et les conceptions historiques de son temps', [en hébreu] dans *'Iyunim be-sifrut HZ"L* (Mélanges E.Z. Melamed) (Ramat-Gan, 1982), pp. 48–74. Voir également M. Awerbuch, *Christlich-jüdische Begegnung im Zeitalter der Frühscholastik* (Munich, 1980).

[44] C'est, bien sûr, essentiellement au niveau de la *littera* ou de l'*historia* qu'est prise en compte l'exégèse juive, à ses différents niveaux, critique textuelle aussi bien qu'étude du contexte historique (voir *supra*, notes 6 à 8).

[45] G. Dahan, 'L'article *Iudei* de la *Summa Abel* de Pierre le Chantre', *Revue des études augustiniennes*, xxvii (1981), pp. 105–26.

[46] Canons 67 à 70, Mansi, xxii, pp. 1055–58.

[47] Cf. *Summa de Sacramentis*, éd. J.-A. Dugauquier, iii/2b, p. 728.

Chantre et ses prédécesseurs, devait encore accueillir ces interprétations juives, mais, accordant plus de place qu'eux aux éléments traditionnels de la polémique, traduisait, sur le terrain même de l'exégèse, le malaise de cette attitude double.[48]

Textes

Nous donnons ici le texte des interprétations juives mentionnées par Pierre le Chantre dans ses commentaires du Pentateuque, d'après les manuscrits suivants:

— pour le *Genèse*, l'*Exode* et le *Lévitique*, Paris, Arsenal, ms 44, du XIIIe siècle (= A);[49]
— pour les *Nombres* et le *Deutéronome*, Oxford, Balliol Coll., ms 23, de la fin du XIIe siècle (= B).[50]

Outre un numéro d'ordre en tête de chaque passage, nous ajoutons l'identification des lemmes bibliques, dans le texte même. Nous faisons suivre chacun des fragments de l'identification de la source de Pierre le Chantre, suivie, quand cela est possible, d'un très schématique résumé de la tradition de l'interprétation donnée. Nous proposons également, dans un certain nombre de cas, sous la dénomination de 'sources juives', des textes rabbiniques qui peuvent être rapprochés, sans qu'il s'agisse nécessairement de la source proprement dite; à ce niveau plus qu'ailleurs, nous savons combien nous sommes fragmentaire et incomplet—l'absence d'indication ne traduisant pas l'inexistence d'une 'source juive', mais bien plutôt notre propre ignorance: nous n'avons dépouillé que les principaux textes rabbiniques et les instruments les plus courants.[51]

---

[48] Voir G. Dahan, 'Exégèse et polémique dans les Commentaires de la *Genèse* d'Étienne Langton', dans *Les Juifs au regard de l'histoire. Mélanges en l'honneur de B. Blumenkranz* (sous presse). Les éléments polémiques (notamment à travers les 'figures' des Juifs et de la Synagogue), ne sont bien entendu pas absents des commentaires de Pierre le Chantre; mais ils nous paraissent y avoir moins de vigueur anti-juive et y être en moins grand nombre. Chez André de Saint-Victor ils étaient relativement rares—mais André ne s'intéressait pas à l'allégorie.

[49] Description sommaire de ce ms: H. Martin, *Catalogue des mss de la Bibl. de l'Arsenal* (Paris, 1885), i, p. 20. Les commentaires contenus dans ce ms (Gen., Ex., Lév., Nb., Deut., Macch., Josué, Rois, Chron., Tobie, Judith, Esther) sont anonymes.

[50] Description: R.A.B. Mynors, *Catalogue of the MSS of Balliol College, Oxford* (Oxford, 1963), pp. 15-16; Petrus Cantor, sur Nb., Deut., Josué, Juges, Ruth.

[51] Les traités talmudiques seront précédés des mentions TB (= Talmud de Babylone) ou TJ (= Talmud de Jérusalem); l'indication des folios renvoie aux éditions

1. (*Gen.*, i. 6) Nota: cum opus huius diei bonum non fuerit ut ceterorum, non legitur Deus dixisse ut de ceteris operibus 'Et uidit Deus quod esset bonum' etc. Cuius causam tradunt hebrei quod ea die angelus factus est diabolus, quibus consentire uidentur qui ea die, scilicet secunda feria, missam de angelis cantare consueuerunt, quasi in laudem stantium angelorum (*A*, p. 5[a]).

Source latine: Pierre Comestor (*PL* cxcviii, 1058–9). *Sources juives*: explication généralement différente; cf. TB *Pesahim*, f. 54a. Cf. *supra*.

2. (a) *Crescite et multiplicamini* (*Gen.*, i. 22). Et sic benedixit eis, id est piscibus et uolatilibus. Dicit iudeus: non reptilibus, inter que erat serpens, qui in sequenti maledicturus est. (b) Querit iudeus: quare non dixit in hac distinctione 'Factum est'? Ita primo scilicet quia nondum omnia animalia fecerat: quedam enim facturus erat de terra (*A*, p. 6[b]).

Source latine: ? Sources juives: (a) cf. Rashi.

3. *Faciamus* (*Gen.*, i. 26). Secundum iudeum loquitur ad angelos; secundum christianum Pater loquitur ad Filium et Spiritum Sanctum, uel est uox communis trium personarum (*A*, p. 7[a]).

Source latine: Hugues de Saint-Victor (*PL* clxxv, 37) – ne l'attribue pas aux Juifs. *Sources juives*: cf. *Gen. R.* xvii. 4; Rashi.

4. (*Gen.*, iii. 1) Iudeus dicit quod serpens uenustus fuit et muliere abuti uoluit ... (*A*, p. 11[a]).

Source latine: ? *Sources juives*: cf. Rashi.

5. *Possedi hominem per Deum* (*Gen.*, iv. 2) ... Hebreus habet 'Cooperata sum cum Deo'; in primis parentibus solus Deus operatus est, in ceteris Deus operatur per auctoritatem, parentes cooperantur per ministerium (*A*, p. 14[a]).

Source latine: André de St-Victor (BN, ms lat. 356, f. 17ra). *Sources juives*: cf. Rashi.

---

standard. Pour la *Glossa Ordinaria*, nous utilisons l'éd. d'Anvers, 1634, i, qui contient également le commentaire de Nicolas de Lyre. A titre indicatif, nous mentionnons la présence de certaines interprétations chez Rupert de Deutz, éd. R. Haacke, dans le *CCCM*, xxi et xxii. Les mentions de commentateurs juifs renvoient aux versets considérés.

6. (*Gen.*, iv. 10) ... (a) Vel alio iudicio sic: Vox sanguinis fratris tui clamat ad me de terra, id est eorum qui sunt sanguis et parentes fratris tui conqueruntur de tua crudelitate michi. (b) Vel uox sanguinis, id est posteritatis [tue], que de sanguine fratris tui descendere posset, si eum non interfecisses (*A*, p. 14^b–15^a).

Source latine: André de Saint-Victor (ms cité. f. 17rb). *Sources juives*: cf. Rashi d'après *Gen. R.* xxii. 9, d'après TB *Sanhedrin*, f. 37^a (seulement interprétation *b*).

7. *Septuagies septies* (*Gen.*, iv. 24) ... Hebreus dicit mulieres suas sepe eum male tractare, unde sepe iratus ad terrorem dicebat eis se pati hoc pro duplici homicidio quod commiserat, quasi diceret: Vultis interficere, sed sciatis quod *septuplum dabitur de* interfectore *Cain quam de Cain*, id est multo plus punietur quam eo, qui me interficiet (*A*, p. 16^a).

Source latine: Pierre Comestor (*PL* cxcviii, 1079), d'après André de Saint-Victor (ms. cité, f. 19ra). *Sources juives*: cf. Rashi, Joseph Bekhor Shor, citant Joseph Qara (mais assez différents);[52] tradition également rapportée par Nicolas de Lyre (col. 125).

8. *Enoch* (*Gen.*, iv. 26), quod sonat 'homo' uel 'uir', id est rationalis et fortis. Iste enim cepit uocare nomen Domini; forte inuenit uerba deprecatoria ad inuocandum Deum. Hebreus dicit quod imagines inuenit ad honorem Dei et incitandum deuocionem, ut modo fit; uel forte errauit et ydolatria prima coluit (*A*, p. 16^a).

Source latine: Pierre Comestor (*PL* cxcviii, 1080). d'après André de Saint-Victor (ms. cité, f. 19ra) ou *Glossa* (col. 128), citant Jérôme (*Hebr. quaestr.*, *CCSL* lxxii, p. 8). *Sources juives*: cf. TB *Shabat* f. 118^b, *Lam. R.* (proem.) etc.

9. *Quia tulit eum Dominus* (*Gen.*, v. 24) ... Quidam iudei attribuunt huius translationis causam pocius septenario (ms septimo) quam eius sanctitati, cum multi eo sanctiores legantur. Alii dicunt hebrei quod fuerit Finees Eleazari sacerdotis, sed falsum est (*A*, p. 16^b).

Source latine: Pierre Comestor (*PL* cxcviii, 1080). *Sources juives*: Pesiqta de-Rav Kahana (cf. *supra*).

10. *Gigantes autem erant super terram* (*Gen.*, vi. 4). Immanes corpore, superbi uiribus, inconditi moribus; unde gigantes filii terre dicuntur in hebreo 'cadentes'. Vnde dicunt quidam hebrei quod angeli de celo cadentes assumpserunt sibi uxores, quos supra dixit 'filios Dei' (*A*, p. 17^a).

---

[52] Joseph Bekhor Shor, éd., Jellinek, p. 13.

Source latine: André de Saint-Victor (ms cité, f. 19vb), d'après Jérôme (*Hebr. quaest.*, *CCSL* lxxii, p. 10); également chez Rupert de Deutz (*CCCM* xxi, p. 298). *Sources juives*: cf. *Gen. R.*, xxvi. 7; *Pirqe R. Eliezer* xxii; Rashi.

11. (*Gen.*, vi. 16) Dicunt hebrei cristallinam fenestram fuisse, que in hebreo dicitur meridianum; a Simacho dicitur diluculum (*A*, p. 17^b).

Source latine: Pierre Comestor (*PL* cxcviii, 1083), d'après *Glossa* (col. 145–6), d'après Jérôme (*Hebr. quaest.*, *CCSL* lxxii, p. 10); cf. également André de Saint-Victor (ms cité, f. 20rb). *Sources juives*: cf. TB *Sanhedrin* f. 108b; *Gen. R.* xxxi. 11; Rashi etc.

12. *Dilatet Dominus Iaphet et habitet in tabernacula Sem* (*Gen.*, ix. 27) ... Hebreus hoc refert de gentibus que fuerunt de Iaphet et in magnis solempnitatibus in Ierusalem conuenire solebant (*A*, p. 20b).

Source latine: André de Saint-Victor (ms cité, f. 23vb). *Sources juives*: ? (tradition également rapportée par Nicolas de Lyre, col. 175–6).

13. (*Gen.*, xi. 28)) Dicit iudeus quod Thare uultificus fuit et ydolatra et fecit uultus quos distraere uoluit, quos Habrae commisit, ut deferret eos ad forum. Qui obtemperans in hoc, cum secum ferret, eorum crura fregit et bracchia, et reuersus respondit patri quod contencio orta est inter eos in sacco, quia constringebantur sacci angustia et mutuo sibi fregerunt crura. Cum pater impossibile esse respondit, cum sint ligna et lapides et motu careant, Cur ergo, dixit Habraám, decipis tuos? Tunc pater promulgauit filios nolle idolatrare et positi sunt in igne Aram et Habram, sed Aram consumptus est, quia infirmus in fide; Habraam, quia firmus, euasit auxilio Dei. Vnde: *Ego sum qui eduxi te de Vr Chaldeorum* (*Gen.*, xv. 7), in ciuitate, secundum Iosephum, et ibi adhuc eius ostenditur sepultura.[53] Hebrei *Vr* dicunt 'ignem', ut dictum est (*A*, pp. 21^b–22^a).

Source latine: cf. Pierre Comestor (*PL* cxcviii, 1091), d'après (?) *Glossa* (col. 185), citant Jérôme (*Hebr. quaest.*, *CC* lxxii, p. 15); cf. aussi Rupert de Deutz (*CCCM* xxi, p. 333) et André de Saint-Victor (ms cité, f. 25rb)—mais tous ces textes beaucoup moins complets que Pierre le Chantre. *Sources juives*: cf. notamment *Gen. R.* xxxviii. 13.

14. *Segor* (*Gen.*, xiv. 2). Ieronimus: hanc dicunt Hebrei uitulam conternantem [ms consternantem] ... et in Isaia dicitur uitula trima,

[53] Cf. Fr. Blatt, *The Latin Josephus* (Copenhague, 1958), p. 143 (*Ant.* i. vi. 151).

id est trium annorum, quia, quatuor igne sulfureo combustis et submersis, hec tercio terremotu, postquam exiuit Loth, submersa est (*A*, p. 23^b).

Source latine: Glossa, d'après Jérôme (*Hebr. quaest., CCSL* lxxii, p. 17), mais non littéral (cf. aussi Rupert de Deutz, *CCCM* xxi, p. 343). *Sources juives:* ?

15. *At uero Melchisedec rex Salem* (*Gen.*, xiv. 18)... Hunc dicunt hebrei fuisse Sem filium <Noe> et usque ad Ysaac uixisse et omnes primogenitos a Noe usque ad Aaron pontifices fuisse (*A*, p. 24^b).

Source latine: André de Saint-Victor (ms cité, f. 26vb), d'après Jérôme (*Hebr. quaest., CCSL* lxxii, p. 19); également dans *Glossa* (col. 205–6), Rupert de Deutz (*CCCM* xxi, p. 346), Pierre Comestor (*PL* cxviii, 1094–5). *Sources juives:* cf. Rashi, citant *Midrash Tehilim;*[54] *Num. R.* iv. 8. etc.

16. (*Gen.*, xvi. 2) Nota diligenter quod procreatio filiorum apud hebreos dicitur 'edificatio'. Legitur enim ibi: *Ingredere ad ancillam meam,* si quo modo edificer ex ea; forte hoc est quod legitur in Exodo (cf. *Ex.* i. 20–1): Benedixit Deus obstetricibus et edificauerunt sibi domos (*A*, p. 25^b).

Source latine: Glossa (col. 218), citant Jérôme (*Hebr. quaest., CCSL* lxxii, p. 20). *Sources juives:* cf. Rashi.

17. (*Gen.*, xvii. 5) Dicunt hebrei quod Dominus de nomine suo tetragramaton addidit *e*, quod tamen sonat *a*; ydioma enim est eorum scribere *e* et sonare *a* et e contrario; et quia tempore circumcisionis mutatum est ei nomen, hebrei in circumcisione imponunt nomina (*A*, p. 26^a).

Source latine: Pierre Comestor (*PL* cxviii, 1097), d'après *Glossa* (col. 224), citant Jérôme (*Hebr. quaest., CCSL* lxxii, p. 21); également chez Rupert de Deutz (*CCCM* xxi, p. 263). *Sources juives:* ? (Rashi ne dit pas que la lettre *he* ait été prise au Tétragramme).

18. (*Gen.*, xvii. 15) Sicut superius de Habraam, dicunt quidam quia, cum Sara prius per unum *r* scribitur, nunc per duo uel e contrario, et quantum ad nos nulla, id est substracta et nulla addita; ad hebreos additur *a* et scribitur *e* (*A*, p. 26^b).

---

[54] Commentaire 'midrashique' sur les *Psaumes*, de date indéterminée; voir la traduction anglaise de W.G. Braude, *The Midrash on Psalms*, 2 vols. (New Haven, 1959), ii, p. 15, (sur *Ps.* lxxvi. 3).

Source latine: Pierre Comestor (*PL* cxcviii, 1098), d'après *Glossa* (col. 227), citant Jérôme (*Hebr. quaest.*, *CCSL* lxxii, pp. 21-2). *Sources juives*: ? (seule la fin est d'origine juive).

19. *Ascendit Loth de Segor* (*Gen.*, xix. 30). Responsio: uera est hebreorum coniectura quod frequenti terre motu territus Loth est. Segor enim terre motu frequenti mouebatur... (*A*, p. 29^b).

Source latine: *Glossa* (col. 250), citant Jérôme (*Hebr. quaest.*, *CCSL* lxxii, p. 23); cf. également Rupert de Deutz (*CCCM* xxi, p. 389) et Pierre Comestor (*PL* cxcviii, 1101). *Sources juives*: ?

20. *At ille non sensit* (*Gen.*, xix. 33), nec quando accubuit filia, nec quando surrexit. Responsio: hebrei hoc apungunt desuper quasi incredibile, quia rerum non capit natura coire quempiam nescientem; sed nos dicimus quod nesciuit esse filiam, sed sciuit esse feminam (*A*, p. 30^a).

Source latine: Pierre Comestor (*PL* cxcviii, 1102), d'après *Glossa* (col. 250), citant Jérôme (*Hebr. quaest.*, *CCSL* lxxii, p. 24); cf. Rupert de Deutz (*CCCM* xxi, pp. 389-90). *Sources juives*: cf. *Num. R.* iii. 13.[55]

21. *In terram uisionis* (*Gen.*, xxii. 2), illam partem Iudee que est in montanis... In summitate uero montium Iudee monticulus erat eminentior, qui dicitur Mons Moria, quem monstrauit Deus Habrae ad immolandum filium. In quo tradunt hebrei templum post esse factum, in quo Habraam altare fecit et Dauid angelum reponentem gladium uidit in area Ornam Iebusei (*A*, p. 31^b).

Source latine: Pierre Comestor (*PL* cxcviii, 1104-5), d'après André de Saint-Victor (ms cité, f. 31ra), d'après (?) *Glossa* col. 266, citant Jérôme (*Hebr. quaest.*, *CCSL* lxxii, p. 25); également chez Rupert de Deutz (*CCCM* xxi. p. 405). *Sources juives*: cf. Rashi.

22. *Buz* (*Gen.*, xxii. 21), a quo Eliu dicitur Buzites, quem putant hebrei fuisse Balaam de genere Buz, qui Eliu in Iob dicitur (*A*, p. 33^a).

Source latine: *Glossa*, col. 271-2; également chez Pierre Comestor (*PL* cxcviii, 1105), d'après André de Saint-Victor (ms cité, f. 31rb), d'après Jérôme (*Hebr. quaest.*, *CCSL* lxxii, p. 27); également chez Rupert de Deutz (*CCCM* xxi, p. 413). *Sources juives*: cf. TJ *Sotah* v. 5.

---

[55] Assez différent tout de même; cf. trad. citée (n. 15), iii, p. 92: 'He knew not when she lay down, but he knew when she arose'.

23. *Pone manum* (*Gen.*, xxiv. 2)… Tradunt hebrei quia in sanctificatione, id est in circumcisione, iurauit. Nos autem dicimus eum iurasse in semine Habrae, id est Christo de eo nascituro (*A*, p. 33ᵇ).

Source latine: Glossa, (col. 282), citant Jérôme (*Hebr. quaest.*, *CCSL* lxxii, p. 28); cf. également André de Saint-Victor (ms cité, f. 31ᵛᵃ), Rupert de Deutz (*CCCM* xxi, p. 417), Pierre Comestor (*PL* cxcviii, 1106). *Sources juives*: cf. Rashi, d'après *Gen. R.* lix. 8.[56]

24. *Cethura* (*Gen.*, xxv. 1), que interpretatur 'copulata' uel 'coniuncta'. Vnde dicunt iudei hanc fuisse Agar, quod dicunt in excusatione Habrae, ne senex ducens uxorem etiam iuuenculam uideretur lasciuisse (*A*, p. 35ᵃ).

Source latine: Glossa (col. 295), citant Jérôme (*Hebr. quaest.*, *CCSL* lxxii, p. 30); également chez Rupert de Deutz (*CCCM* xxi, p. 427), Pierre Comestor (*PL* cxcviii, 1108). *Sources juives*: cf. *Gen. R.* lxi. 4; *Pirqe de-R. Eliezer* xxx (tous identifient Kethura et Agar, mais aucun ne donne l'explication proposée ici).

25. (*Gen.*, xxvii. 11) Nota: ubi habemus *homo pilosus*, hebreus ponit Seir… Item dicunt hebrei primogenitos officio sacerdocii functos et sacerdotale uestimentum habuisse, quo induti uictimas offerebant, antequam Aaron eligeretur in sacerdocium (*A*, p. 38ᵃ).

Source latine: Jérôme (*Hebr. quaest.*, *CCSL* lxxii, p. 34); également *Glossa* (col. 317–8), Rupert de Deutz (*CCCM* xxi, p. 445), Pierre Comestor (*PL* cxcviii, 1111). *Sources juives*: ?

26. (*Gen.*, xxix. 30) Iudeus plures <uxores> adhuc duceret, nisi propter tradicionem quam constituerunt sub anathemate, ut unicus duceret unicam. Ad cautelam hoc est constitutum, quia sepe propter concupiscentiam lecatores ducebant lecatrices, uetulis contemptis (*A*, p. 40ᵇ).[57]

Source latine: ? *Sources juives*: ?

27. *Turrim gregis* (*Gen.*, xxxv. 21): hunc locum dicunt hebrei ubi post edificatum est templum et quasi quodam uaticinio uocatur *turrim gregis*, id est congregationis future ad templum. Ieronimus dicit locum esse iuxta Betleem (*A*, p. 45ᵇ).

---

[56] Joseph Bekhor Shor, éd. Jellinek, p. 35, mentionne l'interprétation chrétienne: 'Les hérétiques (*minim*) disent que c'est parce que Jésus est issu de là'.

[57] La polygamie a été interdite aux Juifs d'Occident par Gershom Meor ha-Gola (fin Xe s.–début du XIe); le décret (*taqanah*) était accompagné de menaces d'excommunication (*herem*) pour les contrevenants; il semble bien que ce soit ce que nous décrit Pierre le Chantre.

Source latine: Pierre Comestor (*PL* cxcviii, 1123), d'après *Glossa* (col. 375), citant Jérôme (*Hebr. quaest.*, *CCSL* lxxii, p. 43); également chez Rupert de Deutz (*CCCM* xxi, p. 501). *Sources juives*: ?

28. *Putiphari eunucho* (*Gen.*, xxxvii. 36). Hunc uocat Iosephus Petefre,[58] sed Ieronimus non bene translatum nomen asserit. Hic habuit uxorem et liberos, quia et Ioseph eius filiam duxit in uxorem, nec de eunuchis regis fuit, qui paruuli castrabantur. Sed tradunt hebrei quod uidens Ioseph elegantem emit eum, ut ei misceretur; sed Dominus custodiens adeo infrigdauit ut deinceps impotens coire fuerit, tamquam eunuchus esset, ita quod uidentes eum ierofanti arefactum de more suo eum pontificem Heliopoleos creauerunt et honoratior erat quam ante in principatu (*A*, p. 47ᵃ).

Source latine: Pierre Comestor (*PL* cxcviii, 1126–7), d'après *Glossa* (col. 392), citant Jérôme (*Hebr. quaest.*, *CCSL* lxxii, p. 45); également chez Rupert de Deutz (*CCCM* xxi, p. 514). *Sources juives*: cf. TB *Sotah* f. 37b; *Gen. R.* lxxxvi. 3.[59]

29. *Donec ueniat qui mittendus est* (*Gen.*, xlix. 10)... Hebreus dicit: donec ueniat Silo, id est usque ad Saulem, qui unctus est in Silo; post tamen rediit ad Iudam, qui eripuit Ioseph de manibus fratrum suorum (*A*, p. 55ᵃ).

Source latine: Pierre Comestor (*PL* cxcviii, 1137), d'après Andrè de Saint-Victor (ms cité, f. 39ʳᵃ), d'après Hugues de Saint-Victor (*PL* clxxv, 59). *Sources juives*: addition au *Midrash Tanhuma* ?[60]

30. *Beniamin lupus rapax* (*Gen.*, xlix. 27). Hunc locum ita hebrei edisserunt [ms disserunt]: altare quod erat in templum Domini in parte tribus Beniamin situm erat. Hoc ergo altare uocat lupum sanguinarium et rapacem propter hostias que in mane offerebantur et igne qui erat super in altari deuorabantur. Hoc est quod dicit *mane comedat predam*. Quod uero sequitur: *uespere diuidet spolia*, ad sacerdotes pertinet, quia ea que per diem de sacrificiis altaris a populo consequebantur, uespere inter se diuidebant (*A*, p. 56ᵇ).

---

[58] Cf. *Ant.*, ii. iv. 39 (éd. Blatt de la trad. latine, p. 174).
[59] Voir également Ginzberg, *The Legends of the Jews*, ii, p. 43, et v, p. 337.
[60] Cf. A. Posnanski, *Schiloh. Ein Beitrag zur Geschichte der Messiaslehre* (Leipzig, 1904), p. 42: 'Im Tanchuma, Ms Oxford Nr 183, befinden sich folgende zwei Randglossen, die von S. Buber ... verzeichnet werden ... Eine zweite Auslegung: bis der Prophet Samuel in Silo auftrat (I *Sam.* i, 24) und Saul aus Benjamin zum Könige erhob'. Mais il semble étonnant que ce soit là véritablement l'origine de cette tradition. Le ms cité par Posnanski est en fait le Hunt. Don. 20 (Neubauer 153).

Source latine: André de Saint-Victor (ms cité, f. 40rb), d'après *Glossa* (col. 467), citant Jérôme (*Hebr. quaest.*, *CCSL* lxxii p. 56). *Sources juives*: cf. *Gen. R.* xcix. 3, Rashi.

31. *In flamma* (*Ex.*, iii. 2)... Aiunt hebrei ideo in rubo Deum apparuisse Moysi, ne possent in ydolum sculpere iudei. Semper enim Deus ydolatrie occasionem rescidit illis (*A*, p. 60^b).

Source latine: André de Saint-Victor (ms cité, f. 41va), d'après *Glossa* (col. 501–2), citant Isidore de Séville (*Quaest. in V.T.*, *PL* lxxxiii, 290). *Sources juives*: ? présent chez Nicolas de Lyre (col. 501–2).

32. *Impeditioris* (*Ex.*, iv. 10) etc. Secundum ebreos gracilem et tenuem habuit uocem. Necesse erat uoce [...]^{61} uti, quia regio fastu prope accedi non permittebatur (*A*, p. 62^a).

Source latine: ? *Sources juives*: ? (pour le début, cf. Nicolas de Lyre, col. 529: 'sicut dicunt Hebraei habebat uocem gracilem').

33. (*Ex.*, iv. 25–6) Angelus dimisit eum, id est Moysen, quod in hebreo patet, in quo habetur: Relaxauit eum angelus, qui prius eum coarctabat usque ad mortem. Hinc uolunt quidam morem circum-cidendi cultellis petrinis habuisse principium, uel a Iosue in Galga-lis. Vbi tamen habemus *petram*, ebreus habet aciem, quam dicit *nouaculam*; unde iudei nouaculis circumcidunt. Fabulantur tamen quidam, dicentes quod usque ad Dauid petra facta est circumcisio ... (*A*, p. 63^a).

Source latine: Pierre Comestor (*PL* cxcviii, 1147), d'après André de Saint-Victor (ms cité, f. 43va et 43rb). *Sources juives*: cf. TJ *Nedarim*, iii. 9. (assez éloigné).

34. (a) *Immobiles* (*Ex.*, xv. 16), ad persequendum uel resistendum non moueantur. Hebreus habet 'taciturni' uel 'silentes', ut nec mutire audeant. (b) *Possedisti* (*ibid.*) in hereditatem, unde *Iacob funiculus hereditatis*. Hebreus habet 'comparasti' uel 'emisti', in quo notatur quod eos caros habebat (*A*, p. 78^a).

Source latine: André de Saint-Victor (ms cité, f. 52ra). *Sources juives*: (a) cf. *Mekhilta de-R. Ishma'el* (cf. *supra*); (b) cf. Mishnah *Avot* vi. 10; Rashi.

35. *Combusit* (*Ex.*, xxxii. 20)... Tradunt hebrei quod filii Israel bibentes aquam uituli puluere [ms puluerem] infectam, qui com-miserant ydolatriam in barba puluerem auri preferebant. Quo signo

---

^{61} Nous ne lisons pas un mot: un adjectif signifiant sans doute 'puissant, fort, qui porte'.

rei uel immunes sceleris apparebant, et rei interficerentur (*A*, p. 116ᵃ).

Source latine: *Glossa* (col. 840); également chez Rupert de Deutz (*CCCM* xxii, p. 783) et Pierre Comestor (*PL* cxcviii, 1190), mais n'est attribuée aux Juifs que par la *Glossa* (Rupert dit: 'Aiunt quidam'). *Sources juives*: cf. *Pirqe de-R. Eliezer* xlv (un peu différent).

36. *Qui peccauerit michi* (*Ex.*, xxxii. 33)... Angelus quem huc usque non deputaueram populo iudaico, tamquam funiculo hereditatis mee; custodem non me ipsum de cetero putabo eis, custodem angelum uobis delegabo, et dicunt hebrei quod tunc deputatus est eis Michael (*A*, p. 117ᵃ).

Source latine: Pierre Comestor (*PL* cxcviii, 1191). *Sources juives*: cf. Rashi.

37. *Diliges* (*Lev..*, xix. 18)... Sed iudeus proximum religione uel beneficii collatione, non proximum pre natura male intellexit (*A*, p. 200ᵇ).

Source latine: ? *Sources juives*: *Eccl. R.* viii. 4.[62]

38. (*Num.*, iii. 2) De Aaron nati sunt Nadab, Abiu, Eleazar et Ytamar. Ecce quatuor qui dicuntur singuli uel uiri sub uno nomine uel uno capite. Ideo dicunt hebrei per omnes tribus hunc ordinem et numerum tam diligenter esse obseruatum, quia preceptum erat ut omnes filii de quacumque tribu secundum matrem essent, in ea tribu numerarentur de qua pater eorum esset et ideo totiens, ut aiunt, replicantur secundum generationes, quia proprie generatio pertinet ad patrem (*B*, f. 3ʳᵇ).

Source latine: ? *Sources juives*: ?

39. *xxii milia* (*Num.*, iii. 39). xxii numerus in diuinis scripturis principalibus causis ascriptus sepe reperitur. Nam xxii prima apud hebreos elementa tradunt esse litterarum et ab Adam usque ad Iacob, ex cuius semine initium duodecim tribus sumunt, xxii patres fuisse memorantur. Tradunt etiam omnium creaturarum Dei species xxii numero colligi (*B*, f. 10ᵛᵃ).

Source latine: *Glossa* (col. 1187), citant Origène, *Hom. iv in Num. Sources juives*: ?[63]

---

[62] Où il est question du prêt à intérêt. Cf. aussi TB *Ketuvot*, f. 37b (même contexte).
[63] Que les vingt-deux lettres de l'alphabet aient été aux origines de la création est une notion exposée par plusieurs textes juifs classés comme 'mystiques' (*Alphabet de R.*

40. *In libro bellorum Domini* (*Num.*, xxi. 14), id est in relatione bellorum Domini, quasi diceret: quando relegentur uel tractabuntur gloriosa bella Domini et eius uirtutes, mentio erit de Arnon. Ibi enim, ut dicunt hebrei, potenti manu Domini deleti sunt amorrei. Veritas hebraica habet: sicut dicetur in relatione bellorum Domini, id est quando hystoriographi uel alii retractabunt que facta sunt in populo Dei, referent quod filii Israel sicco pede transierunt Arnon ut Mare rubrum (*B*, f. 35^{va-b}).

Source latine: André de Saint-Victor (ms cité, f. 84ra); également chez Pierre Comestor (*PL* cxcviii, 1235). *Sources juives*: *Num. R.* xix. 25.

41. *Scopuli torrentium* (*Num.*, xxi. 15) etc. Dicunt hebrei innumeram multitudinem amorreorum fuisse in conualle torrentium Arnon, israelitis insidiantes, ut ex inprouiso illac transeuntes perimerent, et deinde scopulis torrentium in conualle eos oppressisse et rupibus hinc inde cooperuisse, ita ut hec inclinatio rupium requiesceret, id est finiret *in Arnon et recumberent* etc. (*B*, f. 35vb).

Source latine: André de Saint-Victor (ms cité, f. 84rb); également chez Pierre Comestor (*PL* cxcviii, 1235). *Sources juives*: *Num. R.* xix. 25; Rashi (tradition citée par Nicolas de Lyre, col. 1236).

42. *In peccato suo mortuus est* (*Num.*, xxvii. 3), naturali morte inflicta uniuersitati ex peccato Ade uel, ut dicunt iudei, ligna collegit in sabbato, ut dictum est supra (cf. *Num.*, xv. 32–6) (*B*, f. 46vb).

Source latine: cf. Pierre Comestor (*PL* cxcviii, 1229). *Sources juives*: cf. Rashi, d'après TB *Shabat*, f. 96b (tradition reprise par Nicolas de Lyre, col. 1391).

43. (*Deut.*, v. 21) Hec duo precepta Origenes colligit in unum. Preterea dicit Augustinus tria fuisse in una tabula et vii in alia; Iosephus et hebrei .v. in utraque (*B*, f. 66rb).

Source latine: Pierre Comestor (*PL* cxcviii, 1164), d'après *Glossa* sur *Ex.* xx, citant Augustin (*Quaest. in Heptateuchum* ii. 71, *CSEL* xxviii/2, p. 136). *Sources juives*: ?

44. *Ego steti* (*Deut..*, x. 10). Dicit iudeus ter Moysen ascendisse in montem et singulis uicibus .xl. diebus moram fecisse: primo quando primas tabulas attulit; secundo quando secundas; tercio

---

Aqiba, etc.); Agobard en a connaissance (*De Iudaicis superstitionibus*, *PL* civ, 87). Un commentateur du début du XIIe siècle, Rainaud de Saint-Éloi parle également, comme étant une tradition juive, des vingt-deux éléments primordiaux (dans son prologue au Pentateuque, que nous allons publier).

quando ait Domino: 'Dimitte huic populo aut dele me de libro
uite'. Sed hoc non est uerum (*B*, f. 72rb).

Source latine: ? *Sources juives*: cf. Joseph Bekhor Shor.[64]

45. *Et nunc Israel quid petit a te Dominus* (*Deut.*, x. 12) etc. Glosa.
Quidam tres dicunt esse celos... Quidam uero septem... Sed
theologus has non sequitur uisiones, ut iudei qui dicunt septem esse
fundamenta terre (*B*, f. 72va).

Source latine: *Glossa* (col. 1532–3), pour le début seulement. *Sources juives*: cf. *Deut.
R.* ii. 32 (liste des sept cieux).

46. *Non intrabit eunuchus* etc. *ecclesiam* (*Deut.*, xxiii. 1), secundum
atrium mundorum; tercium uero atrium cum immundis gentibus
poterat intrare. Ad litteram sic est expositio (ms expositione). Non
enim habet locum hic expositio hebreorum, qui exponunt *intrare
ecclesiam* 'ducere uxorem de israelitis', quod in sequenti locum
habebit (*B*, f. 87vb).

Source latine: Pierre Comestor (*PL* cxcviii, 1255), mais assez différent dans son
appréciation ('Hebraeus uerius tradit...'). *Sources juives*: cf. Rashi.

47. *Quia noluerunt occurrere* (*Deut.*, xxiii. 4) etc. Tradunt hebrei
quod hee gentes propinque sibi exeuntibus de Egipto cum pane
tantum occurrerunt, cum scirent eos maxime in deserto siti labo-
rare, et ideo huic maledictioni subiecti sunt (*B*, f. 88ra).

Source latine: *Glossa* (col. 1605–6) ou André de Saint-Victor (ms cité, ff. 89vb–90ra).
Sources juives: ?

48. *Memento* (*Deut.*, xxv. 17) etc. Tradunt hebrei quod leprosos et
semine fluentes extra castra positos interficiebat Amalech et hos
dicunt extremos agminis (*B*, f. 92vb).

Source latine: *Glossa* (col. 1627), d'après ps.-Jérôme (*Quaest. hebr. in lib. I Regum*, *PL*
xxiii, 1402); également chez Rupert de Deutz (*CCCM* xxii, 1060) et Pierre
Comestor (*PL* cxcviii, 1253). *Sources juives*: ?

49. *Quando compleueris* (*Deut.*, xxvi. 12). Hic sequenda est traditio
hebreorum. Vide quia hoc preceptum datum est pro remotis
quibus, quia non poterant singulis annis uenire in Ierusalem,
indulgebatur tantum uenire tercio anno. Hii sicut alii separabant

---

[64] Parle des secondes tables et de la demande adressée à Dieu de pardonner le péché
du Veau d'or (éd. Jellinek, p. 22).

decimas et has remoti apud se reseruabant primo et secundo anno. Tercio anno, quo ipsi ueniebant in Ierusalem, separabant tres decimas: prima semper dabatur leuitis et tercia, tercio anno collecta, dabatur pauperibus. Secunde tribus annis collecte tercio anno deferebantur in Ierusalem et inde fiebant expense et oblationes. Sic se habet rei ueritas. (*B*, f. 93vb).

Source latine: cf. Pierre Comestor (*PL* cxcviii, 1251–2). *Sources juives*: cf. Flavius-Josèphe.[65]

50. *Dominus uenit de Syna*, in quo data est lex, *et nobis ortus est de Seyr et apparuit de monte Pharan* (*Deut.*, xxxiii. 2). Hoc ad litteram de populo iudaico stare non potest. Seyr enim mons est in Ydumea, quam nunquam intrauerunt iudei. Hebreus tamen sic ad litteram exponit, dicens: quia Dominus primo obtulit forte per angelum gentibus (*add. intralin.* hismaelitis) legem in Pharan, secundo ydumeis in Seyr et similiter noluerunt recipere et ideo primo obtulit utrisque, quia erant semen Abrahe, cui facta est promissio et, utrisque respuentibus, uenit ad filios Israel in monte Syna, quem diu circuerunt et aliqua precepta ibi acceperunt et legem receperunt, dicentes: Omnia que dixerit nobis Dominus faciemus, et ita uenit ad eos de Pharan et Seyr (*B*, f. 106rb).

Source latine: André de Saint-Victor (ms cité, f. 93$^{rb–va}$) ou Pierre Comestor (*PL* cxcviii, 1260). *Sources juives*: *Lam. R.* iii. 1 etc. (voir supra).

51. *Et non cognouit homo sepulchrum eius* (*Deut.*, xxxiv. 6). Iudei autumant hoc factum fuisse ne iudei, semper ad idolatriam proni et prompti, mortuum colerent tamquam deum. Hac etiam causa Ezechias et Iosias eneum serpentem comminutum in torrentem proiecerunt... (*B*, f. 111vb).

Source latine: André de Saint-Victor (ms cité, f. 94vb); également chez Pierre Comestor (*PL* cxcviii, 1260). *Sources juives*: ? (tradition citée par Nicolas de Lyre, col. 1706).

Centre national de la Recherche scientifique, Paris.

---

[65] Voir Merchavia, *The Church*, p. 178.

POVERTY, PREACHING, AND ESCHATOLOGY IN THE REVELATION COMMENTARIES OF 'HUGH OF ST CHER'*

by ROBERT E. LERNER

T HIS article is dedicated to advancing three propositions, all in elaboration of research by Beryl Smalley:

(1) that the Revelation exegesis of Hugh of St Cher, O.P. (c. 1195–1263; regent master at St Jacques, 1230–1235)[1] can be securely located;
(2) that much of the content of this exegesis is extraordinary; and
(3) that Hugh of St Cher the great Dominican commentator on Scripture is a figment of bibliographers' imaginations.

If the third proposition seems too preposterously at odds with the first to be maintained seriously, the reader is respectfully requested to be patient.

To begin with the most straightforward question—'where is the Revelation exegesis of Hugh of St Cher?'—is to begin with a question posed by Beryl Smalley almost thirty years ago. In a careful study of the Revelation commentary produced in 1292–3 by the Cambridge Franciscan John Russel, she noticed that Russel frequently quoted passages from an earlier Revelation commentary he attributed to 'Magister Hugo', but that none of Russel's quotations came from either the Revelation postill beginning *Aser pinguis*, printed in the *Opera omnia* of Hugh of St Cher, or the thirteenth-century 'Pseudo-Hugo' Revelation postill beginning

* Research for this article was subsidized by the American Academy in Rome and Northwestern University. The author is deeply grateful to both institutions for their support.
[1] For biography and bibliography, see A. Paravicini Bagliani, *Cardinali di curia e 'familiae' cardinalizie dal 1227 al 1254*, 2 vols. (Padua, 1972), i, pp. 256–65; Kaeppeli, *Scriptores*, ii, pp. 269–81.

Vidit Iacob in somniis.[2] 'Here is a puzzle', wrote Beryl Smalley; and I am chagrined to say that I too have found no solution for it.[3] Yet I believe my very failure bears significance: namely, that whoever Russel's 'Hugo' was, he could not have been Hugh of St Cher because the Revelation exegesis of the authoritative Dominican commentator was bound to have circulated widely, whereas the text ascribed by Russel to 'Hugo' clearly did not take the late-medieval *scriptoria* by storm.

If we put the Russel puzzle aside, can we then return to the *Opera omnia* text, *Aser pinguis*, and say simply: here is Hugh's Revelation commentary? Assuredly the answer must be 'no' because a daunting amount of evidence exists to support the proposition that *Vidit Iacob* is not by 'Pseudo-Hugo', but is rather a genuine Revelation commentary of Hugh of St Cher.[4] Clearly *Vidit Iacob* must be assigned to a Dominican because it gives precedence to the founder of the Order of Preachers in a hitherto unnoticed reference to 'Saint Dominic and Saint Francis'.[5] Furthermore, assuming that a 'true

---

[2] B. Smalley, 'John Russel O.F.M.', *RTAM*, xxiii (1956), pp. 277–320, at pp. 305–7. *Aser pinguis* was printed in numerous early-modern multi-volume collections of Hugh's biblical commentaries: I have not attempted to locate all of them, but can attest to its appearance in collections of Hugh's *opera* published in Basel, 1498–1502; Basel, 1504; Paris, 1531; Venice, 1600; Cologne, 1621; and Lyons, 1645. In all cases the text is the same, save for insignificant typesetters' variants; fortunately even the foliation is the same in the three last editions I refer to: *Aser pinguis* appearing in all of them at ff. 363–429. Here I will cite the Cologne ed., correcting it when necessary with readings taken from a fourteenth-century MS, BAV, Pal. lat. 96 (prov., Schönau, near Heidelberg, O. Cist). *Vidit Iacob* appears in published form in the nineteenth-century *Opera omnia* of St Thomas Aquinas, ed. Parma (1860–2), xxiii, pp. 325–511, with a reprint, ed. Paris: Vivès (1871–80), xxxi, pp. 469–661, xxxii, pp. 1–86. I will cite from the corrupt Parma edition and correct it with readings taken from a fifteenth-century MS: BAV Pal.lat.297 (prov. Southern Germany).

[3] Beryl Smalley has already properly excluded Hugh of St Victor, who wrote no Revelation commentary. In addition I can exclude the commentaries on Revelation by Nicholas of Gorran (below, nn. 9–10), and 'Pseudo-Albert'—*B. Alberti Magni ... opera omnia*, ed. A. and E. Borgnet (Paris, 1890–9), xxxviii, pp. 465–792—as well as the *Super Apocalypsim* of Geoffroy d'Auxerre, ed. F. Gastaldelli (Rome, 1971), and the three variants of the mid-thirteenth-century Franciscan Revelation commentary as Stegmüller, *Bibl.*, 2961, 2963, 2964. For the last three I consulted respectively: MS Todi 68, BAV, Ross. lat. 470, and Benedictus Bonellus, ed., *Supplementum operum S. Bonaventurae*, 2 vols. (Trent, 1772–3), ii, pp. 5–103.

[4] For reasons which will later become obvious, Hugh's name will appear without quotation marks at this stage.

[5] Ed. Parma, p. 342a; corrected by BAV, Pal. lat. 297, f. 243[ra]: ' ... *sicut beatus Dominicus, beatus Franciscus, beatus Nicolaus ...*'.

Hugh' postill would have circulated very widely, *Vidit Iacob* fills that bill nicely inasmuch as approximately fifty-three medieval manuscript copies of it are known to exist.[6] Moving to the most important point, of these fifty-three copies at least thirteen—from widely diverse provenances—bear medieval attributions to Hugh of St Cher under such guises as 'Hugo', 'Hugo de Vienna' (St Cher was near Vienne), or 'Hugo Cardinalis', weightiest among which are an English attribution dating from around 1300 ('Frater Hugo Predicator') and a Parisian one of the mid-thirteenth century ('Magister Hugo Cardinalis').[7]

---

[6] My count is based initially on the assumption that entries 2727, 3771, and 3772 in Stegmüller all refer to the same postill. Adding the MSS listed by Stegmüller for these entries—minus one on the grounds that Paris Mazarine 155 appears twice—produces a total of forty-two. (Note the following corrections—Stegmüller 2727: for BN 15604, ff. 317–74, read ff. 371^r–74^v; Stegmüller 3771: for Oxford, Bodl. 760, read 716; for Oxford, Oriel College 6, does such a MS with a copy of *Vidit Iacob* really exist?; for Paris, Arsenal 186 (XIV), read (XV).) To this figure one must add seven more MSS, as listed by Kaeppeli, *Scriptores*, ii, p. 274 (Kaeppeli gives eight, but BN lat. 15605 is *Aser pinguis*), thereby reaching forty-nine. Finally, to this number I can add the following four MSS: Naples, Biblioteca Nazionale I. H. 42 (XV): see C. Cenci, *Manoscritti francescani della Biblioteca Nazionale di Napoli*, 2 vols. (Quaracchi/Grottaferrata, 1971), i, pp. 151–2; Oxford, Balliol College 14, ff. 6^r–123^v (XV): see R.A.B. Mynors, *Catalogue of the Manuscripts of Balliol College, Oxford* (Oxford, 1963), pp. 10–11; BN lat. 12030 (XIII): see C. Spicq, *Esquisse d'une histoire de l'exégèse latine au moyen âge* (Paris, 1944), p. 321; and Pisa, Biblioteca Sta Caterina MS 16: see Spicq, p. 321. Virtually all this information comes to me at second hand and some of it may be imperfect: unfortunately Beryl Smalley's call for a critical study of the MS tradition of Hugh of St Cher's postills (*Bible*, p. 271) has not been answered, nor appears likely to be yet.

[7] According to Stegmüller and/or the relevant MS catalogues, medieval hands in the following MSS ascribe *Vidit Iacob* to 'Hugo': Arras 95; Cambridge, Gonville and Caius 244; Cambridge, Trinity College 99; Copenhagen, Gl. Kgl. S. Fol. 48; Hereford Cathedral O. 2,. iii; Kiel, Bordesholm Fol. 64; Oxford, Balliol College 14; Oxford, Bodleian Bodl. 444; Oxford, Bodleian Bodl. 716; Paris, Mazarine 156 (apparently not Mazarine 155, as Stegmüller); Pisa, Sta Caterina 16; BAV Pal. lat. 297. In addition, Nigel Palmer has kindly informed me that Oxford, Bodleian Lat. th. b. 5, p. 827 gives: '*Explicit liber Hugonis de Wyenna ... super Apoc.*'. The English attribution I allude to is in Bodl. 444, and the Parisian one is Mazarine 156. It should finally be added that an inventory of the holdings of the Dominican convent of Perugia made in 1430 lists *Vidit Iacob* as 'postilla domini Ugonis card.': see T. Kaeppeli, *Inventari di libri di San Domenico di Perugia* (Rome, 1962), p. 57 (repeated in inventory of 1446: see p. 97); and St John of Capestrano attributed *Vidit Iacob* to Hugh of Digne, obviously a mistake for Hugh of St Cher: see R. Rusconi, 'La tradizione manoscritta delle opere degli Spirituali nelle biblioteche dei predicatori e dei conventi dell '*Osservanza*', *Picenum Seraphicum*, xii (1975), pp. 63–137, at p. 87.

Nor does the evidence that *Vidit Iacob* must be given to Hugh of St Cher stop there. Rather, in addition to the numerous direct attributions, there are at least six thirteenth-century indirect ones—six thirteenth-century cases, that is, in which *Vidit Iacob* was copied together with one or more other postills by Hugh of St Cher on other books of the Bible. To mention only the earliest datable example, the present Reims MS 165—copied in the Abbey of St Denis, Reims, before 1263—offers *Vidit Iacob* anonymously but presents it after genuine postills by Hugh on Proverbs, the Canticle, and Isaiah: surely the Reims scribe must have assumed he was working on a set of commentaries by the same author.[8]

A final external argument in favour of assigning *Vidit Iacob* to Hugh of St Cher lies in the hitherto unnoticed facts that this postill was drawn upon heavily by the authors of two subsequent thirteenth-century Dominican Revelation commentaries—Nicholas of Gorran and 'Pseudo-Albertus Magnus'. The former's postill, *Cognovit Dominus*, which must be dated to between *c.*1263 and *c.*1285 and localized to Paris, at one point tantalizingly cites 'Hugo'.[9] Alas, however, the passage given comes from neither *Vidit Iacob* nor *Aser pinguis*, but instead comes from the Revelation commentary of 'Pseudo-Albert'.[10] Since Beryl Smalley has already observed that Nicholas misidentified his 'Hugo' in two citations he offered in his commentaries on the Sapiential Books, this false

---

[8] In addition to MS Reims 165, similar thirteenth-century 'indirect attributions' are found in Oxford, Bodleian Laud Misc. 466; BN lat. 15604; Paris, Mazarine 155; Poitiers 22; and Toulouse 55. The first dated appearance of a set of Hugh's postills occurs in 1239, when a sequential collection was copied in the Abbey of Fleury; but as the set now survives (Orléans, MSS 23–30) it goes no further than the Gospels: see R.H. and M.A. Rouse, 'The Verbal Concordance to the Scriptures', *AFP*, xliv (1974), pp. 5–30, at p. 8, n. 11.

[9] Gorran's authorship of *Cognovit Dominus* (Stegmüller, 5810) is firmly established by L. Meier, 'Nicholas de Gorham, O.P., Author of the Commentary on the Apocalypse Erroneously Attributed to John Duns Scotus', *Dominican Studies*, iii (1950), pp. 359–62. My dating and localization are based on the known facts of his scholarly career as reported, for example, by B. Smalley, 'Some Latin Commentaries on the Sapiential Books in the Late Thirteenth and Early Fourteenth Centuries', *AHDLMA*, xviii (1950–1), pp. 103–28, at pp. 106–7.

[10] Cf. Gorran, *Cognovit Dominus*, in *In Acta Apostolorum ... et Apocalypsim Commentarii, authore R.P.F. Nicolao Gorrano ....* (Antwerp, 1620: I use BAV, Barb. A.V.82; another copy is BL, 692 f. 5), p. 187ª: '*Hugo autem dicit ab aurum et calcos malum: quasi malum aurum, quia solum auri colorem habet, non valorem*', with 'Pseudo-Albert' (as above, n.3), p. 493ᵇ: '*Vel aurichalcum dicitur ab auro ... quod est malum, quasi malum aurum, quia habet colorem aureum, non valorem*'.

citation need not cause worry. In fact, as she has shown, Nicholas's postills on the Sapiential Books drew extensively on the genuine Hugh of St Cher postills on the same texts, but always without name.[11] Thus, when we see Nicholas drawing extensively on *Vidit Iacob* in his Revelation commentary—but again always without name—we must assume that he was himself confused about authorship, but had a multi-volume collection of postills at his disposal in St Jacques, to which he attributed great authority, and which all were part of one set by Hugh of St Cher.

As for 'Pseudo-Albert', a recently announced discovery renders it virtually certain that the Revelation postill, *Confitebor tibi* (Stegmüller, *Bibl.*, 1040), published among the works of Albertus Magnus, was really written by Peter of Tarentaise, O.P. (later Pope Innocent V), who would have composed it during his teaching career at St Jacques between 1259 and 1269.[12] Since Peter's Revelation postill also draws on *Vidit Iacob* extensively but without name,[13] its witness would confirm the authority of *Vidit Iacob* within the thirteenth-century Parisian Dominican exegetical tradition. Admittedly, proof that *Vidit Iacob* was considered to be an authoritative source on Revelation in mid-thirteenth-century St

---

[11] Smalley, 'Some Latin Commentaries', p. 109. She makes the same observation here about the citation of Hugh (i.e., 'Hugh' passages not found in the printed postills; real Hugh passages used anonymously) in a postill on Proverbs probably done at St Jacques *c.*1270 by John of Varzy.

[12] Stegmüller, *Tomus VIII: Supplementum*, entry 1745, reports evidence that should end all doubt concerning the authorship of *Confitebor tibi*. For Peter of Tarentaise's teaching career see R. Creytens, 'Pierre de Tarentaise, Professeur à Paris et Prieur Provincial de France', *Beatus Innocentius PP. V (Petrus de Tarantasia O.P.): Studia et Documenta* (Rome, 1943), pp. 73–100, at pp. 83–96. See *Beatus Innocentius*, at pp. 76, 178–9, 238, 366, for evidence that Peter was a disciple of Hugh of St Cher. Even before his studies at St Jacques, Peter received schooling in the Dominican cloister of Lyons (Creytens, pp. 74–6), where he must have come under the influence of Guillaume Pérault, whom I take to have been a member of Hugh of St Cher's Parisian circle: see n. 74, below.

[13] Cf., e.g., Peter, ed. Borgnet, p. 598ᵃ (citation of St Bernard, '*Felix lacryma* ...') with *Vidit Iacob*, ed. Parma, p. 387ᵃ; Peter, ed. Borgnet, 625ᵇ ('*Demonium ereum sermocinalis scientia* ...') with *Vidit Iacob*, ed. Parma, p. 405ᵃ. It should also be recalled that John Russel quoted extensively from *Vidit Iacob* in 1292–3, not naming the author but calling him by the flattering title of *expositor*: see Smalley, 'John Russel O.F.M.', pp. 308–9, and, on the thirteenth-century meaning of *expositor*, Smalley, 'The Gospels in the Paris Schools in the Late Twelfth and Early Thirteenth Centuries, I, II', *Franc Stud*, xxxix (1979), pp. 230–54; xl (1980), pp. 298–369, at xl, p. 327.

Jacques would not constitute proof that *Vidit Iacob*'s author was Hugh of St Cher if taken alone, but combined with the mass of direct and indirect attributions it ought to settle the matter.

What, then, about *Aser pinguis*? By the brute popularity test it runs a poor second—thirteen surviving copies as opposed to *Vidit Iacob*'s fifty-three.[14] Yet three of these attribute *Aser pinguis* to 'Hugo', including one from the late thirteenth century which specifies that *Aser*'s author was 'Hugo Predicator'.[15] Moreover, at least four of the thirteen copies place *Aser pinguis* together with indisputably genuine postills by Hugh of St Cher.[16] And, finally, *Aser pinguis* passes the thirteenth-century Dominican citation test just as well as *Vidit Iacob*. It is true that Nicholas of Gorran did not draw on *Aser pinguis*, but Peter of Tarentaise drew on it heavily,[17] and I have discovered as well that *Aser pinguis* was used by the Strassburg Dominican Hugh Ripelin as a source for his *Compendium theologice veritatis* of c.1265.[18]

[14] My *Aser pinguis* count is based on the assumption (still to be tested) that Stegmüller 3769 and 3770 refer to basically the same text. From the nine MSS listed for 3769, BN 12030 has to be subtracted because it apparently contains *Vidit Iacob*; but it can be replaced by Cambridge, Gonville and Caius 244, ff. 57–122. It might be noted that at least three of the surviving total of *Aser* MSS are of German or Austrian Cistercian provenance: Erlangen 30; Heiligenkreuz 206; and BAV, Pal. lat. 96.

[15] See Erlangen MS 30 ('Hugo Predicator'); Cambridge, Gonville and Caius MS 244; Prague, University Library MS 1857.

[16] Cambridge, Gonville and Caius 244; Erlangen 30; BN lat. 156; Toulouse 24: the last three date from the thirteenth century.

[17] Peter's borrowings from *Aser pinguis* have already been amply documented by I.-M. Vosté, O.P., 'S. Albertus in Apocalypsim', *Angelicum*, ix (1932), pp. 328–35. Vosté, however, goes too far in branding the author of *Confitebor tibi* 'plagiarius Hugonis a S. Caro' pure and simple because—aside from Peter's borrowings from *Vidit Iacob* (above, n. 13) that show him picking and choosing rather than slavishly copying—he misses Peter's genuine originality, especially in the presentation of *dubitabilia* at the end of each chapter, which lend Peter's work its own distinctive character. (Vosté was unaware that in belittling the author of *Confitebor tibi* he was belittling his Order's first pope.) D.M. Solomon, 'The Sentence Commentary of Richard Fishacre and the Apocalypse Commentary of Hugh of St Cher', *AFP*, xlvi (1976), pp. 367–77, argues that Richard Fishacre's Sentence commentary of 1241–5 borrows from *Aser pinguis*, but in fact Fishacre's *quidam expositor super Apoc.*, whom Solomon takes to be the author of *Aser pinguis* (pp. 369–72), is Haimo of Auxerre (see *PL* cxvii, 1070–5; note too that whenever Nicholas of Gorran refers to the *expositor* on Revelation he means Haimo).

[18] Ripelin, *Compendium*, ed. A. Borgnet,   *Aser pinguis*, ed. Cologne, ff. 390ra, B. *Alberti Magni ... opera omnia*   399va–vb (Paris, 1890–9), xxxiv, p. 245^a

From the foregoing it can easily be seen that either *Vidit Iacob* or *Aser pinguis* would comfortably be accepted as Hugh's Revelation postill by modern scholarship if it were not for the disconcerting existence of the other. Faced with the awkward presence of the surplus text, several twentieth-century scholars have been inclined to leave *Aser pinguis* to Hugh, in accordance with the *Opera omnia* tradition, and tentatively assign *Vidit Iacob* to Hugh's near contemporary, Guerric of St Quentin, who was regent at St Jacques from 1233 to 1242.[19] But this simply will not do, for not only was *Vidit Iacob* widely attributed to Hugh of St Cher, but it was never once during the Middle Ages attributed to Guerric; nor does any medieval evidence concerning Guerric's works include mention of a Revelation commentary.[20]

Quantum autem spatium sit inter illos quadragintaquinque dies et finem mundi nemo sit	*Quantum vero spatium sit inter illos quadragintaduos* [MS BAV, Pal. lat. 96, f. 33ra: xlv] *dies et finem mundi nemo scit ....*
Judei vero tunc convertentur ad fidem	*Tunc enim omnes Iudei convertentur ad fidem Christi*
et sancta ecclesia usque ad finem pacificata quiescet	*et sancta ecclesia, quasi dimidie hore silentio, sc. tempore quod sequitur usque ad finem mundi, pacificata quiescet* [MS BAV, Pal. lat. 96, f. 44vb: conquiescet]
quia tunc fraudulentia et sevitia diaboli penitus ubique deficiet	*quia extunc fraudulentia et sevitia diaboli penitus deficiet*

Ripelin's treatment of Gog and Magog also follows *Aser pinguis*: cf. Ripelin, ed. Borgnet, xxxiv, pp. 243–4, with *Aser pinguis*, ed. Cologne, f. 421a. Note that G. Steer, *Hugo Ripelin von Strassburg* (Tübingen, 1981), pp. 237–8, independently suspected the influence of Hugh of St Cher on bk i of Ripelin's *Compendium*: most likely Ripelin owned and used a set of Hugh's postills that ended with *Aser pinguis*. In my 'Refreshment of the Saints: the Time after Antichrist as a Station for Progress in Medieval Thought', *Traditio*, xxxii (1976), pp. 97–144, at p. 122, I mistakenly credited Hugh Ripelin with originality for lines actually borrowed from Hugh of St Cher.

[19] P. Glorieux, *Repertoire des maîtres en théologie de Paris au XIIIe siècle*, 2 vols. (Paris, 1933–4), p. 56; Spicq, p. 291, n. 3; Stegmüller, *Bibl.*, 2727; Solomon, p. 377.

[20] Stegmüller, *Bibl.*, 2727 (following Glorieux) misleadingly gives 'Guerricus?' for BN, MS lat. 15604, but in fact this MS does not offer any attribution for *Vidit Iacob*, and presents it after the genuine Hugh of St Cher postill on Luke, reporting it as such, f. 370v: '*Expliciunt postille Sancte Lucam secundum fratrem Hugonem de*

Hence we are inevitably left with one conclusion: that both *Vidit Iacob* and *Aser pinguis* must be accepted as genuine Revelation postills belonging to the corpus of Hugh of St Cher. This finding is not entirely new, for oral tradition reports that Fr. M. Perrier, O.P. (1908–81) came to the conclusion from his unpublished research that Hugh's enormous corpus actually includes two postills on every book of the Bible.[21] Moreover, in arguing specifically that both *Vidit Iacob* and *Aser pinguis* were by Hugh of St Cher I have one illustrious predecessor: namely, the fifteenth-century Cambridge doctor of theology John Beverley (Fellow of Gonville Hall *c.*1425–41) who wrote that his multi-volume collection of Hugh's postill's ending with *Aser pinguis* and *Vidit Iacob* (in that order) contained *Viena super ... Apocalipsim bis.*[22]

If it is granted that both *Aser pinguis* and *Vidit Iacob* were by Hugh of St Cher, which came first? Fortunately, *Aser*'s temporal precedence can be established by the following demonstration that

---

Ordine Fratrum Predicatorum' (I am grateful to Professor E.A.R. Brown for having looked at this MS for me). The most exhaustive study of Guerric's works remains F.M. Henquinet, 'Les écrits du Frère Guerric de Saint-Quentin, O.P.', *RTAM*, vi (1934), pp. 184–214, and 'Notes additionnelles sur les écrits de Guerric de Saint-Quentin', *RTAM*, viii (1936), pp. 369–88: Henquinet knows nothing of a Revelation commentary for Guerric. Note finally that any perceived similarities between the content of *Vidit Iacob* and Guerric's genuine exegetical work could easily be explained on the grounds that Hugh of St Cher's postills notoriously took ideas from wherever they found them (what Beryl Smalley calls Hugh's 'paste-and-scissors method'), or even that Guerric contributed to the composition of *Vidit Iacob* as a 'team member' (see below); on the other hand, however, *Vidit Iacob* and Guerric's Isaiah commentary—as described by B. Smalley, 'A Commentary on Isaias by Guerric of Saint-Quentin, O.P.', *Miscellanea Giovanni Mercati*, 6 vols. (*ST*, cxxi–cxxvi) ii, pp. 383–97—are fundamentally different in conception, *Vidit Iacob* being characterized by an extraordinary proliferation of moralities, but Guerric's Isaiah commentary 'keeping to the work of exegesis' and restraining itself in the employment of digressive moralizations.

[21] I was told this by Fr. L.-J. Bataillon, O.P. Presumably drawing on the same unpublished research by Fr. Perrier, Beryl Smalley reports in 'The Gospels in the Paris Schools, I', p. 250, that Hugh's '*Postilla super Totam Bibliam* survives in two versions, a longer and a shorter. The longer is printed in early editions'. Assuming that *Aser pinguis* and *Vidit Iacob* are both by Hugh, they provide an exception to the latter rule, for *Aser*, printed in the early-modern editions, is the shorter of the two.

[22] For Cambridge, Gonville and Caius College MS 244, see M.R. James, *A Descriptive Catalogue of the Manuscripts in the Library of Gonville and Caius College*, 2 vols. (Cambridge, 1907–8), i, p. 295. On Beverley himself, *BRUC*, p. 60.

its author borrowed from the twelfth-century Revelation commentary of Richard of St Victor, and *Vidit Iacob* in turn from *Aser*:

Richard of St Victor, *In Apocalypsim (PL* cxcvi, 795A)	*Aser pinguis* (Cologne, 1621), f. 399vb	*Vidit Iacob*, BAV, MS Pal. lat. 297, f. 311vb
Iam dicitur non fiet, sed factum est, quia extunc fraudulentia et sevitia diaboli penitus deficiet et Deus in suis fidelibus universis perpetua pace et tranquillitate regnabit.	*Et propter hoc etiam dicitur hic* factum est, *et non fiet, quia extunc fraudulentia et sevitia diaboli penitus deficiet et in suis fidelibus universis Deus perpetua pace et tranquillitate regnabit.*	*Sed dicitur tunc finis eorum, quia fraudulentia et sevitia diaboli, que diu regnavit in mundo, penitus deficiet et Deus in suis fidelibus in tranquillitate et pace perpetua regnabit.*

Better still, it is possible to attach reasonably firm dates to both of the Hugh of St Cher commentaries. I shall argue later that *Aser pinguis* can be dated *c.*1236, because it must have been written during the height of the Parisian plurality of benefices controversy. As for *Vidit Iacob*, preliminary *termini* for its composition are July 1234, because of its recognition of the canonization of St Dominic, and 1263, because of its appearance in Reims MS 165. But greater precision than this is attainable because of a revealing allusion made in *Vidit Iacob* to the missionary successes achieved by 'the preaching of the modern preachers'.[23] Specifically, *Vidit Iacob* exults in the

---

[23] Ed. Parma, p. 470^b, corrected by BAV, Pal. lat. 297, f. 363vb: '*Talis terremotus sic magnus respicit hoc tempus presens, in quo multi ad predicationem modernorum predicatorum sunt conversi ad fidem. Nam de solis Cumanis conversi sunt ad fidem, et baptizati in duobus vel tribus annis, i.e. in modico tempore, centum millia. Multi etiam de Georgianis, etiam de Barberia, multi de Africa, multi heretici, et quamplures de aliis partibus mundi. Nam per gratiam Dei fere ad omnes predicatur modo Evangelium Domino nostri Iesu Christi*'. *Vidit Iacob*'s proud reference to the accomplishments of the 'modern preachers' almost certainly refers to the Dominicans, for the Cumans were converted, *c.*1227–30, by Dominican efforts: see on this, J. Richard, *La papauté et les missions d'Orient au moyen âge (XIIIe–XVe siècles)* (Paris, 1977), pp. 24–5. *Vidit Iacob*'s implicit naming of Hugh's Order links up with its explicit naming of St Dominic and St Francis as martyrs before St Nicholas (see quotation above, n. 5) and provides noteworthy contrast to Beryl Smalley's observation that in the Gospel postills 'Hugh never mentions either his Order or its founder' (Smalley, 'Gospels in the Paris Schools, II', p. 311).

conversion of 'many Georgians', yet says nothing about the Mongols: almost certainly the Georgian 'conversion' alludes to the Georgian acknowledgement of Roman primacy in 1240, and the foundation of a Dominican convent in Tiflis in the same year, while lack of reference to the Mongols suggests a *terminus ante quem* of *c.*1250, for by then Dominican and Franciscan missionaries had made sufficient inroads to allow Adam Marsh to write that news of the Tartar conversions had 'spread across the world'.[24] Hugh of St Cher's promotion to the cardinalate in May of 1244 must finally narrow the dates down still further, because Hugh definitely remained associated in some way or another with scholarly work at St Jacques while he was Dominican Provincial of France from 1236 to 1244, but as cardinal he left the realm of formal scholarly activity for good.[25] Taking all these indicators into consideration, it appears warranted to assign *Vidit Iacob*'s composition to the period between late 1240 and early 1244.

Proceeding to matters of content, it is evident that *Vidit Iacob* represents a thoroughgoing revision of *Aser pinguis*.[26] The two texts are very similar, but *Vidit Iacob* continually appears to be moderating extreme positions taken in *Aser pinguis*, while frequently adding new material and developing more prudent positions of its own. These tendencies may be viewed initially by comparing the expressions and attitudes of the two commentaries to Greek philosophy. Simply stated, *Aser pinguis* emerges as being more ardently pro-philosophical, and *Vidit Iacob* more formally 'scholastic' and 'correct'. The compiler of *Aser pinguis* establishes his receptive position towards philosophy early in his exposition when he comments on the Lord's use of Greek in the saying 'ego sum *alpha* et *omega*' (*Rev.*, i. 8). Christ uses Greek here rather than

---

[24] On the Georgian events, Richard, p. 55; on the mendicant missions to the Mongols and Adam Marsh's boast, *ibid.*, pp. 70–80.

[25] On Hugh's extraordinarily energetic activities as cardinal, J.H.H. Sassen, *Hugo von St. Cher, seine Tätigkeit als Kardinal 1244–1263* (Bonn, 1908).

[26] The same conclusion was reached by Solomon, pp. 373–7, primarily on the grounds of passages other than those upon which I comment here. Spicq, p. 321, mistakenly states that the conclusions of both commentaries are identical; but they are indeed very close. I should make clear here that neither *Aser pinguis* nor *Vidit Iacob* was transmitted as a *reportatio*, for both speak consistently in the first person: *Aser*, ed. Cologne, e.g., f. 382[vb]: '*ut diximus*'; *Vidit Iacob*, as Smalley, 'John Russel', pp. 302, 309.

Hebrew, *Aser pinguis* states, 'because wisdom literally began in
Greece and with the Greeks'. Moreover, Christ wanted men to
know that 'not only knowledge of Divine Scripture comes from
God, but also the knowledge of the philosophers'.[27] This passage is
missing in *Vidit Iacob*, and indeed seems counteracted by two
passages found there but not in *Aser pinguis*. In one, *Vidit Iacob*'s
compiler states that 'Jonathan's arrow', designed for Christian
students, is not 'Aristotle, or Plato, or any other inane philosophy',
and in the other he denigrates philosophy even more by branding it
as the source of heresy.[28]

If there is any doubt that *Vidit Iacob*'s omission of *Aser*'s praise of
Greek philosophy was motivated by a difference in attitude towards the subject, it should be removed by a comparison of the
following passage on philosophers, glossing *Revelation*, viii. 8,
which appears in both commentaries but differs in essentials:

Aser pinguis (Cologne,
1621), f. 392va

*Horum tres sunt partes. Quia eorum
quidam per bona naturalia preparati
fuerunt ut reciperent gratiam fidei,
sicut Dionysius et multi alii Philosophi. Alii per auditum honeste doctrine Apostolorum. Tertii vero nec sic
nec sic.*

Vidit Iacob (ed. Parma)
p. 393a

*Horum tres sunt partes. Una pars per
solam diligentiam et inspirationem divinam fuerunt conversi. Alia pars per
auditum predicationis. Tertia pars nec
sic nec sic.*

We can see that *Aser pinguis* reiterates its highly positive evaluation of Greek philosophy by stating that 'Dionysius' and *many other*

---

[27] Ed. Cologne, f. 367va: '*Item Grecis et non Hebreis quia ad literam sapientia incepit in
Grecis et a Grecis. Item ut sciremus quia non solum scientia divinarum Scripturarum est a
Deo, sed etiam scientia philosophorum;* Eccl. 1a: "*Omnis sapientia a Domino Deo est*"'.
This passage is taken over in the Revelation postill by Peter of Tarentaise: see ed.
A. and E. Borgnet, p. 488a.

[28] Ed. Parma, p. 373b: '*Non quas jacit Aristoteles, vel Plato, vel inanis quelibet philosophia
... Quia studendum est ad honorem Dei, non ad lucrum mundi vel laudem hominum*'. Also
Parma, p. 458a: '*Et super fontes aquarum, i.e. super philosophos, a quibus sunt orte
insipide doctrine et varie unde heretici originem duxerunt; Et factus est sanguis, i.e.
occisio sanctorum, vel doctrina hereticorum et philosophorum*'. Although Peter of
Tarentaise and Nicholas of Gorran both drew on *Vidit Iacob*, neither of them
appropriated either of these passages.

philosophers were prepared by *natural* gifts to receive the grace of faith (note the foreshadowing of St Thomas!), whereas *Vidit Iacob* says nothing about Dionysius or 'many philosophers', and instead of praising natural gifts refers to divine diligence and inspiration as the source of some philosophers' conversion. Perhaps most striking is *Vidit Iacob*'s omission of reference to 'Dionysius', who, according to thirteenth-century French lore, was at once the Athenian who 'clave' to St Paul 'and believed' (*Acts*, xvii. 34), the author of what today is known as the Pseudo-Dionysian corpus, and finally, 'St Denis', the patron saint of France. For *Aser*'s compiler it was entirely appropriate that this revered figure began his career as a Greek philosopher endowed with natural gifts, but the reviser behind *Vidit Iacob* clearly decided that St Denis's memory should not be so profaned.[29]

If *Vidit Iacob* censored *Aser pinguis* regarding the natural dignity of philosophy, *Vidit Iacob* certainly was more conventionally scholastic in its methods and citations, presumably because its compiler wished to follow the fashions of the times. The clearest example of this can be seen in *Vidit Iacob*'s appropriation of the four Aristotelian causes. Beryl Smalley has previously emphasized that Hugh of St Cher's printed postill on Isaiah employed a division based on a late twelfth-century moralizing system associated with Stephen Langton, whereas the slightly later Guerric of St Quentin looked more to the scholastic future in his Isaiah commentary by employing the Aristotelian system of four causes.[30] If we compare *Aser pinguis* and *Vidit Iacob* on this subject, we can see that the former alludes in passing to the four causes, but does not use them prominently, whereas the latter uses them as a principle of division much as Guerric did on Isaiah.[31] Hence it seems likely that the

---

[29] Of the two texts it may be that *Aser* is more 'Hugh-like' inasmuch as Hugh quotes Dionysius in his *Questio de prophetia* (see ed. J.-P. Torrell, *Théorie de la prophétie et philosophie de la connaissance aux environs de 1230: la contribution d'Hugues de Saint-Cher* (Louvain, 1977), p. 8), in his postill on John (see Smalley, 'The Gospels in the Paris Schools, II', p. 309), and at least once in *Aser pinguis* itself: see ed. Cologne, f. 363ra. Peter of Tarentaise accepts *Aser*'s reading here rather than *Vidit Iacob*'s: see ed. Borgnet, p. 607[a]. On Pseudo-Dionysius in thirteenth-century Paris, see H.-F. Dondaine, *Le corpus dionysien de l'Université de Paris au XIIIe siècle* (Rome, 1953).

[30] Smalley, 'A Commentary on Isaias', p. 390.

[31] *Aser*, ed. Cologne, 1621, f. 411ra: '*Unde li in notat hic causam efficientem*'; *Vidit Iacob*'s Aristotelian disposition appears in its opening lines: '*Quattuor sunt cause huius operis, sc. efficiens, materialis, formalis, finalis*'.

compiler of *Vidit Iacob* was trying to demonstrate that he could be *au courant* of the Parisian fashions.

Similarly, *Vidit Iacob*'s author rewrote a passage in *Aser pinguis* to highlight his preference for logic among the studies of the *trivium*,[32] and though he denigrated Aristotle by name once, in another passage he singled out the 'false philosophers' as 'Plato and Pythagoras', sparing Aristotle.[33] Apparently wishing to show that he had really absorbed the wisdom of 'the Philosopher', he cited him approvingly three times. As it happens, all three of *Vidit Iacob*'s citations of Aristotle are bogus (i.e., none comes from a genuinely Aristotelian work[34]), but with an Aristotelian tide beginning to flow at Paris the presence behind *Vidit Iacob* apparently tried to swim with it as best he could.

Aser pinguis's receptive attitude towards Greek philosophy is remarkable enough, but when reading the commentary on the main subjects of this article—its treatment of poverty, preaching, and eschatology—one can hardly trust one's eyes, for a pristine mendicant fervour pervades *Aser pinguis* that one would hardly expect to find in schoolbook exegesis. We may plunge in at a point where *Aser*'s author excoriates contemporary pluralists in moraliz-

---

[32] *Aser pinguis*, ed. Cologne, f. 395ᵛᵇ

| |
demonium ereum est sermocinalis scientia, que est in trivio contenta

Vidit Iacob, ed. Parma, p. 405ᵃ, corrected by MS BAV, Pal. lat. 297, f. 300ʳᵇ

demonium ereum est sermocinalis scientia, i.e. logica, que plus aliis sonat, immo etiam quasi mute essent alie nisi ab ista reciperent sonum

Note that Peter of Tarentaise, who knew both texts, chose to follow *Vidit Iacob* here (ed. Borgnet, p. 625ᵇ).

[33] Ed. Parma, p. 405ᵃ: '*Vel capita eorum sunt doctores falsorum philosophorum, sc. Plato, Pythagoras, et huiusmodi*'.

[34] The first, ed. Parma p. 328ᵃ, reads: '*Hic enim duplici modo acquiritur scientia, sc. per inventionem studendo aut per doctrinam audiendo, ut dicit Philosophus*'; this does not appear in *Auctoritates Aristotelis, 1. Concordance*, ed. J. Hamesse (Louvain, 1972) and I am unaware of its real source. The second, ed. Parma, p. 346ᵃ—'*Propter hoc dicit Philosophus: "Utinam inspiciendo mulieres aut lynceos oculos haberemus, aut nullos"*'—comes by way of Boethius, *Consolation of Philosophy*, bk. iii, prose 8. The third, ed. Parma p. 385ᵃ—'*Philosophus: "Sapientia est hominis sui ipsius cognitio"*'—appears to derive ultimately from the Jewish physician Isaak b. Solomon (†c.933); cf. Dominicus Gundissalinus, *De divisione philosophiae*, ed. L. Baur (Münster, 1903), p. 7: '*philosophia est integra cognitio hominis de se ipso*', and Baur's commentary, p. 176.

ing on the text 'I will put upon you no other burden' (*Rev.*, ii. 24):

> If only all bishops would say just this to those having many prebends! For a single prebend is a burden if they would attend to it well, but another prebend is another burden. Yet many say: 'have no fear my lord, give me many burdens, for I am strong and can carry them easily'. Indeed you are strong—like an ass in his hindparts, i.e., temporal things. But in your foreparts, i.e., spiritualities, you are weak .... Such are even worse than the wolf, who is said to be weak in his hindparts but strong in his foreparts.[35]

Doubtless this diatribe reads like a passage from a very daring sermon rather than an extract from an exegetical reference work, but in *Aser pinguis* such outbreaks are by no means rare. Indeed, even at this point the 'preacher' has not finished, for in glossing the succeeding line—'that which you have, hold fast' (*Rev.*, ii. 25)—he reaches a still more fervent pitch:

> Whatever they may say to you, these words are taken approvingly by them [pluralists] regarding the holding of many prebends. For such know not how to say that it is a sin. ... *Hold fast*: this is against absentees who wish to draw fruits when they do not deserve them. But these say 'we can hold on well because we have long hands, for we are sons of noblemen', adducing this doctrine of Ovid in the Church of God. 'Don't you know that long hands are signs of royalty?' But whenever they say this they are really citing *Canticles*, i: 'they made me the keeper of the vineyards, but mine own vineyard have I not kept'.[36]

---

[35] Ed. Cologne, f. 373vb: '*Utinam sic dicerent omnes Episcopi habentibus plures prebendas. Pondus enim est una prebenda si bene attenderent, sed aliud pondus est alia prebenda. Sed dicunt multi: "non curetis domine, date mihi multa pondera, fortis sum, bene possum portare illa". Verum dicis fortis es, ut asinus in posterioribus, i.e. in terrenis, sed in anterioribus, i.e. spiritualibus, debilis. ... Tales etiam peiores sunt lupo, de quo dicitur quod in posterioribus sit debilis, sed fortis in anterioribus*'. In BAV, Pal. lat. 96, f. 15va, a fifteenth-century hand from the Cistercian monastery of Schönau adds marginally: '*Utinam sic dicerent Cardinales et Episcopi nepotibus*'.

[36] Ed. Cologne, f. 376: '*Quicquid dicant vobis, verba sunt consulentium sibi invicem de habendo plures prebendas. Nesciunt quidem dicere quod sit peccatum ... Tenete: Hoc est contra absentes qui volent percipere fructus et non deserviunt. Sed dicunt ipsi "bene possumus tenere, quia longas habemus manus: sumus enim filii nobilium", illam doctrinam*

Unquestionably these philippics against pluralism must be read within the context of the controversy on the plurality of benefices that swept Paris between 1235 and 1238. Always simmering within the high-medieval Church, the issue of pluralism boiled over in Paris with the arrival of the mendicants. Wedded to poverty, these regarded the holding of multiple benefices for the sake of added income as an intolerable scandal. In the event, it was none other than the Dominican theological regent, Hugh of St Cher himself, who launched the mendicant attack on pluralism in the spring of 1235 by proposing in a formal *questio disputata* that 'no one is able to hold two benefices without mortal sin if one suffices for food and clothing'.[37] Although it might seem as if defending pluralism would have been like defending matricide, Hugh surprisingly met with some resistance from representatives of the Parisian secular clergy—most prominently the Cathedral Chancellor, Philip (†1236). Thus it was only in 1238, when the Bishop of Paris convoked all the Parisian masters of theology to pronounce upon pluralism in the chapter-room of the Dominican convent of St Jacques, that the controversy was laid to rest. Probably the announced venue itself suggested the outcome. At any rate, when the Bishop formally ruled on the theologians' advice that 'no one can hold two benefices as long as one is worth 15 Parisian pounds', it was a Dominican triumph.

Beryl Smalley has already reported that Hugh's published post-ills on Luke and John contain attacks on pluralism.[38] Yet these lack the fever pitch of those found in *Aser pinguis*. Given that Hugh postillated the books of the Bible in canonical order, it seems likely that his Gospel postills originated *c.*1235, and *Aser pinguis* roughly a year later, when the pluralism controversy was at its height.[39] On

---

Ovidii adducentes in ecclesiam Dei. "An nescis longas regibus esse manus?" Sed aliquando dicent ipsi, illud Cant. 1b: "Posuerunt me custodem in vineis, vineam meam non custodivi".

[37] For this and the Parisian plurality of benefices controversy, see F. Stegmüller, 'Die neugefundene Pariser Benefizien Disputation des Kardinals Hugo von St. Cher O.P.', *HJb*, lxxii (1953), pp. 176–204.

[38] 'Gospels in the Paris Schools, II', pp. 315–16.

[39] The dating raises the question as to whether Hugh's association with biblical scholarship continued after he left his theological regency late in 1235 for the position of Dominican Provincial of France. In my view the answer certainly has to be 'yes', not only because his *Vidit Iacob* has to be dated after 1240 on grounds

that reconstruction, the Hugh of *Aser* appears to have decided in the
heat of battle that no invective was too strong, and hence did not
shrink from calling pluralists 'asses' and highborn but shameless
'Ovidians'. Most likely in addressing 'bishops' he was implicitly
appealing to the Bishop of Paris. Once the Bishop actually stepped
in, however, the issue was over, and *Aser*'s shrillness must have
seemed inappropriate. Hence it is not surprising that in *Vidit Iacob*
the diatribes against pluralism have disappeared.

Religious who did not adhere strictly to their vows of poverty
were also exposed to *Aser*'s wrath. Of the three religious vows of
chastity, obedience, and poverty, the last alone was being openly
'smitten' [flouted] in *Aser*'s day.[40] Nor did *Aser*'s author care for
ecclesiastical administrators, finding them to be 'avaricious and
unlearned' as a class.[41] Again, both passages were too inflammatory
for *Vidit Iacob*'s compiler. Thus he cut out *Aser*'s lament about the
flouting of poverty and rewrote the passage about administrators to
divest it of its provoking insults.[42]

Nonetheless, poverty was so fundamental a first principle of
early Dominican ideology that *Vidit Iacob* did not invariably
suppress or mute *Aser pinguis*'s commitment to it: indeed, in one
ringingly rhetorical passage *Vidit Iacob* expanded on *Aser* rather
than censored it. Beryl Smalley's work again provides helpful
background, for she finds greater 'tenderness towards poverty' in
Hugh's published Gospel postills than anything displayed by

explained above, but also because the St Jacques biblical *correctorium* associated
with his name was still unfinished at the time of the Dominican General Chapter
of 1236: see on the latter, G.G. Sölch, *Hugo von St. Cher O.P. und die Anfänge der
Dominikanertheologie* (Cologne, 1938), p. 14.

[40] Ed. Cologne, ff. 392vb–393ra: '*Per stellas* [*Rev.*, viii. 12] *religiosi, quorum tres partes
sunt tria vota: continentie, obedientie, paupertatis. Prima ac secunda adhuc ita aperte non
est percussa; sed tertia, sc. paupertas, est aperte percussa. Omnes enim iam divites volunt
fieri, et propter hoc incedunt in tentationes et in laqueos diaboli*'. The essence of this
passage is retained by Peter of Tarentaise: see ed. Borgnet, p. 609^b.

[41] Ed. Cologne, f. 392vb: '*Per lunam* [*Rev.*, viii. 12] *medii prelati ecclesie intelliguntur,
quorum sunt tres partes. Prima cura temporalium, secunda administratio sacramentorum,
tertia administratio pastus, vel temporalis vel spiritualis. Sed hec tertia pars percutitur, quia
ipsi sunt et avari et inscii*'. This is also retained, though muted, by Peter of
Tarentaise: see ed. Borgnet, p. 609^b.

[42] Ed. Parma, p. 395^a: '*Per lunam clerici designantur. ... Horum autem sunt tres partes:
nam alii scholares qui frequentant scholas, alii sunt chorales, qui sequuntur chorum, alii
curiales, qui sequuntur curias principum et prelatorum. Et hec tertia pars fere tota percussa
est, et utinam non mortua*'.

Hugh's Parisian Franciscan contemporaries Alexander of Hales and John of La Rochelle in theirs.[43] Yet adjurations that appear in Hugh's Gospel exegesis, such as 'he who preaches poverty lies, unless he be poorly clad' seem mild in comparison to what we find in both *Aser pinguis* and *Vidit Iacob*. According to both, the 'flood of the dragon's mouth' in *Revelation*, xii (15–16) can be understood as temporal wealth—flooding because of its abundance and fluid in its impermanence. This very flood was infused into the Church by the 'dragon' (i.e., Satan) when Constantine endowed the Church with temporal rule over the Western Empire. According to *Aser pinguis*, the flood let loose by the Donation of Constantine was certainly poisonous, since nothing comes from a dragon except poison, whereas *Vidit Iacob* went further in stating that in addition to poison a dragon emits hissing—temporalities being 'hissing' because they dissipate so quickly. Both commentaries agreed, however, on what might be called the punch line: that since the dragon's temporalities were poisonous it was entirely fitting that when Constantine granted his Donation, angelic voices were heard in the air lamenting that 'today poison has been poured into the Church'.[44]

The full account of the Donation of Constantine story in *Aser pinguis* and *Vidit Iacob* has never been noticed, and is significant because of its date and context. Gerald of Wales told the story shortly before 1200, but in a weaker version which had the devil rather than an angel uttering the portentous words; and Walther von der Vogelweide set it to verse in the first decade of the

---

[43] 'Gospels in the Paris Schools, II', pp. 314–15, 365.

[44] *Aser*'s version appears in ed. Cologne at f. 403ra, but since *Vidit Iacob*'s is fuller I give it here, correcting ed. Parma, pp. 430^{b}–1^{a}, with BAV, Pal. lat. 297, f. 324$^{ra–b}$: '*Vel per* aquam fluminis *significatur abundantia terrenorum, que fluunt continue sicut aqua* .... *Et de hac aqua fluminis ... significat abundantiam quam misit draco Domino permittente in ecclesiam Dei, quando Constantino datum est imperium occidentalis ecclesie. Et signanter dicit, quod "draco sive serpens ex ore suo misit aquam post mulierem"* [*Rev.*, xii. 15]. *Quia ex ore serpentis non exit nisi sibilus et venenum. Et ista temporalia non sunt nisi sibilus unus, quia cito transeunt, et plena sunt vento vanitatis et litis. Et etiam venenosa sunt, quia bibentes occidunt. Unde tunc audita fuit vox angelorum in aere dicentium, "hodie infusum* [MS; *effusum*] *est venenum in ecclesia Dei", sicut legitur in Apocrifo Sylvestri. Et iam appropinquat venenum ad cor ecclesie*'. Both Peter of Tarentaise and Nicholas of Gorran refrained from telling the Donation of Constantine story in their respective Revelation postills that otherwise drew heavily on *Aser pinguis* and *Vidit Iacob*.

thirteenth century, but in German.[45] Excluding these cases, the only presently known Latin account of the story that antedates its appearance in *Aser pinguis* is one included by Odo of Cheriton in his Canticle commentary of 1226.[46] But Odo's commentary was written outside Paris and had a very limited manuscript circulation, whereas *Aser pinguis* and *Vidit Iacob* were read by thousands. Moreover, an account of the Donation of Constantine story by the Dominican Guillaume Pérault, which must have been related to its appearance in *Aser pinguis*, was also read by thousands.[47] Thus it was almost certainly the appearance of the angelic lament in Hugh of St Cher's exegesis that helped ensure its subsequent popularity.

'Poison in the Church', said Hugh about temporalities, but 'poison in the Church' must surely have been the response of many among the established ecclesiastical ranks when they witnessed the friars streaming into Europe's cities and towns to preach their uncompromising gospel, and inevitably embarrass the traditionalists in so doing.[48] Yet much as the traditionalists may have balked, the friars possessed the momentum, as may be seen from *Aser pinguis*'s

---

[45] G. Laehr, *Die konstantinische Schenkung in der abendländischen Literatur des Mittelalters* (Berlin, 1926), pp. 72, 76; Smalley, 'Gospels in the Paris Schools, I', p. 245, n.29.

[46] J. Leclercq, 'Hélinand de Froidmont ou Odon de Cheriton?' *AHDLMA*, xxxii (1965), pp. 61–69, at p. 65. On Odo's activity *c.* 1226, Albert C. Friend, 'Master Odo of Cheriton', *Speculum*, xxxii (1948), pp. 641–58, at pp. 649, 655.

[47] C.T. Davis called attention to the appearance of the story in Pérault's *Summa de vitiis* in *Speculum*, l (1975), p. 349. It appears in tr. iv, pars II, ch. 11, as in Guilelmus Peraldus, *Summae virtutum ac vitiorum*, 2 vols. (Antwerp, 1571), ii, f. 83^r: '*Sed magis occupata est hodie ecclesia in temporalibus quo ad magnam partem sui, quam fuerit synagoga, unde quando datum fuit a Constantino occidentale imperium, facta est vox de celo, dicens: "Hodie infusum est venenum ecclesie Dei"*'. Pérault, who came from the same area around Lyons as did Hugh of St Cher, studied at St Jacques from *c.*1236–40 and wrote his *Summa de vitiis* during that period (in one thirteenth-century MS it is dated to 1236): see A. Dondaine, 'Guillaume Peyraut: Vie et oeuvres', *AFP*, xviii (1948), pp. 162–236, at pp. 171–2, 186–7. His knowledge of the story, then, must have come from its having been discussed at St Jacques around the time it appeared in *Aser pinguis*. Cf. n. 74, below.

[48] Evidence of such hostility is presented by H. Grundmann, *Religiöse Bewegungen im Mittelalter* (Berlin, 1935, repr. Hildesheim, 1961), pp. 153–6, and J.B. Freed, *The Friars and German Society in the Thirteenth Century* (Cambridge, Mass., 1977), pp. 88–90. Yet there is also plenty of evidence for a generous reception of the friars by prominent members of the secular clergy: see Lerner, 'Weltklerus und religiöse Bewegung im 13. Jahrhundert', *Archiv für Kulturgeschichte*, li (1969), pp. 94–108, and Leclercq, pp. 67–9.

stinging rebuke to those who tried to impede the public preaching of the new orders. Glossing *Revelation*, vii. 1—'I saw four angels ... holding the four winds of the earth'....—the author of *Aser pinguis* strayed from his text to say that 'demons attempt to impede these winds and the men who aid them are members of the Devil'. Such in particular are those who try to impede the free preaching of the mendicants in echoing the evil Amaziah's words to Amos: 'O thou seer, go flee thee away into the land of Judah ... But prophesy not again any more in Bethel, for it is the king's chapel, and it is the king's court' (*Amos*, vii. 12–13).

For the author of *Aser pinguis*, the contemporary relevance of the passage from Amos was clear. When Amaziah said 'flee to the land of Judah', he spoke like contemporaries who said to the friars 'preach in your own cloisters'; when he said 'no more in Bethel', he foreshadowed those who said 'not in my own parish'; and when he said 'it is the king's chapel, and it is the king's court', he was like those who said 'I am king and lord here', or 'since my church is a cathedral, it is a royal house and the poor should not preach in such a royal dwelling'. But *Aser*'s author had an answer ready for those who forbade the friars from preaching, which was just that of Amos to Amaziah: 'Because of this the Lord saith: "Thy wife shall be an harlot in the city and thy sons and thy daughters shall fall by the sword, and thy land shall be divided by line; and thou shalt die in a polluted land. ..."' (*Amos*, vii. 17).[49]

Short of literally hurling acid, the St Jacques Dominican who penned this attack *c.*1236 could hardly have been more vitriolic. It is almost as if he himself had been turned away from preaching in a cathedral by a prelate who had mocked his poverty and then had rushed back to his *scriptorium* to seek a scholar's revenge. In fact

---

[49] Ed. Cologne, f. 388ra: '*Hos ventos demones impedire conantur, et homines qui eos impediunt sunt membra diaboli. De quibus dicitur Amos 7c:* Qui vides gradere fuge in terram Iuda [vii. 12]. "*Vade*", *dicunt ipsi*, "*et predica in claustro tuo*, et in Bethel, *i.e. in parochia mea*, non adicies ultra, *ut* prophetes, *i.e. ut predices*, quia sanctificatio regis est, et domus regni est [vii. 13], *quasi ego sum rex et Dominus ibi. Vel quia ecclesia cathedralis est, ecce domus regni, et non est consuetudo quod pauperes predicent ibi*". *Ita dixit unus malus sacerdos ad Amos, sc. Amasius. Sed audiant et timeant isti illud quod Amos respondet ei, dicens:* "Propter hoc *quia me prohibes predicare in tua parochia* hec dicit Dominus: uxor tua in civitate fornicabitur ... de terra sua" [vii. 17]. *Et hoc est mirabile, quod isti prohibent quos Dominus vocat, et vocari precepit a propheta; Ezech.* 37a: A quattuor ventis veni spiritus et insuffla super interfectos istos'.

Aser's invective was too vitriolic to be accepted by the revising presence behind *Vidit Iacob*, who cut out the entire long passage. But *Vidit Iacob*'s compiler himself did not shy away from making a similar point by saying: 'demons try daily to impede preachers from preaching ... for they know that nothing is as salutary as the preaching of the word'.[50]

Possessed by an intense sense of calling for his own militant 'Preaching Order', the author of *Aser pinguis* formulated a remarkably radical eschatology. Indeed, with the exception of Joachim of Fiore, *Aser pinguis*'s author was surely the most chiliastic commentator on Revelation in the West since the patristic era. *Aser*'s chiliasm appears in three separate yet interrelated expositions, the first of which pertains to the vision of the seven seals (*Rev.*, v–viii).[51] Following a well-established medieval tradition, *Aser*'s author interpreted Revelation's seven seals as seven successive periods in the history of the Church: Apostles; persecution of martyrs by the Roman Empire; onslaught of heresy; blandishments of hypocrites and 'false brothers' (i.e., the present); an extrahistorical time of glorification of martyrs and consequent promise of eternal rewards for the elect; reign of Antichrist; and, finally, a 'brief time' of peace before the Last Judgement.[52] In this there would have been nothing intrinsically unusual, had it not been for the fact that *Aser*'s conception of the final time stressed a highly affirmative and hitherto unique element—that is, whereas the

---

[50] Ed. Parma, p. 381ᵃ: '*Demones conati sunt et conantur quotidie impedire predicatores ne predicent. ... Sciunt enim demones quod nihil adeo prodest ut predicatio verbi*'. Neither Peter of Tarentaise nor Nicholas of Gorran borrowed from either *Aser pinguis* or *Vidit Iacob*'s language as cited here or in n. 49.

[51] Since none of the passages I deal with below mentions the imminence of the final earthly Sabbath expected by *Aser pinguis*, it is well to make clear here that *Aser* expects it to come soon: ed. Cologne, f. 411ʳᵃ: '*hic loquetur de poena futura malis in tempora Antichristi, que cito erit*' (the Sabbath was to follow immediately on the reign of Antichrist).

[52] Ed. Cologne, ff. 385ʳᵃ–7ʳᵃ, 390ʳᵃ: see also the convenient summary by R.E. Kaske, 'The Seven *Status Ecclesiae* in *Purgatorio* XXXII and XXXIII', in *Dante, Petrarch, Boccaccio: Studies in the Italian Trecento in Honor of Charles S. Singleton*, ed. A.S. Bernardo and A.L. Pellegrini (Binghamton, 1983), pp. 89–113, at pp. 93–4. On the prior tradition, see, e.g., Lerner, 'Refreshment of the Saints', pp. 103–4, p. 116, n. 61. Note that while *Aser pinguis*'s author always calls the final age brief, following a precedent established by Haimo of Auxerre (see 'Refreshment', p. 107) he considers its exact duration to be a matter of uncertainty: '*Quantum vero spatium sit inter illos quadragintaduos dies et finem mundi nemo scit*'.

authoritative tradition of Jerome, Bede, Haimo of Auxerre, the *Glossa ordinaria*, and Richard of St Victor conceived of the time after Antichrist as being designed constrictively for testing or penance, or at best for a certain 'refreshment of the saints' or transitional glimpse into paradise,[53] *Aser pinguis* introduced the proposition that the time would be characterized by the 'freedom of preaching'. Indeed, *Aser*'s author was so intent on driving this point home that he repeated it three times, stating at his most expansive that after the death of Antichrist, 'the saints will preach freely and without obstacle, and will announce the truth and the faith, nor will anyone attack or afflict them'.[54]

Determined himself to 'preach freely and without obstacle', *Aser*'s author reiterated his chiliasm in commenting on two more of Revelation's septenaries—the seven angels with seven trumpets (*Rev.*, viii. 2–xi. 15) and the seven angels with seven vials (*Rev.*, xvi). In these instances, moreover, he broke new ground. For the septenary of angels with trumpets, *Aser*'s immediate source was the Revelation commentary of Richard of St Victor, based on Bede. According to Richard, the first six figures in this septenary stood for successive 'orders of preachers' leading the Church's respective struggles against Jews, gentile persecutors, heretics, hypocrites, the prior three together (historicizers often had trouble with their fifth term!), and the worst persecutions waged by Antichrist himself. Given Richard's acknowledgement that the opening of the seventh seal stood for a brief time of peace on earth before the Judgement, one might have thought that he would have interpreted the seventh angelic trumpeter as standing for that time. But, like Bede before him, Richard was too averse to chiliasm to pursue this route. Instead, Richard followed Bede in placing the seventh trumpet-blower at the moment of judgement itself, rather than representing any historical age: for Richard the seventh angel stood for a seventh

---

[53] Lerner, 'Refreshment', pp. 101–10.
[54] Ed. Cologne, f. 390ra: '*Tunc enim libere et sine obstaculo sancti predicabunt veritatem et fidem, nec aliquis eos impugnabit vel affliget*'. Also f. 382vb: '*Septimum modica ecclesie requies post Antichristum extinctum, quando libere predicabunt fideles, annunciantes tam preterita quam futura de reprobis et electis*'; f. 390ra: '*erit pax bonis qui libere predicabunt verbum Dei*'. Note also f. 397va: '*Hoc erit post mortem Antichristi, ubi libere postea predicabunt, sed tempore Antichristi non audientur, unde nec tunc predicabunt*'.

order of preachers, who blew their trumpets at the final hour to announce the supernatural peace of eternity.[55]

Recognition of *Aser pinguis*'s source allows us to see how intent the Dominican author of *c.*1236 was upon advancing chiliasm, for while accepting some of Richard of St Victor's words regarding the marvellous tones blown by the seventh order, the Dominican exegete altered Richard's reading to apply it to a final earthly state. For *Aser pinguis* the seventh angel is an 'order of preachers who will come after the death of Antichrist', and the *'great voices in heaven'* (*Rev.*, xi. 15) are those that say *'the Lord shall comfort Zion: He will comfort all her waste places'* (*Isaiah*, li. 3). These voices proclaim 'comfort' twice because during the reign of Antichrist the Church will suffer a twofold desolation, afflicted by many persecutions and unable to work miracles. Accordingly: 'after the death of Antichrist, during the time of the seventh angel, there will be a twofold consolation: namely, peace and propagation of the faith, for then all the Jews will be converted to the faith of Christ'. Moreover, in proclaiming that *'the kingdoms of this world are become the kingdoms of our Lord, and of his Christ'* (*Rev.*, xi. 15), the *'great voices in heaven'*, can be understood to be saying that 'the tranquillity of Christ's kingdom will already begin when Christ kills Antichrist *"with the spirit of his mouth"* [II *Thess.*, ii. 8], for then the Holy Church will rest peacefully *"as if for a half hour of silence"* (*Rev.*, viii. 1), i.e., the time that will follow until the end of the world'. Finally, the *'great voices'* declare 'the kingdoms *are become'* rather than 'the kingdoms will be', because 'from that moment on the fraudulence and ferocity of the Devil will be entirely cast off and God will reign in perpetual peace and tranquillity with all of his faithful'.[56]

---

[55] *PL* cxcvi, 794–5: '*In fine visionis agit de fine temporis* ... '. Note Richard's explicit attack on chiliasm, *'ut quidem heretici putaverunt'*, at 795A. The best analysis of Richard's Revelation commentary remains W. Kamlah, *Apokalypse und Geschichtstheologie: die mittelalterliche Auslegung der Apokalypse vor Joachim von Fiore* (Berlin, 1935), pp. 38–53; according to Kamlah, Richard came to Bede's periodizations indirectly, by way of the *Glossa ordinaria*.

[56] Ed. Cologne, f. 399$^{va–vb}$, corrected by MS BAV, Pal. lat. 96, f. 44vb, with bold-face indicating verbal borrowings from Richard of St Victor, *PL* cxcvi, 794–5: '*Per hunc etenim angelum designatur ordo* [MS: *status*] *predicatorum qui erunt post mortem Antichristi.* ... "*Voces magne in celo*". ... *Bis dicit consolabitur, quia ecclesia tempore Antichristi duplicem desolationem sustinebit. Unam quidem quia erit multos persecutoribus vexata. Et aliam quia non faciet miracula. Et propter hoc post mortem Antichristi in tempore septimi angeli duplex erit consolatio, sc. pax et multiplicatio fidei.*

Aser pinguis's source for the seven angels with the seven vials was also Richard of St Victor, yet again where Richard drew back from chiliasm, *Aser* welcomed it. For Richard of St Victor the first six angels with vials symbolized six orders of preachers, campaigning respectively against Jews, gentiles, heretics, Antichrist, gentiles supporting Antichrist, and Christian apostates supporting Antichrist, whereas the seventh angel stood for an order to appear after the death of Antichrist, for a moment at 'the end of time'. In Richard's view this last angel did not preach on earth but 'poured out his vial into the air' (*Rev.*, xvi. 17)—i.e., preaching to demons to expect the imminent advent of Christ.[57] Revealingly enough, *Aser pinguis* followed all of this exegesis, altering it only at the end. *Aser*'s first six angels were the same as Richard's, and *Aser*'s seventh appeared, like Richard's, after the death of Antichrist, but instead of floating in the air, *Aser*'s seventh angel represented a final order 'securely preaching' during a wondrous time on earth when the saints would work miracles.[58]

The pervasive chiliasm of *Aser pinguis* proves that 'post-Antichrist' chiliasm could exist in the thirteenth century apart from the influence of Joachim of Fiore. Admittedly, *Aser*'s author knew something about Joachim's Revelation commentary, for in one passing reference he alluded to the possibility of calling the Church 'a book with seven seals, as Joachim, who expounded on this book, has said'.[59] But to say that *Aser pinguis* 'bears marks of Joachim's

---

[57] *Tunc enim omnes Iudei convertentur ad fidem Christi.* ... "*Et Christi eius.*" ... **Huius regni tranquillitas etiam tunc in mundo incipiet, quando Christus spiritu oris sui Antichristum interficiet** [II *Thess.*, ii. 8] **et sancta ecclesia** *quasi dimidie hore silentio* [*Rev.*, viii. 1], *sc. tempore quod* **consequenter usque** *ad finem mundi,* **pacificata conquiescet.** ... *Et propter hoc etiam* **dicitur** *hic* **factum est** *et* **non fiet quia extunc fraudulentia et sevitia diaboli penitus deficiet et in suis fidelibus universis Deus perpetua pace et tranquillitate regnabit**'.

[57] *PL* cxcvi, 830.

[58] Ed. Cologne, f. 412rb, with borrowings from Richard in bold-face: '*Iste ergo* **septimus angelus** *sunt* **predicatores ultimi post mortem Antichristi**, *secure predicantes, in quorum tempore* **certissime scient** *demones* **instare diem iudiciii** ... Qualis nunquam fuit: *Etiam hoc legitur per recapitulationem de opere Antichristi. Vel potest lege de tempore novissimo post mortem Antichristi, in quo sancti facient miracula, et multi movebuntur ad penitentiam*'.

[59] Ed. Cologne, f. 382vb: '*Vel sicut ecclesia dicitur liber cuius septem sunt sigilla, sicut Ioachim distinxit, qui hunc librum exposuit*'. This reference was first noticed by Solomon, p. 372. Assuming the passage was written *c*.1236, it apparently

influence'[60] is unwarranted, because the chiliastic interpretation of the septenaries in *Aser* is unrelated to the interpretation of the same septenaries in Joachim's exegesis, and, above all, because there is no instance in which *Aser*'s author demonstrably borrows from Joachim. Rather than being a Joachite, the St Jacques Dominican built on the foundation of an earthly Sabbath after Antichrist located in mainline exegesis, combined with a chiliastic version of Richard of St Victor's seventh 'order of preachers' who would 'blow their trumpets' or 'empty their vials' at the end of time. Obsessed by what he perceived as intolerable restraints on the 'free preaching' of his own Preaching Order, he interrelated the borrowed concepts of an earthly Sabbath and an eschatological preaching order to yield his forecast that there would come a wondrous time when 'the Holy Church [would] rest peacefully' and the saints, or 'seventh order of preachers', would 'preach freely and without obstacle'.

About six years later, the Hugh of St Cher who wrote *Vidit Iacob* muted this chiliastic doctrine somewhat but did not completely abandon it. Reworking the 'seventh seal' passage, he stated that the final time would be *valde parum* instead of just *parum* and he omitted his exemplar's words that the saints then 'will announce the truth of the faith'. But he did not deny the existence of a final time meant for free preaching. Similarly, regarding the seventh trumpeter, he let the notion of a seventh eschatological preaching order stand, and he allowed a double final consolation of 'peace and propagation of the faith', although he subtracted a line from his exemplar about the Holy Church resting peacefully until the end of the world. Finally, his interpretation of the seventh angel was the most muted of all, for he allowed this figure to stand for a preaching order arising after the death of Antichrist, but he returned to Richard of St Victor's view that this order's preaching would be to demons, not mortals.[61]

---

provides the earliest datable evidence of knowledge of Joachim's Revelation commentary at Paris, although it is probably roughly contemporaneous with the reference by William of Auvergne discussed by M. Reeves, *The Influence of Prophecy in the Later Middle Ages: A Study in Joachimism* (Oxford, 1969), pp. 41–2.

[60] Solomon, p. 372.

[61] Ed. Parma, pp. 387^{b}–8^{a}, 416^{a}, 417^{a}, 462^{a}.

Ironically, the Hugh of *Vidit Iacob* knew Joachim of Fiore's Revelation commentary very well, and drew on it more heavily than did the Hugh of *Aser pinguis*. As Beryl Smalley has observed, *Vidit Iacob*'s author once cited Joachim explicitly to support his position that the two witnesses of *Revelation* xi might stand for two eschatological orders preaching against Antichrist, and Marjorie Reeves has called attention to the fact that *Vidit Iacob* several times elsewhere quarries out chunks of Joachim's Revelation commentary without identifying the source.[62] Yet though *Vidit Iacob* quarries from Joachim, it never does so to build chiliasm. Clearly *Vidit Iacob*'s author admired Joachim's fertile exegetical imagination, and felt free to pick from his readings as he chose; but his choice never extended to the heart of Joachim's teachings because he was averse to them. An original passage from *Vidit Iacob* that associates untrammeled chiliasm with the materialistic errors of the Jews underlines this.[63] Apparently, then, *Vidit Iacob*'s muted acceptance of *Aser*'s forecasts about the time after Antichrist was a compromise: *Vidit Iacob*'s author probably would not have accepted *Aser pinguis*'s exultation about the coming earthly Sabbath at all had the doctrine not rested upon a well-established exegetical tradition.

This verdict brings me inevitably to my third section, because it raises the question of how an author can be understood to have compromised with himself. In my view, 'Hugh' could compromise with 'Hugh', because 'Hugh' was never really one author but always a consortium. Although such has long been suspected—Fr. H.-F. Dondaine expressed his suspicion over thirty years ago that Hugh of St Cher worked on his postills with collaborators[64]—I

---

[62] Smalley. 'John Russel', pp. 302–3; Reeves, *Influence of Prophecy*, pp. 87–8. *Vidit Iacob*'s discussion of the red dragon's seven heads [*Rev.*, xii. 3], ed. Parma, p. 452[b], is taken extensively verbatim from Joachim.

[63] Ed. Parma, p. 493[a]: '*Dicunt quidam Iudei ... et tunc reedificabunt Ierusalem auream et erunt in ea gloria magna, et* ducent uxores et facient convivia, *et sic mille anni erunt et postea transferentur in celum. ... Nos autem magis volumus glossis sanctorum adherere....*' The non-italicized words repeat language used by *Vidit Iacob* to describe the conduct of the sinful after the death of Antichrist in commenting on *Revelation*, viii. 1 (ed. Parma, p. 388[a]) and derive ultimately from a condemnatory passage in *Matthew*, xxiv. 38.

[64] H.-F. Dondaine, 'L'objet et le "medium" de la vision béatifique chez les théologiens du XIIIe siècle', *RTAM*, xix (1952), pp. 60–130, at pp. 82–3. See also

believe that the dates I have located for *Aser pinguis* and *Vidit Iacob* serve to prove the *travail d'équipe* thesis more resoundingly than ever before. Moreover, the contents of the two postills suggest that when the real Hugh of St Cher 'signed his name' to a finished commentary he may not even have known all that was in it.

Aser pinguis and *Vidit Iacob* both have to be regarded as the products of teamwork on the grounds of the incongruous relationship between Hugh of St Cher's circumstances when they were compiled and the 'friar-hours' of labour that must have gone into their production. Assuming that *Aser* was completed *c.*1236, Hugh then was finishing a six-year term as Dominican theological regent at Paris, the last three of which overlapped with his tenure of the prior's office at St Jacques. Had Hugh written nothing else within his teaching years, it is just conceivable that he could have composed *Aser* unaided, but chalked up to his credit during that period are no less than a Sentence commentary, at least sixteen 'disputed questions', many sermons, the first complete biblical concordance, and postills on the entire Bible before the Apocalypse![65] Bearing in mind that *Aser pinguis* runs to 132

Smalley, *Bible*, p. xiii: 'The *Postilla super totam Bibliam* of Hugh of St Cher has turned out to be even more composite, so much so that it would be more correct to call the Postillator "Hugh's team"'. An excellent review of disparate evidence for the practice of team work in thirteenth-century St Jacques is Y. Congar, '"In dulcedine societatis quaerere veritatem": Notes sur le travail en équipe chez S. Albert et chez les Prêcheurs au XIIIe siècle', *Albertus Magnus, Doctor Universalis: 1280/1980*, ed. G. Meyer and A. Zimmermann (Mainz, 1980), pp. 47–57; note the quotation from St Thomas, p. 53: '*precipue in acquisitione scientie plerumque societas multorum studentium prodest, quia interdum alter ignorat quod alius invenit*'.

[65] My count of the disputed questions comes from adding the one edited by Stegmüller (as above, n. 3) with fifteen others treated by D. Van den Eynde, 'Nouvelles Questions de Hugues de Saint-Cher', *Mélanges Joseph de Ghellinck*, 2 vols. (Gembloux, 1951), ii, pp. 815–35, and Torrell (as above, n. 29). Schneyer, *Repertorium*, ii, pp. 758–85, lists 429 sermons for Hugh, of which many must have been composed during his Parisian years, given their clustering in Parisian MSS. Finally, regarding the concordance, the doubts of R.H. and M.A. Rouse, 'The Verbal Concordance', pp. 7–8, regarding Hugh's association with the earliest St Jacques concordance should be removed by Salimbene de Adam, *Cronica*, *MGH SS*, XXXII, p. 175 (drawing in part on the chronicle of Martin of Troppau): '*Concordantiarum in Bibliotheca primus auctor fuit. Sed processu temporis facte sunt Concordancie meliores*'. Strong evidence that the first concordance was completed by *c.*1236 appears in the fact that *Aser pinguis* uses its system of subdividing biblical chapters by letters: see not only the printed editions but BAV, Pal. lat. 96, at ff. 24ra, 44vb.

double-column folio-sized pages in its densely printed seventeenth-century editions, the conclusion that Hugh of St Cher could not have produced it single-handed is inescapable. As for *Vidit Iacob*, it is even longer (186 double-column, folio-sized pages in the Parma edition), and hence could hardly have been produced by Hugh alone in the early 1240s, when he was serving as Provincial of the Dominican province of France, presumably a full-time job.

Taking the team-work thesis as proven, the intriguing question arises of whether freedom allotted to individual team members, shifting memberships of teams, and perhaps changing captaincies of teams between 1231 and 1244 combined to create such variety within 'Hugh's' exegetical *oeuvre* as to render the real Hugh of St Cher's authorship of the entirety no more than a convenient bibliographical fiction. My response, inevitably impressionistic, is this: individual friars did have leeway to work as they liked; yet some direction existed to produce a modicum of common outlook within a given postill; yet this direction need not always have been that of the real Hugh.

Two fairly clear-cut examples should prove the team members' freedom. The first lies in the disagreement found between *Aser pinguis* and *Vidit Iacob* about the number of days granted for rest on earth following the death of Antichrist—*Aser* offering forty-two days and *Vidit Iacob* forty-five. As it happens, not only is the figure of forty-five days more traditional, but the rest of 'Hugh's' biblical exegesis votes with *Vidit Iacob* on this detail: 'Hugh' on *Daniel* (xii. 12). *Matthew* (xiv. 36), and I *Thessalonians* (v. 3) consistently gives forty-five rather than forty-two days.[66] Yet the number of forty-two days was not picked by *Aser*'s team member at random, for a gloss of much authority in Parisian circles offered this alternative, and forty-two days consequently appear in the works of several prominent thirteenth-century Parisian theologians.[67] Clearly, then,

---

[66] 'Hugh's' gloss on I Thessalonians derives from language used by Haimo of Auxerre but may have been based on the intermediary of Peter Lombard's *Magna glossatura*. Unfortunately Migne's edition of the latter (*PL* cxcii, 306D) gives '40', instead of the correct '45' which appears in the best early MSS such as BN lat. 649, 17246, and 17247, and BAV, Vat. lat. 144 and 695. (I wish to thank Helen Feng for checking the readings in the Paris MSS for me.) The faulty *PL* edition led to mistakes made in 'Refreshment', p. 109, and in Solomon, p. 371.

[67] The same 'gloss' which gives forty-two days for penance after the death of Antichrist on the analogy of the forty-two years given to the Jews for penance

the friar working on *Aser* who was responsible for the seven seals exegesis followed his own source on the number of days after Antichrist, and no one intervened to stop him.

My second example is perhaps even more revealing because it shows some atypical 'brushwork' in the midst of a single canvas. According to Beryl Smalley, classical citation is minimal in Hugh's postills on the Gospels, and I can confirm this finding for 'Hugh's' Revelation exegesis, with one dramatic exception.[68] Although *Aser pinguis* and almost all of *Vidit Iacob* rarely adduce classical sources, chapter xvi of *Vidit Iacob* must win a prize for thirteenth-century erudition, for this chapter not only cites two relatively rare Christian authorities—Cyprian and Zozimus—and five different lines of sententious medieval verse, but also three tags from

---

between the Passion and the destruction of the Temple is cited independently by Nicholas of Gorran in his Revelation commentary, *Cognovit Dominus*, p. 222[b], and in his *Commentaria in Quatuor Evangelia* (Cologne: P. Quentel, 1537), f. 124A, and by William of St Amour [?], *Liber de Antichristo*, ed. Martène and Durand, *Collectio*, ix, pp. 1271–1446, at p. 1439 (a new edition is currently being prepared by Robert Adams). On the basis of remarks in Gorran's *Commentaria*, it appears that the forty-two-day thesis may ultimately have derived from St John Chrysostom. In addition to its appearance in *Aser pinguis*, Gorran, and Pseudo-[?] William of St Amour, it may also be found in Pseudo-Hugh of St Victor, *Questiones in Epistolas Pauli*, PL clxxv, 592A (a work apparently written between 1180 and 1230; see *Traditio*, xii (1957), p. 384) and St Bonaventure, *Collationes in Hexaemeron*, ed. F. Delorme (Florence, 1934), p. 185.

[68] Smalley, 'Gospels in the Paris Schools, II', p. 307. Apart from the dramatic exception in ch. 16 of *Vidit Iacob*, described as follows, the appearance of pagan sources in *Aser pinguis* and *Vidit Iacob* is minimal. In *Aser*, I note the following: a few citations of Seneca; two of 'Tullius' (both at f. 364[rb]), which, however, are definitely not by Cicero; a story from *historie romanorum* about 'Crassus' and the Carthaginians (f. 411[ra]), which is certainly confused or apocryphal (*Vidit Iacob's* re-telling—ed. Parma, p. 460[b]—changes the Carthaginians to the Parthians); a reference from *fabulae poetarum* about Antaeus (f. 402[rb]); and, most interesting, a citation of the Arabic philosopher Algazel (f. 396[ra]). The source for the last is clearly a Latin translation of Algazel's *Metaphysics*, known today in only six MSS: see J.T. Muckle, *Algazel's Metaphysics: A Mediaeval Translation* (Toronto, 1933), p. 1, lines 24–5; p. 4, line 1 (Fr. L.-J. Bataillon kindly called my attention to Muckle's edition); note that Peter of Tarentaise (ed. Borgnet, p. 625[b]) retained this citation but changed the ascription (which he had via the intermediary of *Vidit Iacob*, ed. Parma, p. 405[a]) from 'Agazel' to 'Philosophus'! Exclusive of ch. 16, *Vidit Iacob* mentions Aristotle occasionally (above, n. 34) as well as introducing a few citations from Seneca and Boethius. Of these the most interesting is a story from a *liber tragediarum Senece qui intitulatur liber de nugis senum* (ed. Parma, p. 385[b]), which I cannot identify, but which is definitely not by Seneca: in retelling it Nicholas of Gorran (ed. Antwerp, p. 221[a]) gives *in quibusdam apocryphis Senece*.

Horace, two anecdotes from unidentified pagan histories, two tags from Seneca, one from Cicero, one from Sidonius Appollinaris, and one attributed to Socrates![69] The conclusion follows that some apprentice in the St Jacques workshop assigned to comment on chapter xvi of Revelation was obviously more citation-happy than his *confrères*, and no overseer intervened to cloud this happiness.

The freedom of team members in the St Jacques *équipe* to pursue their work largely as they deemed best must have rested on three practical assumptions. First, since 'Hugh of St Cher's' postills were academic and/or homiletic reference works, they offered a range of legitimate possibilities, elucidating the meaning of any biblical book or passage rather than insisting on one correct interpretation. Thus the range produced by one 'research assistant' was likely to be as good as that of another. Secondly, 'Hugh's' postills, also featured interspersed 'moralities'—rhetorical declamations, witticisms, and barrages of interrelated scriptural citations and *exempla*, recommending the good and chastizing the bad—all to serve as grist for the mills of preachers.[70] Since lively figures of speech, jokes, and absorbing or moving anecdotes just right for a given occasion are always at a premium, it must have been preferable to have semi-independent team members compile such material than to put the burden on a single shoulder, or to tell a team member censoriously that a certain trope or joke 'wasn't quite right'.[71] And, finally, what was there to worry about? Any friar at St Jacques had to have been a Dominican who had gained a good education, and

---

[69] See ed. Parma, pp. 460[b]–470[a]. Of the five quotations of *versus*, three have rough parallels in Munich, Bayerische Staatsbibliothek Clm 16101 (XIII)—see H. Walther, *Initia carminum ac versum medii aevi*, 2nd ed. (Göttingen, 1969), nos. 10528, 9368, 3449—suggesting the use of a similar source by the compiler of this section of *Vidit Iacob*. Otherwise, I have been able to locate the three tags from Horace (all from the *Epistles*), the one from Cicero (*Post reditum ad Quirites*, 21), and the one from Sidonius (*Epistolae*, VII, 7: see *MGH AA*, VIII, p. 134; Sidonius is mistakenly called Suetonius in the printed edition).

[70] 'Hugh's' motivation of providing moralities as an aid to preachers emerges clearly, for example, from *Vidit Iacob*'s explicit warning, ed. Parma, p. 470[a], that it is offering an *exemplum*. BAV, Pal. lat. 96 gives ample evidence in its margins that *Aser pinguis* was indeed used that way: e.g., f. 30[vb]: 'Exemplum'; f. 67[rb]: 'In dedicatione ecclesie'.

[71] Hence Beryl Smalley's finding, 'Gospels in the Paris Schools, II', p. 363, that 'a reader of Hugh's postills will risk disturbing his neighbours in the library by chuckles of laughter'.

who presumably joined because he hated heresy and vice. Given a more or less finite range of library resources, such a person presumably would have produced more or less the same kind of exegesis and moralizing as any of his fellows.

This reconstruction may help to explain what is already well known: that 'Hugh's' exegesis is vast, that it is mostly unadventurous, and that it often does not hang together very well, seeming, as Beryl Smalley so tellingly puts it, like 'a house furnished at random from a second-hand furniture store with pieces of various styles and periods'.[72] Yet the evidence of *Aser pinguis* seems to offer a hitherto unperceived difficulty, for here is a postill rife with passages that are adventurous in the extreme. Nor are these passages limited in their occurrence to one particular section of the work: rather, they appear throughout and support one another in such a way as to give the postill a distinctive character.[73] Hence one is forced to conclude that during the heat of the plurality of benefices controversy in Paris the director of the exegetical enterprise at St Jacques instructed his charges to take off their kid gloves, or else that a particularly zealous friar assigned to work on *Aser pinguis* managed to persuade his *confrères* to see things his way, with the director's implicit approval.[74]

In either event, I doubt if the captain of the *Aser pinguis* effort would have been Hugh of St Cher himself. From all we know of Hugh, he was a man of 'good sense'—well-informed, diplomatic, and shrewd, but not inflammatory or particularly daring. One has only to look at the text of Hugh's 'disputed question' of 1235 on pluralism to see that when working on his own (I have to assume that Hugh composed at least this text himself!) he could be dogged in defending a principled cause, but was lacking in incendiary ardour. Such a man was just the person to manage the French

---

[72] Smalley, 'A Commentary on Isaias', p. 395.

[73] In addition, there are technical common denominators such as the system of biblical citation by chapter number and letter (see above, n. 65) and the use of *li*, as in ed. Cologne, ff. 383va, 411ra. Neither of these traits reappears in *Vidit Iacob*.

[74] The likelihood that one member of Hugh's team between *c.*1236 and 1240 was Guillaume Pérault, O.P. appears to be very strong, for not only was Pérault definitely a student at St Jacques during that period, and not only was he a compatriot of Hugh of St Cher's, but his *Summa de vitiis*, apparently written in 1236, retells the 'poison in the Church' story and devotes much space to the sin associated with holding a plurality of benefices.

Dominican province and be named the first Dominican cardinal, but such a man would hardly have countenanced calling pluralists 'asses' or warning narrow-minded prelates that they would 'soon die in a polluted land'.

This appraisal of Hugh's personality does allow the possibility that he could have given orders to censor *Aser pinguis*'s boldnesses in the revision that became *Vidit Iacob*. But such is mere speculation, for it is just as conceivable that a different St Jacques team working in a different atmosphere in the early 1240s could have censored *Aser pinguis* on its own. Moreover, even if Hugh did send word to a team of friars to excise *Aser pinguis*'s provocations, it is highly unlikely that he was responsible for much of *Vidit Iacob*'s distinct character beyond that. Assuming that *Vidit Iacob* does have its own character, there was probably one major guiding presence behind its composition at St Jacques; but given Hugh of St Cher's administrative activities during the early 1240s, it seems improbable that it was his.

If it is true that the real Hugh of St Cher had little to do with the composition of *Aser pinguis* and *Vidit Iacob* there are some final ironies. About the time when *Aser pinguis* was written, Pope Gregory IX was publicly invoking the Donation of Constantine as a charter which licensed papal jurisdiction 'over things and bodies throughout the whole world', and after the composition of *Vidit Iacob*, scenes glorifying the Donation were painted on the walls of the oratory of St Sylvester in the Roman church of SS. Quattro Coronati as part of a propaganda programme justifying papal claims to temporal rule.[75] Had Hugh of St Cher, raised to the cardinalate in 1244, really known that two Revelation commentaries circulating under his name castigated the Donation as a malign bequest which had 'spread poison into the Church', he might well have been quite embarrassed.

Worse, he would surely have been embarrassed could he have learned that during the later Middle Ages the story of angels weeping in the skies because of the Donation's 'pollution of the

---

[75] Gregory IX's letter to Frederick II of October 1236 invoking the Donation of Constantine, is ed. *MGH Epp Saec XIII*, I, p. 604. A good introduction to the Donation frescoes, executed during 1244, is J. Mitchell, 'St. Sylvester and Constantine at the SS. Quattro Coronati', *Federico II e l'arte del duecento italiano*, ed. A.M. Romanini, 2 vols. (Galatina, 1980), ii, pp. 15–32.

Church' was to be used as a weapon by Waldensians, Wyclif, and Hus in their diverse attacks against the Roman ecclesiastical regime.[76] Given that *Aser pinguis*, and especially *Vidit Iacob*, were among the most widely circulated orthodox texts which contained the 'poison in the Church' story, it is not impossible that 'Hugh of St Cher's' postills were the direct or indirect source for its heretical appropriation. And even if not, had Hugh of St Cher—one of the most prominent members of the first generation of an order founded primarily to fight heresy—been able to know that a story he licensed to circulate would be turned against the Church hierarchy by various stubborn heretics, he surely would have wondered how well he had earned his red hat.[77]

Yet there is more. In 1255, while Cardinal Hugh was serving as one of the most learned lieutenants of Pope Alexander IV, word came to the curia in Anagni of a stir created in Paris by the proclamation of some shocking Joachite doctrines by the Franciscan zealot, Gerardino of Borgo S. Donnino. Accordingly, Alexander created a commission of three cardinals, one of whom was Hugh, to look into the matter and pronounce upon the orthodoxy of both Gerardino and Joachim of Fiore himself.[78] Did Alexander know that two decades earlier Hugh, as putative author of *Aser*

---

[76] The earliest evidence of heretical appropriation of the story of which I am aware appears in the 'Anonymous of Passau', a treatise against heresy written in the diocese of Passau between 1260 and 1266, probably by a Dominican inquisitor; see the 'first error' of the Waldensians in the edition by A. Patschovsky and K.-V. Selge, *Quellen zur Geschichte der Waldenser* (Gütersloh, 1973), p. 77: '*quod ecclesia Romana non sit ecclesia Iesu Christi … et quod defecit sub Silvestro, cum venenum temporalium in ecclesiam est infusum*'. Evidence for fourteenth-century Waldensian use appears in R. Rusconi, *L'attesa della fine* (Rome, 1979), pp. 190–1; 198, n. 53. Examples of the use of the story by Wyclif and Hus are provided by H. Kaminsky, *A History of the Hussite Revolution* (Berkeley, 1967), pp. 39, 54–5.

[77] In fact, *Aser pinguis* contains numerous attacks on heresy and is worthy of study as a source for heretical doctrines c.1236. E.g., ed. Cologne, f. 383[va]: '*Hic insurgunt Manichei, qui dicunt [Christum] habuisse phantasticam carnem*'; f. 404[ra]: '*blasphemabit sanctos, sc. qui iam sunt in celo, et dicet esse damnatus in inferno: sicut iam faciunt quidam heretici qui dicunt beatum Nicolaum et ceteros omnes confessores qui fuerunt in ecclesia a tempore Silvestri Pape damnatos esse et in inferno*'; f. 406[vb]: '*Primum celi … est vetus testamentum, per hoc volant Iudei. Ultimum celi est novum testamentum, per hoc volant Manichei, qui non recipiunt vetus testamentum …*'.

[78] The standard work on this subject remains H. Denifle, 'Das Evangelium aeternum und die Commision zu Anagni', *ALKG*, i (1885), pp. 49–142. Extracts from the protocol of Anagni are translated by B. McGinn, *Visions of the End* (New York, 1979), pp. 165–6.

pinguis and *Vidit Iacob*, had been one of the earliest Parisian theologians to cite Joachim approvingly? It is doubtful if he did, or if Hugh—had he himself known of his 'own' citations of Joachim—would have told him. To be sure, in a limited sense Hugh need not have had much on his conscience regarding 'his' citations of Joachim, because neither *Aser pinguis* nor *Vidit Iacob* espoused Joachim's 'pattern of threes' centrally at issue in 1255. But in a larger sense the commission of Anagni's deliberations should have given him some pause, inasmuch as the chiliasm espoused in *Aser pinguis* and *Vidit Iacob* was potentially just as subversive of the ecclesiastical order as Joachim's three *status* doctrine. Indeed, generations of heretics were to look forward to a 'coming kingdom of peace' wherein the elect would freely preach, just as much as they would criticize the wealth of the 'carnal Church'.[79] Who knows, then, but that *Aser pinguis*'s and/or *Vidit Iacob*'s expressions of faith in the coming of a similar kingdom helped inspire them in this respect as well? 'Frère Jacques', were you sleeping?

Northwestern University, Evanston, Illinois

---

[79] See Lerner, 'Refreshment', pp. 140–2.

SIMILITUDINES ET *EXEMPLA DANS LES SERMONS DU XIIIe SIÈCLE*

par LOUIS-JACQUES BATAILLON

L A PUBLICATION parmi les fascicules de la *Typologie des sources du moyen âge occidental* du volume de Cl. Bremond, J. Le Goff, et J.-Cl, Schmitt sur l'*exemplum*[1] montre les progrès qui ont été faits dans ce domaine depuis 1927, date à laquelle était parue la thèse de J.-Th. Welter du même titre.[2] Si ce dernier reste encore un remarquable instrument, toujours utile et souvent nécessaire à consulter, c'est dans le récent livre collectif que l'on trouvera désormais des définitions plus élaborées et des études plus précises sur la place et le rôle de l'*exemplum* dans le sermon, des analyses plus affinées de sa structure, des appréciations plus fournies et plus nuancées sur la portée historique et sociologique de ce genre littéraire.

Parmi les éléments neufs de ce volume, il y a un chapitre sur les aspects rhétoriques de l'*exemplum* dans lequel J.-Cl. Schmitt, entre autres remarques fort intéressantes, montre les relations et les différences entre les *exempla* et les *similitudines*; il note combien il est difficile de tracer une frontière nette entre les deux procédés, difficulté déjà perceptible au moyen âge. Il part du fait que, tandis que les *Artes praedicandi* comptent trois types d'argumentation: *auctoritates, rationes, exempla*, Jacques de Vitry bien auparavant parlait plutôt d'*auctoritates*, de *similitudines* et d'*exempla*. Et l'auteur développe:

> Par rapport aux autorités, ... les *similitudines* ont un rôle explicatif, et donc une position subordonnée. Par ailleurs elles se distinguent nettement des *exempla* par des marques d'énonciation spécifiques dont le dédoublement souligne l'articulation

---

[1] Cl. Bremond, J. Le Goff, J.-Cl. Schmitt, *L'"exemplum'* (Turnhout, 1982), avec une très riche bibliographie. Ajouter: J. Berlioz, 'Quand dire c'est faire dire. Exempla et confession chez Etienne de Bourbon (†v.1261)', *Faire croire* (Rome, 1981), pp. 299–335.

[2] J.-Th. Welter, *L'"exemplum dans la littérature religieuse et didactique du moyen âge* (Paris et Toulouse, 1927).

structurelle. ... Pourtant certaines similitudes sont qualifiées d'*exempla* dans les rubriques des manuscrits. ... La confusion entre *exempla* et *similitudines* est surtout fréquente lorsque celles-ci ont un caractère narratif embryonnaire qui les rapproche effectivement des premiers.[3]

En effet il serait souvent assez facile de transformer certaines de ces courtes comparaisons en petits *exempla*. Quand Thomas d'Aquin dit: *Sed istis accidit sicut alicui eunti ad curiam regis qui uolens uidere regem credit quemcumque bene indutum uel in officio constitutum regem esse*,[4] il n'y aurait guère de difficulté à traiter la même image sous forme d'*exemplum*: 'Il y avait une fois un paysan qui devait aller à la cour du roi ... '. On peut aussi assimiler à ces comparaisons des phrases à forme conditionnelle, parfois elles aussi désignées comme *exemplum*. Ainsi nous lisons dans un sermon anonyme pour la fête de saint André: *Exemplum. Si aliquis dominus diligit seruum suum a quo annuatim habet centum meretrices, multo magis diabolus diligit meretricem a qua annuatim habet plus quam mille animas.*[5]

A côté de ces *similitudines* brèves proches des *exempla*, on en rencontre de beaucoup plus longues et développées, parfois sous forme de chaînes de comparaisons, qui tiennent dans un sermon une place analogue à celle des *distinctiones* et sont en fait une forme dérivée de ces dernières. Si la distinction est construite sur l'analyse des diverses significations d'un mot ou d'une expression pris dans le *thema* du sermon, la longue *similitudo* consiste essentiellement à développer une image tirée elle aussi de la péricope biblique liturgique.

Je voudrais ici esquisser le rôle différent joué dans les sermons par les comparaisons longues d'une part et les *similitudines* brèves et *exempla* de l'autre.

Avant de prendre un exemple de sermon bâti sur des *similitudines* longues, il ne sera pas inutile de rappeler d'abord le modèle usuel de division par *distinctiones* proprement dites. Si l'on regarde le sermon

[3] Bremond, L'"exemplum", pp. 154–6.

[4] *Collationes in Symbolum*, ii: *S.Thomae Aquinatis Opera omnia*, 34 vols (Paris, 1871–80), xxvii, p. 206a.

[5] Sermon *Venite post me ... Notandum est cur Dominus*, BAV, Vat.lat.13931, ff. 49ᵛ–50ʳ. Texte publié dans I.B. Lotti, *Sermones qui divi Thomae tribuuntur* (Udine, 1896), p. 76. Aucun des sermons de cette collection n'a de rapport avec Thomas d'Aquin.

Similitudines *et* exempla

de Thomas d'Aquin pour le premier dimanche de l'Avent, *Ecce rex tuus uenit tibi mansuetus*, on voit que le prédicateur commence par découper son thème en quatre éléments:

> ... *possumus quatuor uidere: primo aduentus Christi demonstracionem, ibi: 'ecce'; secundo aduenientis condicionem, ibi: 'rex tuus'; tercio aduenientis humilitatem: 'mansuetus'; quarto aduentus utilitatem: 'tibi'.*

Thomas propose ensuite pour chacune de ces expressions quatre sens, en redoublant le deuxième membre de la division principale en distinguant successivement *rex* et *rex tuus*; chaque signification s'appliquera ensuite à la venue du Christ. Voici la première de ces *distinctiones*:

> *Per 'ecce' quatuor intelligere possumus, primo certificacionem: de rebus enim que nobis constant dicimus: 'ecce'; secundo temporis determinacionem; tercio rei manifestacionem; quarto hominum confortacionem.*[6]

Voici maintenant un sermon structuré par deux *similitudines*; j'ai choisi un texte inédit de Guillaume de Mailly, un religieux français probablement actif durant le troisième quart du treizième siècle. C'est un sermon pour le troisième dimanche de Carême avec pour thème le verset de l'Evangile de *Luc*, xi. 14: *Erat Iesus eiciens demonium et illud erat mutum.*[7]

Après une courte introduction basée sur un proverbe donné assez exceptionnellement en latin: *Bonam dietam facit qui de fatuo se liberat,*[8] et consistant en une brève comparaison entre le diable et un mauvais hôte, avec un bien joli adage en français: *Hostel besoigneus cuers de pecheor*, Guillaume annonce deux parties, la première traitant de la bonté de Dieu, manifestée par l'expulsion du démon, la seconde partie montrant la nocivité de ce dernier.

---

[6] Publié par J. Leclercq: 'Un sermon inédit de Saint Thomas sur la royauté du Christ', *Revue Thomiste*, xlvi (1946), p. 159. Je cite d'après les Mss Salamanca, Biblioteca Universitaria, ms 2187, f. 170rb, et Sevilla, Biblioteca Colombina, ms Capit. 83. 2.15, f. 121vb contenant une reportation un peu différente.

[7] Schneyer, *Repertorium*, ii, p. 485, n° 30. Mss utilisés: BN, ms lat.15956, ff. 44va–46vb, et Venezia, Biblioteca dei Redentoristi della Fava, ms 39, ff. 42v–44v. Sur Mailly, cf. Kaeppeli, *Scriptores*, ii, p. 118.

[8] J. Morawski, *Proverbes français antérieurs au XVe siècle* (Paris, 1925), p. 10, n° 276: 'Bonne jornee fait qui de fol se delivre'.

La première partie nous montre donc que le diable peut être chassé de bien des manières:

> *Primo enim eicitur dolore siue lacrimis contritionis sicut mastinus de coquina cum aqua calida.... Secundo eicitur sicut homo de domo sua tedio litigiose mulieris, id est consciencie remordentis ... hec est uxor data in adiutorium uiri.... Sed nota quod quidam ita consueuerunt audire litigium mulieris quod quasi nichil reputant; sic multi non multum reputant remorsum consciencie. Exemplum de eo qui recolens uitam suam incipiebat lacrimari et quia uolebat repellere remorsum consciencie ludebat ad scaccos. Tercio eicitur demonium sicut homo de domo sua stillicidio predicationis.... Quarto eicitur demonium sicut homo de domo sua fumo deuocionis, scilicet ex consideracione dominice passionis prouenientis.... De isto triplici modo eiciendi dicitur Prou.* secundum aliam litteram: Tria expellunt hominem de domo sua, fumus, stillicidium et mala uxor.[9] *Quinto eicitur demonium sicut ribaldus de hospicio siue sicut histrio, scilicet uirga penitencie, id est carnis afflictione, scilicet per opera penitencie.... Sexto eicitur ieiunio sicut lupus de nemore eicitur fame.... Septimo eicitur sicut coluber de cauerna carmine oracionis siue diuini nominis inuocacione.*

Après une digression presque aussi longue que le développement précédent entraînée par la mention du nom du Seigneur, la seconde partie montre comment le diable se rend maître de l'âme du pécheur: il fait comme un homme qui veut se reposer dans sa maison:

> *Et notandum quod quando diabolus uenit in hominem per peccatum, aufert ei omnes sensus spirituales. Facit enim ad modum diuitis qui uult 'se aaisier' in aliqua domo. Primo enim ingressus domum claudit post se ostium et precipit familie ne dicat esse intus nec alicui indicet.... Secundo clauso ostio extinguit lumen ut quietius dormiat; sic diabolus lumen sciencie et uisum cognicionis ne homo cogitet uanitatem et dampnabilitatem peccati.... Tercio obstruit fenestras propter radios solis ne introeant; sic diabolus fenestras aurium ne radii doctrine intrent et ipsum inquietent.... Quarto precipit familie quod sit in pace ne ipsum inquietet; sic tollit diabolus actum bone operationis.... Sic diabolus aufert etiam homini olfactum, id est odorem peccati, ut non*

---

[9] Adage inspiré de *Prov.*, xxvii.15 selon les Septante. Cf. Walther, ii, p. 215, n° 30832: '*Sunt tria damna domus: imber, mala femina, fumus*'.

sentiat eius fetorem. Nota de angelo transeunte ante iuuenem pulcrum, qui obturauit nares, non autem quando transiuit ante corpus mortuum.... Nota de demoniaco qui habebat tres diabolos quorum unus dicebatur Clobourse, alius Clobouche, alius Clocuer.[10]

On trouve donc quelques *exempla* dans ce sermon de Guillaume de Mailly, mais celui-ci, en dehors de la digression centrale qui est dans le mode de la *distinctio*, est structuré par deux grandes *similitudines*, la première constituée par une chaîne de comparaisons sur le thème de l'expulsion, la seconde par l'analyse détaillée d'un comportement global; toutes deux sont essentielles à la composition même du sermon.

Pour voir maintenant comment fonctionnent dans un sermon l'*exemplum* et la comparaison courte, je prendrai d'abord un sermon de Servasanctus de Faenza, franciscain italien de la seconde moitié du XIIIe siècle, auteur de plusieurs ouvrages destinés à secourir les prédicateurs, dont un *Liber de exemplis naturalibus* et le recueil de sermons dont est tiré notre exemple;[11] il est caractérisé par un goût pour les traits de l'antiquité gréco-romaine qui lui mériterait une bonne place parmi les 'classicising friars' si magistralement dépeints par Beryl Smalley; il était également très attiré par l'histoire naturelle. Voici un sermon pour la fête de la Conversion de saint Paul sur le thème: *Surrexit Saulus de terra apertisque oculis nichil uidebat.*[12] Le sujet traité est la vision du Christ qui doit être contemplé *penis afflictum, rebus destitutum, humilem et abiectum.* La passion de Jésus nous invite à renoncer au luxe et aux plaisirs; sur ce point les chrétiens actuels sont pires que les paiens, et ici viennent les exemples de Pontius et de Virginius qui tuèrent leurs filles plutôt que de les voir violées. La pauvreté du Christ nous incite à fuir toute cupidité et nous voyons que les philosophes Cratès et

[10] *Exemplum* de l'ange, cf. Tubach, n° 2559. *Exemplum* des trois diables, cf. Hauréau, ii, pp. 144, 149.

[11] A. Teetaert, 'Servasanctus de Faenza', *DTC*, xiv, col. 1963–7 (bibliographie). Ajouter: V. Gamboso, 'I sermoni festivi di Servasanto da Faenza nel codice 490 dell'Antoniana', *Il Santo*, xiii (1973), pp. 3–88; *idem*, 'I sermoni *De communi* et *De proprio sanctorum* di Servasanto nei codici 520 e 530 di Assisi', *ibid.*, pp. 211–78. Welter, *L'exemplum*, pp. 181–6.

[12] Schneyer, *Repertorium*, v, p. 385, n° 144. Edité dans *S. Bonaventurae Opera omnia*, 15 vols (Paris, 1864–71), xiii, pp. 522b–25a.

Démocrite ont abandonné toutes leurs richesses. Enfin l'humilité de Jésus nous met en garde contre tout orgueil et l'histoire romaine nous montre le fuite des honneurs chez Marcius Rutilius et Fabius Maximus. Si l'*exemplum* de Cratès vient de Jérôme, tous les autres ont été fournis par Valère Maxime.[13]

Chez Servasanto, les *exempla* sont assez fortement intégrés dans la structure même du sermon en tant qu'ils servent de repoussoir à la conduite des chrétiens contemporains de l'orateur. Ainsi, après avoir raconté comment Xénocrate n'avait pas fait attention aux avances d'une *mulier insana*, il s'écrie: *Magna ergo Christianis est uerecundia dum inter gentes paganas magis quam inter eos inuenitur continentia.*[14]

Mais, plus souvent, les *exempla*, et avec eux les comparaisons courtes, pourraient être ôtés du sermon sans que le sens général de celui-ci en soit affecté. Prenons maintenant un sermon effectivement prêché, probablement en français, et connu par une reportation; il est particulièrement riche en *exempla*. L'auteur en est le dominicain français Pierre de Remiremont qui parlait un septième dimanche après la Trinité, vers 1270, sur le thème: *Nunc autem liberati a peccato, serui autem facti Deo.*[15] Tout le développement porte sur les qualités du véritable serviteur de Dieu; le sermon à la messe matinale les énumère: intelligence, solidité, conduite filiale, humilité et joie; il explique ensuite pour chacune d'elles pourquoi elle est requise, puis comment elle est abîmée ou détruite par le péché; la *collatio* du soir montre comment sont guéries ces blessures. Nous avons ainsi quinze subdivisions: deux fois cinq pour le sermon du matin, cinq à la prédication des vêpres. Neuf d'entre elles sont illustrées par un *exemplum* ou une *similitudo* brève. Six ne tiennent chacune que quelques lignes:

> *Sapiencia diuina habet naturam olei: oleum semper uult totum uas habere, uel si est cum eo liquor alius, eum semper supernatat, sic*

[13] Cratès: Hieronymus, *Comm. in Matheum* I.III (*Matt.*, xix. 28), *CC* lxii, p. 172, 922–955. Autres *exempla*: Valerius Maximus, *Facta et dicta memorabilia*, éd. C. Kempf (Berlin, 1854): Pontius: l.vi., c.1, n° 3, p. 462; Virginius: *ibid.*, n° 2; Democritus: l.vi, c.7, Ext.n° 4, p. 628; Rutilius: l.iv.c.1, n° 3, p. 313; Fabius: *ibid.*, n° 5.
[14] Sermon *Vas electionis*: Schneyer, *Repertorium*, v, p. 385, n° 145. Ed. S. Bonaventurae Opera (Paris), xiii, p. 527b. Cf. Valerius Maximus, l.iv.c.3, Ext. n° 3, p. 342.
[15] Schneyer, *Repertorium*, iv, p. 724, n° 1–2; Soissons, Bibliothèque municipale, ms 125, ff. 66vb–71ra. Cf. Kaeppeli, *Scriptores*, iii, pp. 257–8.

sapiencia diuina ...—*Sicut pueri qui uolunt ludere ad pilam querunt palum in sepi, et cum inueniunt malum fortiter se tenentem in terra uadunt quousque inueniunt palum uacillantem et illum concuciunt donec extrahant; sic diabolus* ...—*Dolent serui principum quando fideliter seruiunt domino et non coram domino suo, quia adulator uel detractor retrahit dominum <quin> ipsum remuneret; seruit aliquis domino alicui V annis; dicit: 'Vtinam dominus meus sciret quam fideliter seruiui et uellem aliquam mercedem'.—Fatuus esset qui traheretur ad suspendium per pratum plenum floribus et ridet de amenitate <prati> et non recoleret patibuli; sic est mirabile quomodo potest quis gaudere in peccato.—Legitur de beato Anthonio quod ibat de loco ad locum; uerberant eum demones, et tunc dixit: 'Domine adiuua me'. Et postquam dimiserant apparuit ei Dominus et dixit beatus Anthonius: 'Domine, ubi eras?' Dixit Dominus: 'Presens eram sed expectabam uictoriam'.—Narratur quod rusticus intrauit lutum, boues et carruca, et ille clamauit: 'Deus adiuua me'. Et dixit ei Mercurius: 'Tu ipse appone manum tuam'.*[16]

Les trois autres exemples sont beaucoup plus développés:

Miles quidam confitebatur cuidam simplici sacerdoti et ille absoluit eum. Dixit miles: 'Volo ire Romam uidere caput Ecclesie'. Dixit sacerdos: 'Nolite quia timeo michi ne ita bene credatis postea sicut modo'. Miles iuit ad curiam, uidit notarios, id est usurarios Domini Pape, sedere in porta, et meretrices; miratus est et reuersus est domi. Dixit sacerdos: 'Quomodo est? Timeo ne ita bene credatis sicut prius'. Dixit miles: 'Immo perfectius credo modo, quia in Deo; et illi qui deberent fidem christianam fulcire nituntur eam peruertere; ergo miraculose stat fides nostra'.—Sicut uidimus quando due situle intrant puteum, quando una deponitur altera alleviatur, sic quando corpus affligitur et anima liberatur.... Legitur in quodam libro Iudeorum quod uulpes siciens intrauit situlam ut posset potare, descendit ad aquam et bibit, et tunc ascendere non potuit. Venit Ysengrinus et dixit ei: 'Quid facis ibi, Reinarde?' Dixit uulpes: 'Hic sunt multa bona', et nominauit illa que Ysengrinus maxime desiderabat; 'Ysengrine pone te in situla illa et statim descendes ad me'. Fecit sic; et cum uulpes ascenderit cum situla, in aqua erat quia Ysengrinus ponderosior fuit ipso. Dixit lupus: 'Quo uadis, frater mi?' Dixit uulpes: 'Ego sum

---

[16] S. Antoine, cf. Tubach, n° 277; le paysan embourbé: *ibid.*, n° 3646.

deliberatus et tu capieris pro me'.—Fuit quidam pauper homo in terra sancta; habuit filium et fuit senex, et dixit filius: 'Pater, non potestis michi relinquere multa bona temporalia; doceatis me aliquid de sapiencia uestra': Dixit pater: 'Libenter'. Habuit pater asinum. Dixit filio quod duceret asinum secum cum ueniret in ciuitate. Dixit filio: 'Ascende'. Obuiauerunt ei quidam dicentes: 'Iste rusticus fatuus est: plus diligit filium quam se ipsum'. Dixit filio: 'Descende'; Et ipse tunc ascendit. Obuiauerunt alii qui dixerunt: 'Impius et crudelis est iste rusticus, non habet de isto iuuene paruo; rusticus habet longa et forcia crura, ascendit equum et permittit istum puerum iuuenem ire pedes'. 'Audis, fili', dixit pater; 'ascende mecum'. Et obuiauerunt ei alii qui dixerunt quod: 'Crudelissimus est iste rusticus: non habet pietatem de bestia muta; ambo eam equitant; ad minus unus deberet ire pedes'. Dixit pater: 'Descendamus ambo'. Et obuiauerunt alii qui dixerunt: 'Fatuus est iste rusticus: plus diligit bestiam suam quam se ipsum et filium suum; ad minus unus deberet ascendere'. Dixit pater: 'Non restat nisi quod portemus asinum: nichil possumus facere de quo non loquantur homines. Hoc dico tibi pro tanto quia cum bene feceris non debes attendere ad uerba hominum, sed semper debes bene operari, quia si uelis attendere ad uerba hominum, nunquam bene facies'.[17]

Dans trois autres des subdivisions, nous avons des allusions bibliques, une au centurion dont le serviteur a été guéri, deux à l'enfant prodigue, dont il est difficile de dire exactement s'il s'agit d'une *auctoritas* ou d'un *exemplum* ébauché. Ailleurs se trouvent de courtes incises qui pourraient être 'dilatées' en *exempla*:

Aliqui sunt ita indurati quod ludunt ad scaccos ut obliuiscantur amaritudinis peccati.—Faciunt aliqui mutatoria equorum et domorum ut obliuiscentur peccati.—Quando clericus est pauper, nullus parentum curat de ipso; quando diues, omnes recurrunt ad ipsum usque ad quartum gradum.

Le sermon de Pierre de Remiremont est donc plein d'*exempla* et de *similitudines* plus ou moins développés. On peut même se demander si, dans les subdivisions qui n'en comportent pas dans le texte tel qu'il nous est parvenu, il s'agit d'un choix de l'orateur ou

---

[17] Le chevalier à Rome, cf. J.-Th. Welter, *La tabula exemplorum secundum ordinem alphabeti* (Paris et Toulouse, 1926), p. 106; Tubach, n° 4173; Le renard et le loup: Tubach, n° 5247; les paysans et l'âne: Tubach, n° 4173.

d'une omission du reportateur. Mais quelle que soit l'abondance des *exempla* et des comparaisons, il est clair qu'aucun n'est indispensable à la structure du sermon et qu'un schéma pourrait fort bien les supprimer; le sens général n'y perdrait pas grand chose, mais tout le charme de ce sermon très familier et concret aurait disparu.

Nous sommes en effet plus à la merci des choix, ou des inattentions des reportateurs pour les *exempla* et les comparaisons courtes que pour les *similitudines* longues, bien que celles-ci ne soient pas à l'abri de tout dommage. Voici le cas d'un sermon prêché le 15 février 1260, probablement par Robert de Sorbon. Le texte nous en est parvenu en trois reportations. La première, dûe à Pierre de Limoges, nous transmet le sermon du matin et la collation du soir; une autre, dans un manuscrit de la Vaticane, ne nous a conservé que le sermon; enfin nous avons quelques extraits d'une troisième reportation.[18] Le thème de la prédication était tiré de l'épître du jour, la Quinquagésime: *Si linguis hominum loquar ... factus sum sicut es sonans.* La deuxième partie, consacrée à l'éloge de la charité, est bâtie sur la comparaison de la cloche, le bronze qui sonne, et le mauvais prédicateur privé de charité. Nos trois témoins s'accordent en gros: la cloche fait beaucoup de bruit au point qu'elle risque d'éclater, mais elle-même est sourde; elle fait entrer les paroissiens dans l'église, mais elle ne bouge pas de sa place; elle est ouverte et large en bas, vers les biens temporels, mais fermée et étroite en haut; elle doit son nom de cloche à ce qu'elle boite; elle fait un bruit terrible tandis que la cithare a un son agréable, mais qu'on prêche sur l'enfer ou sur le ciel, on perd son temps sans la charité; enfin on peut mettre les paroles qu'on veut sur la musique des cloches. Et ici la reportation de Pierre de Limoges ajoute un *exemplum*:

> *Item campana conformat se omnibus que homo cogitat. Exemplum de muliere que uolens ducere famulum suum set non audens propter*

---

[18] Reportation de P. de Limoges: BN, ms lat. 15971, ff. 71ra–2ra (sermon), 72ra–vb (collation). En marge de 71ra est écrit: *Rob.*, abréviation usuelle de Pierre pour R. de Sorbon; mais la marge inférieure porte, également de la main de Pierre: *frater henricus remensis.* Je ne sais comment expliquer ce fait. Autres reportations: BAV, Vat.lat.1211, ff. 51ra–va; BN, ms lat. 15957, f. 113va–vb (abrégé copié par Etienne d'Abbeville).

parentes suos, cui dixit uetula quedam rogata a famulo, quod Deus mandabat ei per campanas suas quod duceret famulum suum, et cum campane pulsarent, dicit ei uetula: 'Ecce, domina,' quod dicunt campane: 'Pren tun gargo, pren tun gargo'. Et duxit eum. Sic quando episcopus aliquis non audet conferre alicui indigno nepoti uel aliquo famulo aliquam prebendam, ueniunt iste campane, scilicet magni magistri, et sonant in aure eius quod ipse uolebat multum facere et consulunt ei: 'Domine, detis hoc famulo uestro qui diu uobis seruiuit'.[19]

Dans le cas présent, les diverses reportations ont plus ou moins choisi parmi les propriétés de la cloche: Pierre de Limoges ne parle pas de la boiterie; la reportation vaticane omet le fait qu'on puisse faire dire à la cloche n'importe quoi; les extraits sont naturellement encore plus avares, mais tous les témoins gardent l'essentiel de la *similitudo* alors que deux sur trois ignorent l'*exemplum* final.

D'autre part, le même *exemplum* peut-être rapporté de façon assez différente selon les auditeurs. Dans ce même sermon de Quinquagésime 1260, la reportation vaticane nous dit:

Exemplum. Rex Francie est in Ardania ubi non est uini copia. Si esset aliquis qui presentaret duos cados uini, multum libenter rex reciperet et danti gracias redderet; plus illud uinum diligeret quam Parisius dolium si esset. In Ardania est Deus modo quia omnes ardent gula et luxuria.

Les auditeurs pouvaient d'autant plus apprécier le jeu de mots sur *Ardania-ardere* qu'ils savaient fort bien que Robert de Sorbon était lui-même ardennais. Mais dans la reportation parisienne toute allusion a disparu:

Si quis uellet mittere duos potos uini regi Francie existenti in deserto ualde pauperrimo et diceret: 'Volo expectare quod rex sit Parisius antequam mittam ei exennium', cum tamen Parisius non indiget uino nullius, musardus diceretur. Sic Christus modo hiis tribus diebus pauper est quia pauci mittunt ei encenia.[20]

---

[19] Même *exemplum* dans Welter, *Tabula*, p. 67, enregistré par Tubach, n° 4295b sous le lemme: *Servant, ugly, loved,* sans allusion à la cloche.

[20] BAV, Vat.lat. 1211, f. 74va; BN, ms lat. 15971, f. 71rb.

Similitudines *et* exempla

De même un sermon de Ranulphe de la Houblonnière nous a été transmis par deux manuscrits qui donnent la même reportation, mais un des copistes a supprimé un des huit *exempla* et en a résumé deux autres de telle façon qu'ils seraient difficilement compréhensibles sans la reportation complète.[21]

La suppression des *exempla* et des comparaisons brèves est en effet une des premières opérations de quelqu'un qui abrège. Un bon exemple est le sermon de Bonaventure pour la Translation de saint François dont la version longue, publiée par Robert E. Lerner, est remplie d'épisodes de la vie de saint François, avec en plus deux autres *exempla*, tous omis dans le résumé imprimé dans la grande édition.[22]

Il serait donc assez risqué de se baser sur des reportations pour savoir dans quelle mesure un prédicateur use de l'*exemplum* et dans quelles circonstances il l'emploie. On peut cependant avoir quelques présomptions. Ainsi Nicole Bériou a-t-elle remarqué que, dans deux sermons de même thème et de plans très voisins prêchés par Ranulphe de la Houblonnière pour la Purification, la même idée est appuyée devant l'Université par une *auctoritas* alors que chez les béguines elle est illustrée par une comparaison courte ou un *exemplum*.[23]

Il faudrait vérifier sur d'autres cas si la prédication dans les paroisses ou dans les communautés féminines était plus riche en *exempla* que celle qui s'adressait aux clercs et surtout aux universitaires. Nous pouvons constater que dans les sermons de Thomas d'Aquin transmis comme tels, qui auraient été prêchés *coram Uniuersitate*, il y a bien peu d'*exempla* ou de comparaisons; mais il n'y en a pas plus dans les *Collationes* données à Naples au peuple en langue vulgaire; il est vrai qu'ici, outre le travail de reportation et de traduction en latin, il semble qu'il y ait eu aussi une sévère abréviation. Les premières collations sur le *Credo* comportent quelques comparaisons courtes proches de l'*exemplum*, mais elles

[21] N. Bériou, *Sermons aux clercs et sermons aux "simple gens": la prédication de Ranulphe de la Houblonnière à Paris au XIIIe siècle* (Thèse de Paris IV, Paris-Sorbonne, à paraître chez Etudes Augustiniennes, Paris).

[22] R.E. Lerner, 'A Collection of Sermons given in Paris *c*.1267, including a New Text by Saint Bonaventura on the Life of Saint Francis', *Speculum*, xlix (1974), pp. 466–98. *S. Bonaventurae Opera omnia*, 10 vols (Quaracchi, 1882–1902), ix, pp. 534–5.

[23] Bériou, *Sermons aux clercs*.

disparaissent vite et l'on n'en compte pratiquement pas dans les autres séries.[24]

On trouve les mêmes difficultés en passant à Bonaventure: dans ses collations sur le Décalogue, je compte six *exempla* pour sept sermons, et sept pour neuf sermons dans celles sur les dons du Saint-Esprit; ces deux séries, sans être proprement universitaires, étaient adressées aux frères de Paris, en grande partie étudiants. Le sermon universitaire de Noël et les trois de l'Epiphanie n'offrent aucun *exemplum*, mais celui de saint Etienne prêché devant l'Université, en compte quatre dont trois tirés de *miracula*. Par contre, si le sermon de saint Marc adressé aux moniales de Saint-Antoine de Paris a un *exemplum* et celui donné aux béguines pour la même fête en a trois, deux sermons d'Assise pour Noël, un aux Clarisses et l'autre au peuple, n'en ont aucun.[25] Il est donc difficile de tirer une conclusion tant soit peu solide dans l'état actuel de la recherche. Ce qui semble au contraire plus assuré est que l'usage des comparaisons longues structurant le sermon est pratiquement absent de la prédication universitaire, construite normalement sur les *distinctiones* proprement dites.

Si nous passons maintenant aux collections de sermons rédigées par des prédicateurs pour aider leurs confrères en leur fournissant des modèles,[26] nous y trouvons aussi une assez grande variété de cas. Welter avait déjà noté que l'un des recueils de Jacques de Vitry ne comporte pas d'*exempla* alors que les deux autres en sont pleins, et que Jean Halgrin d'Abbeville, dont des témoignages disent qu'il

---

[24] Seuls comportent un *exemplum* les sermons: *Attendite a falsis prophetis*: Schneyer, *Repertorium*, v, p. 579, n° 6; *Opera omnia*, xxxii, p. 676ᵃ. *Beata gens*: Schneyer, p. 581, n° 23; *Opera*, p. 802ᵇ. *Ecce rex tuus*: Schneyer, p. 580, n° 15; éd. Leclercq, 'Un sermon', p. 166. *Homo quidam erat diues*: Schneyer, p. 580, n° 24; *Opera*, p. 792ᵇ. *Lux orta est*: Schneyer, p. 582, n° 30; *Opera*, p. 686ᵃ. *Osanna filio David*: Schneyer, p. 582, n° 3; éd. Th. Kaeppeli, 'Una raccolta di prediche attribuite a S. Tommaso d'Aquino', *AFP*, xiii(1943), pp. 74–5. *Puer Iesus*: Schneyer, p. 569, n° 4; *Opera*, p. 666ᵇ. *Collationes in Symbolum*, cf. note 3.

[25] *S.Bonaventurae Opera omnia* (Quaracchi), v: *De X preceptis*: pp. 511ᵃ, 514ᵃ, 517ᵇ, 525ᵃ, 528ᵃ; *De VII donis*: pp. 470ᵃ, 472ᵇ, 477ᵃ, 486ᵃ, 489ᵃ. *Sermones*, ix: *In Nativ*.II, pp. 106–10; *In Epiph*.I–III, pp. 145–60; *De S. Stefano* I, pp. 483–4; *De S. Marco* I, p. 521ᵃ; *De S. Marco* II, pp. 526ᵃ, 527ᵃ,ᵇ; *In Nativ*.I, pp. 102–6; *In Nativ*.III, pp. 110–12.

[26] Nous disposons maintenant sur le sujet des sermons modèles de l'ouvrage de D.d'Avray, *The Preaching of the Friars* (Oxford, 1985).

usait largement de l'*exemplum*, n'en a mis aucun dans sa collection.[27]

Nous ne trouvons pas non plus d'*exempla* dans les plus anciens recueils dominicains italiens dont les *processus* sont plutôt des schémas que des sermons développés; chez Aldobrandino Cavalcanti, plusieurs sont construits sur des similitudes longues: ainsi le thème *Ecce sanus factus es* l'invite à comparer les vertus aux signes cliniques de la bonne santé.[28]

Cet usage de la comparaison fournissant le plan du sermon est systématique chez le dominicain français Pierre de Reims: c'est ainsi que pour le commun des Apôtres, le thème *Tollite iugum meum* lui permet de comparer ceux-ci aux boeufs tandis que le verset *In omnem terram exiuit sonus eorum* est l'occasion d'un parallèle avec le tonnerre, la trompette et la cloche prise cette fois en bonne part:

> *Item nota de proprietatibus campane, scilicet quod integra bene sonat sed fracta horride.... Item campana in qua multum est argenti dulciter sonat.... Item sonus campane, ut dicitur, se conformat omnibus cantilenis et cuilibet cantat quod uult; sic Apostoli linguis loquuntur omnium. Item sonus campane de aquis resultans dulcior efficitur ....*[29]

Pierre de Saint-Benoît, franciscain, use aussi, mais plus sporadiquement, de la comparaison longue. Il prévoit aussi des *exempla* qu'il se contente d'évoquer en quelques mots. Ainsi dans le court sermon *Mane nobiscum Domine*, chaque subdivision a au moins un *exemplum*; les voici:

> *Exemplum de Amon et Thamar. Nota de societate taberne.... Nota de moniali et beata Virgine in die Ascensionis.... Nota de rege et milite et castro in quo rex moratur.... Exemplum de tribus amicis.... Exemplum de rege Philippo. Nota de regina quam nullus principum audet contempnere quamdiu admittitur ad amplexus regis. Nota de illo*

---

[27] Welter, *L'exemplum*, pp. 118–19, 129, et note 27.

[28] Schneyer, *Repertorium*, i, p. 162, n° 180; Milano, Biblioteca Ambrosiana, ms o.1.sup., ff. 300rb–^{va}.

[29] Les sermons de Pierre de Reims ont été imprimés plusieurs fois sous le nom d'Antoine de Padoue. J'utilise: *S.Francisci Assisiatis ... et S.Antonii Paduani ... Opera omnia ... ... opera et labore ... Ioh. de la Haye* (Paris, 1641). Sermon *Tollite iugum*, pp. 428–9; Schneyer, *Repertorium*, iv, p. 753, n° 469. Sermon *In omnem terram*, pp. 420–2; Schneyer, n° 463; je cite d'après Assisi, Biblioteca Comunale, ms 452, ff. 97ra–98rb.

qui ibat ad suspendium propter societatem.... Et nota de uxore que plangebat suum dampnum.... Nota quomodo Dominus uenit in monte ad obsequium hospitis sue Marte....[30]

Nous avons vu que Servasanctus de Faenza usait largement d'*exempla* tirés de l'antiquité classique ou de l'histoire naturelle. Il lui arrive aussi de construire certains sermons sur des *similitudines* développées; c'est le cas du très joli sermon publié par le P.V. Gamboso où, à propos de Jean Baptiste dont il est dit: *Vinum et siceram non bibet*, il compare les différents cépages aux divers états spirituels, depuis le muscat, apanage des bienheureux, jusqu'à la *vernaccia* réservée aux damnés qui ne sont pas trop à plaindre en l'occurrence.[31]

Mais celui qui semble avoir employé le plus souvent et avec le plus d'art la *similitudo* longue est Guillaume de Mailly. Nous en avons déjà vu un exemple; il serait facile de les multiplier: comparaison du navire et de la sainteté, du traitement médical et de la conversion, du vieillard mal voyant, perdant ses dents, aux cheveux blancs, au dos courbé tellement qu'il ne peut plus voir le ciel, tremblant de tous ses membres, *mocheus et baveus*, plein de rides, avec le pécheur endurci.[32]

Ces comparaisons longues, dont on trouverait aisément bien d'autres exemples chez d'autres prédicateurs du temps, mériteraient une étude analogue à celles qui ont été faites sur les *exempla*. En dehors des qualités littéraires ou des intérêts documentaires éventuels, elles témoignent surtout d'un effort très notable des prédicateurs pour se mettre plus à la portée du public des paroisses et correspondent donc à une meilleure prise de conscience au plan psychologique de la mentalité des auditeurs et au plan pastoral des besoins spirituels du laïcat chrétien. Par le développement d'images

---

[30] Schneyer, *Repertorium*, iv, p. 787, n° 62; Venezia, Biblioteca Marciana, ms 1897 (fondo ant.lat. 92), f. 44rb.

[31] Gamboso, 'I sermoni festivi', pp. 78–80.

[32] Cf. note 7. Navire: *Domine salua nos*: Schneyer, *Repertorium*, ii, p. 484, n° 19; BN, ms lat. 15956, ff. 30va–32vb. Traitement médical: *Sanata est*: n° 26; ff. 42vb–44va. Vieillard: *Expurgate uetus fermentum*: p. 485, n° 40; ff. 59vb–62va.

Similitudines *et* exempla

tirées de l'ecriture, elles montrent aussi que, sans pour cela négliger les sens spirituels, les prédicateurs faisaient davantage place au sens littéral des péricopes liturgiques. Ainsi s'inséraient-t-ils dans le grand mouvement exégétique si bien étudié par Beryl Smalley.

Commissio Leonina, Grottaferrata, Rome

THE GOSPEL OF THE MARRIAGE
FEAST OF CANA AND MARRIAGE
PREACHING IN FRANCE*

by DAVID d'AVRAY

THE history of attitudes to marriage is a fashionable subject and has been so for some time.[1] This does not mean that it is an overworked subject, for the field is large enough to provide work for many labourers. A corner of it which has scarcely been touched is the development of marriage doctrine in bible commentaries and sermons, two types of source which medievalists will always associate with Beryl Smalley. This paper deals only with the second class of source, but it is nevertheless about exegesis, since the sermons which will be examined have the pericope or Gospel reading of the marriage feast of Cana as their starting-point. Thus they are not sermons delivered at wedding services, but sermons for a particular Sunday, the second after Epiphany.[2] There would presumably have been many weddings around this time of year, however, for one of the periods during

* I am grateful to Julia Walworth for helpful suggestions. The essay was completed during leave of absence which the Alexander von Humboldt–Stiftung made possible.

[1] Cf., for example, *Love and Marriage in the Twelfth Century*, ed. W. Van Hoecke and A. Welkenhuysen [Colloquium, Louvain, 1978] = *Medievalia Lovanensia*, series 1/studia viii (Louvain, 1981); *Settimane di Studio del Centro italiano di studi sull'alto medioevo 24: Il matrimonio nella società altomedievale* [Spoleto, 1976] 2 vols. (Spoleto, 1977); *Marriage and Society. Studies in the Social History of Marriage*, ed. R.B. Outhwaite (New York, 1982) (especially C.N.L. Brooke, 'Marriage and Society in the Central Middle Ages', pp. 17–34, and K.M. Davies, 'Continuity and Change in Literary Advice on Marriage', pp. 58–80); G. Duby, *Le Chevalier, la femme, et le prêtre. Le mariage dans la France féodale* (Paris, 1983); L. Stone, *The Family, Sex and Marriage in England 1500–1800* (London, 1977). Medieval preaching has also become a popular subject. For a survey of recent work see C. Delcorno, 'Rassegna di Studi sulla Predicazione Medievale e Umanistica (1970–80)' in *Lettere Italiane* (1981), pp. 235–76. The best introduction is L.-J. Bataillon, 'Approaches to the Study of Medieval Sermons', *Leeds Studies in English*, ns,xi (1980), pp. 19–35. On seventeenth-century preaching see P. Bayley, *French Pulpit Oratory 1598–1650* (Cambridge, 1980).

[2] In England, however, the Gospel of the Marriage Feast at Cana seems to have been read on the third Sunday after Epiphany according to the Sarum use.

which it was not permitted to celebrate marriage would just have come to an end.[3] Sermons for this Sunday became a vehicle for marriage teaching around the turn of the twelfth and thirteenth centuries. From then on, the genre flourished until well into the eighteenth century, and very probably beyond. It is therefore an appropriate subject for a comparative study of two periods. The body of material even from the medieval period alone is large, much larger than the modest *corpus* of marriage sermons in medieval *ad status* collections, for instance.[4] To keep it within bounds, I will here confine myself to France, and to the thirteenth and seventeenth centuries.

By now the comparative method is a traditional rather than a new form of history. A comparison between two centuries is a short cut to discovering what the long-term continuities in popularized marriage preaching were. It also helps us to define the specific characteristics of marriage preaching in each period, and to notice significant absences to which we would otherwise scarcely have averted. I shall argue that sermons of both periods lay emphasis on the goodness of marriage, on love in marriage, and on a strict moral code governing married life; but that the seventeenth century differs in an interesting way from the thirteenth in its emphasis on at least two ideas. The first is the connection between grace and marriage. Seventeenth-century preachers are very concerned that the couple should be in a state of grace for the wedding, and they have much to say about the graces which marriage itself confers. Moreover, in the second half of the century (if not earlier) they also speak of a special grace of vocation without which no one

---

[3] BN, lat.14952, f. 24va/b^: '*A prima dominica adventus usque modo secundum consuetudinem matris ecclesie cessaverunt nuptie, quia tunc fiebat sollempnitas et memoria de regalibus nuptiis, scilicet filii dei cum humana natura, et indecens erat, sive inhonestum, rusticum, celebrare nuptias quando deus pater celebrabat* (col. b) *nuptias filio suo. Nunc ergo secundum consuetudinem matris ecclesie redit tempus nubendi et amplexandi. In signum huius ad instructionem nubentium hodie evangelista Iohannes proponit verba de nuptiis ...*' (from a sermon by Peter of Tarentaise, O.P., on the text *Nuptiae factae sunt* (*John*, ii. 1), Schneyer, *Repertorium*, iv, p. 803, no. 8). Cf. the opening words of a sermon for the second Sunday after Epiphany in Clm 2702, f. 22^v^: '*Nuptie facte sunt et cetera. Io. Quia hoc tempore homines maxime cogitant de nuptiis, igitur hoc modo ewangelium legitur de nuptiis ...*' (Schneyer, *Repertorium*, viii, p. 573, no.32). Cf. also a remark by Jacques de Vitry about the times when it was forbidden to get married, cited in D.L. d'Avray and M. Tausche, 'Marriage Sermons in *ad status* collections of the Central Middle Ages', *AHDLMA*, xlvii (1980), pp. 71–119 at p. 112, n. 9.

[4] On this genre see d'Avray and Tausche, 'Marriage Sermons'.

should marry. The idea of marriage as a personal vocation, a critical choice, like the vocation to the priesthood, is in fact the second idea which I have found to be conspicuous in the seventeenth century and conspicuous by its absence in the thirteenth.

Why these two centuries? In some ways they invite comparison—both are periods of Catholic reform and reaction against heresy—but in a sense it would not have mattered greatly which centuries were chosen, provided that they were widely spaced. If the same distinctive *topoi* are found in the same genre in both periods, it is likely that they are also to be found in the intervening period. Once they have been identified, it may be relatively easy to establish that they have a continuous history. This is a more systematic and efficient way of establishing the *longue durée* of mental attitudes than trying to swallow half-a-dozen centuries at one gulp, without a clear idea of what to look for. If major differences between the two periods compared come to light, on the other hand, then the path for further investigation is again well defined. Historians of the periods in between are automatically presented with a precise questionnaire: When was this or that theme introduced? Once the questions are formulated, it may not be long before solutions are found.

Even a few comparative soundings would have saved some early-modern historians from the elementary misconception that medieval theology had a negative attitude to marriage. So good a historian as Jean Delumeau can speak of 'a virulent hostility—which was above all current in intellectual milieux—to marriage'; assert that the truth that man could be saved in all states of life was 'too much forgotten ... by medieval clerics'; and give Erasmus the credit of exalting marriage 'against a medieval theology which had forgotten it and a clerical literature which had scoffed at it'.[5] Similar misconceptions turn up more often than one might expect in serious studies by post-medievalists,[6] a fact which should remind

---

[5] J. Delumeau, *La Civilisation de la Renaissance* (Paris, 1967), pp. 442–4 (my trans.).
[6] L.L. Schücking, *Die puritanische Familie in literar-soziologischer Sicht* (Bern and Munich, 1964), p. 30: '... dem Mittelalter war die Ehe mehr oder weniger ein notwendiges Übel gewesen...'; R. Tavenaux, *Le Catholicisme dans la France classique, 1610–1715* (Paris, 1980), ii, pp. 349–50; cf. too Stone, *The Family*, p. 135. C. B. Paris, *Marriage in XVIIth Century Catholicism. The Origins of a Religious Mentality: the Teaching of 'L'Ecole française' (1600–1660)* (Tournai and Montreal, 1975), leaps from Augustine to Trent and the seventeenth-century 'Ecole française'.

us that concentration on one period only can make one less rather than more scholarly. For any medievalist who has done serious work on clerical attitudes will know that the goodness of marriage was heavily stressed in medieval theology.

The emphasis is if anything still more unmistakeable in preaching, if not so well known. Certain recurrent *topoi* are the usual vehicle for this positive evaluation of matrimony. They crop up again and again in varying combinations and patterns. A number of them are grouped together at the beginning of a schematic summary sermon by the Dominican Paris master, Hugh of St Cher (†1263):

Nuptie facte sunt in Chanan[7] Galilee et cetera. Primo commendatur matrimonium ab auctoritate, quia deus ipsum instituit. Secundo a loco, quia in paradiso. Tertio commendatur a tempore, quia factum fuit ante peccatum. Quarto a causa, quia spe prolis. Verumptamen datum [col. b] est post peccatum non solum ob causam prolis, sed in remedium vitande fornicationis. Quinto a corporali Christi presentia, ut patet in ewangelio. Sexto a miraculorum operatione, ut patet ibi quia aquam mutavit[8] in vinum.[9]	There was a marriage in Cana of Galilee, etc. Marriage is commended first from authority, because God instituted it. Secondly, from place, because in paradise. Thirdly, from time, because it had been done before sin. Fourthly, from cause, because with hope for children. Nevertheless, it was given after sin, not only for the sake of children, but as a remedy to avoid fornication. Fifthly, by the bodily presence of Christ [at the marriage feast of Cana], as is clear from the Gospel [reading]. Sixthly, by the working of miracles, as is clear because he turned water into wine ....

Another *topos* is that marriage is the oldest 'religious' order, founded not by a saint, but by God himself. There is an especially interesting case in a sermon preached at Paris by the Dominican Henry of Provins:

Vos videtis quod noster ordo et fratrum minorum non est diu quod incepit; et similiter alii ordines post	You see that our Order [i.e., the Dominicans] and that of the Friars Minor began not long ago; and

[7] Sic.
[8] *mut* or *nuit* MS?
[9] BN, MS lat. 15946 f. 6[va]/[b]. Schneyer, *Repertorium*, ii, p. 759, no. 18.

incarnationem inceperunt; sed iste ordo incepit a principio mundi. Plus, quidam homo mortalis de Hyspania fecit nostrum ordinem; quidam homo de Lumbardia ordinem fratrum minorum; sed istum ordinem fecit ipse deus, et non de novo, sed a principio mundi... [10]	similarly other orders began after the Incarnation; but this Order began from the beginning of the world. Furthermore, a certain mortal man from Spain made our Order, a certain man from Lombardy the Order of Friars Minor; but God himself made this Order, and not newly, but from the beginning of the world.

Nevertheless, a quantitative survey, if such a thing were possible, would probably show that the most common *topos* of all, perhaps throughout the whole history of the genre, was that God instituted marriage in paradise, then honoured it with his presence at Cana, and that it must therefore be good. We have already seen that these are among the reasons which Hugh of St Cher gives for commending marriage. We may take another example from the sermon on the text *Vocatus est Iesus (John*, ii. 1) by Guibert of Tournai,[11] a Franciscan Paris master:

Nuptialem societatem inter virum et mulierem dominus honoravit. Hoc[12] *enim fuit primum sacramentum, et a principio mundi institutum, et a domino ordinatum, et in paradyso terestri*[13] *factum in principio veteris testamenti, et a domino confirmatum in primo miraculo quod fecit in tempore*[14] *novi testamenti...*[15]	The Lord honoured the partnership of marriage between man and woman. For this was the first sacrament; it was established from the beginning of the world, set up in due form by the Lord, made in the earthly paradise at the beginning of the Old Testament, and confirmed by the Lord in the first miracle which he performed in the age of the New Testament...

We meet exactly the same *topos* in a sermon for the second Sunday after Epiphany by Etienne Molinier, a celebrated preacher who

[10] N. Bériou and D.L. d'Avray, 'Henry of Provins, O.P.'s Comparison of the Dominican and Franciscan Orders with the "Order" of Matrimony'. *AFP*, xlix (1979), pp. 513–17, at p. 514.

[11] Schneyer, *Repertorium*, ii, p. 283, no. 10. It is from his collection of *Sermones de tempore et de sanctis*. For his *ad status* sermons to wives see d'Avray and Tausche, cited above, n.3.

[12] *hic* MS.

[13] *Sic.*

[14] In margin with omission signs.

[15] BN, MS lat. 15941 f. 83[ra].

died in 1647. 'Marriage is honourable ... says the Apostle. God instituted it in the earthly Paradise. Jesus Christ, the Virgin, and the Apostles honoured it by their presence, and Jesus Christ by his first miracle'.[16]

Yet another *topos* which turns up in both periods is that of the three goods of marriage: *fides*, *proles*, and *sacramentum*. The formula itself has been part of the enduring structure of thought about marriage in Christian Europe,[17] though it has not always meant quite the same thing. How naturally this prefabricated combination of ideas was built into the fabric of a marriage sermon depended on the preacher. Hugh of St Cher sticks it in rather awkwardly:

Septimum malum est luxuria. De qua Prover.:[18] *Ne des fornicariis honorem tuum et cetera. Et idem: animam suam et cetera. His breviter prenotatis,*[19] *sciendum est quod—sicut dicit beatus Augustinus super* [f. 7ra] *illum locum i^a ad Cor. vii. [1]: Bonum est homini mulierem non tangere—tria sunt bona matrimonii, scilicet:*
Fides, ne cum alio vel cum alia commisceatur. Eccli. xxxiii[20] *[32]: Omnis mulier, et cetera.*
Proles, ut religiose educetur. Thob. viii [9]: Domine, tu scis, et cetera.
Sacramentum coniugii, ut non separetur. Mt. xix [6] Quod deus coniunxit, homo non separet, et cetera.[21]

The seventh evil [which arises from adultery] is lust, about which Proverbs says: Do not give your honour [*sic*] to prostitutes, etc. And the same: his soul, etc. These things briefly noted, it should be known that—as Augustine says in regard to that passage in I *Corinthians*, vii, 'It is good for a man not to touch woman'— there are three goods of marriage, namely:
Faith, lest there be intercourse with another man or woman. *Ecclesiasticus*, xxxiii: Every woman, et cetera.
Children, that they may be brought up in a religious way. *Tobias*, viii: Lord, you know, etc.
The sacrament of matrimony, that they may not be separated.

---

[16] E. Molinier, *Sermons pour tous les dimanches de l'année* ..., 5th ed. (Paris, 1639), i [BN call no. D. 44936], p. 226: '*Les nopces sont honorables ... dit l'Apostre. Dieu les a instituées dans le Paradis terrestre. Jesus-Christ, la Vierge, & les Apostres les ont honorées de leur presence, & Jesus-Christ de son premier miracle* ...'.

[17] Cf. d'Avray and Tausche, 'Marriage sermons in *ad status* collections', pp. 92–3.

[18] *Prover.* followed by space in MS, perhaps for chapter number. '*Ne des fornicariis animam tuam in ullo* ...' is *Eccli.*, ix. 6, but cf. *Prov.*, v. 2 and ff., vi. 24 ff., and xxix. 3.

[19] *pernotatis* MS.

[20] *Ecc.*, xxxii MS.

[21] BN, MS lat. 15946 f. 6vb–7ra (from sermon on the text *Nuptiae factae sunt* (John., ii. 1), Schneyer, *Repertorium*, ii, p. 759, no. 18).

> *Matt.*, xix: What God has joined
> together, let man not put asunder,
> et cetera.

On the other hand, Guillaume de Mailly (also thirteenth century)
slips the three-goods *topos* neatly into his elaborate structure of
divisions and subdivisions. For Jesus, that is, salvation, to be
present in matrimony—the allusion is to his presence at the
marriage feast of Cana—three things are required: a right intention
in contracting it, fidelity in preserving it, and an inseparable life
together. Each of these three points becomes the basis of a
subsection, and one of the 'three goods' is smoothly introduced in
each subsection.[22]

An awareness of the function of a *topos* in context, and a
recognition of the individuality—or lack of it—in the use to which
it is put,[23] are important when a particular preacher is being
assessed. Our main concern here, however, is with the survival of
the *topos* into the seventeenth century, which may be illustrated
from a sermon by the Franciscan Jean Boucher. The three goods of
marriage are in fact the subject of the greater part of his sermon for
the second Sunday after Epiphany. He introduces the *topos* in the
following manner:

Or ceste vnion coniugale que nous appellons Mariage, est quelque chose [p. 57] de grand, non seulement à	Therefore this conjugal union which we call marriage is something great, not only because of

---

[22] Clm 14702, ff. xxvi[ra]–xxvii[ra]: '*Secunde nuptie sunt sacramentales, que sunt in matrimonio carnali, et iste nuptie sunt ad literam [sic] de quibus agit presens ewangelium. Docemur autem in isto ewangelio quo modo debent iste nuptie conservari et fieri in hoc quod Iesus fuit ibi vocatus. Ad hoc enim debet fieri matrimonium ut sit ibi Iesus, id est salus. Ad hoc autem quod sit ibi salus tria sunt necessaria, scilicet rectitudo intentionis in contrahendo, fidelitas in conservando, inseparabilitas in vivendo. Primo dico debet esse rectitudo intentionis in contrahendo, ut sit bonum prolis, quod fit quando intentione prolis procreande et ad cultum dei educande contrahitur, non sicut usurarii vel cupidi qui propter divitias aggregandas contrahunt. ...* [f. xxvi [rb]] *... Secundo debet esse fidelitas in matrimonium contractum conservando, ut sit ibi bonum fidei. Ista autem fidelitas in iiii attenditur. Primo* (prima ms.) *in mutua cordium dilectione. ...* [f. xxvi[va]] *... Secundo consistit ista fidelitas in temporalium mutua amministratione. ... Tertio* (Terci MS.) *consistit in mutui honoris impensione. ... Quarto consistit in mutua inviolabi-*[col. b] *li iuris thori conservatione. ... Tertio requiritur inseparabilitas in vivendo, ut scilicet sit ibi bonum sacramenti. ... In talibus nup-*[f. xxvii[ra]]*-tiis in quibus ista tria concurrunt est Iesus ...*'. From a sermon on the text *Nuptiae factae sunt* (John, ii. 1), Schneyer, *Repertorium*, ii, p. 484, no. 17.

[23] To borrow the phrase of P. Dronke, *Poetic Individuality in the Middle Ages. New Departures in Poetry 1000–1150* (Oxford, 1970), p. 11.

| cause du temps & du lieu de son institution, qui est au temps d'innocence, & dans le Paradis terrestre; mais de plus à raison de trois grands biens, desquels son autheur, qui est Dieu, l'a voulu enrichir, car il porte auec foy la foy ou fidelité coniugale, la procreation des enfans, & la gloire du Sacrament, qui est vne viue representation de l'vnion de Jesus auec son Eglise, qui son trois biens d'vn haut prix & d'vne valeur inestimable[24] | the time and place of its institution, which is at the time of innocence, and in the earthly paradise, but more by reason of the three great goods, with which its author, who is God, wished to enrich it, for it carries with faith [?] conjugal faith or fidelity, the procreation of children, and the glory of the sacrament, which is a live representation of the union of Jesus with his Church, which are three goods of great price and of an inestimable value. |

It will have become clear (if the matter was ever in doubt) that marriage was not regarded by preachers in France as 'no more than an unfortunate necessity to cope with human frailty',[25] in either the thirteenth or the seventeenth century. That virginity was a higher state would have been the orthodox assumption in both periods, but that would make marriage a lesser good, not a lesser evil.[26]

Furthermore the assumption that there was some sort of contradiction between 'the medieval Catholic ideal of chastity' and the 'ideal of conjugal affection' is undoubtedly mistaken.[27] Educated medieval clerics were sure that love and marriage should go together.[28] Moreover, both they and their seventeenth-century counterparts put over their view of married love to the laity through the medium of preaching. The following passage, from the collection of sermons on the Sunday Gospels by Guillaume Peyraut, O.P. (thirteenth century), will serve as an example.

[24] J. Boucher, *Sermons, ou Thresors de la pieté chrestienne, cachez dans les Evangiles des dimanches de l'année. Nouvelle édition* ... (Paris, 1627) [BN call no. D. 26737] pp. 56–7.

[25] The phrase is used by Stone, *The Family*, p. 135, to characterize Bellarmine's view of marriage.

[26] BN, lat. 12423, f. 83rb: '*Tamen sicut solet dici: Vinum bonum non eicit aliud bonum de domo, nec, secundum Philosophum, Bonum bono est contrarium, licet ergo virginitas et viduitas maiora bona sint, nichilominus tamen matrimonium est bonum et sanctum*' (from a sermon on the text *Nuptiae factae sunt* (*John*, ii. 1) by Odo de Castro Radulphi (= Eudes de Chateauroux), Schneyer, *Repertorium*, iv, p. 400, no. 78).

[27] Stone, *The Family*, p. 135 (though it is a little unfair to use as Aunt Sally a book which is so valuable when taken as a whole).

[28] J. Leclercq, 'L'amour et le mariage vus par les clercs et les religieux', in *Love and Marriage*, ed. Van Hoecke and Welkenhuysen, pp. 102–15, with further references in the notes.

Amare etiam debet vir uxorem. Eph. v [25]: Diligite uxores vestras sicut Christus dilexit ecclesiam, et tradidit semetipsum pro ea. Et potest attendi hec similitudo in duobus. Primo in hoc ut zelet pro salute uxoris. Christus etiam pro salute ecclesie mortuus est. Secundo in hoc quod si adulterat et post peniteat a viro misericorditer recipiatur. Osee. iii. [i]: Diligite mulierem dilectam ab amico et adulteram, sicut diligit dominus filios Israel, et ipsi respiciunt ad deos alienos. Item Eph. v [28]: Viri debent diligere uxores suas ut corpora sua. Ibidem: Qui suam uxorem diligit, seipsum diligit. Item in eodem [v. 33]: Unusquisque uxorem suam [col. b] *sicut seipsum diligat*[29]....[30]

Furthermore a man ought to love his wife. *Ephesians*, v: 'Love your wives as Christ loved the Church, and gave himself up for it'. And we may note two things from this analogy. Firstly, that he should long ardently for the salvation of his wife. For Christ died for the salvation of his Church. Secondly, that if she commits adultery, and should afterwards repent, she should be received with mercy by her husband. *Hosea*, iii: 'Love the woman who has been loved by the friend and committed adultery, just as the Lord loves the sons of Israel, and they look to alien gods'. Again, *Ephesians*, v: 'He who loves his wife, loves himself'. Again, in the same, 'Everyone should love his wife as he loves himself'...

The difficult problem of how much common ground there was between the conceptions of love in marriage sermons and in love lyrics and romances may be left aside for the special study it deserves.[31] It would be necessary to face the question of how normal it was for courtly love and marriage to be associated; to ask whether love was considered a normal preliminary to marriage in either preaching or in courtly literature; and to analyse the respec-

---

[29] *diligit* MS.

[30] Clm 23385 f. 141$^{va/b}$; from a sermon on the text *Nuptiae factae sunt* (*John*, ii, 1), Schneyer, *Repertorium*, ii, p. 535, no. 21. In this manuscript, no. 21 seems to be divided into two sermons. The second (from which this passage comes) has, confusingly, a similar *incipit* to the sermon which follows it in the manuscript, and also to no. 22 in Schneyer's list.

[31] For the evidence of *ad status* sermons on this point see d'Avray and Tausche, 'Marriage Sermons in *ad status* collections', pp. 78, 80, and 114–16. I hope to extend the discussion to the *Nuptiae factae sunt* genre. Van Hoecke and Welkenhuysen (eds.), *Love and Marriage*, and Brooke, 'Marriage and Society', both approach the problem from the point of view of different kinds of source. For the doctrine of the canonists, see J. T. Noonan, 'Marital Affection in the Canonists', in *Collectanea Stephan Kuttner*, ii = *SGra*, xii (1967), pp. 479–509. The bibliography on courtly love is considerable: see, for example, P. Dronke, *Medieval Latin and the Rise of the European Love Lyric*, 2nd ed. (Oxford, 1968), especially i, ch. 2.

tive notions of 'love', in order to determine whether it is even the same sentiment which is in question in these very different media. As a preliminary hypothesis, it may be suggested that the notions differ in at least two important respects. Firstly, the preachers' notion of love does not imply sexual attraction (while not necessarily excluding it). Secondly, love is for them a feeling which belongs to the domain of free will and choice. One of the most interesting things about the modern idea of falling in love is the assumption that one cannot decide to be or not to be in love; it just happens to one. The roots of this assumption may very probably be found in courtly literature, but the preachers would have rejected it.[32] In their view married love was a moral obligation, and one which married people could be persuaded by arguments to fulfil.

However it may be with courtly love, the thirteenth-century preachers' 'voluntarist' concept of married love is unmistakeably recognizable in the seventeenth century. Jean Pierre Camus asks married couples why they do not cherish each other with an *amour tout diuin*;[33] Claude Joly, asking rhetorically what particular *devoir* is demanded of married people, replies that it is *Un esprit d'amour et d'union*;[34] François Bourgoing tells married people that they should follow St Paul's injunction to love their wives, so that there should be between them but one heart, one will, one soul, namely, that of Jesus.[35]

---

[32] Discussion with Eleanor Searle convinced me that my original antithesis between a medieval and a modern concept of love should be turned into an antithesis between two medieval concepts of it.

[33] Jean Pierre Camus, *Premières Homélies dominicales* (Paris, 1619) [BN call no. D. 27707], p. 66: '*Ce fut Dieu qui de sa main paternelle et visible, façonna vne Conforte à nostre premier Pere, & la luy donna pour compagne, & c'est ce mesme Dieu qui de son inuisible main vous a choisi celles que vois possedez: ô Maris c'est luy qui a fait le saint nœud de vostre liaison, ô Femmes pourquoy donc, ô Mariez, ne vous cherissez vous d'vn amour tout diuin, & que ne recognoissez vous l'honneur & le bon-heur que vous receuez de main liberale de Dieu en ceste association*, qui vous ioint vne ayde semblable à vous, *pour vous soulager és trauerses de ce mortel pelerinage*'. The punctuation looks wrong. It could be emended by making 'Maris' and 'Femmes' each the end of a clause, and making 'pourquoy' the beginning of a sentence.

[34] Sermon LV. Pour le second dimanche d'après les Rois, *Sur les devoirs de personnes mariées*, Quodcunque dixerit vobis, facite (*Joan.*, II)', J.P. Migne, *Collection intégrale et universelle des orateurs sacrées*, xxxii (Paris, 1853), col. 744: '*Dans cette diversité d'états il y a de différentes graces, et Dieu, outre les devoirs généraux, en demande de particuliers.... Mais que faut-il aux personnes mariées? Un esprit d'amour et d'union*'.

[35] François Bourgoing, *Homelies chrestiennes sur les évangiles des dimanches et des festes principales de l'année* (etc.), (Paris, 1665) [BN call no. D. 15301] pp. 91–2: '... *que*

In that these thirteenth- and seventeenth-century preachers bring love within the sphere of moral principles it may be regarded as an aspect of the by-no-means easy code of behaviour which they believed should govern marriage. The sermon on the text *Nuptiae factae sunt* in Bourdaloue's *Dominicale* includes, in the *partie* which deals with the 'obligations' of marriage, a passage on married love,[36] in the course of which love is broken down into a series of *devoirs*, moral duties.[37] In a somewhat similar manner, Guillaume de Mailly takes the concept of *fidelitas* and breaks it down into a series of moral obligations.[38] This code of virtues and obligations

---

vous suiuiez l'vn & l'autre cét aduertissement de Saint Paul; Maris, aymez vos femmes, comme Iesus-Christ a aymé son Eglise; femmes, soyez soûmises à vos maris, comme l'Eglise à Iesus Christ; qu'il n'y ayt entre vous deux (p. 92) *qu'vn cœur, qu'vne volonté, & qu'vne ame; sçauoir celle de Iesus'.* For other texts on married love from sermons see Paris, *Marriage*, pp. 108–14.

[36] I refer to the passage beginning '*Il ne s'agit point seulement icy d'une société apparente, mais d'une société de cœur ...*', Bourdaloue, *Sermons ... pour les Dimanches*, i (Paris, 1716), p. 61 (from a 'Sermon pour le second Dimanche après l'Epiphanie, sur l'estat du Mariage. *Nuptiae factae sunt ...*', p. 61. (I use the Bretonneau version, which is defended by Jean Pierre Landry, 'Bourdaloue: l'Etablissement du Texte et ses Problèmes', in *Journées Bossuet. La Prédication au xviiᵉ siècle. Actes du Colloque ... 1977*, ed. T. Goyet and J.-P. Collinet (Paris, 1980), pp. 69–77, with discussion 77–9.)

[37] *Ibid.*, pp. 62–3: '... *Aimez-vous d'un amour respectueux, d'un amour fidelle, d'un amour officieux & condescendant, d'un amour constant & durable, d'un amour chrestien. Tout cela, ce sont autant de devoirs renfermez dans cette foy conjugale, que vous vous estes promise de part & d'autre, & qui vous a unis. Prenez garde: je dis d'un amour respectueux, parce qu'une familiarité sans respect porte insensiblement & presqu'infailliblement au mépris. Je dis d'un amour fidelle, jusqu'à quiter, pour un époux ou pour une épouse, pere & mere, puisque c'est en termes formels la loy de Dieu; mais à plus forte raison jusqu'à rompre tout autre nœud qui pourroit attacher le cœur, & à se déprendre de tout autre object qui le pourroit partager. Je dis d'un amour officieux & condescendant, qui prévienne les besoins ou qui les soulage, qui compatisse aux infirmitez, qui lie les esprits & qui maintienne entre les volontez un parfait accord. Je dis d'un amour constant & durable, pour resister aux fascheuses humeurs qui le pourroient troubler, aux soupçons & aux jalousies, aux animositez & aux aigreurs. Enfin je dis d'un amour chrestien: car c'est icy que je puis appliquer, & que se doit verifier la parole* (p. 63) *de saint Paul, que la femme chrestienne & vertueuse est la sanctification de son mari'.*

[38] Cf. above n. 22, the passage beginning: '*Ista autem fidelitas in iiii attenditur ...*'. The first of the four will serve as an example, Clm 14702 f. xxviʳᵇ/ᵛᵃ: '*Primo (prima MS) in mutua cordium dilectione. Eph. v [25] Viri diligite uxores vestras. Hoc est enim unum quod summe placet deo. Eccli. xxv [1–2]: In tribus beneplacitum est spiritui* [f. xxviᵛᵃ] *meo, que sunt probata coram deo et hominibus: concordia fratrum, amor proximorum, vir et mulier, scilicet in bono, sibi consentientes. Non enim debent se inordinate diligere, quia omnis vehemens amator uxoris adulter est, inmo peior quam*

(and, the obverse, vices and sins), of which Bourdaloue's remarks on love, and Guillaume's on *fidelitas*, may be seen as an expression, cannot easily be reduced to one or two clearly defined *topoi*. There are stereotyped features common to both periods, but the code to which they belong is a general attitude of mind. It is too broad and diffuse to be briefly summarized within the compass of this essay, including as it did the relations between husband and wife both inside and outside the sexual sphere, as well as their duties as parents. Perhaps it is in any case a rather obvious point that preachers should have presented marriage in terms of a moral code. All the same, it is important to bear in mind that they thought of marriage as a state of life which made many demands on the virtue of those who entered it. In this regard their view of marriage is somewhat analogous to their view of the priesthood and the religious life. That is no doubt why it was easy for the idea of marriage as religious order to become a *topos* in the thirteenth century.[39]

In the seventeenth century, however, this view of marriage as a high but demanding state of life found expression in two ideas which I have not found in thirteenth-century marriage sermons. They are not common or normal in marriage sermons by French

---

adulter, quia de eo quod datum est sibi in remedium, facit venenum. Ad hoc enim institutum est matrimonium ut sit remedium contra incontinentiam. I. Cor. vii [9]: Si non continent, nubant. Melius est enim nubere quam uri'.

[39] I have not yet found this *topos* in a seventeenth-century French sermon, but think it quite possible that there are cases of it awaiting discovery. Cf. (as a German case) the following passage from Bartholomaeus Wagnerus Augustanus, *Homiliarum Centuria de Tempore & Sanctis Postill* ... (Freiburg im Breisgau, 1613) [Munich, Staatsbibliothek, call no. 2° Hom. 524], p. 93: '*Ich will gleich den anfang machen mit dem ersten Wasserkrug darauss die boese Eheleuth trincken/ durch ein vnordenliche Hausshaltung/ die zwar wol inn Ehestandt tretten/ nicht das sie Gottes Willen ein genuegen thetten/ sondern Fleisch vnnd Blut vnd dem leiblichen Wollust koenden ausswarten/ die allein betrachten vnnd vor ihnen haben den zeitlichen verdamblichen Wollust/ vnd dergleichen sich im eingang boesen* religiosen *welche allein inn Orden begeren zukommen/ das sie im zeitlichen weren* benadicti, *dem Leib nach durch vnd durch versorgt. Also die boese Eheleuth tretten wol in den Orden dess H. Ehestandts/ aber verkehrter weiss/ dann sie ein solches leben vnd wandel mit einander fuehren/ das alles muss seyn der Welt nach gebenedeyt vnnd gesegnet...*' (the words not in italic are those not in Gothic print). However, in this sermon the idea evolves into something entirely different from the medieval *topos*, as described in Bériou and d'Avray, 'Henry of Provins'.

preachers of the period. In observing these differences between the two periods, it should be emphasized, we are establishing negative facts about the thirteenth century as well as positive facts about the seventeenth.

One major difference is that the idea of grace is constantly associated with marriage in the seventeenth-century sermons. Thus Jean Boucher says that the dowry given in the marriage of man and woman (which he is comparing with the marriages of soul and body, and of God and man) 'is the spiritual life which consists in grace'.[40] Etienne Molinier says that 'those who receive the sacrament of marriage with the required intention and disposition, draw from the power (*vertu*) of the sacrament a grace and a force which, like a strong and powerful wine, alleviates and assuages all the troubles of so heavy a charge'.[41] Jean Pierre Camus says that the third good of marriage is the grace of the sacrament, which augments sanctifying grace, like the other 'sacraments of the living', and which also has a special grace. This consists in the special helps from God, by which those who are united by this sacred bond are given *une force particulière* to cope with the difficulties which are inseparable from marriage.[42] Adrien Gambart calls marriage '... a means of salvation, and a sacrament which confers grace...'.[43] In Claude Joly we again meet the idea that

---

[40] Boucher, *Sermons*, pp. 53–4: '... *au second la vie spirituelle* [p. 54] *qui consiste en la grace ...*'.

[41] Molinier, *Sermons*, p. 229: '... *ceux qui reçoiuent le Sacrement du Mariage auec l'intention, & disposition requise, ils tirent de la vertu du Sacrement vne grace, & vne force, qui comme vn vin fort & puissant allege, & soulage toutes les incommoditez d'vne si pesante charge*'.

[42] *Prosnes Catech-Evangeliques* (etc.) (Paris, 1651) [BN call no. D. 15529] p. 46: '*Et le 3. c'est la grace du Sacrement, lequel comme tous les autres Sacremens appellez des viuans, augmente la grace sanctifiante en ceux qui l'ont desia en habitude, & dauantage a vne grace speciale, comme les autres Sacremens qui ont chaqu'vne la leur. Cette grace consiste en des assistances speciales de Dieu, par lesquelles ceux qui sont conioints par ce lien sacré, reçoiuent vne force particuliere pour supporter auec patience, les trauaux, les peines, & les sollicitudes inseparables de cét estat ...*'.

[43] Migne, *Collection intégrale*, lxxxix (Paris, 1866), col. 59: '... *les fiancés doivent prendre garde à trois circonstances de leur engagement. La première, qu'étant une condition pour toute la vie, un moyen de salut, et un sacrement qui confère la grâce; il le faut aussi traiter saintement ...*'. From 'Prone VII .... De la bonne vocation au mariage, etc. *Nuptiae factae sunt in Cana Galileae; vocatus est et Jesus (Joan., ii, 1.)*'. (The sermon is described, col. 56, as being for the *third* Sunday after Epiphany, rather than the second, but this is probably a misprint.)

marriage confers two kinds of grace. He asks rhetorically what the effects of marriage are, and answers that 'One is general, I mean the augmentation of sanctifying grace; the other particular, I mean the infusion of actual graces proper to the state of life which the two who have been joined together are obliged to lead'.[44]

The relative rarity[45] of references in thirteenth-century marriage preaching to the grace conferred by matrimony should not surprise us when we remember that it was only in the course of that century that theological doctrine on the point crystallized.[46] If we allow for a time-lag between the development of speculative theology and popularization through sermons, their silence is natural enough.

The idea of marriage as vocation is quite probably a later development. There seems to be something very like it in a sermon by Johannes Nider,[47] in the fifteenth century, so it is perhaps in this

---

[44] Migne, *Collection intégrale*, xxxii, col. 743: '*Quels sont ses effets? l'un est général, je veux dire l'augmentation de la grâce sanctifiante; l'autre particulier, je veux dire l'infusion des grâces actuelles propres à l'état de vie que les deux conjoints sont obligés de mener*'. (from the sermon cited above, n. 34).

[45] So far I have found the following. Firstly: '*quia sciatis certissime quod magna gratia confertur in matrimonio*'. BN lat. 16481 f. 87ra. (This is from a sermon on the text *Nuptiae factae sunt* (John, ii, 1) by André 'de Caro Loco', Schneyer, *Repertorium*, i, p. 286, no. 1. It was preached on the second Sunday after Epiphany at the church of Saint-Leufroi in 1273: cf. Bériou and d'Avray, 'Henry of Provins', p. 514 n. 2.) The other two writers in whom I have found the idea are Italians, who do not strictly speaking come within the scope of this essay. Aldobrandino da Toscanella O.P. may mark a turning-point, for he writes at some length about the connection between marriage and grace in two sermons of the genre under review (Schneyer, *Repertorium*, i pp. 225–6, nos. 46 and 48; BAV, MS Ottob. lat. 557 ff. 61rb–61va, and f. 63$^{va/b}$. I am not yet certain whether he is referring to the same kind of grace as the later preachers. Remigio de'Girolami O.P. (who belongs as much to the fourteenth as to the thirteenth century), makes at least one clear reference to the grace conferred by marriage, Florence, Bibl. Naz., MS conv. soppr. G 4. 936, f. 25vb: '*4° in aliis invenitur vini experientia, in illis scilicet qui gustando sentiunt quod in ipso matrimonio etiam laicali confertur gratia, cum sit sacramentum nove legis*'. (From a sermon on the text *Deficiente autem vino* (John, ii. 3), Schneyer, *Repertorium*, v, p. 67, no. 31). There may be other such passages in Remigio, on whom I have not worked systematically. There may well also be other thirteenth-century preachers who link marriage and grace. My point is that the impact of the doctrine, at least in France, is definitely small by comparison with the seventeenth century.

[46] Cf. D. Burr, *The Persecution of Peter Olivi = Transactions of the American Philosophical Society*, ns, lxvi, part 5 (Philadelphia, 1976), pp. 45–6.

[47] J. Dahmus, 'Preaching to the Laity in Fifteenth-Century Germany: Johannes Nider's "Harps"', JEH, xxxiv (1983), pp. 55–68, at p. 63. (Nicole Bériou gave me the reference.)

period that the origins of the idea, and its entry into the genre, should be sought. All the same, it is worth considering the possibility that a different flavour was imparted to the idea in the seventeenth century as a result of another development. In the seventeenth century there appears to have been a qualitatively new interest in the process of choice and self-examination which should precede the decision to become a priest.[48] (Here, incidentally, one must distinguish the secular priesthood from the religious life. Something quite similar to the idea of vocation may be discerned, where entry into a religious order was concerned, from at least the second third of the twelfth century.) This development in the attitude to the priesthood, which in Catholic Europe implied celibacy, may have helped to sharpen the focus on the idea of vocation to the main alternative.

The two ideas of marriage as vocation and marriage as vehicle of grace were closely linked. Jean Richard l'Avocat, an interesting layman who was a prolific author of sermons, gives the following explanation of why marriages without *la grace de la vocation* are almost always unhappy (*funestes*):

Pourquoy? parcequ'il y a dans le mariage des voies obliques & mauvaises qu'il faut eviter, qu'il y en a de droites & de bonnes qu'il faut prendre; que pour éviter les unes & prendre les autres il faut un sage discernement, que ce discernement a besoin de certaines graces propres à cet état; que ces graces ont relation à une premiere qui est celle de la vocation...[49]	Why? Because there are crooked and evil ways in marriage that must be avoided, and straight and good ones that must be taken; because to avoid the one sort and take the other sort a wise discernment is necessary, and this discernment has need of certain graces which go with this state of life; because these graces connect with a first grace, that of vocation ...

[48] I have done no first-hand research on the idea of priestly vocation, but follow R. Tavenaux, *Le Catholicisme dans la France classique, 1610–1715* (Paris, 1980), i, pp. 157–9.

[49] [Jean Richard, avocat à la Cour du Parlement], *Discours moraux sur les évangiles de tous les dimanches de l'année ...*, i (Paris, 1680) [BN call no. D. 50523], p. 225 (from his 'Sermon pour le II. Dimanche d'après les Rois. Du mariage. *Vocatus est Jesus & Discipuli ejus ad nuptias. Joan. 2...*'). Cf. *ibid.*, p. 226: '*Toutes sortes de graces peuvent-elles nous mettre dans ce juste milieu, nous détourner de ces extremitez fâcheuses, nous faire acquitter de ces devoirs? non sans doute, autres sont les graces des Ecclesiastiques, autres celles des Religieux, autres celles des Vierges, autres celles des mariez; il en faut d'immediates, de speciales, de propres à ce dernier état, & elles dependent d'une premiere qui est la grace de la vocation ...*'.

The ideas of grace and vocation are particularly neatly integrated in a sermon by Bourdaloue, one to which reference has already been made for its remarks on married love.[50] It is a good sermon with which to end, since it draws together most of the ideas discussed in this paper: both the ideas which the two centuries under review share—love, the demanding ethical code of marriage, its holiness as a state of life—and the ideas which are absent, or at least well hidden, in the thirteenth century. To be more specific, he uses the latter, the ideas of grace and vocation, to synthesize the former. (I am not speaking of his specific intentions, but of the functional connections between the ideas in the sermon.) The sermon is an illustration of the way a distinguished mind, working within a well-defined tradition, can impress his personality on the repertory of ideas at his disposal, by welding them together to make a unified whole.

Here there is room for no more than a dry and highly selective summary of a long and carefully constructed sermon. On the one hand, Bourdaloue devotes a great deal of the sermon to the obligations, troubles, and dangers of the married state. We have already noted that he includes among the obligations the duty of the couple to love each other, which he sees as part of the conjugal faith which the couple have promised. This leads on to a long discussion of the way husband and wife should behave towards each other. Later on in the sermon Bourdaloue alludes to rules governing the specifically sexual sphere, though he deliberately refrains from going into details.[51]

The interesting thing is that Boudaloue's emphasis on the obligations, troubles, and perils of marriage stiffens rather than weakens his initial remarks about the goodness of marriage; in fact, the duties, difficulties, and dangers are each seen as arising necessarily out of his version of the three goods of marriage. Even the dangers of sin which married people face have heroic goodness as their counterpart. There is a striking passage in which he argues that interior detachment from worldly affairs and goods must in no way detract from the vigilance required for conserving material goods and supporting the family. 'Therefore, to join the one and

---

[50] Above, nn. 36 and 37.
[51] *Sermons ... pour les Dimanches*, i, pp. 86–8.

the other together, that is what I call the heroic virtue of your state of life'.[52]

Bourdaloue argues that it is impossible to achieve this point of evangelical purity without *la grace de la vocation*,[53] and indeed the concepts of vocation and grace cement the argument of the whole of the sermon together. In a key paragraph in which the duties, etc., of marriage are linked with its three goods, he proceeds to reason that 'one can neither satisfy these obligations, nor support these troubles, nor preserve oneself from these dangers without the grace and the vocation from God. From which I conclude that there is no condition of life among men for which this divine vocation is more necessary'.[54]

It is easier to take snapshots of a genre at two points in its development than to make a motion picture of its whole history, and the former is a sensible preparation for the latter. We know that we should look for the following in late-medieval and sixteenth-century sermons of the genre: firstly, for the probable constants, like the three-goods *topos* and the 'voluntarist' concept of love, and secondly, for the points in the genre's history at which the ideas of grace and of vocation became prominent.

Moreover, a comparison between the thirteenth and the seventeenth century is an end in itself as well as a means to a future consecutive history of the genre. Two snapshots cannot show us the actual process of change, but they can give us a strong sense of change: a historical sense in fact. 'It was [so Isaiah Berlin], I think, L.B. Namier who once remarked about historical sense that there

---

[52] *Ibid.*, p. 93: '*Car il vouloit que ce detachement interieur ne vous ostast rien de toute la vigilance necessaire pour la conservation de vos biens & pour l'entretien de vos familles. Or de joindre l'un & l'autre ensemble, c'est ce que j'appelle la vertu heroïque de vostre estat ...*'.

[53] *Ibid.*, pp. 93–4: '*Et comment en effet, me direz-vous, atteindre à ce poinct de pauvreté évangelique? A cela je vous reponds ce que repondoit JésusChrist luy-mesme sur un sujet à peu prés semblable: la chose est impossible aux hommes, mais elle ne l'est pas à Dieu. Elle est impossible à ceux qui s'ingerent d'eux-mesmes & saus la grace de la vocation dans le mariage; ou qui l'ayant cette grace, n'en font pas l'usage qu'ils doivent. Mais à ceux qui y sont fidelles, tout devient* [p. 94] *possible*'.

[54] *Ibid.*, p. 55: '*Or je soutiens qu'on ne peut ni satisfaire à ces obligations, ni supporter ces peines, ni se preserver de ces dangers sans la grace & la vocation de Dieu. D'où je conclus qu'il n'y a donc point d'estat parmi les hommes, où cette vocation divine soit plus necessaire*'. This is the central argument of the sermon. Only at the end (*ibid.*, pp. 94–6) does he give some words of comfort to people who have already got married without the appropriate vocation.

was no *a priori* short-cut to knowledge of the past; what actually happened can only be established by scrupulous empirical investigation, by research in its normal sense. What is meant by historical sense is the knowledge not of what happened, but of what did not happen'.[55] But the question of what did not happen can also be answered by empirical investigation. The historians of the early-modern period cited at the beginning of this paper had a mistaken sense that certain ideas about love and the goodness of marriage were not medieval, and even a 'still' shot of the thirteenth century is enough to show that they are mistaken. The less obvious point is that by looking at the seventeenth century our attention is drawn to subjects, in this case vocation and grace, on which thirteenth-century French preachers say nothing or little. We could hardly have become aware of the significance or even the existence of this fact about thirteenth-century marriage preaching without looking outside the thirteenth century.

University College London

---

[55] I. Berlin, 'The Concept of Scientific History' [first published 1960] in *Concepts and Categories. Philosophical Essays* (Oxford, 1980), pp. 103–42, at p. 140.

THE BIBLE AND RIGHTS IN THE FRANCISCAN DISPUTES OVER POVERTY

by GORDON LEFF

A MONG the more far-reaching consequences of the disputes over absolute poverty in the Franciscan Order was the emergence of a doctrine of natural rights. Or rather conflicting doctrines, drawn from conflicting interpretations of the life of Christ and the apostles, which crystallized in the debates between Pope John XXII and members of the Order in the 1320s and 1330s over Christ's absolute poverty. Both the Pope, in denying that Christ had ever lived in absolute poverty, and his Franciscan opponents, who upheld the Franciscan doctrine that he had, arrived at rival conceptions of the rights involved in either possessing or renouncing temporal things. Although still largely inchoate as self-conscious doctrines of natural rights, nevertheless, as represented by John XXII and Ockham in particular, they can be regarded as the first explicit statements that men naturally have certain rights or powers which are the foundation of legal rights or, in the case of the Franciscans, and even more significant, their renunciation. In what follows I wish to examine the development of those ideas principally by reference to the contributions of Bonaventure, John XXII, and Ockham.

What they had in common was their appeal to an accepted repertory of biblical texts to support their opposing positions of what can be called the hierarchical and evangelical conceptions of Christ's earthly existence which evolved in the twelfth and thirteenth centuries. For both sides, as for so many others unconnected with the particular disputes over poverty, the historical figure of Christ as a man, portrayed in the Gospels, provided the norm for a Christian life: a life which, when taken literally in its evangelical interpretation, as one of renunciation of all rights and possessions, as it was by the different apostolic groups, such as the Arnoldists and Waldensians, and diverse individuals, like Dante and Marsilius of Padua, could challenge the very existence of the Church as an institution with its own juridical and material identity. Although that challenge was also implicit in the attitude of the Franciscan Spirituals, it was not an issue in the disputes over the legitimacy of Franciscan poverty as the absolute and unqualified renunciation of all legal titles to possession and ownership of property. The issue was its scriptural title in the life of Christ and the apostles; and it was the claim to that which lent legitimacy to the arguments and counter-arguments of the contending parties, not only over Franciscan poverty, but the very nature of religious life from the twelfth to the fifteenth centuries.

In that sense the debates over poverty were but one aspect of a universal debate which had Christ as the focus: or perhaps, more accurately, they were a heightened example. For they had their origin in the very intensity of St Francis's own desire to relive Christ's gospel life, both in himself and among his companions who formed the nucleus of his Order. The opening words of the first extant Rule of 1221 are, 'This is the life of Jesus Christ's gospel'; and although modified in form in the second Rule of 1223, they remained the substance of his own life, and that which he enjoined on the Order until his death in 1226. It was that immediacy of St Francis's vision of Christ's earthly life of spiritual and material renunciation in a life of poverty, humility, obedience, and chastity, which made him so uncompromising in its pursuit.

Already in St Francis's lifetime[1] it raised the two problems which were at the heart of Franciscan poverty: of how to reconcile renunciation and non-appropriation of possessions with the need to use goods to sustain daily life and the Order's increasing religious activities, as well as—against St Francis's will— its growing pursuit of learning; and second how to define the material conditions of a life of poverty to conform to a level of indigence in keeping with the vow of poverty. St Francis had prescribed much of the second in the provisions of the Rule, concerning tattered tunics, no shoes or riding of horses, as well as the avoidance of all contact with money; and he had overcome the first when it had arisen by what

---

[1] For an account of these events and the development of the Order, see R.B. Brooke, *Early Franciscan Government* (Cambridge, 1959); M.D. Lambert, *Franciscan Poverty* (London, 1961); and G. Leff, *Heresy in the Later Middle Ages* (Manchester, 1967), i, chs 1 and 2, and further references there to citations which follow.

could be described as direct action in rejecting or withdrawing from anything which could be construed as a possession. But neither problem would go away. The second, over the quality of the Order's life, was the one which rent the Order, and although it does not directly concern us here, it largely arose from the first, which does. It came to be expressed in the legal distinction between use and possession by which Pope Gregory IX sought to resolve it in 1229. By declaring that all goods used and consumed by members of the Order belonged not to them but to their donors, including those procured by a third party (*nuncius*) to meet their needs, the Pope thereby regularized the Order's status of absolute poverty as owning nothing either individually or in common.

The distinction between use and possession remained canonical for nearly a hundred years until repudiated by John XXII in 1322. It thus gave a legal definition to an evangelical conception of life which would have been alien both to Christ, who inspired it, and St Francis, who re-enacted it, and was treated as such by the Franciscan zealots, who saw themselves as the continuators of both. For a purely legal definition of poverty came before long to enshrine a purely legalistic meaning of a life of poverty without reference to the quality of life involved, which in its material conditions became indistinguishable from those of any other order, and indeed of the Church, not pledged to absolute poverty. And it was precisely over its practice in a life of poverty that the schism within the Order arose, beginning in the generation after St Francis's death between what became the two parties of the Conventuals, the majority pledged solely to its legal definition of renunciation of all ownership, and the Spirituals, for whom poverty consisted in actual penury or poor use (*usus pauper*), restricted to only the necessities specified in the Rule and supported by Christ's and St Francis's own injunctions and examples. By the time of the appearance in 1254 at Paris of the young Franciscan Gerard of Borgo San Donnino's *Introduction to the Eternal Gospel*, the lives of Christ and St Francis and their followers had been fused into the single life of the Gospel, of which Christ was the founder and St Francis and his true disciples the renewers: an identification which became one of the hallmarks not only of the Spirituals, but the Order as a whole, if diversely interpreted, and underlay the very notion of Franciscan poverty as it became reformulated by St

Bonaventure and defended by the conventual leaders of the Order half a century later against the attacks of John XXII.

It was on that biblical basis, as the direct continuation of the life of Christ and the apostles, that Bonaventure produced his defence of absolute Franciscan poverty in his *Apologia Pauperum*, written probably in 1269.[2] It formed the point of departure for all subsequent discussion, both among the contestants within the Order and against its detractors outside it, beginning with the Franciscans' opponents among Bonaventure's contemporaries such as Gerard of Abbeville, at Paris university and culminating in the attacks and effective destruction of the doctrine of absolute poverty by John XXII.

Our interest here is in Bonaventure's central distinction, on which the disputes over the validity of Franciscan poverty turned, between a natural, non-legal obligation, binding upon all men, to use the necessities of life for self-preservation, and the legal forms of ownership, possession, and use, which were not binding. It was founded, as the whole of Bonaventure's vindication was, upon Christ as the norm both of perfect virtue, which was, naturally, unattainable, and of the relative perfections attainable in this world by following his example contained in the Gospels. It was there, historically in Christ's own life, that the justification for absolute poverty was to be found. And much of Bonaventure's treatise consisted in glossing passages from the books of the New Testament to witness to its apostolic nature, while at the same time providing a place for the other religious forms—of the monks and the secular Church—not vowed to absolute poverty. With characteristic inventiveness, Bonaventure identified the exemplar of each within the same historical figure of the life of Christ and the apostles. If the life itself, of preaching and renunciation, was that of the Franciscans, characterized among other examples by Christ's injunction to his disciples to take nothing with them when he sent them to preach (*Matthew*, x. 7–12)—the passage which had first shown St Francis his path—the apostles' bag of money carried by Judas corresponded to both the communal form in which wealth was held by the monastic orders, and to the role of the Church in dispensing it to support its priests and relieve the poor.[3] Far then from derogating from Christ's perfection, they represented it in its external acts of imperfection by condescending to human infirmities. Actions in themselves imperfect, performed by Christ became perfect in serving higher religious ends. Among them was owning the goods enjoyed by the Franciscan Order as the condition of its state of absolute poverty modelled on Christ's. For only if their ownership lay elsewhere could the Franciscans renounce their possession. And that must embrace consumables, such as food, whose use entailed their consumption. The case against the Franciscan claim to absolute poverty, by opponents like Gerard of Abbeville, was precisely that where goods were consumed their use could not be separated from their possession because they could belong only to those who consumed them:[4] an argument revived by John XXII.

It was to overcome it that Bonaventure made the distinction mentioned above between natural—which he called simple—use and legal use and possession which alone carried legal rights.[5] The latter could be renounced: the first could never be because mortal life depended on it. That had been the state in which Christ and the apostles had lived, and it was that of their Franciscan disciples. It involved the abdication of all rights, which at that time, in keeping with their derivation from Roman law, were regarded exclusively as property rights. To that extent neither Bonaventure nor Pope Nicholas III, who in 1279 confirmed Bonaventure's distinctions and made them more precise in his bull *Exiit qui seminat*, giving them the force of law—until again rescinded by John XXII— conceived natural use as a right, but rather as its antithesis, as something given naturally and independently of any legal right.

The contrast was sharpened by Nicholas III,[6] on the one hand, by adding a further legal category, of the right of use, to Bonaventure's three existing rights of ownership, possession, and usufruct, and, on the other, by amplifying Bonaventure's term 'simple use' into 'simple use of fact', to emphasize its natural,

---

[3] *Ibid.*, p. 90.
[4] *Ibid.*, p. 93.
[5] *Ibid.*, pp. 94–5.
[6] *Ibid.*, pp. 97–100.

non-legal character. He did so from the same evangelical grounds as Bonaventure's in the example of Christ's life as the path to perfection, and he used the same argument to explain Judas's bag, now explicitly making the Church of Rome the owner of everything in Franciscan hands.

Neither Bonaventure nor Nicholas III took the application of simple use beyond the immediate justification which it provided for a voluntary religious state of poverty. Nevertheless, the recognition of an inviolable claim which everyone had on goods necessary for survival contained the germ of a natural right, not only in the power which it gave of being able to use and consume such goods, but even more in being able to renounce legal rights. In that second aspect it represented a potentially religious and political negative liberty, to be without legal rights or to abdicate them to someone else, which was to be the basis of contract theory three centuries later. For Bonaventure and Nicholas III and their successors among the Franciscan leaders of the Order in the 1320s and 1330s, such as Michael of Cesena and Bonagratia of Bergamo, the liberty which it provided was to follow Christ, and was subsumed under his absolute poverty. It was with John XXII, in rejecting both natural use and Christ's absolute poverty, and then Ockham, in countering John, that they became an issue of natural rights. Between them John XXII and Ockham extended the arguments to include the nature of dominion itself and its origin in Adam; they therefore also extended their range to the Old Testament, as well as giving them increasingly the form of endless biblical exegesis of both the Old and New Testaments.

John XXII opened that latest phase with a series of papal bulls in 1322 and 1323, which between them legally annulled Franciscan poverty and anathematized the doctrine of Christ's absolute poverty.[7] He thereby knocked away the twin props of the Order as it had existed for a hundred years. He achieved the first by making all use entail a legal right of use, which in the case of consumables was indistinguishable from ownership, reaffirming Gerard of Abbeville's contention sixty years earlier. John XXII thus turned Nicholas III's category of a right of use against the very distinction between natural and legal titles to goods which it had been designed

---

[7] *Ibid.*, pp. 163–6, 241–9.

to reinforce. All natural titles now became legal titles. He gave practical expression to his abolition of a separate natural use of goods by withdrawing papal ownership of Franciscan goods, except those, including churches, which had a divine use; all other forms of use must carry rights of ownership. Independently therefore of the Pope's theoretical arguments, he had abolished the legal basis of Franciscan poverty. He did the same for its religious basis in the third bull of the series, *Cum inter nonnullos*, in November 1323,[8] by denying and pronouncing heretical the doctrine that Christ and the apostles had lived in absolute poverty, on the scriptural grounds that there were many references in the Bible to their having possessions. To deny them would be to deny Christ and the apostles their right to their use, which would be impiety.

These remained the two threads in the exchanges between the Pope and his opponents, a combination of legal and scriptural arguments, with a growing concentration on the niceties in each. They were inseparable because the status of the Franciscans and Christ was inseparable, as it had been from the beginning with St Francis. Hence, however interpreted, the first must conform to the second, which meant finding scriptural support for the religious and legal interpretations of both. The Bible gave them their sanction. That applied equally to John XXII's argument reversing the status of both from possessionlessness to possession.

In his final declarations on the question, *Quia quorumdam* in 1324, and *Quia vir reprobus*[9] in 1328, replying to the counter-attacks of the Franciscan leaders reaffirming Christ's and the apostles' exclusive reliance on simple use and treating property as the result of the fall, John completed his sanctification of property rights and lordship by making them at once the source of justice and divinely instituted. Far from their renunciation representing a higher state of perfection, lack of legal rights meant lack of justice, of which legal rights were part, and so lack of perfection of which justice was part. Hence to have only simple use, without rights of use and ownership, was to be less acceptable to God than it was in possessing them. It could not, therefore, have been the state of Christ and the apostles, as Judas's bag, among other examples, showed; nor could

---

[8] *Ibid.*, pp. 165–6.
[9] *Ibid.*, pp. 241–9.

they have used it to dispense money to the poor if they had not had a legal right to it.

With *Quia vir reprobus* that legal right was derived directly from God; given to mankind with Adam's creation before any human society or kings. At first it had been lordship over the whole earth; after the fall God had then introduced private property, as *Genesis*, iii. 19 testified, when God told Adam that he would eat his bread in the sweat of his own brow. He did no less for Christ and the apostles, who also had property and temporal ownership from the beginning, as well as rights of litigation over what they possessed in common. That, too, was proved in numerous places in the Bible, including the very passage of Christ's injunction to the apostles to take nothing with them on their preaching missions (*Matthew*, x. 7–12), which for St Francis and Bonaventure had been testimony to their poverty. For the Pope, on the other hand, it proved that ordinarily they had possessions which they were temporarily relinquishing. The *impasse* was complete. It came from diametrically opposed interpretations of common beliefs.

The overriding effect of John XXII's interpretation was to endow all men with inalienable rights of property over everything they used and possessed. Hence, there could be nothing which they used or consumed which did not bear a legal title to it. In cutting the ground from under the Franciscans, by displacing rightlessness by dominion not only in Christ but in all mankind and directly vested by God in Adam, the Pope made all men the beneficiaries, direct or indirect, willing or unwilling, of the same universal rights. In that sense John XXII can be regarded as the originator, in the Middle Ages at least, of an explicit doctrine of rights. But only at the expense of denying liberty as a natural right. At John XXII's hands, scriptural truth presented men with rights which were more obligations that could not be renounced, as the Franciscans discovered.

In asserting their freedom from them, the main spokesmen of the Order, Bonagratia of Bergamo and Michael of Cesena, based themselves on two main defences.[10] The first was the familiar one of the self-sufficiency of simple use, as a natural state freed from all legal rights, which had been Christ's and the apostles' state, and

<hr>

[10] *Ibid.*, pp. 239–49.

was now that of the Franciscan Order. As expounded by Bonagratia and Michael against the Pope's pronouncements, they contained little that was unfamiliar, apart from Michael of Cesena's introduction of a further category of a licence of use from a superior, as a temporary grant of permission to use goods beyond the necessities which fell under natural law. It did not, therefore, Michael claimed, constitute a legal right of either use or possession. Although it was also adopted by Ockham it did little to change the terms of the debate, which now took on a predominantly legal and exegetical character, where the same arguments supported by chapter and verse from the Bible were endlessly repeated and glossed by both sides.

The second defence did bring a new element into the debate, although it originated in a notion of far longer standing than the doctrine of absolute poverty, going back to Augustine and the early Fathers, and had recently been revived by Duns Scotus.[11] It was that private property was the result of the fall; from which Bonagratia of Bergamo drew the conclusion that Christ and the apostles in adopting a life of poverty were returning to a state of innocence.[12] That became the Franciscan riposte to John XXII's exaltation of dominion as divinely ordained from the beginning in Adam and renewed in Christ. Christ the possessionless wanderer faced Christ the lord of the world. They came from two different readings of Christian history taken from the Bible; the conflict between them was as unresolved at the end of the Middle Ages as it had been from the beginning in the twelfth century, and was resolved in the Franciscan Order only with the gradual fading away of its main contestants in the second half of the fourteenth century.

Before then, though, Ockham had capped the Franciscan case in his defence of both those positions. In doing so, against John XXII's denial of the freedom to relinquish property rights, Ockham took two decisive steps in the direction of a counter-doctrine of individual liberty as a divine dispensation, to which his initial defence of Franciscan poverty ultimately led him. The first and

---

[11] R. Tuck, *Natural Rights Theories* (Cambridge, 1979), p. 21, who was the first to recognize an issue of rights in these disputes, although I disagree with his interpretation of Duns Scotus as the originator of this particular doctrine.

[12] Leff, *Heresy*, i, p. 240.

[13] *Ibid.*, pp. 249–53 and G. Leff, *William of Ockham* (Manchester, 1975), pp. 618–9.

major one was to naturalize the use of necessities into a natural right by accepting with John XXII that all use entailed a right of use, and making that of natural use a right deriving from natural law; it accordingly owed nothing to a legal right or human law. Ockham thus trumped John XXII's conversion of all use into a legal right by converting use into a right founded in nature to refuse legal rights, and so realized the potential in Bonaventure's and Nicholas III's category of natural use as the ground for a natural right of negative liberty. Like John XXII's rights of use and dominion it was no less irrevocable, but in also carrying with it the power to refuse or renounce all rights, it was not only radically different; it was, potentially, the source of all other rights, which, as his successors Gerson and John Major were to recognize, must be founded on individual liberty. In upholding it against John XXII's set obligatory rights, we thus have the remarkable spectacle of the defence of liberty as a natural right against the imposition of legally binding rights.

Ockham's other step was to establish the autonomy of natural rights from the independence of natural law of positive law, in defence of the other Franciscan position of private property and dominion as the consequence of the fall. It was not, therefore, as John XXII contended, something immutable. In opposition to the Pope, before the fall Adam and Eve had needed neither coercive power nor possessions, even in common, because they had ruled over the world with reason, and had had the use of the things they had needed in common with the animals. It was that and not, as misconstrued by John XXII, ownership of everything, that had constituted their dominion. And it was just that state of spiritual ascendancy and material possessionlessness, belonging to a state of innocence, which Christ's earthly life had re-enacted, and which the Franciscans took for their model.[14] Ockham thus followed Bonagratia of Bergamo and Michael of Cesena in identifying Christ's absolute poverty with a return to man's original unfallen state. But he also went further in directly separating the natural law, under which they had lived, from human positive law which came with the fall, and the institution of private property.

He contrasted them in the same work, the *Opus Nonaginta*

---

[14] *Opus Nonaginta Dierum*, ed. H.S. Offler, *Opera Politica*, ii (Manchester, 1963), ch. 14, p. 432; Leff, *ibid.*, p. 626.

Dierum,[15] a blow by blow reply to John XXII's final statement on the issue of poverty, in *Quia vir reprobus*, and of the same legal and exegetical character; like the Pope's bull, on the other side, it was by far the most substantial reply on the Franciscan side. Natural law (*ius poli*) was immutable, and conformed to right reason, and could be known naturally or as revealed in the Bible. It was therefore interchangeable with divine law, and, as Ockham developed its different meanings subsequently in the *Dialogus*, an extension of the principles contained in the Bible, explicitly or implicitly.[16] Hence it was independent of positive law (*ius fori*), which was not immutable, and did not have to conform to right reason, though it should. Although the power of enacting human law was from God, it was the outcome of sin, designed to regulate the dominion and private appropriation which had resulted from the fall. They had come into being only with Cain and Abel, who had used the power of dividing and appropriating goods which God had given to Adam and Eve, who had not used them, after they had sinned.[17] Accordingly, natural law and positive law belonged to two different states, and what held by natural law, in being inviolable, could never be altered or overriden by human, positive law. That was the very case over evangelical poverty. As a natural right of use from natural law it was immune from the legal rights which belonged to positive law.

Ockham thus completed the defence of Franciscan poverty by giving a theoretical frame to both the freedom to renounce rights as a natural right and the legitimacy to do so under natural law. Both had their source in divine law, and their exemplification in Christ's life, and both were revealed in God's word in the Bible. Within a decade of the *Opus Nonaginta Dierum* God's law in the Gospel had become the law of liberty against spiritual oppression and every believer had a voice in matters of faith.[18] Even if the struggle over poverty did not survive the Middle Ages, the issue of rights, which it first raised, did.

University of York

---

[15] *Opus Nonaginta Dierum*, ch. 65, pp. 573–5; Leff, *ibid.*, pp. 620–3.

[16] *Dialogus*, III, II, bk iii, ch. 6, *Opera Plurima*, i (Lyon, 1494, reprinted London, 1962), f. 263vb; Leff, *ibid.*, pp. 622–3.

[17] *Opus Nonaginta Dierum*, ch. 88, pp. 656–7; *Leff, ibid.*, pp. 626–7.

[18] Leff, *ibid.*, pp. 616–17, 638–40.

... novo sensu sacram adulterare Scripturam: CLEMENT VI AND THE POLITICAL USE OF THE BIBLE*

by DIANA WOOD

MEDIEVAL biblical commentators traditionally inter-preted the Bible in terms of the 'four senses' of Scripture—the literal-historical and the three 'spiritual' senses, the allegorical, the tropological or moral, and the anagogical.[1] Recently attention has been focused on the use of a variation of the allegorical sense, namely, political allegory.[2] This was the application of a biblical text to a current political situation or argument. The Roman revolutionary Cola di Rienzo, after hearing Pope Clement VI preach in consistory, gave it another name altogether—*sensum adulterum*. Clement had apparently deli-vered the customary papal allegorization of the two-swords pas-sage (*Luke*, xix. 38), according to which both swords, that of spiritual authority and of physical power, were in the hands of the priesthood.[3] This inspired Cola's accusation that the Pope was

* I should like to thank Katherine Walsh and Vincent Packford for their advice and encouragement in the preparation of this paper.

[1] For a definition see B. Smalley, 'Use of the "Spiritual" Senses of Scripture in Persuasion and Argument by Christian Scholars in the Middle Ages', *RTAM* (in press). On the 'four senses' in general see H. de Lubac, *Exégèse médievale. Les quatre sens de l'Ecriture* (Paris, 1959–64).

[2] I.S. Robinson, '"Political Allegory" in the Biblical Exegesis of Bruno of Segni', *RTAM*, l (1983), pp. 69–98. See also Smalley, *Becket*, pp. 30–6.

[3] 'Il commento di Cola di Rienzo alla *Monarchia* di Dante', ed. P.G. Ricci, *StM*, 3rd series, vi, pt II (1965), pp. 679–708 at pp. 705–6. It has not been possible to trace the sermon to which Cola referred. Since Cola said Clement delivered it during the first or second year of his pontificate, during processes against Louis of Bavaria, and Cola was at Avignon from January 1343 until the summer of 1344, Ricci has identified it with that preached on Maundy Thursday, 10 April, 1343 (ed. H.S. Offler, 'A Political *collatio* of Pope Clement VI, O.S.B.', *RB*, lxv (1955), pp. 125–44). This sermon contains no reference to the 'two-swords' passage, nor to the subsequent quotation by Cola of Clement's rendering of the 'great tree' of Nebuchadnezzar's dream (*Daniel*, iv. 7–9). The interpretation of the two-swords passage is the one normally quoted by Clement in his political *collationes*, and is taken from Bernard, *De Consideratione*, iv, 3.

endeavouring to adulterate Holy Scripture with his new sense: *hodie suo satagit novo sensu sacram adulterare scripturam.*[4] The bearer of the keys of St Peter was being encouraged to shed blood and the sword bearer to brag about himself, Cola lamented, and thus the *sensum adulterum* was being added to the words of Christ.[5]

In fact, the idea of 'adulterating' the words of Scripture was not new. As Beryl Smalley has shown, for several writers of the late twelfth and early thirteenth centuries the terms 'gloss' or 'postillate' could be used in the derogatory sense of adulterating the words of Scripture: they could mean glossing over, or making unwarranted additions to, the sacred page.[6] Cola's originality was in applying the word to political allegory. Although he saw this as a new 'sense' of Scripture, its use to bolster papal arguments was far from novel in the fourteenth century. Beryl Smalley has traced its origins to the polemical literature of the Investiture Contest.[7] Between then and Clement's pontificate it had been widely used by the papacy and its supporters.[8] More generally, from the time of Leo I (440–61) the popes had based their justifications of the theory of papal monarchy, and of the uniqueness and universality of the Christian society, on the application of biblical texts in their literal sense. The Petrine commission of *Matthew*, xix. 17–18 was the most obvious one.[9] From the twelfth century onward, when the idea of the vicariate of Christ developed,[10] it became possible to apply any biblical text which referred to Christ either directly or prophetically to his earthly vicar, the pope.

The writing of Clement VI encompasses all the traditional papal texts and allegories. The ship of St Peter, the seamless garment of

---

[4] Cola di Rienzo, 'Il commento', p. 705.

[5] *Ibid.*

[6] B. Smalley, 'The Gospels in the Paris Schools in the late twelfth and early thirteenth centuries, II', *Franc Stud*, xl (1980), pp. 366–9.

[7] Smalley, *Becket*, p. 32.

[8] *Ibid.*, pp. 30–6; de Lubac, *Exègèse médiévale*, ii, 2, pp. 380–1.

[9] W. Ullmann, *The Growth of Papal Government in the Middle Ages* (London, 1955), pp. 7–14; 'Leo I and the Theme of Papal Primacy', *JTS*, ns, xi (1960), pp. 25–51. For the influence of the Bible on medieval principles of government in general see Ullmann, *Law and Politics in the Middle Ages* (London, 1975), pp. 41–50, especially p. 43, n. 1, where further bibliography is given.

[10] Ullmann, *Growth of Papal Government*, pp. 426–37; M. Maccarrone, '*Vicarius Christi*'; *Storia del titolo papale* = *Lateranum*, xviii (Rome, 1952), especially pp. 91–118.

Christ, the sheepfold and the good shepherd, the Noah's ark, the fishing-net, the stone which builders rejected: these and others are given extensive currency. So too is the application to the pope of such familiar texts as *Jeremiah*, i. 10: 'See, I have this day set thee over the nations and over the kingdoms, to root out, and to pull down, and to destroy, and to throw down, to build, and to plant'; *John*, xxi. 17: 'Feed my sheep', and I *Corinthians*, ii. 15: 'He that is spiritual judgeth all things, yet he himself is judged of no man'. More original, however, is Clement's use of the Bible in some of his political *collationes*. These consistory sermons expand on the abbreviated and well-tried formulae of papal letters, and afford precious insights into the Pope's political principles and motives. Clement liked to preach on occasions of political significance. There are, for example, several connected with his plan to rid Europe of the heretical 'emperor' Louis IV of Bavaria and to promote the election of Charles, son of John of Bohemia, to the imperial office. There are pieces about the deposition and subsequent reinstatement of the tyrant Archbishop Giovanni Visconti of Milan, about the crusade, the jubilee year of 1350, and many other political topics. There are two about the creation of a king of the Fortune (or Canary) Islands. And there are several connected with the cardinals' appointments, promotions, or legations. In all there are over thirty extant political discourses, many of them unpublished.[11]

In structure these *collationes* are much like other sermons of the period in that they have a biblical theme, which is then divided into distinctions and subdistinctions to illustrate particular points. These are weighted with biblical, patristic, and other authorities.[12] This is not to suggest, however, that all of them follow a uniform plan, far less that they all adhere strictly to the guidelines recommended by writers such as 'Henry of Hesse'.[13] What distinguishes the political

---

[11] On Clement's sermons see G. Mollat, 'L'oeuvre oratoire de Clément VI', *AHDLMA*, iii (1928), pp. 329–74; P. Schmitz, 'Les sermons et discours de Clément VI', *RB*, xli (1929), pp. 15–34; D. Wood, '*Maximus sermocinator verbi Dei*; the Sermon Literature of Pope Clement VI', *SCH*, xi (1975), pp. 163–72.

[12] On the structure of late-medieval sermons see H. Caplan, *Of Eloquence. Studies in Ancient and Medieval Rhetoric*, ed. A. King and H. North (Ithaca and London, 1970), pp. 235–59.

[13] See his tract, *De arte praedicandi*, ed. Caplan, *Of Eloquence*, pp. 143–59. Caplan points out that the attribution to Henry of Langenstein, once thought likely, is now considered doubtful: *ibid.*, pp. 135–6.

collationes from the 'pulpit sermons' is that their biblical themes are generally adapted to expound a political rather than a purely theological or moral message. To the extent that all the discourses are based on a biblical theme, they all exemplify Clement's political use of the Bible. But here their homogeneity ends, for Clement uses the Bible in a number of different ways and on different levels. Sometimes a text will be given specific political application throughout the sermon, as in his best-known piece, that on the approval of Charles of Bohemia as king of the Romans, on the theme of III *Kings*, i. 35: Solomon 'shall sit upon my throne, and he shall reign for me'.[14] By contrast, a text such as *Et iste bonus est nuntius* (II *Kings*, xviii. 26), the basis of a sermon preached on the return of a cardinal legate from abroad,[15] provokes a lot of generalities about the qualities required of papal nuncios, but little in the way of hard political application of the Bible.

Clement himself said little during his pontificate about the Bible, but two years before becoming pope he declared that the privilege of containing nothing *fermentum aut contagium falsitatis* God had reserved for Holy Scripture alone. The work of no doctor of the Church, neither Augustine, nor Aquinas, nor any other was entirely free from error.[16] Some twenty years earlier, in his role as a master in theology at the University of Paris, he had made an interesting statement about the pope's inability to alter the sacred text. Scripture had been written by the Holy Ghost, for according to II *Peter*, i.21: 'Holy men of God spoke, inspired by the Holy Ghost', and he added significantly, *non potest in ea [scil. scriptura sacra] aliquod per* eum qui inferior est, cuiusmodi est papa.[17] Given this unassailable reverence for the truth of Scripture, it would be somewhat surprising to find Clement VI, even in his capacity as

---

[14] *MGH Const.*, VIII, no. 100, pp. 142–63.

[15] Paris, Bibliothèque Ste Geneviève, MS 240 [hereafter referred to as St G 240], ff. 26ʳ–41ᵛ.

[16] Pierre Roger, St Thomas Aquinas Day Sermon, 1340, St G. 240, f. 399ᵛ: '*Bene ergo [Thomas] conscripsit rectissimos sermones et veritate plenos, licet enim sunt aliqua pauca que communiter non tenentur, tamen ex hoc non est doctrina eius abicienda, sicut nec doctrina Augustini nec aliorum. Hoc enim privilegium Deus solam divinam scripturam habere voluit, ut in ea sola nullum firmentum aut contagium falsitatis*'.

[17] Pierre Roger, *Postill on 'Quia quorundam mentes'*, Brussels, Bibliothèque Royal Albert Iᵉʳ, MS 359 (11437–40), f. 26ᵛ.

pope, justifying Cola's accusation by 'adulterating' the words of Christ.

Clement's political use of the Bible appears to fall into three main categories, although they are by no means watertight. He was a man who set much store by precedent, and he therefore used biblical precedents to justify his policies and actions. Secondly, he would try to explain a particular situation as a fulfilment of a prophecy, or, occasionally, would try to use prophecy prospectively, that is, he would argue that by taking a particular course of action he would be assisting the fulfilment of a prophecy. Finally, he would use 'political allegory' to illustrate a theoretical point.

The use of biblical precedent involved the application of the literal and historical sense of a text to a contemporary situation. Generally biblical figures would be used to signify both the pope himself and those whom his theories or actions affected. The best-known examples are those from the Old Testament which justify Clement's institution and control of lay officials. The New Testament provided no suitable examples.[18] Underlying all of them is the familiar identification of the people of the universal Christian society with the people of Israel. The obvious precedents for Charles of Bohemia when Clement instituted him as king of the Romans and approved of his personal suitability for office were Solomon, Saul, and David. The theme, Solomon 'shall sit upon my throne and rule for me, and I have appointed him to be ruler over Israel and over Judah', emphasized the point that even after papal confirmation and institution Charles would still be totally under the pope's control. As Clement admitted, he had not the slightest intention of renouncing the throne himself. 'He shall rule for me', he expanded, 'when he reigns for my honour and that of my see. When he reigns on my behalf he will totally direct his rule to the honour of God and the Holy See'.[19] The text also implied that it was the pope alone who invested Charles with his powers, who appointed him to be ruler over Israel. The other precedents, those of Saul and David, reinforced this. Both kings had been appointed directly by Samuel. 'Not at the election of the people, but at their

[18] Cf. J. Chydenius, *Medieval Institutions and the Old Testament* (Helsinki, 1965), pp. 11–12; 44–52; 73–9.
[19] *MGH Const.*, VIII, no. 100, pp. 151–2.

petition Samuel, according to the counsel of God, gave them King Saul', Clement announced, and pointed out that the same was true of David.[20] When Samuel elevated Saul he was instituting the office of kingship, which was previously unknown among the Israelites: every time the pope instituted a king, the Old Testament scene was re-enacted. To support this, the Pope quoted from Hugh of St Victor: the *sacerdotium* was instituted first, and then it instituted the royal *potestas* at God's command. The same still happens today in the *Ecclesia Dei*: the priestly dignity consecrates the royal *potestas*, sanctifying it by benediction and forming it by institution.[21] The salient point, as Clement spelt out to Charles, was that the spiritual power instituted the temporal so that it might exist—*ut sit*—judged it in case it was not good; and consecrated it so that it would be good.[22] The all-important anointing of the kings of Israel had also not escaped Clement. As Augustine had emphasized, the kings of Israel were the only ones to be anointed, and had their immediate *ordo* from Christ, on whom depended all unction. Clement therefore considered it only right that since the Empire was catholic, and whoever was promoted to rule over it received unction, he should have to be approved by the supreme pontiff.[23] In any case, God had always wished that the kings of Israel should be approved or rejected by the priesthood.[24] And this was another aspect of the precedent. It was quite possible for the pope to reject a candidate: instead he might promote David, the least of the sons of Jesse.[25] There was also the abhorrent possibility of deposition. So long as Saul obeyed Samuel he had prospered and done well, but the moment he disobeyed he had been deposed. There were, of course, precedents in more recent history, and Clement reminded Charles of the processes of Innocent IV against Frederick II (1245). Charles was not allowed to forget that *Samuel Saul reprobavit et David approbavit*.[26] The same biblical threat had also been applied to Louis de la Cerda, a minor prince of the French royal house, whom

---

[20] *Ibid.*, p. 155.
[21] *Ibid.*, p. 154. Cf. Hugh of St Victor, *De Sacramentis Christiane Fidei*, ii, II, ch. 4: *PL* clxxvi, 418.
[22] *Ibid.*
[23] *Ibid.* Cf. Augustine, *Enarr. in Ps.*, xliv, 19; *CSEL*, x (1), p. 507.
[24] *Ibid.*
[25] *Ibid.* Cf. I *Kings*, xvi. 6–13.
[26] *Ibid.*, p. 153.

Clement had created King of the Fortune Islands two years earlier.[27] The final inference the Pope drew from the Saul precedent was that the king had been given 'not at the election of the people but at their petition'. It was a neat answer to the pretensions of the imperial College of Electors, whose members thought that the election they made on behalf of the people of the Empire was the vital factor in the king-making process, and that it was from election rather than papal approval that the king received his administrative power over the *imperium*.[28]

Old Testament rulership precedents were not unusual. More original, however, was Clement's use of precedent to justify a controversial decision. Giovanni Visconti of Milan had been a partisan of Louis of Bavaria, even to the extent of accepting a red hat from his antipope, Nicholas V (Peter of Corbara O.F.M.). After being restored to the unity of the Church, Clement had provided him to the archbishopric of Milan. This honour notwithstanding, Visconti occupied the papal territory of Bologna, for which Clement excommunicated him. Yet only two years later the Pope appeared to commit a complete *volte face* by coming to terms with the excommunicate and appointing him his vicar in Bologna for twelve years.[29] This meant that he had to be received back into the grace of the Church, and Clement was faced with the difficult task of explaining why he had appeared to change his mind, despite Visconti's obvious lack of contrition. Clement had to tread carefully, because if a pope reversed a previous decision, either his own or that of a predecessor, it automatically raised the issue of infallibility: could the original pronouncement have been wrong? could papal

---

[27] Clement VI, Coronation *collatio* for Louis of the Fortune Islands, BN, MS lat. 3293, f. 298ʳ: '*Unde in toto libro Regum quamdiu reges servaverunt fidelitate Deo, obediendo eis mandatis ipsum colendo et adorando, tamdiu regnum eorum fuerat prosperatum. Sed quam cito infideliter agebant, erga dominium et multa infortunia patiebantur, et regnum ad alios transferebatur*'.

[28] This idea had been expressed in the anonymous *Weistum* of 1252. See K. Zeumer, 'Ein Reichsweisthum über die Wirkungen der Königswahl aus dem Jahre 1252', *Neues Archiv*, xxx (1902–5), p. 406. For discussion see H. Mitteis, *Die deutsche Königswahl und ihre Rechtsgrundlagen bis zur Goldenen Bulle*, 2nd ed. (Brünn, 1944), pp. 216–17.

[29] On the relationship between Clement and the Visconti during the early years of the pontificate see G. Biscaro, 'Le relazioni dei Visconti di Milano con la Chiesa. Giovanni e Luchino—Clemente VI', *Archivo Storico Lombardo*, liv (1927), pp. 44–95.

decisions be reversed? Clement had to justify his reversal without endangering his sovereignty.[30] He chose to do this on the basis of a biblical precedent combined with the, originally Thomist, idea of *ratione status*, by which a ruler could act above the law in emergency circumstances if the common good demanded it. Clement's sermon text was *Esther*, xv. 11: 'And God changed the king's spirit into mildness',[31] from a chapter which amply demonstrated the majesty of the king and his use of the imperial power of clemency, that is, of voluntary restraint in the use of sovereign power. The Pope thought that God *in hac et consimilia materia facit conversionem mirabilem et gloriosam*.[32] He then moved on to argue that his action was *ex rei publice et universali bono*. The good of the *res publica* was peace, without which the author of peace could not be properly worshipped.[33] The manifest suffering brought about by war in Tuscany, especially in the cities loyal to the Church, was what prompted Clement to his action. The reconciliation was not for his own good, he hastened to assure his audience, but *ex comodo rei publice*.[34] Among the precedents he cited was that of Eleazar (I *Macc.*, vi. 43–46), who *pro bono rei publice* had exposed himself to death in battle. He had slain an elephant, which he had thought was carrying the enemy king, by creeping underneath it and thrusting at it from below. Predictably enough, the elephant had fallen on top of Eleazar and had killed him.[35] And there was also the example of Joab. After the slaying of the traitor Absalom, the people of King David were pursuing the Israelites, the followers of Absalom. But the text (II *Kings*, xviii. 16) said that Joab blew his trumpet to recall his people from pursuing the Israelites because he wished to spare the multitude. If Joab had wanted to spare a multitude of such ungrateful traitors, how, then, should the vicar of Christ act if a

---

[30] On the incompatibility of infallibility and sovereignty see B. Tierney, *Origins of Papal Infallibility, 1150–1350: A Study on the Concepts of Infallibility, Sovereignty and Tradition in the Middle Ages* (Leiden, 1972), especially pp. 1–13.

[31] St G. 240, ff. 458ʳ–63ʳ.

[32] *Ibid.*, f. 458ᵛ.

[33] *Ibid.*, f. 459ᵛ.

[34] *Ibid.*: '*Modo quot bella quot mala sequebantur in Tuscia et in civitatibus que semper fuerunt fideles ecclesie sicut sunt Florentia, Perusina, Senensis manifestum est. Et ideo ... nos ... volumus istam reconciliationem facere, non attendentes tantum ad proprium comodum quantum ad comodum rei publice*'.

[35] *Ibid.*

multitude of grateful and obedient people is likely to suffer such disaster? Clement wondered.[36]

The use of precedent involved the literal and historical interpretation of a text, which was then compared with a contemporary situation. The use of prophetic texts might also entail the use of the allegorical sense. Clement's most sustained use of prophecy occurred in a *collatio* he preached on the deposition of Henry of Virneberg, Archbishop of Mainz, in April 1346.[37] Like Visconti, Henry was also an adherent of Louis of Bavaria, and he was a member of the imperial College of Electors. Quite apart from the desire to be rid of Henry, Clement needed to create a malleable College of Electors to insure that it would elect the imperial candidate he was about to propose, namely, Charles of Bohemia. He wanted to promote a loyal papalist, Gerlach of Nassau, to the see of Mainz, and therefore to the College, in place of Henry. The text he chose was from *Psalm* cviii, 7–8: 'When he is judged, may he go out condemned; and may his prayer be turned to sin. May his days be few: and let his bishopric another take'. These words, as Clement knew, literally expressed a prophecy rather than a wish, and they concerned the traitor Judas. Peter had appreciated this when in *Acts*, i. 16 he had said, 'The scripture must needs be fulfilled which the Holy Ghost spoke before by the mouth of David concerning Judas, who was the leader of them that apprehended Jesus: who was numbered with us, and had obtained part of this ministry'. All these words Clement felt he could apply to Henry of Mainz,[38] which he did throughout the *collatio*. There are many apt comparisons: for example, both were of similar vocation, because Judas had been 'elected' by Christ, Henry by the vicar of Christ.[39] Both held similar office, one being called to be an apostle and the other a bishop, bishops being the vicars of the apostles.[40] Their

---

[36] *Ibid.*: '... *sed dicit textus quod Joab cecinit buccina et retinuit populum volens parcere multitudini. Si ergo iste voluit parcere multitudini proditrici pessime et ingrate, quid debet facere vicarius Christi ne multitudini obedienti et grate tot mala perveniant certe multa mala pati?*'

[37] Ed. J.P. Schunk, *Beyträge zur Mainzer Geschichte*, ii (Mainz and Frankfurt, 1789), pp. 352–75.

[38] *Ibid.*, pp. 352–3.

[39] *Ibid.*, p. 354.

[40] *Ibid.*, p. 355.

transgressions were similar too: Judas had consented to kill Christ, while Henry, through his various iniquities, had wished, in so far as he was able, to subject, to trample underfoot, even to kill Christ in his members and in his spouse Holy Mother Church.[41] In other words, Judas had wanted to destroy the physical body of Christ, whereas Henry wanted to destroy the mystical body of Christ, which was the universal Church. The allegory of the Church as the bride of Christ was a traditional one and was taken to signify its uniqueness, its purity, and its total identification with Christ. Having established Judas as the prototype of Henry, Clement could then go on to apply the words of the prophecy to him. 'When he is judged, may he go out condemned' was simple enough, and it enabled the Pope to expand on his supreme judicial authority, and to stress yet again those iniquities of Henry which had caused his condemnation.[42] 'May his days be few' was also easy to apply. It referred not merely to his physical life, but also to his spiritual and his pastoral lives.[43] Clement then obligingly gave the fulfilment of prophecy a helping hand by deposing Henry from office, and appointing Gerlach in his place: *Episcopatum ergo ejus hodie merito accipiet alter*,[44] he declared triumphantly. Thus had the words of the Prophet been fulfilled.

There were other occasions too when Clement felt inclined to render prophecy a little assistance, usually in connection with the coercion of infidels to embrace the Faith. Coercion was justified on the grounds that it would enable the Church to achieve its prophesied universality.[45] But prophecy could also be used retrospectively, as it was in Clement's unusual rendering of Daniel's interpretation of Nebuchadnezzar's dream. During the approbation *collatio* delivered to Charles, the Pope tried to explain Clement V's controversial legislation, *Pastoralis cura*, which appeared to sanction the fact that the Empire was territorially limited.[46] Clement VI concentrated on the iron-and-clay feet of the image seen in the

---

[41] *Ibid.*, pp. 356–7.
[42] *Ibid.*, pp. 362–73.
[43] *Ibid.*, p. 373.
[44] *Ibid.*, p. 374.
[45] D. Wood, 'Infidels and Jews: Clement VI's Attitude to Persecution and Toleration', *SCH*, xxi (1984), pp. 115–24.
[46] *MGH Const.*, IV, 1, no. 1166 (= *Clem.*, II, xi, 21).

dream, which symbolized the fourth of five kingdoms to hold supremacy, that of the Romans. As Daniel himself had explained, 'the fourth kingdom shall be divided' (*Daniel*, ii. 41) and 'it shall be partly strong and partly broken' (*Daniel*, ii. 42)—*sicut hodie ad litteram cernimus*, added Clement.[47] The papal theory of government had been founded on the idea that *Ecclesia* and *imperium* were identical in extent. They were really two complementary aspects of the one united and universal Christian society, always assuming, of course, the superiority of one aspect over the other. Now, however, the Christian society was partly strong, that is, still theoretically universal, and partly broken, that is, territorially limited since Clement V's decree, hence the kingdom was divided. Clement then went on to refer specifically to *Pastoralis cura*.[48]

The third way in which Clement used the Bible politically was by employing allegory, that is, by using texts in a spiritual sense. One of the best examples again concerns Henry of Mainz, and comes from an earlier *collatio* Clement had preached against him in 1344. The text was from *Deuteronomy*, xxi. 20: 'This our son is stubborn and rebellious; he will not obey our voice'.[49] Clement explained the literal sense of the text: Moses had issued a law which described how a stubborn and rebellious son who ignored the admonitions of his father and mother was to be apprehended and brought before the elders. Moses had meant this law to be applied to a natural son. But because 'all these things happened to them in figure' (I *Corinthians*, x. 11) and 'the law has a shadow of good things to come' (*Hebrews*, x. 1) the Gloss, that is, the *Glossa Ordinaria*, had applied the words to a spiritual son. It identified 'son' as a son by faith, that is, the spiritual son of a priest, and 'mother' as the Church.[50] This gave Clement the opportunity to air his favourite metaphor, that of the marriage of the pope, in his capacity as the vicar of Christ, to the *Ecclesia*. Clement and his predecessors, with Holy Mother Church, had procreated a son, Henry, Archbishop of Mainz: indeed, they had not simply procre-

---

[47] *MGH Const.*, VIII, no. 100, p. 150.
[48] *Ibid.*, p. 151.
[49] Ed. Schunk, *Beyträge*, pp. 332–40.
[50] *Ibid.*, p. 333. Cf. *Biblia Sacra cum Glossa Ordinaria* (Antwerp, 1617), ad *Deut.*, xxi. 20, col. 1592. See the article by B. Smalley, 'Glossa Ordinaria' for the *Theologische Realenzyklopädie* (in press).

ated him, but had also nurtured and lovingly educated him, and
then had exalted him by promoting him to one of the most
important churches. But he had proved stubborn and rebellious,
conspiring against his father and mother by favouring the Church's
enemy, Louis of Bavaria. He had therefore been summoned before
the elders, which signified consistory.[51] The marriage metaphor
was an extension of the customary description of the Church as the
bride of Christ, which Clement was to use in the later sermon
against Henry. Since the pope was Christ's earthly vicar, he
automatically assumed Christ's role as the bridegroom of the
Church. The metaphor demonstrated the total identity of the pope
with the *Ecclesia*. It also provided a convenient way of emphasizing
the corporate nature of the Christian society: it was the *corpus
Christi mysticum*, within which existed an indissoluble unity, both
among the members, and between the head (that is, Christ or his
vicar) and the members. This too was a biblical concept, based on I
Corinthians, xii (12–27).[52]

There seems to be little in Clement's three uses of the Bible to
warrant Cola's accusation of adulterating the sacred page in the
sense of dishonestly glossing it. The only instance to emerge so far
of Clement's actually twisting a quotation for a political end occurs
in his reply to the Roman ambassadors who had requested his
return to Rome, preached in 1343. He was arguing that Rome
rather than Jerusalem was rightly the *propria sedes* of the pope: in
effect, that the see had been translated from Jerusalem to Rome.
Christ had gone to Jerusalem because it was the principal city of the
Israelites. But the Jews had rejected him, and so the disciples had
been forced to turn to the Gentiles. Clement then quoted the words
of Paul and Barnabas to the Jews (*Acts*, xiii. 46), 'It was necessary
that the word of God should first have been spoken to you: but
seeing ye put it from you, and judge yourselves unworthy of
everlasting life, lo, we turn to the Gentiles'.[53] Jerusalem, so
Clement reasoned, had been the principal city of the Jews, so Christ

---

[51] Schunk, pp. 333–4.

[52] See M.J. Wilks, 'The Idea of the Church as *Unus homo perfectus* and its Bearing on
the Medieval Theory of Sovereignty', *Miscellanea Historiae Ecclesiasticae* (Stock-
holm, 1960), pp. 32–49. Further bibliography is given at p. 39, n. 24.

[53] Ed. H. Schmidinger, 'Die Antwort Clemens' VI. an die Gesandtschaft der Stadt
Rom vom Jahre 1343', *Miscellanea in onore di Monsignor Martino Giusti: Collectanea
Archivi Vaticani*, vi (Vatican City, 1978), pp. 344–65, at p. 349. In general see his
'Die Gesandtschaft der Stadt Rom nach Avignon vom Jahre 1342/43', *Römische
Historische Mitteilungen*, xxi (1979), pp. 15–33.

had gone there: Rome was the principal city of the Gentiles, as Augustine's *De Civitate Dei* had proved, and it had therefore been ordained by divine rather than human inspiration that the apostles should go there, and that the see which was most peculiarly Peter's—*propriissima*—should be established there.[54] Clement's intellectual sleight of hand came in attributing the words of Paul and Barnabas to Peter. It made far better sense from the papal viewpoint that the translation of the see should be made by Peter, the first pope, rather than by Paul. But the adaptation is a relatively minor one and hardly enough to substantiate Cola's charge.

With one minimal exception Clement seems to have borne out his own conviction that the pope could not alter Scripture because of its divine authorship. Even allowing for the fact that some of his political interpretations are a little free, they hardly constitute a new sense of Scripture. In any case, his detractor was just as free in some of his own biblical interpretations. The *Libellus* to Ernest Pardubitz, Archbishop of Prague, written in 1350, was probably Cola's most anti-papal work. Among other things, Clement was branded as the hireling of *John*, x. 12, who fled when he saw the wolf coming. This was because the Pope had deserted Rome.[55] In a phantasy conversation with Clement Cola warns the Pope not to destroy himself, for if he destroys the members of Christ, he will crucify Christ, and if he crucifies Christ, then he will be destroying himself, because he calls himself the vicar of Christ.[56] The passage is somewhat reminiscent of Clement's accusations of four years earlier against Henry of Mainz, who had wished to kill Christ in his members and in his spouse Holy Mother Church.[57] In the final analysis, Cola's charges that Clement had adulterated the sacred page sound suspiciously like a case of the medieval pot calling the kettle black.

University of East Anglia

[54] Schmidinger, 'Die Antwort', p. 349.
[55] Cola di Rienzo, *Verus Tribuni Libellus contra scismata et errores, scriptus ad Archiepiscopum Pragensem*, ed. K. Burdach and P. Piur, *Briefwechsel des Cola di Rienzo*, II, iii (Berlin, 1912), pp. 231–78, at pp. 233–4. On Cola di Rienzo, and for bibliography, see J. Wieder, 'Cola di Rienzo', in *Karl IV. und sein Kreis*, ed. F. Seibt = *Lebensbilder zur Geschichte der bömischen Länder*, iii (Munich, 1978), pp. 111–44. Unfortunately M.B. Juhar, 'Der Romgedanke bei Cola di Rienzo' (dissertation, Kiel, 1977) is not available to me.
[56] Cola di Rienzo, *Libellus*, p. 246.
[57] See above p. 246.

PREACHING, PASTORAL CARE, AND *SOLA SCRIPTURA* IN LATER MEDIEVAL IRELAND: RICHARD FITZRALPH AND THE USE OF THE BIBLE

by KATHERINE WALSH

IN THE preface to the third edition of *The Study of the Bible in the Middle Ages* Beryl Smalley pointed out the dilemma posed by the apparently simple solution contained in the mature teaching of Thomas Aquinas, whereby the literal sense of biblical interpretation was *all* that the sacred writer intended.[1] Her question as to what should be included under 'all' preoccupied many medieval students of Scripture. That Richard FitzRalph (†1360) is to be included among their number, we learn both from the theoretical expositions of his personal understanding of exegesis and from the sermons which represent his pastoral approach to the Bible translated into concrete terms. These reflections were to have a considerable impact on his subsequent reputation in the western Church following the Wycliffite, Hussite, and Reformation controversies.[2]

Whereas it is obvious from his academic career at Oxford that FitzRalph must have spent a period lecturing on several books of the Old and New Testament as *baccalaureus biblicus*,[3] no direct record of these lectures and commentaries survives. This state of affairs is in itself not unusual. Surviving biblical commentaries by bachelors are rare, a situation which presumably reflects both their provisional nature and the state of the manuscript notebooks in

---

[1] (Oxford 1983), p. xv.

[2] See K. Walsh, *A Fourteenth-Century Scholar and Primate. Richard FitzRalph in Oxford, Avignon and Armagh* (Oxford, 1981), esp. pp. 318, 378, 452–75. More recently see J.D. Dawson, 'Richard FitzRalph and the fourteenth-century poverty controversies', *JEH*, xxxiv (1983), pp. 315–44; J. Coleman, 'FitzRalph's antimendicant *proposicio* (1350) and the Politics of the Papal Court at Avignon', *JEH*, xxxv (1984), pp. 376–90.

[3] *The Universities of Europe in the Middle Ages by the late Hastings Rashdall*, ed. F.M. Powicke and A.B. Emden, 3 vols. (Oxford, 1936), iii, p. 139, n. 2.

which they were jotted down. They were never intended as an *ordinatio* text, but simply contained raw material for future ventures into the field of homiletics. Much more common is the developed version of the schoolmen's views in the magisterial commentaries and lectures of the regents. Among these may be noted a significant preponderance of masters from the ranks of the regular clergy, especially from the mendicant orders, who were almost exclusively responsible for biblical teaching in the schools.[4] Though the friars frequently complained about having to bear this burden, the more astute among them must have recognized the benefits to be accrued from the situation. Nevertheless, there were, as William J. Courtenay has recently indicated,[5] many cases in which the lectures of a *baccalaureus biblicus* could have a significant intellectual, if not exegetical, content. These, or biblical *questiones* by regent masters, could be structured around problems of moral and speculative theology, continuing the themes and debates of their commentaries on the Sentences, as was the case with FitzRalph and the bachelors William Crathorne and Grafton, who disputed under and shortly after his regency.[6] These underline the need to avoid an exaggerated and artificial distinction between the speculative theology of logically-minded schoolmen, and the exegetical approach of those concerned with spirituality and with problems of the later medieval pastoral scene.

FitzRalph personified this dilemma very clearly, though his attempt towards the end of his life to dramatize his change of attitude from the scholastic to the pastoral-biblical approach to theology as a personal 'conversion' has tended to obscure rather than clarify the development of his views. Elsewhere it has been attempted to show that his change of direction is more likely to have been determined by the practical requirements of the job on hand in each case.[7] Here it is intended to illustrate the development

---

[4] For examples of the wide-ranging implications of the friars' scriptural teaching in and beyond the schools see Smalley, *Friars*, pp. 28–34.

[5] W.J. Courtenay, 'The Lost Matthew Commentary of Robert Holcot, O.P.', *AFP*, l (1980), pp. 103–4.

[6] For these disputations and for the confusion surrounding the identity of the various Graftons see W.J. Courtenay, *Adam Wodeham. An Introduction to his Life and Writings = Studies in Medieval and Reformation Thought*, xxi (Leiden, 1978), esp. pp. 90–112.

[7] Walsh, *Richard FitzRalph*, esp. pp. 16–17, 176–9, 466.

of his approach to the Bible through the internal evidence of his systematic writings and a limited selection of sermons. Our earliest evidence for FitzRalph's thinking about the role of the Bible in theological debate and therefore in the teaching *magisterium* of the Church dates from his regency in Oxford. It falls into the category alluded to by Courtenay and is, for present purposes, unsatisfactory. Furthermore, it is indirect and comes from the numerous references made by the Franciscan bachelor Adam Wodeham, while disputing under FitzRalph's regency, to the latter's *Questio Biblica*.[8] This work, which has not survived in any identifiable manuscript, is clearly not a series of lectures given as *baccalaureus biblicus*, but is to be regarded as a by-product of the author's magisterial teaching. It was composed after the partial revision of his commentary on the Sentences for publication and, as we can deduce from the criticism of the opposing bachelor, contained a reappraisal of his own much-disputed views on future contingents. Hence it would appear that its value in the present discussion may be limited to the confirmation and theoretical justification for that philosophical approach to exegesis, which can be identified in his later work, and which contrasts sharply with the linguistic method of a Nicholas of Lyre.[9] However, the fact that FitzRalph composed a biblical *questio* as regent in theology, when he was not obliged by statutory requirement to do so, when most biblical teaching was in mendicant hands, and he had as yet no reason to minimize the friars' monopoly in that area, suggests that his interest developed personally and independently, and that he was concerned to employ the medium of biblical commentary to convey philosophical opinions.[10]

---

[8] Courtenay, *Adam Wodeham*, pp. 78–9.

[9] A.J. Minnis, '"Authorial intention" and "literal sense" in the exegetical theories of Richard FitzRalph and John Wyclif: an essay in the medieval history of biblical hermeneutics', *PRIA*, lxxv, C(1975), esp. p. 2. See also the same author, 'Discussions of "Authorial Role" and "Literary Form" in Late-Medieval Scriptural Exegesis', *Beiträge zur Geschichte der deutschen Sprache und Literatur*, xcix (1977), pp. 37–65; 'Late-Medieval Discussions of *Compilatio* and the Rôle of the *Compilator*', *ibid.*, ci (1979), pp. 389–421; *Medieval Theory of Authorship: Scholastic literary attitudes in the later Middle Ages* (London, 1983).

[10] Minnis, '"Authorial intention"', pp. 7–8, indicates a number of cases in which FitzRalph was not prepared to follow Lyre, notably when prophecy is related to problems of predestination and future contingents.

More promising material for the present topic is offered by FitzRalph's *Summa de Questionibus Armenorum*, which permits a consideration of his view of the four interpretative senses and of the use of Scripture in ecumenical debate.[11] The lengthy discussions in the *Summa* indicate that, at least by the time he had become involved in the curial debates, FitzRalph had developed an intense and informed interest in the role of the *auctor*, in problems of intention and interpretation of the Scriptures. A major source of this interest and information is likely to have been the Franciscan exegete Nicholas of Lyre, whose *Postilla litteralis* enjoyed enormous popularity in Avignon during the 1330s, and who was involved in the beatific vision controversy on the same side as FitzRalph.[12] In its broadest sense the *Summa* had a secondary purpose in that it provided a general framework for discussion of the uses and limitations of a *sola scriptura* approach to theological debate, and hence throws valuable light on its author's role in later medieval intellectual controversy within and beyond the schools.

Within this framework it will be further attempted to survey the pastoral, practical application of FitzRalph's views on arrival in Ireland, where a sophisticated, theologically-informed public, such as he had been accustomed to in Oxford and Avignon, was not to be expected. Only on rare occasions, such as a provincial synod or in the Carmelite church in Drogheda before the pressure of events closed off such contacts with a mendicant audience,[13] was the preacher able to allow free rein to his talents for the more formal, learned, and demanding type of sermon. The vast majority of those which FitzRalph preached in Ireland were simple pastoral homilies, that set out to offer on the basis of the gospel of the day clear guidelines for morality and charity, for the love of God and fair dealing with one's neighbour. The sample selected here consists of the first five sermons preached by the new Archbishop in the

---

[11] Manuscript circulation and content of FitzRalph's most popular scholarly work is discussed in Walsh, *Richard FitzRalph*, pp. 129–77, 469–71. For a review of recent opinion on the levels of meaning, the senses of scriptural exegesis, see Smalley, *Bible*, pp. viii–xvi.

[12] Minnis, "'Authorial intention'", p. 2.

[13] This sermon has been edited by B.M. Zimmermann, 'Ricardi Archiepiscopi Armacani Bini Sermones de Conceptione B.V. Mariae ... annis 1342 et 1349', *Analecta Ord. Carm. Discalc.*, iii (1931), pp. 179–89.

course of a tour of his diocese after Easter 1348. In many respects unrepresentative of the kind of sermon of which the preacher was capable,[14] they have the advantage in the present context of belonging to a period in which his relations with certain groups in the diocese, the merchants in the towns and the Franciscans in the confessional, were still unclouded by bitterness and open conflict. Hence they may be understood as reflecting first impressions of the pastoral situation and as representative of the programme which the new Archbishop intended to undertake. Here the tone is still moderate, but there are clear pointers of the direction in which he would move, both in terms of homiletic style and biblical practice and with regard to the range of topics that he regarded as burning issues in the ecclesiastical province of Armagh. The social and political tensions of the day, the prelate's denunciations of sexual depravity among laity and clergy alike, of economic corruption, usury, and tax evasion among the mercantile classes in the towns, then led him in the heat of battle to a form of expression, an *ad hoc* interpretation of the Bible, which the uninitiated might identify with the *sola scriptura* teaching of Wyclif's followers outside the schools. These outbursts help to explain the intellectual climate and social context in which the opponent of mendicant poverty, the defender of papal hierarchical structures and dominion, might become within a generation of his death the 'Sa(i)nt Armachaun' of the Lollards and poor priests, whose more extreme teaching FitzRalph would certainly have rejected.[15]

However, it must be stressed that these sermons did *not* represent the main channel whereby interest in FitzRalph's biblical teaching was transmitted to the Lollards. With the single exception of the homily on the Immaculate Conception, delivered to the Carmelites in Drogheda on 25 March 1349, which followed the style of preaching adopted at the papal curia in Avignon, the Irish pastoral

---

[14] For a general characterization of FitzRalph's preaching style, see A. Gwynn, 'The Sermon Diary of Richard FitzRalph, Archbishop of Armagh', *PRIA*, xliv, C (1937), pp. 17–46; Walsh, *Richard FitzRalph*, pp. 182–238; Schneyer, *Repertorium*, v, pp. 150–8.

[15] This title figures regularly in the satirical poems cited by C.M. Erikson, 'The fourteenth-century Franciscans and their Critics', *Franc Stud*, ns, xxxv (1975), pp. 107–35; *ibid.*, xxxvi (1976), pp. 108–47, esp. pp. 117–18. It was also used by Nicholas of Hereford (1382), see A. Hudson, 'A neglected Wycliffite text', *JEH*, xxix (1978), p. 263.

homilies had a very limited circulation by comparison with the anti-mendicant sermons, which had sensational as well as practical appeal, and the formally-structured sermons delivered in Avignon, which were designed to display theological expertise. The informal Irish homilies, preached in the English vernacular and transmitted to us frequently through outline Latin notes in the sermon-diary, which give only an impression of the tone adopted by the preacher, were designed to meet a limited and specific purpose and had little attraction for collectors of sample sermons of general utility. Such collections account for most of the circulation of FitzRalph's formal sermons on the Continent, and especially in the monastic centres of the *Germania Sacra*,[16] whereas these Irish sermons appear not to have had any other circulation independent of the sermon-diary as a whole. Indeed, they represent the core of the *diary* in its most basic form, and its circulation as a complete work was—even in England—very restricted.

Apart from the problem of circulation and availability, it has been established that the chain of contact from FitzRalph to the Lollards, especially with regard to his biblical teaching, is part of a longer chain stretching back to Nicholas of Lyre. Hence it has been suggested that the presumed author of the Prologue to the Lollard Bible, John Purvey, 'reads Lyra with FitzRalph in mind'[17]—it would of course be equally plausible to reverse this pairing and suggest that the Lollards read FitzRalph, either directly or through Wyclif's extensive quotations and paraphrases of the arguments of the *Summa*,[18] with their other model, Nicholas of Lyre, before them. In either case, the fact remains that, surprising as it might seem, the Lollards learned FitzRalph's scriptural teaching in theoretical rather than practical form, through one of his most intellectually demanding works.

FitzRalph's attitude to the Bible presents one of the most important of the many problems that arise from an analysis of the

[16] For example Göttweig (O.S.B.), Klosterneuburg (Can. Reg. O.S.A.), Stams (O.Cist.), and the collegiate church of St Nicholas in Passau.

[17] Minnis, '"Authorial intention"', p. 30. Whether Lollard students of Scripture were able or willing to distinguish between the underlying presuppositions of FitzRalph and of the Franciscan exegete is however open to question.

[18] For the extent to which Wyclif actually read FitzRalph and closely studied extensive portions of his work, see G.A. Benrath, *Wyclifs Bibelkommentar = Arbeiten zur Kirchengeschichte*, xxxvi (Berlin, 1966), pp. 35–6, 293.

Summa. The emphasis on scriptural proof which dominates the work was, as the author was careful to point out, determined by the circumstances which occasioned it. Above all, it was made necessary by FitzRalph's recognition that, whereas his discussion partners at Avignon, the Latinizing Armenians,[19] were receptive to arguments from conciliar decrees and the patristic tradition of the western Church, those whom they would have to convince on their return to the East would be amenable to no arguments other than those of Scripture—and presumably the Greek Fathers, of whom FitzRalph's own knowledge was singularly deficient. He avoided, and leaves the impression that he saw no need for a systematic discussion of, the relation of Scripture to the tradition of the Church.[20] Hence he puts the questions which seem relevant to him into the mouth of Johannes, the 'pupil' and debating partner of Ricardus, who opens the *Summa* with a query as to the sense in which Scripture should be discussed here. The question provides Ricardus with the opportunity to analyse the problems faced by those interpreters of the Bible who were not prepared to evade historical and linguistic difficulties of interpretation by an appeal to the tropological or allegorical senses.[21] This analysis indicates that FitzRalph was receptive to genuine Thomist teaching on the literal sense. Aquinas had already worked out a satisfactory theory of the relations between the senses, and his distinction provided a firm foundation for the view (by then already partly accepted) that all argument must proceed from the literal sense only.[22] FitzRalph adopted this solution and used it as a guideline, not only in the *Summa*, but in sermons to audiences at all levels. He employed it in the form which had been developed and refined by Nicholas of

---

[19] As the *editio princeps* of FitzRalph's *Summa*, that of Johannis Sudoris (Paris, 1511) is notoriously deficient, the text will be cited here from the printed edition for reference purposes, and from one of the better early-manuscripts, BAV, Vat.Lat. 1033, dating from 1393.

[20] For such a discussion by the pre-Reformation preacher in Strassburg, Geiler of Kaisersberg, see E.J. Dempsey Douglass, *Justification in Late Medieval Preaching. A Study of John Geiler of Keisersberg = Studies in Medieval and Reformation Thought,* i (Leiden, 1966), pp. 65–74.

[21] *Summa,* ed. Sudoris, ff. II^{ra}–III^{vb}; Vat.Lat. 1033, fol. 1^v–4^r.

[22] B. Smalley, 'William of Auvergne, John of La Rochelle and St. Thomas Aquinas' on the Old Law', *St. Thomas Aquinas 1274–1974. Commemorative Studies,* 2 vols. (Pontifical Institute of Mediaeval Studies, Toronto, 1974) i, pp. 16, 54–5.

Lyre. The latter permitted a *duplex sensus literalis*, which covered a range of possible meanings of Scripture, and depended on the reader's understanding in accordance with his own intellectual capacities,[23] an approach which could and did lead to controversy later in the fourteenth century. As authority for this view, Ricardus drew on the Pauline distinction between the literal and spiritual senses, when he spoke of the New Law not as a covenant of written letters but of the Spirit.[24] This close dependence on the leaders of biblical scholarship among the friars reflects FitzRalph's conventional scholasticism, developing what he had learned in Oxford and at the papal curia, where, especially during the pontificates of Benedict XII and Clement VI, the climate for biblical studies was favourable.[25]

A further component is introduced into the dialogue—the argument from reason in conjunction with Scripture. Johannes queries how to deal with the problem raised by the Armenians that one can accept the primacy of the Roman Church only if it can be proved by Scripture and reason. He objects to Ricardus' case for the primacy of Peter, and draws on a battery of arguments from the New Testament to show that the same powers were given by Christ to all the apostles equally.[26] The counter-arguments of Ricardus, who takes scriptural examples to give ten reasons for the primacy of Peter, clearly appealed to Wyclif, who took over this lengthy passage in his commentary on the Acts of the Apostles.[27] The argument from reason had its attractions for both of them, though their interest in Peter's primacy stemmed from different premisses—FitzRalph was concerned to defend the special position of the papacy, whereas Wyclif used the passage to demonstrate the exemplary nature of the early Church.

Consistent with his fidelity to the best Thomist tradition, FitzRalph was careful to establish the canon of the books of the Old

[23] Minnis, '"Authorial intention"', pp. 4–8.
[24] II. *Cor.*, iii. 6; *Summa*, I, v, ed. Sudoris, f. III^{rb}; Vat.Lat. 1033, f. 3^v.
[25] For the relevant documents concerning the promotion of biblical studies and the provision of the required linguistic instruction see *Chartularium Universitatis Parisiensis*, ed. H. Denifle and E. Chatelain, 4 vols. (Paris, 1891–9), ii, pp. 154–5, 200–1, 576–88; see also D. Wood, '... *novo sensu sacram adulterare Scripturam*', above, pp. 237–49.
[26] *Summa*, VII, i–v, ed. Sudoris, ff. XLV^{ra}–XLVI^{va}; Vat.Lat. 1033, ff. 45^r–47^r.
[27] Benrath, *Wyclifs Bibelkommentar*, p. 293.

and New Testaments. He returned to the issue in the two concluding books of the *Summa*, upholding the veracity and authority of
the books of the Old Law individually and collectively,[28] and
stressing their value for dealings with the Jews. Once again he
documented his willingness to treat favourably men of a different
religious tradition, paralleling Wyclif's later readiness, on particular
theological grounds, to grant that there may be Christians among
other 'sects'—not only Saracens, but also Jews, Greeks, and other
schismatics.[29] To underline his respect for these, FitzRalph specifically allowed *Acts*, ii. 5–11, to include learned Hebrew doctors
among those present in Jerusalem at Pentecost[30]—surely intended
as a compliment to those in Avignon who had provided him with
information. At the same time he followed Aquinas in the line of
argument establishing the authority of the Mosaic law by means of
the law of the evangelists and other apostolic writers, and concluded the work with an exhaustive discussion of the relationship
between the Old Law and the New, which leaves no stone
unturned, but has little claim to originality.[31] Hence the *Summa*
presents FitzRalph's estimate of the Bible, taken as a whole book,[32]
as an acceptable and effective vehicle for ecumenical discussion:
indirectly he offered a plea for the usefulness of *sola scriptura* in such
circumstances. Despite his disclaimers, which were a political
necessity at the papal curia, he seemed personally to be of the
opinion that for his purposes the Bible was sufficient.

The willingness to engage in dialogue and discussion across
traditional dividing lines, which is a feature of the *Summa*, was also
to mark his pastoral work in Ireland. For all the violence of his
condemnation of the confessional malpractices of the friars, the lack
of discipline, education, and religious disposition among his clergy,
and the moral failings of his flock, he made an important plea for

---

[28] *Summa*, XVIII, i–ix, ed. Sudoris, ff. CXLIIII^va–CXLVII^vb; Vat.Lat. 1033, f. 149^v–52^v.
[29] Cited in Dempsey Douglass, *Justification in Late Medieval Preaching*, p. 65.
[30] *Summa.*, XVIII, vi, ed. Sudoris, ff. CXLVI^v–CXLVII^r; Vat.Lat. 1033, f. 152^r.
[31] All 35 chapters of bk. xix are devoted to the topic.
[32] In this view of the Bible as a book among books, FitzRalph is following Lyre, and his view depends on the distinction between the sacred *auctor* and the human *scriptor*. See Minnis, '"Authorial intention"', p. 11; 'Late-Medieval Discussions', pp. 418–19.

justice, charity, and mutual toleration, and for an end to economic exploitation and social discrimination among the two 'nations' in his ecclesiastical province.[33] He had arrived in Ireland as Archbishop of Armagh by the early spring of 1348, with the obvious intention of making a pastoral impact. It is not clear whether, during the long absence in Oxford, Avignon, and Lichfield, he had maintained sufficient contact with his native area to give him first-hand knowledge of the pastoral problems of the diocese prior to taking up office. We have no evidence that he was a regular visitor in Dundalk during these years, but his contacts with the personnel of the diocese and with his own clerical relatives are well documented. So we can presume that he was returning to an area in which he could expect to be received as a favoured and trusted friend, and that his programme of moral reform was specifically tailored to combat abuses which he knew to be a common and acute problem there.[34] Hence it is unlikely that he was a completely unknown quantity when he set out, during Easter week 1348, on a goodwill preaching tour of that part of the diocese with which he must have been familiar since childhood—the concentration of urban settlement on the eastern seaboard around Drogheda and Dundalk, which also included Ardee, Louth, and Mansfieldstown.

A striking feature of these early sermons in Ireland is their author's readiness to transfer scriptural images to his own person. He depicted his coming in the same biblical language as the gospel narrative used to describe Christ's coming among the Jews, and invited—deliberately, it would seem—comparison with the role of the Saviour in his arrival among his own people, the citizens of Drogheda and Dundalk, as their pastor, mentor, and guide. Skilfully he used the Easter and Pentecostal liturgy to convey this impression, employing a figurative interpretation of the events between the Resurrection and the coming of the Holy Spirit, not only to instil a Christian message, but also for propaganda pur-

[33] For a recent review of the problem of nationality in the Middle Ages see L. Schmugge, 'Über "nationale" Vorurteile im Mittelalter', *DA*, xxxviii (1982), pp. 439–59.
[34] The basis for these views is discussed in Walsh, *Richard FitzRalph*, and requires no further treatment here, though a shift in the argument in favour of greater familiarity with his native diocese may be noted.

poses, to emphasize his own authority, and heighten the impact of his triumphant return home to the most exalted ecclesiastical office in the land. But this was not the place for elaborate rhetoric: considerations of form, the evaluation of FitzRalph's use of the *artes praedicandi*,[35] which might be attempted in the light of the Avignon sermons, are here precluded by the nature of the transmission of the source. The brief jottings in the diary are most precise when giving references to scriptural quotations, thus indicating its function as a handy work of reference for a busy preacher. Hence the sermons can be considered only in terms of subject, content, and choice of biblical example. In these early days the preacher borrowed frequently from earlier sermons, notably those preached in Lichfield, where a similar, simple level of exposition would have been appropriate. Then, within a short time of his arrival in Ireland, he began to adapt his sermons more thoroughly, or to write new ones which took deliberate and direct issue with the changed pastoral context in which he found himself. The question of available books, the homiletical and exegetical tools of the preacher, for FitzRalph's work in Ireland cannot be discussed here. On another occasion, while completing the *De Pauperie Salvatoris*, he complained about the dearth of suitable reference works,[36] but it seems likely that he did have access to a verbal concordance of the Bible such as had become common by the later thirteenth century.[37] An indispensable aid for preachers, it helped them to find reference to the use of words in various contexts, and facilitated the kind of

---

[35] See Th.M. Charland, *Les Artes Praedicandi. Contribution à l'histoire de la rhétorique du moyen âge = Publications de l'institut d'Etudes médiévales d'Ottowa*, vii (Paris and Ottowa, 1936), esp. pp. 327–403 for the text of the *De modo componendi sermones* of Thomas Waleys; see also L.-J. Bataillon, 'Approaches to the study of medieval sermons', *Leeds Studies in English*, ns, xi (1979, for 1980), pp. 19–35, which concentrates mainly on the thirteenth century; Schneyer, *Wegweiser*, pp. xi–xxv.

[36] *De Pauperie Salvatoris*, bks. i–iv, ed. R.L. Poole, in: John Wyclif, *De dominio divino* WS, (1890), p. 277.

[37] See R.H. and M.A. Rouse, 'The verbal concordance to the Scriptures', *AFP*, xliv (1974), pp. 5–30. The only extant manuscript of such a concordance known to have been in circulation in late medieval Ireland is now Dublin, Trinity College, MS 65. Made in Dorchester, *c.*1348, it later passed into Irish Franciscan hands and is unlikely to have been available to FitzRalph. However, in view of the wide circulation of such expensive handbooks among wealthy prelates and at the papal curia, it is possible that he possessed a copy personally, *ibid.*, pp. 21–2. See also C. von Nolcken, 'Some Alphabetical Compendia and how Preachers used them in Fourteenth-century England', *Viator*, xii (1981), pp. 271–88; V. Gillespie, '*Doctrina*

word-play which FitzRalph employed in the more formal Avignon sermons, and of which there are occasional traces among those in Ireland. But, for the most part, his method here was simple: biblical quotation, mainly from the New Testament, was used in a basic, common-sense way, to tell a story and illustrate a message—practical instruction, moral exhortation, and plenty of illustrations drawn from recognizable situations in the daily lives of his audience.

The first sermon, preached in his birthplace, Dundalk, on 24 April 1348, the Thursday of Easter week, was based on the *Pater noster*, and devoted entirely to a minute explanation of the historical and religious significance of the prayer. The notes in the diary are limited to a brief explanation that he had given his audience three reasons for his choice of topic, in which he repeated a sermon previously delivered in London on 11 April 1347.[38] The first two reasons are not specified, though—whether expressed or not—one good reason must have been the practical consideration that the new arrival had a suitable sermon already written out in his baggage. The third reason is worth noting: *et tercia racio fuit adiecta quia exemplo domini nostri, qui iudeos de sanguine suo decem illam oracionem primo docebat, volui eos de sanguine meo illam oracionem primo docere.*[39] Expressedly following the example of Christ (*Matt.*, vi. 7–13), FitzRalph chose this as his personal introduction to his flock. The principal theme of the homily is prayer, and the manner of exposition is typical of much of his preaching: the scriptural account is repeated phrase by phrase, the examination is detailed, but without recourse to any source of authority beyond the literal meaning of the text.

Three days later the Archbishop had moved on to Louth, where he continued the Easter theme of redemption and the coming of the

---

and *predicacio*: the Design and Function of some Pastoral Manuals', *Leeds Studies in English*, ns, xi (1979, for 1980), pp. 36–50; L.J. Bataillon, 'Les instruments de travail des prédicateurs au XIIIe siècle', *Culture et travail intellectuel dans l'Occident médiéval. Bilan des "Colloques d'humanisme médiéval" (1960–1980) fondés par le R.P. Hubert, O.P.,* ed. G. Hasenohr and J. Longère, Institut de Recherche et d'Histoire des Textes, (Paris, 1981), pp. 197–209.

[38] The sermon-diary will be cited here from Oxford, Bodleian Library, MS Bodl. 144. The notes for the extended version of this sermon are on ff. 39ᵛ–42ʳ.

[39] MS Bodl. 144, f. 42ᵛ.

Lord, taking as his text the gospel of the day: *Cum sero esset die illo, una sabbatorum, et fores essent clausae* (*John*, xx. 19).[40] This sermon is constructed around an elaborate interplay of the numbers three and seven, beginning with the three aspects of the coming of Christ to the apostles after the resurrection. Then follows the spiritual development of the apostles—from the doubting of Thomas to general belief and acceptance by all—in the course of the following week. The development of the theme is constructed around the seven deadly sins, a favourite *topos* for medieval preachers and confessors, as it provided the most useful scheme for helping the penitent to examine his conscience or the priest to examine his flock.[41] For each day of the week FitzRalph cites one of the deadly sins, offering in each case three remedies to help his audience combat such failings. While several of the seven are passed over briefly, three are clearly the focus of his attention—lust, anger, and covetousness. These he denounces with a fury more appropriate to a Lenten preacher preparing his flock for repentance and for the Easter ceremonies than a newly arrived pastor introducing himself. It appears that he had already decided that adultery and sexual depravity were major flaws in the social fabric of his diocese, and he was to return to the matter frequently, most extensively in the course of a synodal sermon several years later,[42] when he attempted to provide his priests with a secure guideline in confessional practice—doubtless in order to build up a counter-weight against

[40] MS Bodl. 144, ff. 42ᵛ–43ᵛ.

[41] See S. Wenzel, 'The Seven Deadly Sins: some Problems of Research', *Speculum*, xliii (1968), pp. 1–22; 'Vices, Virtues, and Popular Preaching', *MARS*, vi (1976), pp. 28–54.

[42] This sermon was edited by A. Gwynn, 'Two sermons of Primate Richard FitzRalph', *Archivium Hibernicum*, xiv (1949), pp. 53–63, and the topic in question is alluded to at pp. 56–7. See also Walsh, *Richard FitzRalph*, pp. 326–33. With regard to the tone of this sermon it is worth noting that the synod took place during the second week of February 1352, precisely at the time when the controversy over the disputed provision to the rectory of Stabannon (Co. Louth) came to a head. Apart from the legal problem posed by the nomination of two candidates, respectively under the Great Seal of England and under that of the Irish chancellor, FitzRalph's primary concern appears to have been the question of suitability for office with *cura animarum*, and the issue is a welcome illustration of the pastoral context within which the Archbishop had to work. See G.O. Sayles, 'Ecclesiastical Proceedings and the Parsonage of Stabannon in 1351', *PRIA*, lv (1952), pp. 1–23. I am grateful to Professor J.A. Watt, who drew my attention to the significance of this episode.

the friars, who by the mid-fourteenth century had developed a near-monopoly in marital counselling.[43] With regard to greed and covetousness, the preacher launched a philippic against the failings of the merchants, their insatiable desire for greater riches, and their specious arguments to the effect that the accumulation of wealth is laudable and desirable.[44] These are early rumblings of FitzRalph's criticism of financial juggling in order to show little profit, and therefore a reduced obligation to pay tithes at the end of the year, and (his particular fiscal *bête noir!*) of the view that it is equally meritorious to make a legacy of one's goods for charitable purposes after death, while retaining their unrestricted use in life. At a remarkably early date he struck that note which was to become familiar in his dealings with the population of Drogheda, leading to the crisis of the interdict four years later.[45]

A more harmonious note is introduced when the preacher repeated part of a discourse on wisdom and sanctity, based on *Eccles.*, xxiv. 15, which he had delivered in Lichfield on 15 August 1345, before returning to more serious business.[46] The juxtaposition of these passages reminds us that the pastoral homilies preached in Lichfield are far less combative than their successors in Ireland.

---

[43] For examples see D. d'Avray and M. Tausche, 'Marriage sermons in *ad status* collections of the Central Middle Ages', *AHDLMA*, xlvii (1980), pp. 71–119; D. d'Avray, 'The Gospel of the Marriage Feast of Cana and Marriage Preaching in France', above, pp. 207–24. Apart from the Franciscan Bishop of Ossory, Richard Ledred, there is little literary evidence for mendicant preaching or pastoral activity among FitzRalph's contemporaries, though a large proportion of his fellow bishops were members of the regular clergy, especially friars. See Edmund Colledge, *The Latin Poems of Richard Ledred, OFM, Bishop of Ossory, 1317–1360 =* Pontifical Institute of Mediaeval Studies, Studies and Texts xxx (Toronto, 1974). Polemical in tone, but useful for the documentation contained, is M.H. MacInerny, *A History of the Irish Dominicans from original sources and unpublished records, vol. I: Irish Dominican Bishops (1224–1307)*, (Dublin, Belfast, Cork, and Waterford, 1916). No further volumes appeared.

[44] Even the notes indicate his righteous indignation: 'Quoad detestacionem peccati auaricie et ipsum medicandum dicta fuerunt tria remedia, scilicet, diuiciarum laudabilitas, earum insaciabilitas, et possessoris propter eorum retencionem finalis calamitas. Quoad laudabilitatem dicta fuerunt facta communia mercatorum et principum ...', MS Bodl. 144, f. 42ᵛ.

[45] The most detailed statement of his views on the matter are to be found in the notes in the diary for the sermon preached in Drogheda, 18 December 1351. Briefer notes survive, but the tone is appreciably sterner, for that delivered in the same venue a year later, 2 December 1352. MS Bodl. 144, ff. 58ʳ–62ᵛ, 62ᵛ–63ʳ.

[46] MS Bodl. 144, ff. 20ʳ–22ᵛ.

Were the people of Anglo-Ireland really so depraved, or was FitzRalph's aggression partly provoked by a need to confound his critics at home? The remainder of this sermon is reserved for a discourse on the beatitudes, on the gospel precepts to forgive and to judge as one would wish to be judged,[47] and for an urgent plea for peace and reconciliation with one's neighbour. Such an attitude would, he assured his hearers, enable them to conquer fear, sorrow, and unbelief as the apostles did. The parallel with the role in which FitzRalph saw himself is obvious.

That this was the core of his message to his diocese is demonstrated by the fact that he returned to it yet again two days later on the next stage of his itinerary, in Ardee. Here too the mood reflects little of the joy in the liturgical calendar. Choosing as his text the eschatological discourse foretelling the destruction of Jerusalem and the tribulations of the Jews (*Mark*, xiii. 1–37), he came back yet again to an exposition of the deadly sins, the transitory nature of human love, the deceptive attractions of the material world, and the need for prayer and vigilance to ward off temptation. With unwearying emphasis the central texts on the love of God and of one's neighbour, Matthew's version of the beatitudes and the Lord's Prayer, are repeatedly cited to illustrate the need for fraternal charity even in the face of apparently impossible demands, and the preacher explicitly reminded his audience that *fratres suos* are to be understood as *aliquos christianos*.[48] Presumably his listeners would have grasped the point of these remarks more easily than the concluding passage of the sermon in which, according to the diary, he delivered a brief instruction on the nature of beatitude and its effects on body and soul.

The two remaining sermons in our sample were preached respectively in Drogheda, which in mercantile terms was one of the most important towns in fourteenth-century Ireland, as well as being the major ecclesiastical centre for the 'English' portion of the archdiocese of Armagh, and in Mansfieldstown, a vicarage of some strategic and economic importance.[49] These homilies reflect the

---

[47] MS Bodl. 144, f. 43ᵛ; *Matt.*, v. 2–10, 20–25, vi. 9–13.

[48] MS Bodl. 144, ff. 43ᵛ–44ʳ.

[49] The rectory of St Mary's Mansfieldstown was held by, among others, William Moner, bachelor of laws and proctor of Archbishop Nicholas Fleming at the papal curia (from 1405), and official principal of the archiepiscopal court (from 1407),

same concern for basic instruction to clarify possible points of confusion and—in the Drogheda sermon—the same method of simple exposition of the gospel story and explanation of the literal sense. The sermon at Mansfieldstown is, in one respect, an odd-man-out in the series: quotations from the Old Testament and from Augustine's *De Civitate Dei* abound, and it is possible that here FitzRalph had an ecclesiastical audience (the rural deans?) or other illustrious persons, who were to be impressed by a more liberal sprinkling of learning. At Drogheda on 4 May 1348 he chose the text *Quis crediderit et baptizatus fuit* ... (*Mark*, xvi. 16), and here he stressed the necessity of baptism for salvation, while introducing a reassuring note in his discussion of original sin, grace after the fall, and the capacity for merit. He took great pains to reject the notions that in the Old Law God visited the sins of the fathers on their sons, and that infants who died before baptism were damned.[50] These remarks invite a number of questions, which cannot be answered satisfactorily: had such queries been raised and brought to the Archbishop's notice, had he reason to correct false teaching already in circulation, or to warn against hysterical preachers? We do not know, and the remainder of the sermon gives no indication of special circumstances which might have provoked it, as the concluding portion on baptism in the early Church repeated a discourse which had more topical relevance in its original context: in the cemetery of the hospital of St John the Baptist in Lichfield three years earlier.[51]

At Mansfieldstown, in the last recorded sermon before the Black Death put an end to such assemblies in the area for almost a year—a period in which, as has been noted elsewhere, a fundamental change of attitude occurred in FitzRalph's dealings with his flock[52]—he again struck a conciliatory note, which might suggest

---

see *BRUO*, p. 1293; H.J. Lawlor (ed.), 'A Calendar of the Register of Archbishop Fleming', *PRIA*, xxx C (1912) *ad indicem* (p. 182). It was also held, from before 1431 until at least 1449 by Thomas Hussey, rural dean of the deaneries of Ardee and Dundalk, see D.A. Chart (ed.), *The Register of John Swayne, Archbishop of Armagh and Primate of Ireland 1418–1439* (Belfast, 1935), pp. 133, 189, 193–5. In the assessments of 28 June 1431 it was valued at 10 *s.*, the same sum as the vicar's stipend in the church of Stabannon, *ibid.*, p. 137.

50 MS Bodl. 144, f. 44^r.

51 MS Bodl. 144, ff. 9^r–13^r.

52 Walsh, *Richard FitzRalph*, pp. 284–8.

an audience with which he had a personal rapport. On the theme of
sorrow which will turn to joy (*John*, xvi. 20) he began with the
popular account of the marriage feast at Cana, when the transformation of water into wine prevented the wedding, which should
be a joyous occasion, from turning to one of sorrow.[53] Not only is
the sermon more elaborately constructed, according to the tripar-
tite scheme common to many of the Avignon sermons, but the
range and level of scriptural proof is more ambitious. Apart from
more frequent use of the Psalms and the Epistles of St Paul,
examples from the prophets, the historical and didactic books of
the Old Testament are paraded to illustrate when, and under what
circumstances, God did punish for sin.[54] The seven deadly sins
reappear under a different guise, and the preacher still found time to
warn his audience against pride and the practice of usury. Was this
battery of scriptural scholarship designed to impress, or was the
audience at Mansfieldstown a clerical one, to be provided with
suitable weapons for their own part in the fight against sin and
corruption in FitzRalph's Armagh? The question is more easily
asked than answered.

FitzRalph was a strong believer in the utility of sermons—he
would have approved of Gascoigne's stand in 1447 against Bishop
Reginald Pecock, when the latter defended the bishops in their
neglect of preaching.[55] In this respect both were following a
perfectly orthodox mendicant tradition stretching from, among
others, Humbert of Romans to Bernardino of Siena, which
favoured the sermon over the Mass.[56] This tendency to adjust the
balance between the celebration of the Eucharist and the more
obviously didactic homily continued to have a respectable following in spite of Lollardy, whereas the new emphasis on frequent
communion and on the importance of the Eucharist as a focus of
religious sentiment gave cause for concern.[57] It seems possible
therefore to anticipate the sixteenth-century equation: respect for
the literal sense (which had obvious homiletic value) = *sola*

---

[53] MS Bodl. 144, f. 44[v].
[54] MS Bodl. 144, ff. 45[r-v].
[55] *BRUO*, p. 746.
[56] G.R. Owst, *Preaching in Medieval England* (Cambridge, 1926), p. 93; Dempsey
Douglass, *Justification in Late Medieval Preaching*, pp. 87–90.
[57] See J.I. Catto, 'Wyclif and the Cult of the Eucharist', below pp. 269–86.

scriptura, as the evidence suggests that FitzRalph's understanding of the matter came close to this in practice. It suited his requirements better and complemented his reluctance to accept the authority of the Gloss.[58] His mental and pastoral development is closely linked with that of Wyclif. The latter's move in the direction of *sola scriptura* was not an isolated phenomenon, but one of several possible options in face of a scholasticism which, in the mind of many of its practitioners, had become increasingly theoretical, and which no longer provided satisfactory solutions to the religious problems confronting contemporary theologians. Are these numerous pointers in the direction of *sola scriptura* accidental, or do they, in the light of Wyclif's progress in the same direction, indicate a respected Oxford tradition of academic thinking? Has a post-Lollard and post-Reformation course of events led us to postulate a particular orthodoxy, to presume that such thinking must needs be heretical? It is undeniable that some of the most eloquent Lollard leaders claimed FitzRalph as one of their number, a forerunner of their way of thinking. It is almost certain that the spurious tradition, whereby FitzRalph should have translated the Bible into Irish, is based on a misunderstood source of Lollard provenance. Yet the Lollards' choice of phrase, *Sanctus Armachanus*, does not suggest a revolutionary rejection either of the cult of sainthood or of the traditional episcopal hierarchy. Was there a certain *Freiraum* in the field of biblical scholarship before the lines hardened around the Hussite problem during and after the Council of Constance? Did the generation before Wyclif feel the same need as Gascoigne for authoritative teaching, for a careful theological programme backed by the sanctions of orthodoxy as ammunition in reserve? FitzRalph's death in 1360, as a prominent and respected prelate at the Roman curia, could lead to calls for canonization. Had he lived and died a generation or more later, his fate might have been open to question.

Universität Salzburg

[58] In the course of the anti-mendicant sermons in London in the winter of 1356 he ridiculed those who appealed to the authority of the Gloss, MS Bodl. 144, f. 92^v, cited in Walsh, *Richard Fitz Ralph*, p. 410. See also J.R. Zenner, 'Armachanus über Widersprüche und Irrthümer in der heiligen Schrift', *Zeitschrift für katholische Theologie*, xv (1891), p. 350, and B. Smalley, 'Use of the "Spiritual" Senses of Scripture in Persuasion and Argument by Christian Scholars in the Middle Ages', *RTAM* (in press).

JOHN WYCLIF AND THE CULT OF
THE EUCHARIST

by J. I. CATTO

THE storm centre of John Wyclif's quarrel with the Church was his doctrine of the Eucharist. The critic of clerical dominion over secular things and of the authority of the pope had passed through ecclesiastical censure almost unscathed; but the proponent of a revisionist theology of the eucharistic sacrament would at once lose the countenance of academic colleagues and public opinion alike, and would suffer the consequences. The crisis of Wyclif's career came with striking rapidity after he broadcast, in his *Confessio* or public statement in the Oxford schools on 10 May 1381, his opinion that the presence of the Body of Christ in the Eucharist was figurative, 'sacramental', or in some sense, to anyone not acquainted with the terms of his own mental world, less than real. Though the relationship between Wyclif's opinion on transubstantiation and his views on the Church and philosophical ideas have been studied in some detail, no scholar, so far as I know, has investigated the passionate character, on both sides, of the debate on the Eucharist, or shown why a belief allegedly secondary to larger metaphysical ideas should have precipitated so unprecedentedly violent a debate. This controversy can be distinguished from any previous controversy in the schools by the powerful emotion it evoked among both laity and clergy: in the unmeasured language of friar John Tissington and the painful second thoughts of friar Adam Stockton; in the reported outrage of Wyclif's erstwhile patron, John of Gaunt; in the unwonted cries of heresy among the commons of the 1381 parliament. In the event, Wyclif's *Confessio* can be seen to have inaugurated an age of general religious controversy in Europe, with its consequent wars, persecutions, and divided peoples, which, lasting through three centuries, abated only in the toleration, or indifference, of the eighteenth century.

Why should a statement of belief about the Eucharist have precipitated all this? The answer cannot be found in the usual field of modern Wyclif scholarship, where the tendency is to elucidate his philosophy and ecclesiology in exclusively intellectual terms.[1] Instead, we shall have to consider the religion of his time not as theory but as practice: the cult of the Eucharist both within and outside the Mass, both the miracle of transubstantiation and the celebration of Corpus Christi. In the fourteenth and fifteenth centuries, two recent studies have reminded us, a changing notion of community came to focus on the sacrament of the Eucharist. John Bossy has suggested that the communion, or sacramental element in the Mass, was by then taken as a ritual of unity or integration, to which the 'asocial mysticism' of frequent communion, often outside the Mass, was a threat. At the same time, Mervyn James has pointed out that the rise of the cult of Corpus Christi, with its processions and sacred drama out of doors, related the notion of the social body to that of the Body of Christ, sanctifying the union of particular groups in a larger community: guilds for instance in a town.[2] In both settings the place of the Eucharist in the life of the believer is highly significant. The feelings of members of a population, who after all participated in the sacrament of unity by escorting the Host in procession, and offering their prayers in every enactment of the sacrifice of the Mass, have their place in the theological controversy of the age.

What, first of all, did Wyclif believe on this subject? Though Wyclif's (or his disciples') habit of revising his writings makes it dangerous to put his changing opinion on many topics in a sequence, early reference to the Eucharist in his unrevised biblical lectures and reports of his views by his opponent William Woodford show that the subject had been in his mind for at least a decade

---

[1] S. Harrison Thomson, 'The Philosophical Basis of Wyclif's Theology', *Journal of Religion*, xi (1931), pp. 86–116; G. Leff, *Heresy in the Later Middle Ages* (Manchester, 1967), ii, pp. 494–558, and 'John Wyclif: the Path to Dissent', *PBA*, lii (1966), pp. 143–80. A more rounded view of Wyclif's philosophy is presented by J.A. Robson, *Wyclif and the Oxford Schools* (Cambridge, 1961); see especially on his eucharistic doctrine, pp. 190–5, 218–21. But for an alternative approach see Smalley, *Postilla*; 'Wyclif's *Postilla* on the Old Testament and his *Principium*', *Oxford Studies presented to Daniel Callus* = OHS, ns, xvi (Oxford, 1964), pp. 253–96; 'The Bible and Eternity; John Wyclif's Dilemma', *JWCI*, xxvii (1964), pp. 73–89, reprinted in *Studies*, pp. 399–415.

[2] J. Bossy, 'The Mass as a Social Institution', *PP*, c (1983), pp. 29–61; M. James, 'Ritual, Drama and Social Body in the Late Mediaeval English Town', *ibid.*, xcviii (1983), pp. 3–29.

before 1381, and that he had been unable to settle on a satisfactory position. As we shall see, there is no reason to suppose that the position stated in his *Confessio* was any more satisfactory, and Woodford claimed that he had changed his mind again by 1383 or 1384.[3] We are not witnessing Wyclif's defence of a solidly held position, but stages in a painful and confused internal dialectic, of which his ill-tempered public statements seem to be only the incidental fall-out. However, the doctrine of transubstantiation consistently raised in his mind the same objections, and the kind of difficulty he felt is perhaps more important than the various philosophical solutions which he pondered. He had always maintained, he said, that the identical Body of Christ which suffered on the cross, and who sat at the right hand of the Father, was truly and really the sacramental bread, the consecrated host, which the faithful perceived in the hands of the priest.[4] He was also, however, consistent in his belief that the natural order of things and the supernatural must cohere. The Eucharist was not some supernatural entity beyond the natural order, but must conform to the natural laws of being and coming into being, which metaphysics could determine.

The question, whether the sacramental accidents could exist without a subject of which they were accidents, was the philosophical crux of Wyclif's doctrine of the Real Presence. It is the principal subject of his polemical work *De Eucharistia*, and the account, given briefly by William Woodford, of his arguments as a bachelor in the schools, shows that in this question, more clearly than in the debate on the annihilation of substance, his philosophical preoccupations grappled with the doctrine of the Eucharist.[5] The issue, though posed in scholastic terms, was simple: could appearances subsist without reality? Wyclif found justification for denying that they could in a novel combination of received views. Thomas Aquinas had indeed posited that the sacramental accidents had a subject, which was the quantity of the host (Aristotle had said that quantity was prior to qualities, and that qualities referred to

---

[3] William Woodford, *De Sacramento Altaris Quaestiones LXXII*, qu. 63, Oxford, Bodleian Library, MS Bodl. 703, f. 162ʳ.

[4] *FZ*, p. 114.

[5] *De Sacramento Altaris*, qu. 50, *veritates* 13 and 17, Oxford, Bodleian, MS Bodl. 703, ff. 161ᵛ–62ʳ and 162ᵛ–63ʳ, printed Robson, *Wyclif*, pp. 192 n. 2 and 193 n. 1.

quantity), and that in transubstantiation, the quantity of the bread and wine remained though the qualities were no longer present. In this way, the nature of the Eucharist could be reconciled with a rational explanation of the natural order, and Wyclif, in his early consideration of the subject, seems to have adhered to this opinion.[6] However, the commoner view in the fourteenth century was that of Duns Scotus and his followers, among whom apparently were many of Wyclif's opponents. They proposed that however impossible it may be for accidents to subsist without substance in the world, the case of the Eucharist, by virtue of God's *potentia absoluta*, was different.[7] In his two short treatises on the subject, William of Ockham also subscribed to this view, in addition rejecting the Aristotelian distinction on which Aquinas' explanation rested. Since individualization added nothing to a given lump of matter, what distinguished any individual from another could only be matter, not form. There was, therefore, no reason to distinguish substance from quantity; an individual was *as much as* it was.[8] This was an important idea for the development of physics on the lines of the Merton school, among whom a new mathematical conception of quantity was emerging. Wyclif seems to have combined Ockhamist philosophy with Thomist theology. While retaining the belief that accidents must have a subject, that is to say quantity (a view which Aquinas had maintained, but which Scotus and Ockham rejected) he now also held that the quantity must be identical with a material substance—as Ockham, in contradistinction to Aristotle and Aquinas, asserted. If bread and wine appeared to be there on the altar, then indeed they must be there.

This mixture of old and new ideas is so bizarre and strained that it must raise doubts of the generally accepted view that Wyclif's philosophy led him by ineluctable steps to deny transubstantiation.[9] Far from being inevitable, it was an original point of view formed in

---

[6] Thomas Aquinas, *Summa Theologiae*, pars iii, qu. 77, art. ii: *Sancti Thomae Aquinatis Opera Omnia*, ed. Leonina (Rome, 1882 ff.), xii, pp. 196–7, and cf. Aristotle, *Metaphysics*, M. 8 (1083a); Wyclif, *De Benedicta Incarnacione*, ed. E. Harris, WS (1906), p. 190.

[7] Scotus, *Opus Oxoniense*, lib. IV, dist. xii, qu. 2; *Joannis Duns Scoti Opera Omnia* (Lyons, 1639) viii, pp. 728–38.

[8] Ockham, *De Corpore Christi* (Venice, 1504), ch. 21, f. 137ᵛ; see G.N. Buescher, *The Eucharistic Theology of William Ockham* (Washington, 1950), pp. 123–30.

[9] Leff, *Heresy*, pp. 550, 616 n. 2, and 'John Wyclif', p. 176; Robson, *Wyclif*, p. 195.

the light of well-ventilated issues, and its underlying logic must be sought outside the philosophy of the schools. Aquinas and Ockham were, it seems, merely the instruments of Wyclif's attempt to demonstrate that, in the Eucharist, appearances could not deceive. His own explanation of how the Body of Christ could be present in the sacrament, if the bread and wine remained after consecration, confirms the impression that this was no technical theological argument: rather, he was reasserting a religious idea which had been dormant since the mid-thirteenth century, a hierarchy of being which transcended the distinction of natural and supernatural. 'Crude people', as Wyclif asserted in his *Confessio*, could understand no mode of being except a purely material and substantial being.[10] In the sacrament the *figura* of Christ, a kind of mirror image of the Body of Christ in heaven, was present on the altar: as he explained in the language of optics, 'To understand how the Body of Christ is sacramentally, not dimensionally, present in this venerable sacrament, consider the view of the optical philosophers who tell us that when a clean mirror is placed proportionately opposite a shape, a full likeness of that shape is present in every point of that mirror, although one man may see it in one point and another man in another point, depending on where the mirror falls and reflects'.[11] Thus the form of Christ's Body was in the sacrament, but so was the surface of the mirror, the bread and wine itself. Here, of course, Wyclif was reviving Grosseteste's explanation of being in terms of a light-metaphysic.[12] Indeed, Wyclif's universe was a vast hall of mirrors in which every universal form was the reflection of some higher being; the figurative mode of being by which the Body of Christ existed in the Eucharist was a subtler and a higher mode than merely material being.[13] Wyclif was not, therefore, derogating from the dignity of the Eucharist by denying transubstantiation, but endowing it, as he thought, with a finer, a higher, and even more real presence.

Moreover, the difference between the mode of being of accidents without substance and his own concept of figurative being was not

---

[10] *FZ*, p. 117.

[11] Wyclif, *Sermones*, ed. J. Loserth, 4 vols, WS (1887), iv, p. 352. The sermon was evidently preached at Easter, 18 April 1378: see W. Mallard, 'Dating the *Sermones Quadraginta* of John Wyclif', *Mediaevalia et Humanistica*, xvii (1966), p. 105.

[12] J. McEvoy, *The Philosophy of Robert Grosseteste* (Oxford, 1982), pp. 151–8.

[13] Robson, *Wyclif*, p. 28.

only philosophical but moral. An accident without a substance was the lowest thing in nature, less than *materia prima*, less than a spider's web, as he put it, less even than mud.[14] Refusing to admit that substances might be annihilated in *De Apostasia* and *De Eucharistia*, his argument was simply that it was an abominable notion, incongruent with the dignity of the Eucharist: 'annihilation seems a harmful transaction, since the substance of bread and wine would profit the world more than this obscene transubstantiation of it; God would have profited his Church thus ineptly and ineffectively'.[15] Wyclif's adjectives reveal the quality of his dissent: transubstantiation was improper, material, horrible, gross. He held, then, no coolly philosophical notion of logical impossibility: what was absurd was also blasphemous; and error, above all, consisted in a 'crude' or 'material' misinterpretation of a spiritual reality. Appearance without reality, which his opponents would have it was the nature of the Eucharist, was in fact the mark of the cardinal sin in Wyclif's moral universe, the sin of hypocrisy. Here, it may be inferred, is the essence of Wyclif's rejection of transubstantiation: it attributed to the Eucharist a deception, the mark of Antichrist in contemporary life; an Antichrist who, as explained in his tract *De Antichristo*, incorporated in *Opus Evangelicum*, was manifest in the evil practices and institutions of the Church.[16]

It follows that the stronger the language Wyclif used against transubstantiation, the more evidence there is of the value he placed on the Eucharist. In raising the question, his intention was not it seems to dislodge the sacrament from its place in Christian life, but to dissociate it from the *sacramentalia*, the festoons of additional practices, the cult of saints, the veneration of relics and images, pilgrimages, and so on, which made up the substance of popular religion. Reality had to be disentangled from the 'signs' which, as he lamented, were everywhere confounded with it by the people. It is clear then that Wyclif, the observer and interpreter of his time, was not arguing in the abstract, but had diagnosed and sought to

---

[14] Wyclif, *De Blasphemia*, ed. M.H. Dziewicki, WS (1893), p. 27.
[15] Wyclif, *De Eucharistia*, ed. J. Loserth, WS (1892), pp. 53–4; cf. *De Apostasia*, ed. M.H. Dziewicki, WS (1889), p. 146. See Leff, *Heresy*, ii, p. 553; Robson, *Wyclif*, p. 189.
[16] *Opus Evangelicum*, ed. J. Loserth, WS (1895–6), ii, pp. 106–9.

correct a particular state of affairs. This was the 'idolatry' of the Eucharist, as he called it, prevalent among the laity. He blamed the bishops more for failing to correct the idolatrous cult of the Eucharist than for embracing it themselves.[17] Both laity and clergy, he said, 'are too many of them so faithless on this point, that their belief is worse than the pagan, in that the consecrated host is their God'; and 'this lay faith', as he called it, 'is not a faith to please the lord of truth, but the worst infidelity'.[18] To encourage devotion by means of a false doctrine was to foster idolatry. However it might be sustained by the clergy, the idolatry of the Eucharist was lay superstition. To understand what he objected to, therefore, it is necessary to look beyond the doctrine of the Eucharist and give some consideration to its role in the life of the *simplices devoti* on whom so much of the attention, the hopes, fears, and disappointments of the protagonists were concentrated.

What was in Wyclif's mind when he began to focus on this *fides laica* as the source of so much evil? He was clearly referring to lay belief: but the beliefs of laymen might be expressed in the indirect language of the rites and in the practice of congregations as well as in catechism or creed. If, as he implied, they did not conform to the eucharistic teaching of theologians, they must be established from the sparse and anecdotal evidence of individual responses to the sacrament, and the following pages will attempt so far as brevity allows to trace their general direction. It is evident that they cannot be confined to the Mass, the development of which is reasonably clear from such contemporary expositions as Durandus' *Rationale Divinorum* and William Woodford's *De Sacramento Altaris*.[19] Indeed, the integration of the public sacrifice of the Mass with the reception of the Eucharist seems never to have been absolute, descending as they did from separate antique traditions of public oblation and domestic cult.[20] From the earliest times the Eucharist was evidently reserved, either for communion at home, a *viaticum* for the sick, or even for use as a relic in the consecration of

---

[17] *De Eucharistia*, p. 183.
[18] *De Eucharistia*, pp. 13–14.
[19] William Durandus, *Rationale Divinorum* (Naples, 1859 and many other editions); Woodford, *De Sacramento Altaris Quaestiones LXXII*, Bodl. 703, ff. 102ʳ–83ᵛ.
[20] Bossy, 'The Mass', pp. 51–2.

churches.[21] From about the ninth century, lay communion was incorporated in the canon of the Mass; but the consecrated elements, reserved in church or carried in procession, would retain and increase their importance as the focus of a separate cult. Only the Eucharist among the sacraments, of course, consisting of physical elements, is susceptible to the kind of cult which had long grown up around the relics of saints. Its unique status from this point of view is the consequence of its immediacy in every Christian life. The educated in every age would philosophize after Gregory the Great on the passing of the age of miracles, but the Eucharist was a daily, repeated, and predictable miracle, whose presence summoned every believer, priest or layman, to meet his Maker face to face. It has been argued that as it developed in the West, the Mass proceeded from the diversity experienced in particular prayers for the living or the dead to a sustained, many-sided act of unity.[22] At the same time the Corpus Christi procession, and the plays which developed around it in many of the larger and more self-conscious English towns, could represent the ideal form of the social body, diverse in composition but unitary in function, to a people as receptive to symbolic language outside as inside church.[23] However, it may be timely to note that many of the eucharistic miracles collected in the thirteenth century have quite a different import: they show the Christian soul alone with his hidden sin, brought to the light by the sacramental presence of Christ, or secretly contemplating some blasphemous misuse of the elements' supernatural quality.[24] Lay belief in the Eucharist, therefore, cannot be tied down too closely. There was room for many varieties of emphasis in response to the 'powerful work' of the Mass.

That popular awareness of the Eucharist was sharpened in the twelfth and early thirteenth centuries can scarcely be doubted.[25]

---

[21] S. Mattei, 'La Custodia Eucaristia' in *Eucaristica*, ed. A. Piolanti (Rome, 1957), pp. 898–9.

[22] Bossy, 'The Mass', p. 53.

[23] James, 'Ritual, Drama and Social Body', pp. 6–10.

[24] The most extensive collection of eucharistic miracles is that of Caesarius Heisterbacensis, *Dialogus Miraculorum* (Cologne, 1851), ii, pp. 167–217. In general, see P. Browe, *Die Eucharistische Wunder des Mittelalters* (Breslau, 1938).

[25] J. Leclercq, F. Vandenbroucke, and L. Bouyer, *The Spirituality of the Middle Ages* (London, 1968), pp. 245–7.

The growth of practices in the Mass which dramatized its meaning, such as the elevation of the host to show the people, the new emphasis on eucharistic miracles, and, by the middle of the thirteenth century, the gradual acceptance of the new feast of Corpus Christi, all indicate that in parallel with the theologians' development of the doctrine of transubstantiation, many of the currents of lay devotion were beginning to converge in a cult of the Eucharist. The most obvious feeling expressed in this cult was compassion for the sufferings of Christ, a theme repeatedly expressed in the miracle stories of the twelfth and thirteenth centuries, in which the consecrated host appeared in the form of Christ suffering on the cross.[26] But perhaps the more significant theme is the powerful and largely unpredictable response of congregations to the moment of consecration in the Mass, dramatically manifested at the elevation. The desire to see the host, of which the practice of elevation was a liturgical expression, seems to have excited various forms of religious hysteria or mystical exaltation, which are reflected in the contemporary collections of eucharistic miracle stories.[27] A guilty conscience could incur a horrifying vision of Christ in the flesh appearing on the altar instead of the host: a priest told St Hugh of Lincoln that his transgression of saying Mass in mortal sin had brought him the gory experience of seeing actual flesh and blood in the chalice after he had consecrated it.[28] Caesarius of Heisterbach's two collections of miracle stories for use in preaching, compiled between 1215 and 1230, are a rich source of material on popular attitudes to the Eucharist and its supernatural power. The bulk of his stories concern visions during the Mass, whether of a Virgin and Child, a lamb, the infant or crucified Christ, or mere flesh.[29] A more refined expression, significantly much later, of the desire to see the host was the exaltation of the Blessed Dorothea of Danzig, who was sometimes incapacitated for a time after witnessing the elevation.[30] Eccentric

---

[26] Browe, *Eucharistische Wunder*, pp. 93–100.

[27] E. Dumoutet, *Le desir de voir le hostie* (Paris, 1926); P. Browe, *Die Verehrung der Eucharistie im Mittelalter*, 2nd ed. (Freiburg im Breisgau, 1967), pp. 26–48.

[28] *Magna Vita Sancti Hugonis*, ed. D.L. Douie and H. Farmer (London, 1961–2), ii, pp. 93–4.

[29] Above, n. 24.

[30] John of Marienwerder, *Septililium Beatae Dorotheae*, ed. F. Hipler, *AB*, ii (1883), pp. 381–472; iii (1884), p. 113–40, 408–48; iv (1885), pp. 207–51; cf. iii, pp. 409–10.

or even neurotic as the subjects of these experiences may have been, the common catalyst of their emotion was the sight of the host, within or outside the Mass, but most frequently at the moment of the liturgy when the consecrated elements were manifested to the people.

The vision of the host should perhaps be understood in the light of the abundant vision literature of an earlier age: a dramatic confrontation with a normally unseen world, a shaft of light upon moral reality, contrasting God's perfection with the visionary's corruption. Like the relics of the saints, the Eucharist must be apprehended with fear and humility: God's servants, like the household of an earthly king, must keep their distance. The undoubted power of the elements could not be applied mechanically like an electric current: in Germany, when a woman tried to cure her bees of some infection by bringing them the host to eat, they terrified her by building it a beeswax chapel in their hive.[31] The instinct of the bees accorded with the interior design of churches in the thirteenth and fourteenth centuries. While the host was kept locked in a tabernacle or reserved above the altar to be seen, the choir was often enclosed by the construction of screens to make a more private chamber or chapel fit for the physical presence of God, after the fashion of the private quarters where, during the fourteenth century, the nobility increasingly tended to pass their time.[32] This apprehension of a powerful and distant God in the Eucharist is more understandable as a development of the older but similar worship offered to the saints: a development already implied by Guibert of Nogent in *De Pignoribus Sanctorum*, where he discussed eucharistic miracles in the context of the miracles of the saints.[33] The growing awareness of the Eucharist was, of course, an advance from the diverse cults of the saints towards a common Christianity. But it did not wholly emancipate itself in this period from the aura of miracle and wonder which surrounded the saints. Theologians of the thirteenth century, when they considered the matter, were concerned primarily to define the miracle of transub-

---

[31] Caesarius Heisterbacensis, *Dialogus*, ii, pp. 172–3.
[32] C.N.L. Brooke, 'Religious Sentiment and Church Design of the Later Middle Ages', *BJRL*, l (1967–8), pp. 13–33.
[33] Guibert of Nogent, *De Pignoribus Sanctorum*, lib. i, ch. 2, *PL* clvi, 616.

stantiation, by determining the relation of the Eucharist to the natural world: the mode of Christ's being in the eucharistic elements compared with ordinary being was discussed by Alexander of Hales, Albert the Great, Thomas Aquinas, Richard of Mediavilla, Scotus, Peter Auriol, and finally Ockham. For these theologians, appearance was not necessarily reality: faith, they taught, must supply the defect of the senses. Aquinas' version of the *Pange lingua*, written for the Corpus Christi office, was quite explicit: *praestet fides supplementum sensuum defectui*.

The attitude of the laity is perhaps nowhere more clearly expressed than in the origins and development of the feast of Corpus Christi. The new festival enshrined the conception of the Eucharist as an object of devotion separate from the Mass and communion; it was the logical outcome of permanent reservation of the sacrament in church. The distinctive form of the festival was a civic procession, in which representatives of the community, the guilds in their pageant-waggons and the city officers, exhibited themselves as servants or retainers of God, as he made an *adventus* or 'joyous entry' into his city.[34] Instituted to meet the laity's desire to see the host, the procession exhibited it to the widest of congregations. Its originator, characteristically, was lay, though religious: Juliana of Liège, prioress of Mont-Cornillon, who, like other holy women of the thirteenth century, was profoundly affected by the sight of the host during Mass, sometimes relapsing into silence and seclusion for long intervals afterwards.[35] More originally, it occurred to her to enshrine her devotion in a new feast, which was said to have been suggested to her in a vision early in her life, perhaps about 1218. According to her biographer, she saw a full moon in its splendour, broken or cracked through the middle: the moon, it was revealed, was the Church, while the fault across it represented the absence of a eucharistic feast from the liturgy.[36] It is tempting to guess that the moon was associated in her imagination with the host itself as it was held up at the elevation, and to relate it to other contemporary visions originating

---

[34] James, 'Ritual, Drama and Social Body', p. 5. On the tradition of *adventus* and its religious applications, see P. Brown, *The Cult of the Saints* (London, 1981), pp. 98–100.

[35] *AS, Aprilis*, i, p. 447.

[36] *Ibid.*, p. 459.

at the same moment of the liturgy. Be that as it may, Juliana of Liège supplied an obvious want of those who thought of the Eucharist in the way they thought of the saints. Eventually she repeated her dream to a canon of Liège, John of Lausanne, through whom it became known to the Bishop of Cambrai and a circle of other churchmen, including the future Pope Urban IV. Through them Corpus Christi became a local feast at Liège in 1246; Urban IV made it universal in 1264, and its proliferating office, for one version of which Aquinas' hymn was written, marks its rapid reception throughout the western Church.[37]

As has recently been emphasized, Corpus Christi came to be especially associated with communities' sense of identity. The Corpus Christi guild was perhaps the most popular form of lay religious confraternity among the multiplying pious or charitable associations of the thirteenth and fourteenth centuries, especially where, as at Venice for instance, the sense of corporate identity was well developed. The first English example was founded at Norwich in 1278, but the largest were probably those of York and Leicester, which appear to have flourished particularly in the late fourteenth and early fifteenth centuries. At York in particular, the Corpus Christi guild was responsible for a wealth of pageantry.[38] At other times, when some disaster threatened, the local communities which formed the guilds turned to the Eucharist to perform the traditional role of a saint's relic. At Lynn, early in the fifteenth century, when the town was threatened by fire, Margery Kempe's first reaction was to send for the sacrament: and the people

> notwythstondyng in other tymes thei myth not enduryn hir to cryen & wepyn for the plentyuows grace that owr Lord wrowt in hir, as this day for enchewyng of her bodily perel thei myth suffyr hir to cryen & wypen as mech as euyr sche wolde, & no man wolde byddyn hir cesyn but rathar preyn hir of contynua-cyon, ful trustyng & beleuyng that thorw hir crying & wepyng owr Lord wolde takyn hem to mercy. Than cam hir confes-sowr to hir and askyd yf it wer best to beryn the Sacrament to

[37] Browe, *Verehrung*, pp. 72, 76–80; F. Callay, 'Origine e sviluppo della festa del *Corpus Domini*' in *Eucaristia*, ed. Piolanti, pp. 907–32.
[38] James, 'Ritual, Drama and Social Body', pp. 5–6.

the fyer er not. Sche seyd, 'ys, ser, ys, for owr Lord Ihesu Crist telde me it xal be ryth wel'. So hir confessowr, parisch preste of Seynt Margaretys Cherche, toke the precyows Sacrament & went be-forn the fyer as deuowtly as he cowde.[39]

The incident brings together the exhibition of the sacrament in the manner of a relic with the impulse of a thoroughly lay devotion, extrovert in its manifestations, and untouched as yet by any hint of private or interior feeling. In this world of externals, then, the cult of the Eucharist must, in its original form, be placed. Like devotion to the Virgin, another international cult, it may well have been more efficacious in breaking down the diversity of European religious practices than the canons of popes and councils over two centuries. In this popular form, it was evidently at its height during Wyclif's lifetime.

Idolatry, it seems, was Wyclif's name for the common response of wonder and awe evoked by the sight of the host at the elevation or in procession at Corpus Christi. The doctrine of transubstantiation, with its insistence on the total suspension of the natural order, emphasized the gulf between humanity and the Eucharist. The doctrine of remanence, with which he proposed to replace it, minimized the difference between human and sacramental being: by placing the Eucharist in the context of familiar nature, it brought Christ close to men and invited a more direct relationship. In one of the most eloquent and spiritual passages of his surviving works, in chapter 6 of *De Eucharistia*, Wyclif expounded the proper disposition of the communicant. 'Putting away contentious matter', he developed a sustained analogy of the grain dying to bring forth fruit and the sufferings of the communicant, offered for Christ, 'disposing him in receiving the host to free and unfeigned love of Christ and God'.[40] The immediate relation of the Christian with Christ through the Eucharist was underlined with a long quotation from Gregory's twenty-second Gospel homily on the blood of the Lamb, which culminated in a call to communion.[41]

---

[39] *Book of Margery Kempe*, ed. S.B. Meech, EETS (London, 1940), p. 163.
[40] *De Eucharistia*, pp. 158–70; cf. pp. 158, 169.
[41] *Ibid.*, pp. 164–9, from Gregory, *XL Homiliarum in Evangelia Lib. ii, Homilia xxii*, PL lxxvi, 1178–81.

Independently of differences on the doctrine of transubstantiation, Wyclif's words in the light of the common attitude of the previous century, and of many contemporaries, strike a new note. An experience of Mass or of a eucharistic procession in which the main point is the sight of the host is clearly distinct from an experience of Mass culminating in communion. If the contrast is not absolute, given the prick of conscience which the elevation could administer, it is evident, nevertheless, that communion is much the more powerful stimulus to interior prayer. Concomitantly, its 'asocial mysticism' lessens the impact of Mass as a 'ritual of integration'.[42] Here, then, is a new departure in the practice as in the theory of the Eucharist.

Was Wyclif then a solitary voice crying in the wilderness of popular superstition? In a sense this was so: no other theologian of his time revived the heresy of Berengar of Tours, even in the modified form which he proposed, or resorted to an archaic light-metaphysic to explain the Real Presence. Even the contemporaries or near-contemporaries closest to him in spirit, the Czech reformers, and especially John Hus, did not accept his eucharistic theology. Hus, however, like Wyclif, emphasized the spiritual role of communion and, in addition, the right of the faithful to communion in both kinds. Though Hus denied at Constance that he had ever held that the bread and wine remained (and there is no evidence of such a belief in his writings), he or his followers were responsible for the copying and dissemination of Wyclif's *De Eucharistia*, which survives only in Bohemian manuscripts; and his view of superstition about the sacrament, against which Wyclif's doctrine was directed, was the same.[43] His first public statement on the subject had been the result of the commission to which the Archbishop of Prague had appointed him, in 1405, to investigate the alleged blood of Christ kept in the church at Wilsnack, in Brandenburg; and his subsequent tract, *De Sanguine Christi*, is an *exposé* of the deceit and hypocrisy of the miracles associated with it, which detracted from the real purpose of the sacrament, the

---

[42] Bossy, 'The Mass', p. 59.
[43] Leff, *Heresy*, ii, p. 657; M. Spinka, *John Hus* (Princeton, 1968), pp. 68–9.

communion.[44] Within a few years communion in two kinds had become the potent symbol of the Hussite separation from the visible Church, and the issue would not be debated outside its ecclesiological aspects. But it originated elsewhere—in a significant common ground between Wyclif and his Bohemian counterparts, their sharp sense of the private, spiritual benefits of communion, and distaste for the public cult of the Eucharist.

In fact, the issue had already arisen in Bohemia before Wyclif's writings were widely known outside England, in an argument over frequent communion for the laity provoked by the teaching of Matthew of Janov. The religious views and social circle of the Bohemian reformer bear a striking resemblance to Wyclif's own, and deserve more extensive comparison than is possible here. But it is probably significant that in the Prague of the 1380s a body of Paris graduates, whom city livings had made independent and the task of preaching had brought together, should have come to see a central spiritual value in the practice of frequent communion, perhaps through the influence of Janov. A former student of Paris and prebendary of the Cathedral, he seems to have been the most influential of a group of reformers, until his advocacy of frequent communion was condemned by the Prague synod of 1389. His unfinished *Summa*, the *Regulae Veteris et Novi Testamenti*, shows that, without Wyclif's superstructure of philosophical explanation, his views on the religion and society of his time were in many respects the same.[45] Like Wyclif, Matthew of Janov was obsessed with the contrast between reality and appearance in the modern world. The besetting sin of the age, which confounded the two, was hypocrisy, the subject of the second book of the *Regulae*. The dissolvent of hypocrisy, he believed, was conformity to the rules of life which could be found in the Bible; the various forms of popular

---

[44] *De Sanguine Christi*, ed. V. Flajšhans in *Magistri Joannis Hus Opera Omnia*, i, fasc. iii (Prague, 1904), cf. pp. 32–7. On Wilsnack see now H. Boockmann, 'Der Streit um das Wilsnacker Blut. Zur Situation des deutschen Klerus in der Mitte des 15. Jahrhunderts', *Zeitschrift für historische Forschung*, ix (1982), pp. 385–408.

[45] On Janov see V. Kybal, *M. Matěj z Janova* (Prague, 1905); Leff, *Heresy*, ii, pp. 612–19. E. Valasek, *Das Kirchenverständnis des Prager Magisters Matthias von Janow (1350/55–1393). Ein Beitrag zur Geistesgeschichte Böhmens im 14. Jahrhundert = Lateranum*, ns, xxxvii (Rome, 1971) is a useful summary of modern research, although not particularly original.

religious practice which had not been sanctioned by the Bible, the cult of the saints, the veneration of relics, and the elaboration of ritual, belonged to the specious world of appearances, with the false priests and the monks and friars whose front of piety concealed interior spiritual desolation.[46] Hypocrisy was the mark of Antichrist, whose age was beginning. Matthew of Janov's apocalyptic view of the present, his insistence on the Bible as the only criterion of a genuine Christian rule of life, his repudiation of the proliferating 'private religions' of the age, and antipathy to the forms of popular religion are strikingly reminiscent of Wyclif, though evidently independent of him, and show how radical views on the contemporary world could be held without Wyclif's metaphysics.

Matthew of Janov's teaching on the Eucharist, however, provides an equally instructive comparison with Wyclif's. His most distinctive idea was his insistence on frequent communion as the primary source of grace and an integral part of a true Christian life. The common discouragement of frequent communion, the liturgical practices which emphasized the remote majesty of the consecrated elements, were associated in his mind with the worship of images and other popular forms of idolatry. The desire to see the host, the religious sentiment implicit in the elevation, trivialized the Eucharist, placing it on a level with 'fine pictures and statues and all the other trappings'.[47] The fourth book of the *Regulae* was a sustained exhortation to frequent communion and a Jeremiad against the priests who withheld it from the laity from a false sense of reverence; the desire for communion, which they regarded as audacity and temerity, was in fact grace drawing men to God.[48] Like Wyclif, Matthew of Janov sought to disentangle the Eucharist from the infiltrating weeds of superstition. If Wyclif was silent on frequent communion, he had been explicit on the value of receiving the sacrament, and only a difference of emphasis separates the views of the two reformers.

In the work of Matthew of Janov we can detect a changed atmosphere in the religious climate of Europe. Communion,

---

[46] Matthew of Janov, *Regulae Veteris et Novi Testamenti*, ed. V. Kybal and O Odlozilik (Innsbruck and Prague, 1908–26), i, pp. 45–9.

[47] *Regulae*, v. pp. 303–4; see P. Browe, *Die häufige Kommunion im Mittelalter* (Munster, 1938), pp. 33–5.

[48] See also *Regulae*, v, p. 184.

originally an infrequent duty, has become a right. To refuse it to the laity was to re-enact the massacre of the innocents; it evoked compassion for the faithful thus deprived by those who imagined so 'hard and cruel' a prohibition to come from Christ.[49] Janov appealed to the opinion of his colleagues, canonists and theologians in Prague. He included some of their writings on frequent communion as *pièces justificatives* in the second book of the *Regulae*, and it is clear that a large and influential body of opinion had supported him in maintaining the laity's right of access to the altar.[50] The desire for frequent communion, moreover, was not confined to Bohemia. Catherine of Siena's constant demand for communion, initially resisted by the conventional piety of her confessors, was finally satisfied by a papal privilege which allowed her to communicate at will.[51] The practice of frequent communion could arouse strong feeling, as its passionate defence by Raymond of Capua, Catherine's biographer, proves. At the opposite end of Europe, Dorothea of Danzig was less indulged: her profound desire to communicate, restricted by her confessor, found its outlet in the older devotion of gazing upon the host.[52] Frequent communion was already the practice among some congregations in Bohemia, and it may have been growing in popularity among the Beguines of the Rhineland.[53] Emphasis on the value of communion was a feature of the *devotio moderna*, with its stress on what was common and simple in religious experience. For Thomas à Kempis, it was a bulwark of honest life, and scruples about approaching the altar were to be overridden: 'although I am neither fit nor rightly disposed to celebrate daily, yet I will endeavour at proper times to receive your divine Mysteries, and present myself to receive this great grace'.[54] Eventually even the most solemn authority followed the example of the spiritual leaders of the age, when an exhortation to frequent communion was made in the thirteenth session of the Council of Trent.[55] Wyclif's belief in the indispensable value of

---

[49] *Regulae*, i, p. 53.
[50] *Regulae*, ii, pp. 75–107.
[51] *AS, Aprilis*, iii, pp. 931–2.
[52] *Septililium, AB*, iii (1884), pp. 410–11.
[53] Browe, *Häufige Kommunion*, pp. 109–10.
[54] *Imitatio Christi* iv, p. 3, trans. L. Sherley-Price (London, 1952), p. 189.
[55] *Concilium Tridentinum, sessio* xiii, ch 8, Mansi, 2nd ed., xxxiii, cols. 83–4.

communion, echoed by the spirituality of his time, was finally sanctioned by the Counter-Reformation.

Why then did Wyclif's contemporaries react more strongly against his eucharistic doctrine than against any other aspect of his thought? Some of his lay friends considered it intolerable: John of Gaunt, who had countenanced more subversive notions, commanded him to be silent on the subject.[56] A contemporary master, the Durham monk John Uthred of Boldon, contrasted his arrogance with the faith of the *simplices devoti* whom he impugned.[57] Yet some other opponents were beginning to place more emphasis on communion. William Woodford, his principal contemporary critic, certainly conceived of the Eucharist as a familiar and accessible institution, and the anonymous Austin friar who controverted Matthew of Janov merely argued that the frequent consumption of the host was not necessary to receive its benefits, and was inadvisable for a laity preoccupied with worldly matters; evidently accepting his opponent's main point, the overriding value of communion in itself.[58] There was, then, no direct confrontation of the old devotion with the new. Among religious thinkers there was little agreement as to what the Eucharist was. But on the whole the context in which it was commonly worshipped—the conventional lay religion of the time, the ever-changing cult of saints, the reverence for relics, images, and holy places, the elaboration of pilgrimages and spiritual exercises for the sake of indulgences—was coming under varying degrees of suspicion from theologians, in the Paris of d'Ailly and Gerson as well as in Oxford and Prague. To many intellectuals, popular religion was hypocrisy, the worship of external appearances. But it was a common characteristic to regard the Eucharist as a supremely important focus of religious feeling: at once the gateway to an intensely private world of prayer, and an image of the Church, a *corpus mysticum*. Wyclif was not alone in regarding it as the crown and touchstone of his reformation.

Oriel College, Oxford

---

[56] *FZ*, p. 114.

[57] Uthred of Boldon, *De Eucharistia*, Durham Cathedral Library, MS B.IV.34, f. 1ʳ.

[58] *Augustiniani cuiusdam tractatus contra errores Mathiae de Ianov*, ed. J. Sedlák, in *Mistr. Jan Hus* (Prague, 1915), pp. 21*–44*, esp. p. 35*. See also Valasek, *Matthias von Janow*, p. 91.

WYCLIF'S *LOGIC* AND WYCLIF'S EXEGESIS: THE CONTEXT

by G.R. EVANS

WYCLIF found certain scholars of his time 'in full cry against the unlogical, imprecise language of the Bible and the liturgy'.[1] No commentaries written in that spirit survive,[2] but traces are abundant in contemporary writings of aggressive talk in the schools and disputatious questioning along these lines. The challenge was not in its essence a new one. It is an episode in a series of encounters which had taken place between secular learning and Christian learning from the beginning; and more recently between grammar and logic and the difficulties presented by the Bible's language. But it was perhaps new in degree. These critics of Wyclif's day, it seems, said that the Bible was not logical and found in that a reason to question its truth, rather than to look to their logic for faults, as had been the traditional way.

Wyclif considered himself well placed to meet their objections. He had, he says, travelled the same road himself. A sophist like them, he too had studied by the light of reason, and it had then seemed to him that the Bible did not speak logically.[3] He had come to think differently, and in the *De Veritate Sacrae Scripturae* and elsewhere he makes a vigorous case for Scripture's truth.

He had written a textbook on logic, in which he shows himself familiar with the traditional difficulties.[4] He wrote it 'to sharpen the

---

[1] B. Smalley, 'The Bible and Eternity: John Wyclif's Dilemma', *Studies*, p. 408.

[2] On Wyclif as a biblical scholar and theologian, see S.H. Thompson, 'The Philosophical Basis of Wycliffe's Theology', *Journal of Religion*, xi (1931), pp. 86–116; R. Guelluy, *Philosophie et théologie chez Guillaume d'Ockham* (Louvain, 1947); Smalley, *Postilla*, pp. 186–205; 'The Biblical Scholar', in *Robert Grosseteste*, ed. D.A. Callus (Oxford, 1955), pp. 70–97. On the lack of commentaries carrying the kind of criticism to which Wyclif refers, see Smalley, 'Bible and Eternity', p. 403.

[3] *Ibid.*

[4] On the date of Wyclif's *Logica*, see *De Logica*, ed. M.H. Dziewicki, 4 vols, WS (1893), i, pp. vi ff. Peter the Chanter seems to have been one of the first to make a systematic collection of problems. See my *Alan of Lille* (Cambridge, 1983), pp. 23–9 and Appendix II, and 'A Work of "Terminist Theology"? Peter the Chanter's *De Tropis Loquendi* and some *Fallacie*', *Vivarium*, xx (1982), pp. 40–57.

wits of the faithful', by teaching them those elements of logic which may be of help to them in their study of the Bible (*ponere probaciones proposicionum que debent elici ex Scripturis*). He has seen many taking up logic (*ad logicam transeuntes*) in the belief that they will come to know God better (*per illam proposuerant legem Dei melius cognovisse*), and yet by foolishly muddling technical terms as used by the secular authors on logic with terms used in Scripture (*propter insipidam terminorum mixtionem gentilium*) they fail to come to any valid conclusion (*in omni probacione propositionum propter vacuitatem operis eam deserentes*).[5]

In looking to Wyclif for leadership in directions which were to lead to the thinking of the Reformation, modern studies have perhaps neglected to look closely at the implications of his early training in language and logic for the detailed working out of his own analysis of the Bible. His war was not with logic but with the abuse of logic in exegesis. In this paper I should like to consider in outline some of the assumptions on which he worked and the way he made use of them in his own exegesis. A full discussion must wait; but enough may perhaps be said to throw these important foundations of his later thinking a little more clearly into relief.

Wyclif pursued the usual course of study for his first degrees in the Arts Faculty. We can assume that he spent his three years or more as *scholaris* and *sophista*, took part in the academic exercises required of him, and was familiar with the stock questions raised and answered in the disputations. He taught as a Master of Arts. After a gap of a few years, he returned to Oxford in 1363 to begin his studies in theology; he heard the Bible commented for the statutory three years; he engaged in the required formal disputations; he read the Sentences. Then he went on lecturing in the Oxford schools, until by 1372 he had become their leading master.[6] His *Logica* was written by a practising teacher of the subject, probably rather early in his career (he refers to his fortieth birthday which is yet to come).[7] The Sermons, preached while he was

---

[5] Wyclif, *Logica*, i, p. 1, lines 3–8.
[6] J.A. Robson, *Wyclif and the Oxford Schools* (Cambridge, 1961), pp. 13ff, and J.A. Weisheipl, 'Curriculum of the Faculty of Arts at Oxford in the Early Fourteenth Century', *MSt*, xxvi (1964), pp. 143–85, and 'Developments in the Arts Curriculum', *ibid.*, xviii (1966), pp. 151–75.
[7] Wyclif, *Logica*, i, p. 69, lines 5–6.

teaching at Oxford, are likely to be rather later, but still while he was a practising master (*dum stetit in scolis*).[8] The context of these and other works of the period before Wyclif became a controversial figure, the content of scholarly references, the logicians' jokes, are similar; they belong substantially to the same world of thought.

It was not a quiet world; among logicians as among theologians, there were acrimoniously opposed schools. A climax had been reached in Paris in the 1340s, when the Faculty of Arts condemned a number of teachers who had opposed Augustine's theory of signs and put forward modern views.[9] Something of the same controversy went on in Oxford, but there Walter Burley (*c.*1275–*c.*1344) had provided a strong leadership against such modern opinions and upheld the traditional epistemology. Wyclif was perhaps the last major scholar to support this position at Oxford,[10] a conservative in logic, if not in theology. It is not easy to place either the leaders of the *via moderna* (Henry of Ghent, Scotus and Ockham) or their opponents (Bradwardine and Walter Burley); the technical ramifications of their work as logicians are only now beginning to become clear with the publication of the texts.[11] Wyclif took up a position on many of the issues which were being aired.[12]

It would have been hard to do otherwise. Questions presented themselves everywhere. Preaching on *Matthew*, viii. 13 ('In that hour the boy was healed'), Wyclif notes a *triplex dubium*. The questions he answers are the sort to fuel the objections raised by those challengers of the Bible's truth to whom Wyclif later addressed himself. How can it be that Jesus, who knew everything from eternity, 'wondered' at something he foreknew even as a man (*eciam humanitus*)? (The 'wonder', Wyclif explains, was a response of his power of feeling to the actual experience, for we know that he fully possessed *sensus* and *passiones* from his capacity to grieve

---

[8] On the date of the *Sermones Quadraginta*, see Wyclif, *Sermones*, ed. J. Loserth, 4 vols, WS (1890), iv, p. 5.

[9] Robson, *Wyclif and the Oxford Schools* discusses the affair, p. 97 ff. On terminism, see a convenient discussion and bibliography in *CHLMP*, pp. 180–6.

[10] Robson, *Wyclif and the Oxford Schools*, p. 19.

[11] For a list of texts now in print, see *CHLMP*, pp. 893–977. The new series *Artistarium* (Nijmegen, 1981ff) appeared too late for inclusion in this bibliography.

[12] Wyclif, *De Universalibus*, Cambridge, Gonville and Caius College, MS 337/565, ff. 1–48.

and to grow in knowledge). How was it that Christ 'did not find such faith in Israel' when he found there the faith of his mother and his apostles? That, says Wyclif, is like someone who comes to London with his household and says that he does not find such gratitude among his compatriots as he does in foreigners: we must understand 'except among his household and friends'. How is it that the darkness of Hell is an 'outer' darkness? That is because the darkness of ignorance in the inner man leads rapidly to outer darkness.[13] These answers rest on common sense, and are straightforwardly tried against the text of Scripture which has raised the difficulties; they are, nevertheless, handled by a logician according to principles which contemporaries would recognize as depending ultimately on the formal study of logic, and of grammar in connection with logic.

This technical approach is often quite explicit: 'Assuming the truth of the faith of Scripture, we must examine one by one what the words of this Gospel signify to the faithful. It should be noted that the first word can have a double sense in a perfectly orthodox way. Thus Christ, explaining the difference, sets out how he and others speak equivocally of 'bread' (*John*, vi. 59)'.[14] *Supposita*; *signant*; *sensus*; *ponit*; *equivoce* fall naturally into the sentence, as Wyclif explains how a problem may be resolved by minute study of the way the words of Scripture are being used.

A term is to logic as a word (*dictio*) is to grammar;[15] and a number of the technical terms of later mediaeval logic appropriately owe their origin to technical terms of grammar: *substantivatio*; *copulatio*; *adiectivatio*; *appellatio*; *implicatio*; *incongruus*; *relativum*; *sincathegorema*.[16] An awareness that grammatical rules are working among the logical is noticeable in, for example, William of Sherwood's treatise on *syncategoremata* of the first half of the thirteenth century or a little later, where repeated reference is made to Priscian.[17] Ralph Brito (†1230) is the author of a series of

[13] Wyclif, *Sermones*, XXVIII, iv, p. 236.
[14] *Ibid.*, LXI, ii, pp. 453–7.
[15] Wyclif, *Logica*, i, p. 2, lines 1–5.
[16] *Logica Modernorum*, ed. L.M. de Rijk, 2 vols. (Assen, 1967), i, p. 21.
[17] William of Sherwood, *Syncategoremata*, ed. J.R. O'Donnell, *MSt*, iii (1941), pp. 46–93, *passim*.

Questiones super Priscianum Minorem where logic is brought to bear
on grammar in a discussion of *modi significandi*.[18] Logic and
grammar had developed so closely together in the twelfth century
that such applications of one to the other were natural now.[19]

That is equally true of the working together of theology and
exegesis with grammar and logic. Examples at every technical level
are legion. John Hus (*c.*1369–1415) preached a witty sermon called
Contemplate the Adverb, in which, with the aid, he says, of Donatus,
he examines how various types of adverb may be taken as
directives for the living of a good Christian life. The adverbs of
place show 'where', and 'whither', and 'thither', and 'inwardly',
and 'outwardly' how the Christian should be obedient; adverbs of
time encourage him to be good 'today', although 'yesterday' he
was wicked. If 'once' he was wicked, 'now' he is a lover of virtue;
'tomorrow' he will be more virtuous still—and so on with adverbs
of number, negation, affirmation, demonstration, and a dozen
other varieties.[20] At a less fanciful level we find Bonaventure
(1221–74) discussing the question, 'Who are you?' (*John*, i. 22).
Since the Jews knew who John was, why did they ask him? Priscian
says that *quis* sometimes seeks an answer in terms of a substance
(*aliquando quaerit substantia*) and sometimes a proper name (*propriam
nominationem*). The Jews knew who John was by name, but not
who or what he was.[21] In the statement: 'My hands which made
you were pierced by nails', the relative 'which' refers not to the
bodily hands which were pierced by the nails, but, by a sideways
movement into the figurative (*translative*), to spiritual hands.[22]
This, occurring in a grammatical treatise of the later twelfth or
early thirteenth century, makes plain the intimacy with which
grammar (the discussion of pronouns), logic (the discussion of
relativa), and theology (the subject-matter) worked together in the
development of technical skills of analysis. It is in this spirit and in
this tradition that we find Wyclif describing God as *remunerator*

---

[18] Ralph Brito, *Questiones super Priscianum Minorem*, 12, ed. H.W. Enders and J.
Pinborg (Stuttgart, 1980), p. 130.

[19] *Logica Modernorum*, ii covers aspects of this development.

[20] John Hus, *Sermones*, ed. A. Schmidtová (Prague, 1958), p. 81.

[21] Bonaventure, *In Ioh.*, i. 50, *Opera Omnia*, 10 vols. (1882–1902), vi, p. 257.

[22] C.H. Kneepkens, 'The *Relatio Simplex* in the Grammatical Tracts of the Late
Twelfth and Early Thirteenth Century', *Vivarium*, xv (1977), p. 1.

adverbiorum: for God cares not only what a man does (*quid*), but 'with what' intention (*qua*), and 'in what way' (*quomodo*) he does it.[23] He notes the importance of the choice of a preposition—often a significant matter in theology—for circumventing the *evasiones* of the sophists.[24]

We can see a good deal further into Wyclif's detailed use of logical principles in his exegesis than these general indications that he was able to turn readily to grammar and logic for help and illumination. To take first things first: Porphyry's *Isagoge* taught the beginner to classify those things which are to be the subject of discussion by determining their group or type (*genus*), and then looking at the *differentia* which identify the individual or the species.[25] Bonaventure refers to *differentia* in his attempts to clarify the meaning of *opus* in a particular context.[26] Wyclif does the same: *ponit autem Augustinus differenciam inter temporalia et spiritualia.*[27] *Differunt autem inter se fides et spes.*[28] In the manner of the *Categories* he looks at the properties of the thing under discussion: 'For light has three properties pertinent to the matter in hand',[29] 'As is clear in the *Categories* ...',[30] 'Thus concerning its substance ...'.[31] This sort of comment is utterly commonplace to Wyclif; the elements of logic come as naturally to him in thinking about the text of the Bible as his understanding of the Latin itself.

The arrival of the remainder of Aristotle's logical works in the West[32] had an enlarging effect upon the study of logic, not only because there was now much more textbook material to be worked on, but also because they suggested new emphases and brought to light new problems.

---

[23] Wyclif, *Opus Evangelicum*, ii, 28, ed. J. Loserth, 2 vols. WS (1895), i, p. 346, lines 18ff.

[24] Wyclif, *Opus Evangelicum*, ii, 1, i, p. 238.

[25] On the *Isagoge* and its modification of Aristotle's predicables of definition, property, genus, and accident, see A.H. Armstrong's article in *CHLMP*, p. 281.

[26] Bonaventure, *In Ioh.* vi. 52, Question iii, *Opera Omnia*, vi, p. 327.

[27] Wyclif, *Sermones*, XVII, iv, p. 236, lines 29–32.

[28] *Ibid.*, XXV, iv, p. 221, line 12. For Wyclif's discussion of Porphyry, see *Logica*, i, pp. 8–9.

[29] Wyclif, *Sermones*, XXIV, iv, p. 210, line 5.

[30] *Ibid.*, XXV, iv, p. 221, lines 21–5.

[31] *Ibid.*, XXX, iv, p. 260, line 4.

[32] *CHLMP*, ch. 4.

The *Prior* and *Posterior Analytics*, the *Topics* and the *Sophistici Elenchi* contain further discussions of aspects already covered in the textbooks of the Old Logic. In the *Prior Analytics*, for example, Aristotle looks further at predication and at the underlying metaphysical questions about the nature of things. (All existing things are of certain types: such that they cannot be truly predicated in a universal sense of everything else, as Cleon or any individual and sensible being: such that they are predicated of other things, but other things are not first predicated of them; such that they are both themselves predicated of other things, and have other things predicated of them, as 'man' is predicated of Callias and 'animal' of man; some things are naturally predicated of nothing).[33] There is further talk of necessity and futurity, fuller analysis of the structure of arguments and the ways in which arguments may deceive—and a great deal that was entirely new to students of the *logica vetus*. The result was a striking shift in the level of technical difficulty of the subject as taught in the schools.

Not only a degree of overlap, but also some lack of consistency in Aristotle's arrangement and treatment made it necessary for commentators to review their courses, and to write, in addition to commentaries, and perhaps more urgently,[34] a number of studies of their own, in which they examine individually some of the difficulties the new works of Aristotle have thrown up for them. These new topics ('obligations'; 'consequences'; 'syncategorematic terms') became an established part of the course, and the need for them raised the important question of whether Aristotle had perhaps handed down logic to his posterity *insufficienter* and incomplete.[35] Certainly something in addition came to be needed, and this extra material came to be known as the *logica moderna*.

Both Aristotle and the Augustinian epistemological tradition,[36] which underlay mediaeval work on the relationship of signification between words and things, encouraged an emphasis upon the analysis of modes of signifying (*modi significandi*) and upon the

---

[33] Aristotle, *Prior Analytics*, ed. H. Tredennick (London, 1973), I. xxvii. 43^a.
[34] Commentaries on the *Posterior Analytics* seem to have been made rather slowly.
[35] *Logica Modernorum*, i, p. 15, from a *copulata tractatuum parvorum logicalium* (1493).
[36] On Augustinian sign-theory and its mediaeval development, see M. Colish, *The Mirror of Language* (Yale, 1968, repr. 1983).

theory of terms, which marks Wyclif's work as strongly as that of his predecessors and contemporaries.

Students of the Bible met not only difficulties with terms, but the difficulties posed by the objections of the heretics, now rephrased and stated as formal arguments. Perhaps some of them were no more than schoolroom exercises. Perhaps the intention was to prime those who might encounter heretical objections in their preaching and travelling. In any case, the 'question-literature' of the later Middle Ages is immense, and sets of questions found their way as appendages to commentaries or as *scholia*.[37]

Wyclif gives an example in his *De Mandatis Divinis*:

> *Sed contra istud obicitur*—against this it is objected:
> If every man has whatever is his, then no one can be injured, since everyone will have what is justly his.[38]

Wyclif analyses the terms. He looks closely at the statement that 'every man "has" whatever is his', so as to establish what is meant here by 'having'. He identifies a formal consequence: *nichil est bonum hominis quod non habet, et per consequens omnis homo habet quidlibet quod est suum*.[39] He notes a conditional, too.[40]

The fundamental difficulty raised by the statements of Scripture, and the one most often a prompter of discussion, was that of contradiction or apparent contradiction between one passage and another. It is the first law of logic that two true statements cannot contradict one another. If the Bible does in fact contradict itself, it seemed to some commentators of Wyclif's day that parts at least of it must be false. Wyclif argues that the *veritas evangelica* must be saved (*servatur*), even though there seems some oddity or worse in the words: *licet in linguis disparibus fuerit promulgata*. The *sensus evangelii* is always true even if the words contradict one another: *licet evangelia in verbis aliqualiter discordarunt*. The contradiction is, for him, always apparent not real. The problem lies in false interpretation. A sense which is thus *male elicitum* is simply not

---

[37] Y. Iwakuma, 'Instantiae', *Cahiers de l'institut moyen âge grec et latin, Copenhague*, xxxviii (1981).

[38] Wyclif, *De Mandatis Divinis*, ed. F.D. Matthew (London, 1896), p. 3, lines 15 ff.

[39] On consequences, see *CHLMP*, pp. 300–15.

[40] Wyclif, *De Mandatis Divinis*, p. 5, line 25.

true. No argument can make what is true false, or what is false true. The error of a man's belief does not falsify the true object of that belief: *nec error aliorum sensuum falsificat suum verum obiectum.* The modern scholars who argue that Scripture contradicts itself and is therefore in part false begin from false premises. The contradictions are in their own reading, not in Scripture itself.[41]

Alertness to contradiction is everywhere.[42] But again and again in the interpretation of Scripture, the contradiction is made to vanish by distinguishing the apparent contradiction in form from the reality in which there proves to be no contradiction. A real contradiction is in *res* as well as in word: *contradictio enim non est nominis tantum, sed rei et nominis,* as Wyclif puts it.[43] A typical handling of the apparent contradiction in Scripture is Bonaventure's analysis of Jesus' statement in *John,* v. 31: 'If I bear witness of myself, my witness is not true' and the statement in *John,* viii. 14, 'If I bear witness to myself, my witness is true', taken together with *Numbers,* xxiii. 19, 'God is not a liar like man'. Bonaventure provides several means of resolving the difficulty. We might consider the subject of the sentence. *Ego* may refer in one case to Jesus speaking as man (*secundum humanam naturam*) and in the other to his speaking as God (*secundum divinam*). Or 'my witness is not true', may mean that it will not be taken as true, even though it is true. Or we may be intended to understand Jesus as saying 'If I bear witness to myself' as though he alone did so, although he is not alone but one with the Father, and so his testimony is in fact true because he does not bear witness to it alone.[44] All these devices are familiar in logicians' exercises in resolving contradiction. In another example, Bonaventure identifies with technical exactitude a case where a contradictory pair of texts in John's Gospel is to be understood *per relationem ad diversa tempora*, by thinking of them as referring to different times, or else *per relationem ad diversas personas*, as referring to different persons, directly in the tradition of the *Sophistici Elenchi* commentaries.[45]

---

[41] *Ibid.*, p. 6, line 1.
[42] For example, Wyclif deals in his treatise *De Christo et Antichristo* with the *contrarietas* of the two lords. *Polemical Works*, ed. R. Buddensieg, 2 vols., WS (1883).
[43] Wyclif, *Logica*, ii, p. 203.
[44] Bonaventure, *In Ioh.*, v. 68, Question i, p. 316.
[45] *Ibid.*, vi. 50, Question i, p. 326.

Wyclif does the same, and sometimes makes an image out of the notion of contradiction, so familiar is it. In one of the sermons he refers to those who 'contradict themselves' in their actions (*repugnant contradictorie sibi ipsis*).[46] The assumption which underlies these exercises is that since Scripture cannot contradict itself in reality (if it is wholly true), something has been misread or misunderstood if it appears to do so. The art of resolving contradictions is therefore close to the art of spotting the fault in a fallacious argument—not because Scripture is deceitful, as are the arguments of the sophists, but because human fallibility fails to see clearly what is being said.

If Scripture ever deceived man, then God himself is guilty of lying, and that is impossible.[47] But it must be read with an understanding of its own 'subtle logic' (*logica subtilis*),[48] says Wyclif. That 'subtle logic' is not sophistry. But the study of fallacies became a valued aid in unravelling difficulties of interpretation where opponents of Christian truth pointed to misleading statements in the text of the Bible, and it was necessary to show that they were not misleading at all if properly understood.

The study of fallacies had been possible, and with some technical skill, even before the arrival of Aristotle's *Sophistici Elenchi* in the West in the first half of the twelfth century. Boethius discusses fallacies in his second commentary on Aristotle's *De Interpretatione*,[49] and in his treatise on categorical syllogisms.[50] He mentions six cases where confusion may arise in considering propositions. Sometimes the same word is used with two different significations in the two propositions (*equivocatio*). Sometimes the word is used univocally. Sometimes different parts are referred to (*secundum diversam partem*); sometimes there is a different *relatum*; sometimes a different time (*diversum tempus*), sometimes a different modus (*diversum modum*). He says enough of these—we shall return to them in a moment—to whet the appetite, and the study of sophistry became extremely popular with the arrival of the *Sophistici Elenchi* and the advent of

---

[46] Wyclif, *Sermones*, XXVI, iv, p. 226.1.
[47] Wyclif, *De Veritate Sacrae Scripturae*, ed. R. Buddensieg, 2 vols, WS (1905), ii, p. 67.
[48] *Ibid.*, p. 69, line 21.
[49] Boethius, *De Interpretatione*, ed. C. Meiser (Leipzig, 1886), p. 129, line 14–p. 132, line 21.
[50] See *Logica Modernorum*, i, pp. 22–39.

commentaries.[51] The interest of arguments which looked fair and were not lay in part in the sheer intellectual challenge of determining what was really going on in the propositions, and where the shift from one signification of the key term to another had taken place. Paradoxes in various forms—but all along the lines of the Liar Paradox—appear from at least the time of Adam of Balsham in the early twelfth century, who mentions as well known the puzzle of the man *qui se mentiri dicit*. Paul of Venice lists fifteen attempts to resolve it.[52] Again, the appeal was one of challenge.

No doubt, too, the students in the schools had something to do with fostering the study of fallacious arguments. The inception of much of the vast question-literature of the later Middle Ages must be put down to their direct questioning of their masters. Amongst their honest questions were trick ones, designed to catch the lecturer out.[53] And again, not least among these questions were the problems raised in the course of the study of the text of the Bible. To take an example: 'Every animal was in Noah's Ark' (*Omne animal fuit in Arca Noe*). Man was in Noah's Ark; cattle were in Noah's Ark; and so on for each individual species (*et sic de singulis speciebus animalis*). Therefore, every animal was in Noah's Ark. The confusion here, explains Walter Burley, discussing the *syncategorema omnis*, is in the *distributio pro partibus*. It is a confusion between species and number. It is true to say that every [species] of animal was in Noah's Ark, but not that every [individual] animal was in Noah's Ark.[54]

The standard mediaeval division of fallacies into types proceeded along the lines laid down by Aristotle in his *Sophistici Elenchi*, arranged according to various schemes of classification.[55] The commonest examples of this sort of fallacious reasoning turned to

---

[51] W. and M. Kneale, *The Development of Logic* (Oxford, 1962), p. 227.

[52] Adam of Balsham, *Ars Disserendi*, ed. L. Minio-Paluello (Rome, 1966), p. 107, and see W. and M. Kneale, *The Development of Logic*, pp. 227–9.

[53] See, for example, S. Ebbesen, 'Simon of Faversham on the *Sophistici Elenchi*', *Cahiers de civilisation médiévale*, x (1973), p. 21.

[54] Walter Burley, *De Puritate Artis Logicae Tractatus Longior*, ed. P. Boehner (New York, 1955), pp. 253, line 26–254, line 15.

[55] BN, MS 4720A, p. 7, and see John Buridan, 'The *Summulae, Tractatus VII, De Fallaciis*', ed. J. Pinborg (Copenhagen, 1976), p. 139, line 60, for Buridan's bold moving of stock examples from one category to another.

account on the side of orthodoxy have to do with equivocation. The possibility that a word may have more than one signification is one of the commonest sources of trickery or simple uncertainty in arguments.[56] William of Sherwood outlines the possibilities: a word may signify more than one thing on its own (*de se*), either properly or improperly (transumptively). For example: 'Whatever runs has feet; the Seine runs; therefore the Seine has feet'. Here there is a confusion between a literal meaning of 'runs' and a figurative one. Or a word may signify more than thing as a result of its connection with something else. For instance:

> Whoever was being cured is healthy.
> The sufferer was being cured.
> Therefore the sufferer is healthy.

There is a confusion here between the sufferer considered as a sufferer at present (minor premiss) and the sufferer considered in respect to the past as once a sufferer, who has been cured, and is now healthy. 'The sufferer' is equivocal because of the different connections of the word in the two premisses.[57]

Wyclif's references to equivocation are legion, from simple notes that a word has two or more meanings (mercy;[58] power)[59] to references to the logic of equivocation in Jerome,[60] or Augustine's loose usage compared with Chrysostom's tighter one: *videtur istum sanctum restringere equivocationem regni quam Augustinus racionabiliter magis laxat.*[61] He warns that many are deceived by certain equivocal usages.[62] He puts the knowledge of the signification of terms and their equivocation in the forefront of the task of the commentator: (*terminorum significatio et eorum equivocatio*).[63] He is well aware of the confusion which can result from a lack of clear thinking on this point. 'The scholastics labour upon such 'miserable expressions, confounding themselves vainly in equivocations'; he identifies one

---

[56] See C.L. Hamblin, *Fallacies* (London, 1970), pp. 286–92.
[57] William of Sherwood, *Introductiones in Logicam*, ed. M. Grabmann (Munich, 1937), p. 135.
[58] Wyclif, *Opus Evangelicum*, i, p. 41, lines 21–36.
[59] *Ibid.*, p. 96, lines 35–8.
[60] Wyclif, *De Veritate Sacrae Scripturae*, ii, p. 20, line 22.
[61] Wyclif, *Opus Evangelicum*, i, p. 276, lines 22–3.
[62] *Ibid.*, i, p. 281, line 35.
[63] *Ibid.*, i, p. 281, line 4.

such confusion, an equivocation on which he thinks Anselm worked when he was writing against Gaunilo's criticism of his *Proslogion* argument.[64] Scripture has its own modes of equivocation, and the critic should familiarize himself with them, and learn how to avoid equivocation himself before he attacks the truth of the Sacred Page.[65] Scripture's own equivocations are entirely good and helpful; it is simply a matter of studying them, to see, for example, how 'in this equivocation Christ and John the Baptist differed without contradiction (*sine repugnatia variabant*)'.[66]

Limitations of space make it impossible to follow Wyclif through his applications of the study of topics, consequences, and obligations here, or to look at his use of what he knew about modal propositions in the discussion of necessity and futurity, possibility and probability.[67] But enough has been said perhaps to enable us to take stock of the relationship between his logic and his approach to the study of the Bible.

The most obvious result of his early training in logic, for Wyclif as for his contemporaries, is the utter naturalness with which they think in logical terms when they are confronted by a textual difficulty. Wyclif reads into Scripture logicians' habits which belong to a mediaeval world of thought. Scripture is seen to prove, that is, to furnish material for, arguments or formal arguments.[68] The student is encouraged first to understand the *sensus scripture*, and then to construct his *argumenta* according to that sense (*secundum hunc sensum*), and thus to avoid sophistries.[69]

The test of sound interpretation is *consonantia*; Scripture is a whole, and it is *unum et consonum*. Thus, when Wyclif examines the different versions of the parable of the talents in the Gospels he is able to content himself with saying that, whether or not it is the same parable as told by Jesus, or more than one parable, the moral is the same: *concordat utrobique sentencia*.[71] No gloss ought to be accepted unless it is in harmony with Scripture, or with reason,[72]

---

[64] Wyclif, *De Veritate Sacrae Scripturae*, ii, p. 126.
[65] Wyclif, *Sermones*, XXIV, iii, p. 189.
[66] *Ibid.*, LX, i, p. 400.
[67] On topics, consequences, obligations, and modal logic, see *CHLMP*, ch. 5.
[68] Wyclif, *Sermones*, VI, ii, p. 40; VII, ii, p. 47; XXIII, iii, p. 179.
[69] *Ibid.*, XXXII, i, p. 218, line 19.
[70] *Ibid.*, XXVIII, iii, p. 217.
[71] *Ibid.*, VI, ii, p. 37.
[72] *Ibid.*, I, iii, p. 1.

which Wyclif believes will always accord with the teaching of Scripture if it is properly handled. There are sometimes difficulties here, but if in doubt one must choose the rendering which is most harmonious with Scripture.[73]

For Wyclif, then, logic is a help, uncontroversial in itself, and causing difficulty only when ill-disposed persons bring challenges which may deceive the simple. Such challenges will always prove to involve fallacies or misunderstandings of some sort. But the honest student is obliged to be familiar with the technicalities of logic so as to avoid being deceived. Logic applied to Biblical studies was by now unavoidably a part of the course. The old controversy about its use took a new form. It could not be kept out altogether, as some commentators had hoped in the twelfth century; it must now be contained and directed. Most important of all is the presence of innumerable terms and ideas and principles, often scarcely signalled, which show the study of the Bible shot through with the assumptions of grammarians and logicians about the nature and functioning of Biblical language.

When Wyclif reacted against the conventional approach of his day to certain questions and asserted—among other things, this was surely the most significant—the absolute truth of Scripture, he was doing so within this context of rebuttal of fallacious reasoning and technically inaccurate reading of terms. More was made of what he had said later. But the prompting of the explosive *De Veritate Sacrae Scripturae* was perhaps as much irritation with bad logic as the urge to self-defence under attack. Where the scholars of the Reformation sometimes reject a scholasticism wholly in decay, Wyclif merely asks for a proper application of scholastic methods.

Fitzwilliam College, Cambridge

[73] *Ibid.*, I, i, p. 4, line 16 and p. 7, lines 27–30.

A WYCLIFFITE SCHOLAR OF THE EARLY FIFTEENTH CENTURY

by ANNE HUDSON

TWENTY-FIVE years ago the title of this paper would have seemed to many a contradiction in terms; even now there may be some who will expect the scholar of my title to be a critic of Wyclif, erudite in the heresiarch's manifold outpourings. The scholar was, however, himself a Wycliffite, indeed of the radical wing of that persuasion. His misfortune, from a modern viewpoint, is that he did not in his works reveal his name, and hence a cumbersome periphrasis is unavoidable. The writer reveals most about himself in the *Tractatus de Oblacione Iugis Sacrificii*, despite its title an English work of nearly 4000 lines, dealing primarily but not exclusively with the Eucharist: there it becomes clear that he must have been writing between March 1413, since Henry IV is spoken of as recently dead, and February 1414, since Arundel (*þe grettist enmy þat Crist haþ in Ynglond*) is still said to be archbishop of Canterbury, and that he had previously treated the subject of clerical temporalities in a sermon on the text *Omnis plantacio qu[am] non plantauit pater meus celestis eradicabitur*. The *Tractatus* survives in a single manuscript, now BL, Cotton Titus D.v, of the first half of the fifteenth century and clearly not the author's original.[1] A long sermon with the required text and subject is found in three early fifteenth-century manuscripts (BL, Egerton 2820, CUL, Dd. 14.30(2) and Huntington Library, San Marino, HM 502, of which the first will be quoted here) and one

---

[1] The allusions mentioned are at ff. 7^{r-v}, 13^v, and 8^v respectively, using the modern pencilled foliation. I am preparing an edition of this text and of the sermon next described for the Early English Text Society. All abbreviations are here expanded without notice, and modern punctuation is supplied. That Titus is not the autograph emerges from various points where the text as it stands needs substantial emendation to make it intelligible.

sixteenth-century copy (CUL, Ff. 6.2, ff. 1–70ᵛ).[2] That this is indeed the work alluded to in the *Tractatus* emerges from a similarity of phraseology and, the main subject of the present paper, authority cited, and from an underlying consistency of outlook, despite the somewhat more extreme expression of the later text. The sermon itself exists in a second form as a tract of twelve chapters plus three appendices of authorities; this exists now only in a single manuscript, Lambeth Palace Library 503 of the early fifteenth century, but a second must have been available in the 1530s when extracts from it were printed by an editor of reforming views.[3] The question of the relation between these two versions is a complicated one that needs separate treatment, but it may be accepted as certain that both are by the same author. The *Tractatus* overtly reveals nothing about its audience, though the writer's commitment of judgment to *þe dome of þo þat reden þis* (f. 100ʳ) may suggest a private one; the sermon was, if the observations at the end are credible, delivered orally (despite its length of nearly 3000 lines) and then left in written form for scrutiny by the congregation, with admonitions to note the objections of any adversary who might advance arguments against it, and with a promise to deal with these, and with any queries from the congregation, on the preacher's next visit. It seems safe to assume that at the time of the sermon the writer was a peripatetic Lollard preacher; his audience was probably one of the *scholae* or *conventiculae* of which the records tell so frequently.[4] How long elapsed between the sermon and the

---

[2] All the fifteenth-century copies are defective, though Egerton only by the loss of the final leaf; Egerton and Dd. 14.30(2) are in the same hand. CUL, Ff.6.2 is the only manuscript with any item beyond the sermon, namely *Jack Upland* and the *Epistola Sathanae ad Cleros* [printed respectively by P. Heyworth (London, 1968) and A. Hudson, *Selections from English Wycliffite Writings* (Cambridge, 1978) no. 17].

[3] Printed by F.D. Matthew, *The English Works of Wyclif hitherto unprinted*, EETS, lxxiv (1880, 2nd rev.ed. 1902), pp. 362–404; for the printed text see A. Hudson, '*No newe thyng*: the printing of medieval texts in the early Reformation period', in *Middle English Studies presented to Norman Davis*, ed. D. Gray and E.G. Stanley (Oxford, 1983), pp. 153–74. Lambeth is cited here by page and supplied line number, ignoring all headings; where Egerton is quoted without a following Lambeth reference, it may be assumed that Lambeth does not contain the material.

[4] The autobiographical passage was printed in *Selections* no. 18, lines 100–17. For the schools compare the evidence given in N. Tanner, *Heresy Trials in the Diocese of Norwich, 1428–31* = CSer, 4, xx (1977), and by M. Aston, 'Lollardy and Literacy', *History*, lxii (1977), pp. 347–71.

dated *Tractatus* is not entirely clear, though some passages in the former suggest that Arundel's *Constitutions* of 1407 were already in force.[5]

It should be said straightaway that the amount of citation that will be described in these works is by no means exceptional in Wycliffite writings. The advantage of the present group of texts is that in them we have a substantial body of material (over 8000 lines, counting the material shared between sermon and Lambeth tract only once but that found uniquely in either separately) attributable to a single author, and dated fairly closely between about 1407 and 1414. It is therefore possible from them to assess the erudition of a single Wycliffite a full generation after Wyclif's death.[6] The most frequently cited authority is inevitably the Bible, usually quoted in translation (not that of either version of the Wycliffite Bible) with book and chapter reference, the latter either in the text or in the margin; the writer's familiarity with the text emerges from the constant use of biblical phraseology and allusion.[7] Canon law, often recurrent in Wycliffite works, is rare: two appearances in the *Tractatus* and thirteen in the Lambeth version of the sermon.[8] From patristic sources there is a mass of quotation: the *Tractatus* includes in its argument about 180 quotations or very close references, some of the former extending to over fifty lines. Augustine was the favourite, contributing over a hundred to the *Tractatus*, fourteen to the sermon; compared with him Gregory comes a poor second (seventeen and two respective-

[5] At Egerton ff. 48ᵛ–49ʳ appear allusions to *newe constituciouns statutis*, regarded as acts against the Lollards, restricting preaching on the grounds of preventing heresy, and encouraging what the author regarded as idolatry. Arundel's *Constitutions* (Wilkins, iii, pp. 314–19) seem the likely reference, but earlier anti-Wycliffite legislation could be presented in similar terms.

[6] Many of the other Wycliffite texts that show equal reliance upon learned sources are either much earlier (the *Opus Arduum* of 1389–90 or the *Floretum* compiled before 1396) or are less closely dateable (such as the *Apology for Lollard Doctrines*).

[7] Though it is possible that scribes added some of these, it seems unlikely for the majority; in the sermon the four extant manuscripts usually coincide in their placing of references, whether marginally or in the text, and in those allusions they document.

[8] Titus ff. 19ʳ and 51ᵛ referring to Gratian, III, D. ii, c. 58 and 42 respectively; most of the Lambeth instances are in a group towards the end of the final appendix (Matthew, pp. 403–4) and give the originating authority as well as the canon-law reference, though some of these are utilized in translation earlier.

ly), Jerome third (eleven and two),[9] and a number of others, some of whom will be considered below, even fewer. Many of the quotations are extremely close translations after the style of the early version of the Wycliffite Bible, keeping such Latinisms as the absolute use of the past participle;[10] indeed in the *Tractatus*, for which only the one rather careless copy survives, many textual problems can be resolved only by recourse to the patristic originals.

More interesting than the bulk of quotation is its route into the writer's repertoire: did the patristic citations come direct from the individual texts, or from secondary *florilegia*, handbooks, or indexes? At present only a tentative answer can be given: no single anthology has been found, and there is no clear overlap between the quotations in the works here and the apparently relevant entries in the Wycliffite handbooks, the *Floretum* or *Rosarium*.[11] The nature of any secondary source can be outlined. The references given for quotations are normally detailed: as well as the author's name, the work and often a division (book number often with chapter number, sermon number, and so forth) is provided. Thus, for example, Augustine's *De Civitate Dei* or *De Trinitate* are cited by book and chapter number, his *Ennarationes in Psalmos* by psalm number or by quotation of the relevant verse in Latin or by both, the letters of Augustine or Jerome by number and the name of the addressee.[12] Any secondary *accessus* must therefore have references

---

[9] For the sake of simplicity references where possible will be to the editions of *PL*, save in one case. Gregory's *Moralia* was the chief source, the *Homilia in Evangelia* being cited once in each text, the *Cura Pastoralis* once in the sermon. Jerome's letters were the main quarry, though there is one reference in the *Tractatus* to the commentary on Matthew (f. 5ᵛ, *PL* xxvi, 167).

[10] For instance, Titus f. 60ʳ: '*Soþeli not God, whom þei mai not beþenk, but beþenking hemself for him, þei comparisounen not God but hemself, not to God but to hemself*', which translates *De Civitate Dei*, xii, 17 (*PL* xli, 367), '*profecto non Deum, quem cogitare non possunt, sed semetipsos pro illo cogitantes, non illum sed se ipsos, nec illi, sed sibi comparant*'.

[11] For these see A. Hudson, 'A Lollard Compilation and the Dissemination of Wycliffite Thought', *JTS*, ns xxiii (1972), pp. 65–81, C. von Nolcken, *The Middle English Translation of the 'Rosarium Theologie'*, = *Heidelberg Middle English Texts*, x (1979) and the same author's paper 'Some Alphabetical Compendia and how Preachers used them in Fourteenth-century England', *Viator*, xii (1981), pp. 271–88.

[12] For instance Titus f. 25ᵛ *Austen ... De Ci.Dei li.18 ca.38* (correct for *PL* xli, 598); f. 82ᵛ *Austen ... vpon þe worde of þe prophete 'Si dormiatis inter medios cleros'* (*Enarr. in Ps.*, lxvii, 14, *PL* xxxvi, 823); f. 88ᵛ *Austen Super Genesim ad Litteram li.2 ca.1 in þe ende* (*PL* xxxiv, 263); f. 96ʳ *Ierom...Epistola 54 ad Lucin[i]um* (*PL* xxii, 672, the medieval numeration of Jerome's letters differed from that now used).

of equal detail. The references to Gregory's *Moralia* sometimes cite in Latin the words of Job in addition to the book number.[13] When the patristic author was himself quoting a prior source, that is mentioned: thus, for instance, *Austen ... alegging ... Cypriannys sentence in De Dono Perseuerancie*.[14] If any secondary source provided references such as these, it must be one that supplied all this information, or it is necessary to suppose that the secondary source merely provided a way into the original text and not the only knowledge of it.[15] The texts of the Fathers so far mentioned have been mostly their best-known works. But this is not always the case. As well as those of Augustine already named, and the *De Doctrina Christiana, Super Genesim ad Litteram*, the sermons, and the *tractates* on John, a number of less familiar texts are plundered, *De Natura et Gracia, De Anima, Contra Aduersarium Legis et Prophetarum, De 83 Questionibus, Enchiridion, Retractiones, De Uera Religione, Liber de Spiritu et Anima, De Libero Arbitrio, De Duodecim Abusionum Gradibus, De Dono Perseuerancie, De Mendacio*

Of the Lollards' favourite and most characteristic authorities one is missing and one substantially under-represented: FitzRalph, Ardmachanus or St Richard to the Wycliffites, is not cited by this writer,[16] and Chrysostom, or rather pseudo-Chrysostom on Matthew, so ubiquitous in texts such as the *Glossed Gospels*, is quoted only once in the *Tractatus* and twice in the sermon, on two occasions without detailed reference.[17] Peraldus, under the title of *Parisiensis*, appears four times in the *Tractatus* and once in the

---

[13] For example, Titus f. 19ᵛ *Gregor 18.Moralia super isto uerbo 'Habet argentum venarum suarum principia et auro lotus est in quo conflatur'* (*Moralia*, xviii, 26, *PL* lxxvi, 58).

[14] Titus f. 40ᵛ (correct reference to *PL* xlv, 996); compare f. 95ʳ *Austen rehersing Ciprian ... libro 4 De Doctrina Christiana* (correct reference to *De Doctr.*, iv. 21, *PL* xxxiv, 111).

[15] For an invaluable survey of medieval *accessus* see R.H. Rouse and M.A. Rouse, *Preachers, Florilegia and Sermons: Studies on the 'Manipulus Florum' of Thomas of Ireland* (Toronto, 1979) and bibliography there.

[16] Examples of such references may be seen in T. Arnold, *Select English Works of John Wyclif* (Oxford, 1869–71), iii, p. 281, line 13, p. 412, line 22, p. 416, line 20, and Matthew, p. 128, line 26; more precise references are found in the York version of the *Glossed Gospels*, York Minster Library, MS XVI.D.2, for instance f. 170ᵛ *Ardmacan in x book of þe Questiouns of Armenyes xviij cᵒ.*

[17] Titus f. 33ᵛ; Egerton ff. 52ʳ and 112ʳ. Only the last of these is a detailed reference *Crisostum...upon þis word of þe gospel (Mt. 7) 'Attendite a falsis prophetis'* (*PG* lvi, 737). Other Wycliffite works give homily number and further indication of location, as in York f. 178ᵛ *xv omeli aftir þe bigynnyng, xviii omeli bifore þe myddis*, or ff. 213ʳ–14ʳ marginal references *15.j, 13.1, 13.m, 13.o* using the literal subdivisions of the sermons.

Lambeth version of the sermon; three of these are extracts from the *Summa Viciorum*, one from the *Summa Virtutum*, and one apparently from the less frequently cited sermons.[18] Grosseteste's *Dicta* are quoted twice, the sermon *Natis et Educatis* twice, and there is one specific reference to the commentary on pseudo-Dionysius's *De Ecclesiastica Ierarchia*.[19] This last is also probably the source of a number of quotations from the text itself in both the Wycliffite's works, since Grosseteste's commentary follows each chapter of the translated text.

Another less familiar author of the early thirteenth century is emerging as a further favourite Lollard source. This is Odo of Cheriton, apparently not cited by Wyclif himself, but certainly used by a number of his followers.[20] Three extracts, two from a dominical gospel sermon and one from the *proprium sanctorum* sermons, are quoted in the *Floretum*.[21] Two of these reappear in translated form in the *Apology for Lollard Doctrines*, but the *Floretum* cannot have been the sole source, since one passage extends the translation beyond the short quotation given there; the *Apology* also adds a third passage, this time from the *commune sanctorum* sermons.[22] The present writer quotes Odo in both his works, twice

---

[18] Titus ff. 35ᵛ and 38ʳ, Matthew, p. 399, line 13 to *Summa Viciorum* (ed. Paris, 1669), pp. 72, 106, and 123 respectively; Titus f. 20ʳ to *Summa Virtutum* (ed. Paris, 1668), p. 120; with Titus f. 85ᵛ *Parisiensis rehersing seint Ambrose super isto euangelio 'Ego sum pastor bonus'* compare Oxford, Magdalen College, MS 204, pp. 97–8.

[19] The *Dicta* at Titus f. 38ʳ unspecific and unlocated, and Egerton f. 82ᵛ (Lambeth p. 385, line 30) *Dicto 2* (cf. Oxford, Bodleian Library, MS Bodl. 798, f. 1ᵛ); the sermon *Natis et Educatis* specifically at Titus f. 79ʳ and unnamed at f. 29ᵛ (cf. BL, MS Royal 6.E.v, ff. 122ᵛ–3ʳ); Titus f. 69ᵛ *Lincoln...super Ecclesiastica Ierarchia* (cf. Oxford, Lincoln College, MS Lat. 101, f. 106ᵛ). For the sections where Grosseteste is not mentioned see Egerton f. 102ᵛ (cf. Lincoln f. 124ᵛ) and Titus f. 48ʳ (cf. Lincoln f. 108ʳ).

[20] See A.C. Friend, 'Master Odo of Cheriton', *Speculum*, xxiii (1948), pp. 641–58 and the same author's unpublished D.Phil. thesis, 'The Life and Unprinted Works of Master Odo of Cheriton' (Oxford, 1936). More Wycliffite use of Odo is noted by Helen Spencer in her unpublished D.Phil. thesis, 'English Vernacular Sunday Preaching in the Late Fourteenth Century and Fifteenth Century, with illustrative texts' (Oxford, 1982), pp. 423–534.

[21] Odo's sermons are listed in Schneyer, *Repertorium*, iv, pp. 438–99. Extracts from the sermon for 10 Trinity appear in the *Floretum* under *columba* (BL, MS Harley 401, f. 51ᵛ, cf. Oxford, Bodleian Library, MS Bodl. 420, f. 161ᵛ) and *simonia* (Harley, f. 291ʳ⁻ᵛ, cf. Bodl., f. 161ᵛ), whilst one from the sermon for the feast of St Peter's Chair appears under *prelacia* (Harley, f. 245ʳ, cf. Bodl., f. 225ᵛ).

[22] *Apology for Lollard Doctrines*, ed. J.H. Todd, *CSer* (1842), pp. 57, line 21–58, line 23 has the second exactly, p. 56, lines 9–14 has more of the passage cited in the third; the material not found in the *Floretum* is at p. 75, lines 12–15 from the

in the Lambeth version of the sermon and once (unfortunately
without precise location) in the *Tractatus*. The regular form of
reference in all of these extracts, apart from the last, is to quote in
Latin the text of Odo's sermon.[23] The reason for the appeal of Odo
to Wycliffite authors is not far to seek: though doubtless they
would have disapproved of his collections of *fabulae*, albeit one of
the Lambeth extracts includes two lines of verse, Odo's outspoken
condemnation of the venality of the clergy, and of their reluctance
to perform their evangelical duty, makes his sermons a happy
hunting-ground for antecedents to Wycliffite views.

There are two puzzles amongst the authorities used. The first is
one cited in both sermon and *Tractatus* as 'Gorham on the Apocalypse'. It is fortunate that some sixteen lines of this source are
quoted in Latin in an appendix to the Lambeth version of the
sermon, since this circumvents the problems of hunting from
translation (and hence potentially free rendering or paraphrase).
This quotation deals with *Apocalypse*, xii. 15, explaining that the
water that engulfed the woman and was sent by the dragon
signifies temporal wealth with which the devil has overcome the
Church; this is connected with *Psalm* lxi. 11 (Vulgate, AV, lxii. 10),
and with the story of the angelic voice heard at the Donation of
Constantine. The earth that absorbed the water is understood as the
attempt of secular lords to deprive the church of its temporalities.[24]
The attraction of such a passage to a Lollard author hardly needs
remark. In the English sermon itself Gorham is quoted three times,
two apparently drawing on this same exegesis of xii. 15, whilst the
third alludes to three passages from the biblical book: vii. 1, xi. 3,
and xvii. 2.[25] In the *Tractatus* Gorham on the Apocalypse is twice
mentioned, apparently with regard to the first two verses of

---

sermon for St John's day (Bodl., f. 33ᵛ). The *columba* Odo quotation appears in the
Lanterne of Liȝt, ed. L.M. Swinburn, EETS, cli (1917), pp. 92, line 28–93, line 10.

[23] Matthew, p. 374, line 14 and in the original Latin p. 400, line 27 *Odo in a
sermon...þat bigynneþ...'Ecce nos reliquimus omnia'* (cf. Bodl., f. 271ᵛ), and p. 399,
line 33 *Odo in sermone 'Estote misericordes'* (cf. Bodl., f. 142ʳ, but closer to the
version in CUL, MS Kk.1.11, f. 64ᵛ); Titus f. 15ʳ *Odo...vpon þe gospellus* (a passage
with similar sentiments, but not the source if this is a close translation, is in Bodl.
f. 225ᵛ).

[24] Matthew, p. 401, lines 9–26.

[25] Egerton ff. 72ᵛ (Lambeth p. 380, line 3) and 121ᵛ, and ff. 118ʳ–19ᵛ respectively; the
last of these is not a continuous quotation, but draws on a number of different
passages united in a single argument.

chapter xvii of that book, but in essence repeating the same ideas as appear in the quoted exegesis of xii. 15 in the earlier text.[26]

The Dominican Nicholas Gorham, though he commented on the Apocalypse in the course of his virtually complete bible commentary, seemed an unlikely originator for such radical views on endowment; a quick search in MS Bodley 321 of his genuine exposition of the text showed that the Latin quotation did indeed not derive from there. Two pseudo-Gorham suggestions in Stegmüller (to Guilelmus de Melitona and to pseudo-Albertus Magnus) likewise proved unproductive.[27] A search nearer to the home Wycliffite base offered more. In MS Bodley 716, the manuscript from whose erased colophons Beryl Smalley began her brilliant reconstruction of Wyclif's *Postilla super totam Bibliam*, there appears at the end a second commentary on the Apocalypse not by Wyclif himself.[28] In chapter xii of that work appears a slightly fuller version of the Latin quotation in the Lambeth manuscript; the exegesis of the first two verses of chapter xvii confirmed the suspicion that, despite the references to those verses in the two English texts, the commentary came from the same chapter xii. 15; a fair but not complete agreement emerged between the full text of the commentary on vii. 1 and xi. 3, and the English allusions.[29] In Bodley 716 the commentary is ascribed in both the initial list of contents and at the head of its first leaf to Hugh of Vienne, better known to us as Hugh of St Cher. This attribution, though found in other manuscripts, seems not to be correct; the same text has also been printed as by Aquinas, but its true author is neither and remains uncertain.[30] Why the Lollard author should have thought the work by Gorham is unknown, but he does not seem to have been alone in his ascription.[31] As *accessus* to the text he may well

[26] Titus ff. 35^{r–v}; the reference gives simply *Gorham upon þe Apocalips*, but just before it *Apoc.*, xvii, 1–2 are in question.
[27] Stegmüller, *Bibl.*, no. 5810, with cross references to nos. 2961 and 1040 under 5811–12. For Gorham, see Smalley, *Bible*, pp. 273–4.
[28] Smalley, *Postilla*, pp. 186–205; the text is noted at p. 188.
[29] Respectively ff. 213^{r–v}, 231^r, 193^v–94^r, and 206^r; the whole text is ff. 173^r–246^v and is dated by the scribe at the end 'Oxford 1403'.
[30] See Stegmüller, *Bibl.*, nos. 3771 and 8066; I used the text printed in *Sancti Thomae Aquinatis Opera Omnia*, xxiii (Parma, 1869), pp. 325–511.
[31] Under 3771 Stegmüller's entries suggest attribution to Gorham is found in BL, MS Royal 3 E.x, ff. 173^r–87^r and to Gorham and Lyra in Berlin, Staatsbibl., Theol. Fol. 23 (Rose 493), ff. 122^r–291^r. The library catalogue for the latter

have used the index with which Bodley 716 and other manuscripts are provided; this gives subject headings with references to the commentary by chapter and subdividing letter, and the necessary letters appear in the margins of the text.[32] The only surprise perhaps is that the author did not quote 'Gorham on the Apocalypse' more often, since many entries in the index are of a kind that would have attracted Wycliffite attention.

The second puzzle is a long quotation in the *Tractatus* ascribed to *Fulgencius þat is cald auctor De Diuinis Officiis*, a quotation evidently distorted several times by the bad transmission of the vernacular text.[33] The content of the passage suggested that a later writer than Fulgentius was in question, though one at work before the firm definition of transubstantiation had been reached. The correction of the attribution to Rupert of Deutz, and the identification of the passage in the *Liber de Diuinis Officiis*, solved the editor's problem, but left many questions unanswered.[34] Much more intriguing is the fact that Wyclif also quoted this work, again without correct attribution, and that Thomas Netter puzzled over the possible authorship. Wyclif's longest quotation comes in the *De Apostasia*, chapter vi, a passage which corresponds closely to that translated in the English work, but which the latter cannot have derived straight from Wyclif, since one sentence of Rupert's work is found in the English version but not in Wyclif's quotation.[35] Wyclif introduced his citation thus:

---

confirms the information (and adds that the manuscript was written in 1432); but the former can be accepted only if a colophon at the end of a commentary on Mark in the companion volume, MS. Royal 3 E.xi, f. 89ᵛ, is extended to the rest of the otherwise anonymous compendium.

[32] See, for instance, MSS Bodl. 716, ff. 247ʳ–255ᵛ, CUL, Kk.1.29, ff. 177ᵛ–184ʳ and Oxford, Merton College, MS 42, ff. 166ʳ–70ʳ plus a supplementary index ff. 170ᵛ–73ʳ (listed separately by Stegmüller at no. 2805 and attributed with a query and for no clear reason to Guilelmus de Alvernia).

[33] Titus ff. 70ʳ–71ᵛ. A paraphrased version of part of the same quotation appears in Thorpe's account of his trial before Arundel, Oxford, Bodleian Library, MS Rawlinson C. 208, f. 43, where it is also attributed to Fulgencius.

[34] See the edition by H. Haacke, *CC, Continuatio Mediaeualis*, vii (1967); bk. ii, 9, lines 361–421 and 424–36, not including the long extra passage quoted in the variants there for lines 401 or 426 nor the extra variants given for this chapter by P. Classen, 'Zur kritischen Edition der Schriften Ruperts von Deutz', *DA*, xxvi (1970), pp. 522–7.

[35] *De Apostasia*, ed M.H. Dziewicki, WS (1889), pp. 73, line 25–75, line 25 corresponding to Rupert, book ii, 9, lines 359–85, 393–436; this passage is referred to again p. 123, lines 25–7.

> ... *ad hoc michi opinabiliter notandus est auctor Ambrosius in libro suo De divinis officiis, vel ut aliis placet, autor De divinis officiis, qui cepit istam sentenciam de beato Ambrosio, ut probabiliter creditur, ex secreto medie missę natalis domini. Unde vidi librum solemnem et antiquum intitulatum: 'Ambrosius, de divinis officiis'.*

Apparently, however, the attribution troubled him: a later allusion speaks of the author *qui superius nominatus est Ambrosius*, whilst two further quotations are ascribed simply to *auctor De divinis officiis*.[36] A summary of a brief section in the *Confessio minor de Eucharistia* is again without specific name; the same agnosticism recurs in the third book of the *Opus Evangelicum* written during the last months of his life.[37] Wyclif may have had another reason, beyond the venerable tome in which he had seen the title, for thinking Ambrose to be the author of his text: in the *De Eucharistia* he refers to Ambrose *in libro suo De Officiis et ponitur in De Consecracione, distinccione II, 'Forte dicis'.* Wyclif, had he investigated a little more fully, would have found that the extract does not occur in the *De divinis officiis*, though the sentiments expressed are certainly very similar.[38] Fulgentius, however, is a name that hardly appears in all these works; the only hint comes in a side-note to one allusion in the *De Apostasia*, but since it contradicts the naming of Ambrose in the text it seems unlikely that it can be Wyclif's guess.[39]

---

[36] *De Apostasia*, p. 95, lines 36–9, from Rupert ii, 9, pp. 106, line 36–107, line 16 from ii, 2, lines 93–114 and pp. 248, line 4–249, line 37 from ii, 21, lines 676–746. In a review of Haacke's edition J. Möllerfeld [*Theologische Revue*, lxv (1969), pp. 374–5], referring to some of these passages, suggests that Wyclif's copy of the text may have contained only book ii.

[37] For the former see the text in *FZ*, p. 121 summarizing Rupert, ii, 9, variants to p. 426, line 30; for the latter edition by J. Loserth, WS (1895–6), ii. p. 145, lines 5–8, paraphrasing ii. 9.

[38] *De Eucharistia Tractatus Maior*, ed. J. Loserth, WS (1892), p. 99, lines 26–28; Gratian, III, D. ii, c.43. Since *John*, vi. 68 is quoted in the canon-law passage, it is now easy to verify this; though the verse is quoted in the extra passage added by some manuscripts the rest does not correspond.

[39] *De Apostasia* p. 95, line 37, the manuscript is Vienna, Cvp, 1343; the only surviving manuscript of English origin does not extend so far. The most recent dating of the works by Wyclif mentioned here is that in W.R. Thomson, *The Latin Writings of John Wyclyf: An Annotated Catalog* (Toronto, 1983): *De Apostasia*, p. 64, late 1380; *De Eucharistia*, p. 67, mid-to-late 1380; *Confessio minor*, p. 69, 10 May 1381; *Opus Evangelicum*, p. 220, 1383 to end 1384. The second of these may be a little early, and Thomson makes insufficient allowance for Wyclif's habits of revision.

Netter worried at this problem at various points in his discussion of the Eucharist in the *Doctrinale*, book V. He starts in chapter 47 from the *Opus Evangelicum* and *De Apostasia* quotations, admitting that Wyclif was hesitant about the authorship, reverts to the question in chapter 66 and 81, and again more fully in 93.[40] What is interesting here is not the ill-tempered polemic, nor even the evidence that Netter's story provides that some of Wyclif's historicism had rubbed off onto his opponents (who here thought that they had caught him out),[41] but the indications that there had been considerable interest in the question of the *auctor De divinis officiis* in Oxford in the early years of the fifteenth century. Netter tells how at the request of King Henry IV he had discussed with Oxford men the problem: *Quærebatur author, quærebatur et liber, quibusdam dicentibus, quod Ambrosius diceretur.*[42] Isidore seems to have been suggested. But then *compertum est eumdem Authorem scripsisse diebus Anselmi*; Netter quotes a letter allegedly by Anselm, but then conjectures that it was actually by a contemporary of his, and compares the comment of Guitmund on the followers of Berengar, guilty of the heresy of impanation.[43] Actually some twenty years before this discussion can have occurred (and some forty before Netter was writing), the Franciscan John Tyssington mentioned the vital clue of this letter, but without clearly connecting it with Wyclif's use of the supposedly 'Ambrose' text.[44] Netter seems to have pursued his curiosity after the Oxford discussion: he tells that he looked at several copies of the *De divinis officiis*, but found them

---

[40] I have used the edition by B. Blanciotti (Venice, 1757–9), here ii, cols. 293–7, 404, 485, and 546–9. Notes at the end of the volume, cols. 978–82, identify Rupert of Deutz as the *auctor de diuinis officiis*.

[41] Bk. v, 47 (col. 295); Netter does not candidly reflect the extent of Wyclif's hesitation about the author.

[42] The occasion of these discussions, and the instigation by the King, remains obscure. A possible opportunity would seem to have been during Netter's probable involvement from 1409 onwards in attempts to persuade the university to submit a list of Wyclif's heretical conclusions [see *Snappe's Formulary*, ed. H.E. Salter, OHS, lxxx (1924), p. 169, and J. Crompton, 'Fasciculi Zizaniorum II', *JEH*, xii (1961), p. 159].

[43] Col. 294; the letter is actually by William of St Thierry (*PL* clxxx, 341–2), where precisely the section first quoted in the *De Apostasia* and by the Titus *Tractatus* is singled out for condemnation. The passage of Guitmund is *PL* cxlix, 1430.

[44] *FZ*, p. 156 quoting *PL* clxxx, 342; Tissyngton, though he perceived the date of the letter, describes it as by Anselm *ad auctorem quendam de Officiis Divinis*; he reverts to it pp. 172 and 178–9.

all anonymous and one, even more suspiciously, to lack the first three folios;[45] reading further in the work he came upon a reference to a miracle of 1111, thus proving the origin to be long after Ambrose;[46] finally he found a question by Henry Harkeley that gave the name of the author as 'Waleran, bishop of Memburg'.[47] The later sections add little save one tantalizing point: in chapter 93 Netter says that the Wycliffites claim support from *Fulgentius de divinis officiis, lib. cujus Prologus incipit, 'Ea quæ per anni circulum'* (indeed the opening of the prologue to Rupert's work). Unfortunately the context in which Netter uses this point precludes the deduction that he knew of the *Tractatus*: the discussion at that point concerns utraquism, and the *Wycliffistæ* in question are those of Prague and not England.[48] The whole confusing episode emphasizes the extent to which Wyclif's views on the Eucharist revived interest in the Berengarian dispute.[49]

Beyond the mere citation of authorities, however obscure, in the English works is evidence of an academic bent of mind. The author remarks in the *Tractatus, And hou3 seint Denyse writiþ of þis sacrament aftur þe logic of Goddis law I told in partie before, but for I haue not nou3*

---

[45] Col. 296. Haacke lists fifty-three complete surviving manuscripts and a further twelve partial texts. Many of these are unattributed. It is tempting to think that Netter's defective text was that now Lincoln Cathedral Library, MS 82, which lacks the first four folios and begins at i, 22. By 1501 Oxford, Bodleian Library, MS Laud misc. 412 belonged to Canterbury College, Oxford, but in default of any ascription that would explain either 'Ambrose' or 'Fulgentius' it remains unprovable that this was the text seen either by Wyclif or by the author of the *Tractatus*.

[46] Rupert, viii, 4.

[47] Netter, cols. 296, 485, and 546. For Harkeley see *BRUO*, ii. pp. 874–5. F. Pelster, 'Heinrich von Harclay, Kanzler von Oxford, und seine Quästionen', *ST*, xxxvii (1924), pp. 307–56 at p. 331 mentions Netter's allusions, but wonders whether the attribution is correct; no such question survives. Bale's attribution of a text *De transubstantione, Catalogus*, i, p. 503 goes beyond Netter's information in giving an incipit, *Utrum de necessitate salutis*. Harkeley's author, however, is presumably Bishop Waleram of Naumburg, who corresponded with Anselm of Canterbury on the Eucharist, see *S. Anselmi Cantuariensis Archiepiscopi Opera Omnia*, ii, ed. F.S. Schmitt (Edinburgh, 1946), pp. 223–42.

[48] Col. 546.

[49] For the earlier period see J. de Montclos, *Lanfranc et Bérenger: la controverse eucharistique du XIe siècle* = *Spicilegium Sacrum Lovaniense*, xxxvii (1971), and M. Gibson, *Lanfranc of Bec* (Oxford, 1978), pp. 63–97. The recent biography *Rupert of Deutz* by J.H. van Engen (Los Angeles and London, 1983) has much useful information, but unfortunately nothing on knowledge of Rupert in the later medieval period.

þe copie of his boke I write not his wordis here.[50] One may link with this scholarly desire to verify references the request at the end of the sermon that the congregation, with whom he leaves the copy, should note particularly any scriptural passages produced against it by a hostile observer (ff. 116[r–v]); here a discernment of authorities is implicitly acknowledged. The writer had some knowledge of theories of the continuum, realizing that Plato and Aristotle had disagreed on the subject and on the question of infinity.[51] Academic idiom seems to come naturally to him: the syllogistic method of argument is used, and *Gabriel shal blowe his horn er þei han preued þe minor* is unexplained to the sermon's congregation.[52] Equally, though canon law is rarely specifically cited, legal vocabulary and argument are frequent: *persoone aggregat, fraunchisen togidir, perquisite,* and *entail* are all used in the sermon with a precise legal sense, whilst there is an ingenious argument that the clergy's claim to temporalities is a diversion of the *entail* entrusted by God to the laity, and that their claim to tithes because of the Levitical precepts ignores the interruption of the *entail* at the time of Christ and the apostles.[53] Grammatical terminology is used and again is not explained: *siþþen an aduerbe is worþe a preposicioun wiþ a casuel* seems, not surprisingly, to have escaped the comprehension of the scribe of the *Tractatus* since he corrupts the example that follows.[54] A credible if dubiously correct etymology and gloss is given for Latin *ebrius,* that *aftur þe composicioun of the worde* it means in origin *out of mesure.*[55] One obscure passage in the *Tractatus* condemns the

---

[50] Titus f. 69[v]; the earlier citations are at ff. 16[v], 18[v], and 48[r].

[51] Egerton ff. 28[r–v]; cf. J.E. Murdoch, 'Infinity and Continuity', in *CHLMP*, pp. 564–91. Murdoch points out (p. 576, n. 36) that Wyclif was an indivisiblist; the sermon writer follows him in this.

[52] Titus ff. 10[v]–11[r]; Egerton f. 76[r] (Lambeth p. 382, line 28). Matthew, p. 528, draws attention to the same phrase in one of the articles from Wyclif condemned at the Council of Constance in 1415; see *Fasciculus Rerum Expetendarum*, ed. E. Brown (London, 1690) i, p. 267; the article is a quotation from *Opus Evangelicum*, ii, p. 152, lines 22–6.

[53] Egerton ff. 78[r–v], 99[r], 95[r]–6[v].

[54] Titus f. 76[v]; the argument turns on the reasonable translation of the Pauline Titus ii. 12 that *pie* is equivalent to *in pietate* (corrupted by the scribe to *impietate*), and hence may be rendered *in trew wirschipping of uerri God.* I am indebted to David Thomson for his solution to this obscurity.

[55] Titus f. 33[v]; the author apparently has in mind *sobrius* and has taken *e*- as a negative prefix (not supported by A. Walde revd. J.B. Hofmann, *Lateinisches Etymologisches Wörterbuch* (Heidelberg, 1938–54) i, pp. 387–8).

proposition put forward by adversaries that *no negatif includeþ contradiccioun and þerfor eche negatif is possible.*[56]

There remains the question of the writer's acquaintance with Wyclif's writings. Unlike some Lollard texts Wyclif is never mentioned by name or by allusion. In some cases Wyclif could have provided the material, but equally academic discussion in Oxford at the end of the fourteenth century could well have been the source. The discussion of the distinction between *peyne of harme* and *peine of feling* reflects the *pena dampni* and *pena sensus* examined by Wyclif in *De Statu Innocencie* and elsewhere, but the issue was a lively one at the time.[57] Specifically Wycliffian influence seems most evident in the discussion of various theories of the Eucharistic words in the *Tractatus*. Here the writer outlines different theories about the referent of *hoc* and about the sense of *est* in terms very similar to those used by Wyclif in the fourth book of the *Trialogus*. This last could likewise have provided the information about John de Deo, whose views are mocked earlier in the *Tractatus.*[58]

Who then was this erudite Wycliffite? The options can be narrowed: his education must have been a university one, and one that had progressed beyond the arts to the theology course. His university equally must have been Oxford. Not only is it inherently more likely that he should have learnt his Wycliffism at Oxford than at Cambridge, but he twice mentions the older university. After repeated condemnation of the currently orthodox view of the Eucharist, he adds (Titus f. 72ᵛ) *For men be not ȝit determened in Oxeford houȝ an accident schal be discriued or diffinid.* Earlier he embellishes Augustine on Psalm lvii that he quoted shortly before in a fine rhetorical flourish (Titus f. 15ʳ):

> *So seie I: þat it mai be þat boþ in þis poynt of beleue and also of oþur þat Ion de Deo lieþ; it mai be þat pope Innocent lieþ; it mai be þat alle þe foure ordris of freris lien wiþ munkis and chanouns; also it mai be þat al þe vniuersite of Oxford lieþ and oþur also; it mai be þat aggregat persone*

[56] Titus f. 91ᵛ.

[57] Titus ff. 90ᵛ–91ʳ; see *De Statu Innocencie*, ed. J. Loserth and F.D. Matthew, WS (1922), p. 478, lines 8ff and also *Trialogus*, ed. G. Lechler (Oxford, 1969), pp. 289–92.

[58] Titus ff. 55ʳ–56ᵛ and mention of John de Deo f. 15ʳ; cf. *Trialogus* pp. 247–81 (John de Deo, pp. 251, line 10 and 264, line 22).

þat haþ his see in the chirche lieþ. But in no wise mai it be þat truþe þat is God lieþ.

Though it would be rash to attempt to put a specific name to this argumentative preacher, his writings certainly put into perspective Arundel's eleventh Constitution, which imposed upon the heads of halls of residence the duty of enquiring monthly into their students' views on questions Wycliffite. There is strong temptation to attach the name of one of those very heads of halls to the anonymous English writer—but that is to go beyond the available evidence.

Lady Margaret Hall, Oxford

BIBLIOGRAPHY OF THE WRITINGS
OF
BERYL SMALLEY

Note: Reviews are excluded from this bibliography.

1931   With G. Lacombe, 'Studies on the Commentaries of Cardinal Stephen Langton', *AHDLMA*, v, pp. 1–220.

With G. Lacombe, 'The Lombard's Commentary on Isaias and Other Fragments', *The New Scholasticism*, v, pp. 123–62.

'Stephen Langton and the Four Senses of Scripture', *Speculum*, vi, pp. 60–76.

1933   '*Exempla* in the Commentaries of Stephen Langton', *BJRL*, xvii, pp. 121–9.

1935   'Master Ivo of Chartres', *EHR*, l, pp. 680–6.

'Gilbertus Universalis Bishop of London (1128–1134) and the Problem of the "Glossa Ordinaria", I', *RTAM*, vii, pp. 235–62.

1936   'Gilbertus Universalis Bishop of London (1128–1134) and the Problem of the "Glossa Ordinaria", II', *RTAM*, viii, pp. 24–64.

1937   'La *Glossa Ordinaria*', *RTAM*, ix, pp. 365–400.

1938   'Andrew of St. Victor, Abbot of Wigmore: a Twelfth Century Hebraist', *RTAM*, x, pp. 358–73.

'A Collection of Paris Lectures of the Later Twelfth Century in MS Pembroke College Cambridge 7', *Cambridge Historical Review*, vi, pp. 103–13.

1939   'The School of Andrew of St Victor', *RTAM*, xi, pp. 145–67.

Hebrew Scholarship among Christians in xiiith Century England, as Illustrated by some Hebrew-Latin Psalters = Society for Old Testament Study, Lectio 6, (London).

1941   *The Study of the Bible in the Middle Ages* (Oxford).

1943   With H. Kantorowicz, 'An English Theologian's View of Roman Law; Pepo, Irnerius, Ralph Niger', *MARS*, i, pp. 237–52.

1945   With S. Kuttner, 'The "Glossa ordinaria" to the Gregorian Decretals', *EHR*, lx, pp. 97–105.

1946   'Two Biblical Commentaries of Simon of Hinton', *RTAM*, xiii, pp. 57–85.
'A Commentary on Isaias by Guerric of St Quentin O.P.', *ST*, cxxii, pp. 383–7.

1948   'Some More Exegetical Works of Simon of Hinton', *RTAM*, xv, pp. 97–106.
'Robert Bacon and the Early Dominican School at Oxford', *TRHS*, 4th series, xxx, pp. 1–19.
'The *Quaestiones* of Simon of Hinton', *Studies in Medieval History Presented to Frederick Maurice Powicke*, ed. R.W. Hunt, W.A. Pantin, and R.W. Southern (Oxford), pp. 209–22.

1949   'William of Middleton and Guibert of Nogent', *RTAM*, xvi, pp. 281–91.
'Some Thirteenth Century Commentaries on the Sapiential Books', *Dominican Studies*, ii, pp. 318–55.

1950   'Some Thirteenth Century Commentaries on the Sapiential Books', II, III, *Dominican Studies*, ii, pp. 41–7; 236–74.
'Some Commentaries on the Sapiential Books of the late thirteenth and early fourteenth centuries', *AHDLMA*, xviii, pp. 103–28.
'Gregory IX and the Two Faces of the Soul', *MARS*, ii, pp. 179–82.

1951   'A Commentary by Herbert of Bosham on the Hebraica', *RTAM*, xviii, pp. 29–65.

1952   *The Study of the Bible in the Middle Ages*, 2nd ed. revised and enlarged (Oxford).

1953   'A Commentary on the Hexaemeron by Henry of Ghent', *RTAM*, xx, pp. 60–101.
'John Wyclif's *Postilla super totam Bibliam*', *Bodleian Library Record*, iv, pp. 186–204.

1954   'Thomas Waleys O.P.', *AFP*, xxiv, pp. 50–107.
'Which William of Nottingham?', *MARS*, iii, pp. 200–38.

1955   'Gerard of Bologna and Henry of Ghent', *RTAM*, xxii, pp. 125–9.
'The Biblical Scholar', *Robert Grosseteste Scholar and Bishop*, ed. D.A. Callus (Oxford), pp. 70–97.

1956   'Robert Holcot O.P.', *AFP*, xxvi, pp. 5–97.
'John Russel O.F.M.', *RTAM*, xxiii, pp. 277–320.

1957 'John Ridevall's Commentary on *De Civitate Dei*', *MedA*, xxv, pp. 140–53.

'*Prima Clavis Sapientiae*: Augustine and Abelard', *Fritz Saxl, 1890–1948*, ed D.J. Gordon (London), pp. 93–100.

'Capetian France', *France: Government and Society. An Historical Survey*, ed. J.M. Wallace-Hadrill and J. McManners (London), pp. 61–82.

1959 'Flaccianus, *De visionibus Sibyllae*', *Mélanges offerts à Etienne Gilson* (Toronto and Paris), pp. 547–62.

1960 *English Friars and Antiquity in the Early Fourteenth Century* (Oxford)

1961 'Les commentaires bibliques et l'époque romane; Glose Ordinaire et gloses périmées', *Cahiers de civilisation médiévale*, iv, pp. 15–21.

'Jean de Hesdin O. Hosp. S. Ioh.', *RTAM*, xxviii (1961), pp. 285–330.

1962 'Problems of Exegesis in the Fourteenth Century', *Miscellanea Medievalia, Veröffentlichungen des Thomas-Instituts an der Universität Köln*, ed. P. Wilpert, i, *Antike und Orient im Mittelalter* (Berlin), pp. 266–77.

1963 'Moralists and Philosophers in the Thirteenth and Fourteenth Centuries', *ibid.*, ii, *Die Metaphysik im Mittelalter, ihr Ursprung und ihre Bedeutung*, pp. 59–67.

'The Bible in the Middle Ages', *The Church's Use of the Bible Past and Present*, ed. D.E. Nineham (London), pp. 57–71.

'L'exégèse biblique dans la littérature latine', *Settimane di Studio del Centro Italiano di Studi sull'Alto Medioevo*, x, *La Bibblia nel Alto Medioevo* (Spoleto), pp. 631–56.

'Jean de Hesdin, a Source of the *Somnium viridarii*', *RTAM*, xxx, pp. 154–9.

1964 'Wyclif's *Postilla* on the Old Testament and his *Principium*', *Oxford Studies presented to Daniel Callus* = OHS, ns, xvi, pp. 253–96.

'The Bible and Eternity: John Wyclif's Dilemma', *JWCI*, xxvii, pp. 73–89.

1966 'A Pseudo-Sibylline Prophecy of the Early Twelfth Century in the *Life* of Altman of Passau', *Mélanges offerts à René Crozet*, Société d'études médiévales (Poitiers), pp. 655–61.

1968 'L'exégèse biblique du xiie siècle', *Entretiens sur la renaissance du xiie siècle*, ed. M. de Gandillac and E. Jeaneau =

Decades du Centre culturel international de Cerisy-la-Salle, ns, ix, pp. 273–93.

'Church and State, 1307–77: Theory and Fact', *Europe in the Late Middle Ages*, ed. J.R. Hale, J.R.L. Highfield, and B. Smalley (London), pp. 15–43.

Introduction to *Trends in Medieval Political Thought*, ed. B. Smalley (Oxford).

'Ralph of Flaix on Leviticus', *RTAM*, xxxv, pp. 35–82.

1969 'The Bible in the Medieval Schools', *CHB*, ii, pp. 197–220.

'An Early Twelfth-century Commentator on the Literal Sense of Leviticus', *RTAM*, xxxv, pp. 78–99.

1971 'Sallust in the Middle Ages', *Classical Influence on European Culture A.D. 500–1500*, ed. R.R. Bolgar (Cambridge), pp. 165–75.

'*Privilegium fori*: un dialogue entre la Theologie et le Droit canon au xiie siècle', *Atti del secondo congresso internazionale della Società Italiana di Studio del Diritto*, ii (Florence), pp. 749–55.

1973 *The Becket Conflict and the Schools. A Study of Intellectuals in Politics in the Twelfth Century* (Oxford).

1974 *Historians of the Middle Ages* (London).

'William of Auvergne, John of La Rochelle and St Thomas Aquinas on the Old Law', *St Thomas Aquinas 1274–1974* (Pontifical Institute of Medieval Studies, Toronto), i, pp. 10–71.

1975 'Ecclesiastical Attitudes to Novelty *c.*1100–*c.*1250', *SCH*, xii, pp. 113–31.

1976 'Oxford University Sermons, 1290–1293', *Medieval Learning and Literature. Essays presented to Richard William Hunt*, ed. J.J.G. Alexander and M.T. Gibson (Oxford), pp. 307–27.

1978 'Some Gospel Commentaries of the Early Twelfth Century', *RTAM*, xlv, pp. 147–80.

1979 'Peter Comestor on the Gospels', *RTAM*, xlvi, pp. 84–129.

'The Gospels in the Paris Schools in the Late Twelfth and Early Thirteenth Centuries: Peter the Chanter, Hugh of St Cher, Alexander of Hales, John of La Rochelle, I', *Franc Stud*, xxxix, pp. 230–54.

1980 'The Gospels in the Paris Schools in the Late Twelfth and Early Thirteenth Centuries: Peter the Chanter, Hugh of St

Cher, Alexander of Hales, John of La Rochelle, II', *Franc Stud*, xl, pp. 298–369.

'An Early Paris Lecture Course on St Luke', '*Sapientiae Doctrina': Mélanges de théologie et de littérature médiévales offerts à Dom Hildebrand Bascour O.S.B.* = *RTAM*, numéro spécial, i, pp. 299–311.

1981   'L'uso della Scrittura nei "Sermones" di Sant'Antonio', *Rivista Antoniana di storia dottrina arte*, xxi, pp. 3–16.

Studies in Medieval Thought and Learning from Abelard to Wyclif (London).

1983   *The Study of the Bible in the Middle Ages*, 3rd ed. revised (Oxford).

In press *The Gospels in the Schools c. 1100–c. 1280* (London).

'Use of the "Spiritual" Senses of Scripture in Persuasion and Argument by Christian Scholars in the Middle Ages', *RTAM*.

'Glossa Ordinaria', *Theologische Realenzyklopädie*.

ABBREVIATIONS

AB	*Analecta Bollandiana* (Paris and Brussels, 1882ff)
AFH	*Archivum Franciscanum Historicum* (Quaracchi/Grottaferrata, 1908ff)
AFP	*Archivum Fratrum Praedicatorum* (Rome, 1931ff)
AHDLMA	*Archives d'histoire doctrinale et littéraire du moyen âge* (Paris, 1926ff)
ALKG	*Archiv für Litteratur- und Kirchengeschichte*, ed H. Denifle and F. Ehrle, 3 vols (Berlin, 1885–7, Freiburg im Breisgau, 1888–1900)
AS	*Acta Sanctorum*, ed J. Bollandus, G. Henschenius and others (Antwerp, 1643ff)
AV	Authorized Version
Bale, *Catalogus*	John Bale, *Scriptorum Illustrium Maioris Brytanniae Catalogus*, 2 parts (Basel, 1557, 1559)
Bale, *Index*	John Bale, *Index Britanniae Scriptorum*, ed R.L. Poole and M. Bateson (Oxford, 1902), *Anecdota Oxoniensis*, Medieval and Modern series 9
BAV	Vatican City, Biblioteca Apostolica Vaticana
BEC	*Bibliothèque de l'école des Chartes* (Paris, 1838ff)
BEFAR	*Bibliothèque des écoles françaises d'Athènes et de Rome* (Paris, 1876ff)
BIHR	*Bulletin of the Institute of Historical Research* (London, 1923ff)
BJRL	*Bulletin of the John Rylands Library* (Manchester, 1903ff)
BL	British Library, London
BM	British Museum, London
BN	Bibliothèque Nationale, Paris
BRUC	A.B. Emden, *A Biographical Register of the University of Cambridge to A.D. 1500,* (Cambridge, 1963)
BRUO	A.B. Emden, *A Biographical Register of the University of Oxford to A.D. 1500,* 3 vols (Oxford, 1957–9); *1500–40* (Oxford, 1974)
CC	*Corpus Christianorum* (Turnholt, 1952ff)
CCCM	*Corpus Christianorum, Continuatio Mediaevalis*
CCSL	*Corpus Christianorum, Series Latina*
Cgm	Codex germanicus Monacensis = MS collection, Munich, Bayerische Staatsbibliothek
CH	*Church History* (New York/Chicago, 1932ff)
CHB	*Cambridge History of the Bible*, i, ed P.R. Ackroyd and C.F. Evans (Cambridge, 1970); ii, ed G.W.H. Lampe (Cambridge, 1969); iii, ed S.L. Greenslade (Cambridge, 1963)

CHLMP | *Cambridge History of Later Medieval Philosophy from the Rediscovery of Aristotle to the Disintegration of Scholasticism, 1100–1600*, ed N. Kretzmann, A. Kenny, and J. Pinborg (Cambridge, 1982)

Clem. | *Constitutiones Clementis Papae V*, ed Ae. Friedberg, *Corpus Iuris Canonici*, ii (Leipzig, 1879), cols 1132ff

Clm | Codex latinus Monacensis = MS collection, Munich Bayerische Staatsbibliothek

Colgrave and Mynors, *Bede* | *Bede's 'Ecclesiastical History of the English People'*, ed B. Colgrave and R.A.B. Mynors (*OMT*, Oxford, 1969)

Coll Franc | *Collectanea Franciscana* (Assisi/Rome, 1931ff)

CS | *Cartularium Saxonicum*, ed W. de G. Birch, 3 vols (London, 1885–93)

CSEL | *Corpus Scriptorum Ecclesiasticorum Latinorum* (Vienna, 1866ff)

CSer | *Camden Series* (London, 1898ff)

CUL | Cambridge University Library

Cvp | Codex Vindobonensis Palatinus = MS collection, Vienna, Österreichische Nationalbibliothek

DA | *Deutsches Archiv für [Geschichte* (Weimar, 1937–43)] *Erforschung des Mittelalters* (Cologne and Graz, 1950ff)

Decretales | *Decretales Gregorii IX*, ed Ae. Friedberg, *Corpus Iuris Canonici*, ii (Leipzig, 1879), cols 6ff

DSAM | *Dictionnaire de Spiritualité, Ascétique et Mystique*, ed M. Viller (Paris, 1932ff)

DTC | *Dictionnaire de Théologie Catholique*, ed A. Vacant, E. Mangenot, and E. Amann, 15 vols (Paris, 1903–50)

EETS | Early English Text Society

EF | *Etudes Franciscaines* (Paris, 1899–1938, ns 1950ff)

EHR | *English Historical Review* (London, 1886ff)

Extrav. Comm. | *Extravagantes Communes*, ed Ae. Friedberg, *Corpus Iuris Canonici*, ii (Leipzig, 1879), cols 1237ff

Extrav. J. XXII | *Extravagantes Ioannis Papae XXII*, ed Ae. Friedberg, *Corpus Iuris Canonici*, ii (Leipzig, 1879), cols 1205ff

Franc Stud | *Franciscan Studies* (St Bonaventura, New York, 1941ff)

FZ | *Fasciculi Zizaniorum*, ed W.W. Shirley, *RS*, v (London, 1858)

Gratian | *Decretum Gratiani*, ed Ae. Friedberg, *Corpus Iuris Canonici*, i (Leipzig, 1879)

Hauréau | B. Hauréau, *Notices et extraits de quelques manuscrits latins de la Bibliothèque Nationale*, 6 vols (Paris, 1890–3)

HE | *Historia Ecclesiastica*

HJb | *Historisches Jahrbuch der Görres-Gesellschaft* (Cologne, 1880ff, Munich, 1950ff)

HLF | *Histoire littéraire de la France* (Paris, 1733ff)

HMC | Historical Manuscripts Commission

ABBREVIATIONS

HTR	*Harvard Theological Review* (New York/Cambridge, Mass., 1908ff)
JEH	*Journal of Ecclesiastical History* (Cambridge, 1950ff)
JHI	*Journal of the History of Ideas* (London, 1940ff)
JMedH	*Journal of Medieval History* (Amsterdam, 1975ff)
JTS	*Journal of Theological Studies* (London, 1899ff)
JWCI	*Journal of the Warburg and Courtauld Institutes* (London, 1937ff)
Kaeppeli, Scriptores	T. Kaeppeli, *Scriptores Ordinis Praedicatorum Medii Aevi* (Rome, 1970ff)
LThK	*Lexikon für Theologie und Kirche*, ed J. Höfler and K. Rahner, 2nd ed (Freiburg im Breisgau, 1957ff)
Mansi	J.D. Mansi, *Sacrorum conciliorum nova et amplissima collectio*, 31 vols (Florence/Venice, 1757–98), new impression and continuation, ed L. Petit and J.B. Martin, 60 vols (Paris, 1899–1927)
MARS	*Medieval and Renaissance Studies* (London, 1943–68)
MedA	*Medium Aevum* (Oxford, 1952ff)
MEFRM	*Mélanges d'archéologie et d'histoire*, i–lxxxii (Paris, 1881–1970); *Mélanges de l'école française de Rome. Moyen âge, temps modernes*, lxxxiii ff (Paris, 1971ff)
MF	*Miscellanea Francescana* (Foligno/Rome, 1886ff)
MGH	*Monumenta Germaniae Historica inde ab a.c. 500 usque ad a. 1500*, ed G.H. Pertz and others (Berlin, Hanover, etc., 1826ff)
AA	*Auctores Antiquissimi*
Ant	*Antiquitates*
Briefe	*Epistolae 2: Die Briefe der Deutschen Kaiserzeit*
Cap	*Leges 2: Leges in Quart 2: Capitularia regum Francorum*
CM	*Chronica Minora 1–3 (= AA 9, 11, 13)* ed Th. Mommsen (1892, 1894, 1898, repr 1961)
Conc	*Leges 2: Leges in Quart 3: Concilia*
	4: Constitutiones et acta publica imperatorum et regum
DC	*Deutsche Chroniken*
Dip	*Diplomata in folio*
Epp	*Epistolae 1 in Quart*
Epp.S XIII	*Epistolae 3: Epistolae Saeculi XIII e Registris Pontificum Romanorum Selectae.*
Epp Sel	*4: Epistolae Selectae*
FIG	*Leges 3: Fontes Iuris Germanici Antique*, new series
FIGUS	*4: , in usum scholarum*
Form	*2: Leges in Quart 5: Formulae Merovingici et Karolini Aevi*
GPR	*Gesta Pontificum Romanorum*
Leges	*Leges in folio*

Lib	*Libelli de lite*
LM	*Ant* 3: *Libri Memoriales*
LNG	*Leges* 2: *Leges in Quart* 1: *Leges nationum Germanicarum*
Necr	*Ant* 2: *Necrologia Germaniae*
Poet	1: *Poetae Latini Medii Aevi*
Quellen	*Quellen zur Geistesgeschichte des Mittelalters*
Schriften	*Schriften der Monumenta Germaniae Historica*
SRG	*Scriptores rerum germanicarum in usum scholarum*
SRG ns	, new series
SRL	*Scriptores rerum langobardicarum et italicarum*
SRM	*Scriptores rerum merovingicarum*
SS	*Scriptores*
SSM	*Staatschriften des späteren Mittelalters*
MIÖG	*Mitteilungen des Instituts für Österreichische Geschichtsforschung* (Innsbruck, 1880ff, Cologne, Graz, and Vienna, 1945ff)
Moyen âge	*Le moyen âge. Revue d'histoire et de philologie* (Paris, 1888ff)
MSt	*Mediaeval Studies* (Toronto, 1939ff)
Neues Archiv	*Neues Archiv der Gesellschaft für ältere deutsche Geschichtskunde* (Hanover/Leipzig, 1876ff)
NF	Neue Folge
ns	new series
OHS	Oxford Historical Society
OMT	*Oxford Medieval Texts*
PBA	*Proceedings of the British Academy* (London, 1904ff)
PG	*Patrologia Graeca*, ed J.P. Migne, 161 vols (Paris, 1857–66)
PL	*Patrologia Latina*, ed J.P. Migne, 217 + 4 index vols (Paris, 1841–61)
Plummer, *Bede*	*Venerabilis Baedae Opera Historica*, ed C. Plummer, 2 vols (Oxford, 1896)
PP	*Past and Present* (London, 1952ff)
PRIA	*Proceedings of the Royal Irish Academy* (Dublin, 1840ff)
QFIAB	*Quellen und Forschungen aus italienischen Archiven und Bibliotheken* (Rome/Tübingen, 1897ff)
RB	*Revue Bénédictine* (Maredsous, 1884ff)
RH	*Revue historique* (Paris, 1876ff)
RHE	*Revue d'histoire ecclésiastique* (Louvain, 1900ff)
RS	*Rerum Brittanicarum Medii Aevi Scriptores*, 99 vols (London, 1858–1911), *Rolls Series*
RSCI	*Rivista di storia della chiesa in Italia* (Rome, 1947ff)
RTAM	*Recherches de théologie ancienne et médiévale* (Louvain, 1929ff)
SA	*Studia Anselmiana* (Rome, 1923ff)
SCH	*Studies in Church History* (London, 1964ff)

Schneyer, Repertorium
J.B. Schneyer, *Repertorium der lateinischen Sermones des Mittelalters für die Zeit von 1150–1350*, 9 vols = *Beiträge zur Geschichte der Philosophie und Theologie des Mittelalters*, xliii (Münster, 1969ff)

Schneyer, Wegweiser
J.B. Schneyer, *Wegweiser zu lateinischen Predigtreihen des Mittelalters* = *Bayerische Akademie der Wissenschaften. Veröffentlichungen der historischen Kommission für die Herausgabe ungedruckter Texte aus der mittelalterlichen Geisteswelt*, i (Munich, 1965)

SCR
Sources chrétiennes, ed H. de Lubac and J. Danielou (Paris, 1941)

SF
Studi Francescani (Florence, 1914ff)

SGra
Studia Gratiana, ed J. Forchielli and A.M. Stickler (Bologna, 1953ff)

SGre
Studi Gregoriani, ed G. Borino, 7 vols (Rome, 1947–61)

Smalley, Becket
Beryl Smalley, *The Becket Conflict and the Schools. A Study of Intellectuals in Politics in the Twelfth Century* (Oxford, 1973)

Smalley, Bible
Beryl Smalley, *The Study of the Bible in the Middle Ages*, 3rd ed (Oxford, 1983)

Smalley, Friars
Beryl Smalley, *English Friars and Antiquity in the Fourteenth Century* (Oxford, 1960)

Smalley, Historians
Beryl Smalley, *Historians of the Middle Ages* (London, 1974)

Smalley, Postilla
Beryl Smalley, 'John Wyclif's *Postilla super totam Bibliam*', *Bodleian Library Record*, iv (1953), pp. 186–204.

Smalley, Studies
Beryl Smalley, *Studies in Medieval Thought and Learning from Abelard to Wyclif* (London, 1981)

ST
Studi e Testi (Vatican City, 1900ff)

Stegmüller, Bibl.
Fr. Stegmüller, *Repertorium Biblicum medii aevi*, 11 vols (Madrid, 1950–80)

Stegmüller, Sent.
Fr. Stegmüller, *Repertorium Commentariorum in Sententias Petri Lombardi*, 2 vols (Würzburg, 1947)

StM
Studi Medievali, 1st series (Turin, 1904–13); ns: (Turin, 1928–50); 3rd series (Spoleto, 1950)

TRHS
Transactions of the Royal Historical Society (London, 1871ff)

TU
Texte und Untersuchungen zur Geschichte der altchristlichen Literatur (Leipzig/Berlin, 1882ff)

Tubach
F.C. Tubach, *Index Exemplorum. A Handbook of Medieval Religious Tales* = *Folklore Fellows Communications*, no 204 (Helsinki, 1969)

Walther
H. Walther, *Proverbia Sententiaeque Latinitatis medii aevi. Lateinische Sprichwörter und Sentenzen des Mittelalters in alphabetischer Anordnung* = *Carmina medii aevi posterioris latina*, II, i–vi, 6 vols (Göttingen, 1963–9)

ABBREVIATIONS

WS	Wyclif Society
ZKG	*Zeitschrift für Kirchengeschichte* (Gotha/Stuttgart, 1878ff)
ZRG	*Zeitschrift der Savigny-Stiftung für Rechtsgeschichte* (Weimar)
GAbt	*Germanistische Abteilung* (1863ff)
KAbt	*Kanonistische Abteilung* (1911ff)
RAbt	*Romanistische Abteilung* (1880ff)

INDEX OF MANUSCRIPTS

INDEX OF PERSONS